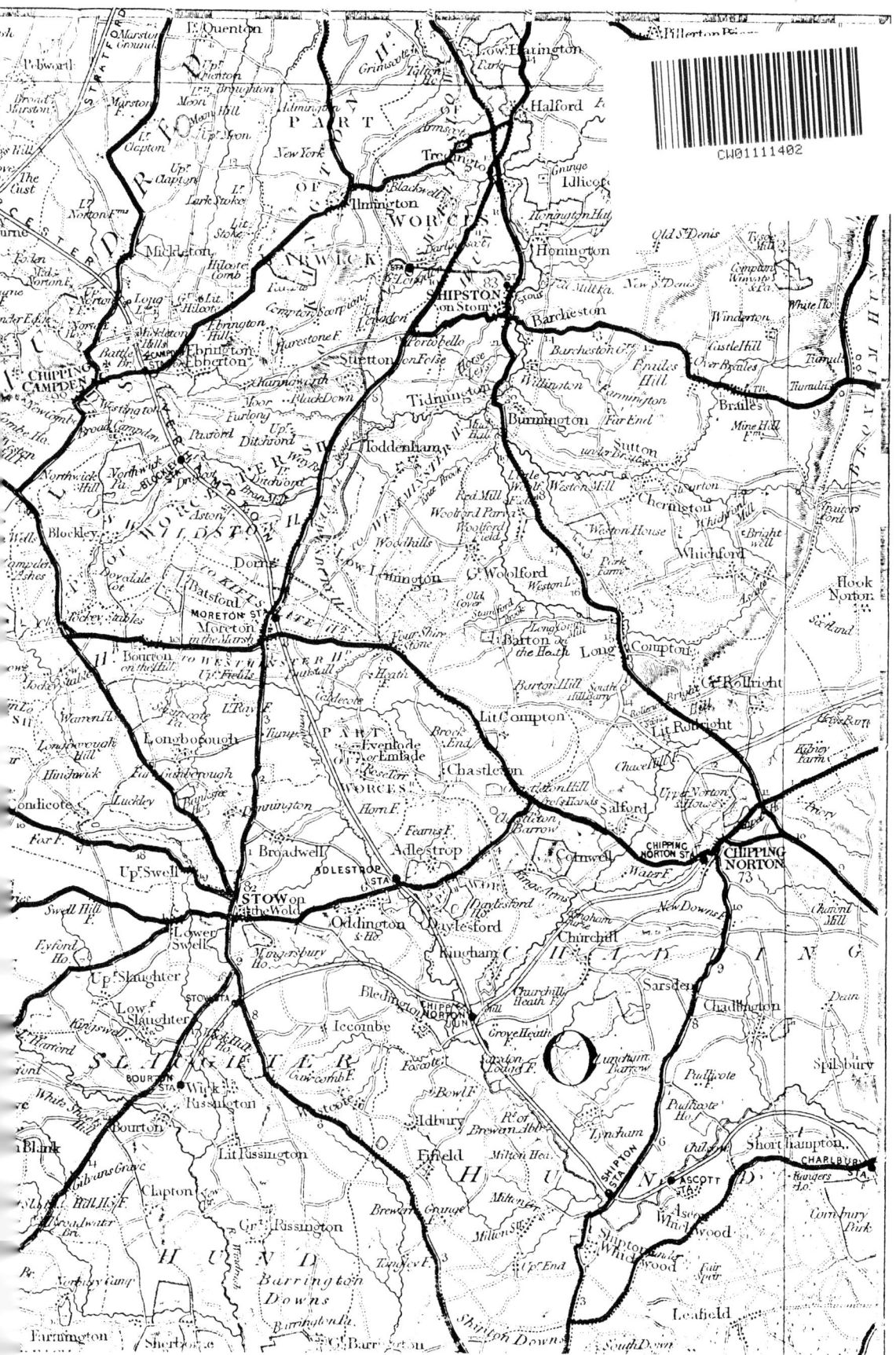

THE COTSWOLDS

The porch of Upper Slaughter Manor House with the arms of the Slaughter family.

THE COTSWOLDS

Anthea Jones

Photographs by Glyn Jones

Phillimore

First edition 1994
Reprinted 1997

Published by
PHILLIMORE & CO. LTD.
Shopwyke Manor Barn, Chichester, West Sussex

© Dr. Anthea Jones, 1994, 1997

ISBN 0 85033 883 2

Printed and bound in Great Britain by
BUTLER & TANNER LTD.
London and Frome

Contents

List of Illustrations vii
List of Colour Illustrations x
Acknowledgements xi
Introduction 1

1. The Cotswold Scene in Domesday 7
2. Anglo-Saxon Estates and Settlements 18
3. Minsters, Rectories and Churches 35
4. Market Charters and Town Councils 52
5. Sheep Downs and Common Fields 74
6. Wool, Wool Churches and Cotswold Sheep 90
7. Knights and Manor Houses 105
8. The Disappearance of the Cotswold Peasant 123
9. The Modernisation of the Church 144
10. Gentlemen and Country Houses 160
11. The Decline of Village and Town 183
12. In Search of Old Cotswold 199

Sources 213
Bibliography 217
Index 221

List of Illustrations

Frontispiece: The porch of Upper Slaughter Manor House with the arms of the Slaughter family

1.	Four Shire Stone near Moreton in Marsh	4
2.	Broad Campden: Norman doorway before restoration	4
3.	Map of Stow on the Wold	9
4.	Stow church: west end	10
5.	Withington church	10
6.	Hazleton: Glebe Farm	11
7.	Team of four oxen drawing a plough in 1992	13
8.	Ascot under Wychwood church	19
9.	Shipton Court	21
10.	Map of Icomb	24
11.	Icomb village centre	25
12.	Harford in Naunton	27
13.	View over Naunton including Sheepwell Lane	28
14.	Clapton Bridge	28
15.	Bourton on the Water church about 1780	29
16.	Little Barrington	30
17.	Windrush church south doorway: detail	31
18.	Syreford Mill in Whittington	33
19.	Syreford pond and Mill in Whittington	33
20.	Guiting Power church	37
21.	Temple Guiting church	37
22.	Great Barrington chancel arch: detail	43
23.	Broadway old church: Norman font	44
24.	Oddington old church: pulpit	44
25.	Hampnett chancel	45
26.	Cutsdean church	47
27.	Great Barrington church	47
28.	Farmington church	48
29.	Greet chapel in 1815	49
30.	Gretton church in 1865	49
31.	Norman doorway at Sherborne	50
32.	Map of Winchcombe	54
33.	Winchcombe parish church	56
34.	Map of Burford	59
35.	Burford: High Street	60
36.	Burford church from Lawrence Lane	61

37.	Stow on the Wold: St Edward's Hall	62
38.	Map of Campden	64
39.	Map of Northleach	67
40.	Bourton on the Hill	69
41.	Moreton in Marsh	69
42.	Map of Moreton in Marsh	70
43.	Broadway hill	71
44.	Map of Broadway	72
45.	Open wold scenery	75
46.	Puesdown Inn sign	76
47.	Hampen Manor: collecting sheep for shearing	78
48.	Stanway tithe barn	79
49.	Ridge and furrow at Broad Campden	80
50.	Campden Hill Farm	82
51.	Lots Barn, Bemborough	82
52.	Taynton 'lots'	83
53.	Map of part of Shipton Oliffe and its open fields in 1764	85
54.	Part of the map of Shipton Oliffe and Solers showing Hampen open field	85
55.	Cutsdean village	88
56.	A river for sheep washing: the Sherborne Brook	92
57.	Northleach church	96
58.	Campden church from the south	97
59.	Sevenhampton church	98
60.	Sheep on Northleach woolmen's monumental brasses	100
61.	A Cotswold 'Lion'	101
62.	Broadfield Farm, Northleach	103
63.	Icomb Place: north front	108
64.	Icomb Place: front in mid-19th century	108
65.	Two knights of Sudeley and ruins of the Presence Chamber	110
66.	Sudeley Castle	113
67.	Bourton on the Hill House	115
68.	Bourton on the Hill House: barn	115
69.	Sherborne House: south front	117
70.	Sherborne House: stable entrance	117
71.	Burford Priory: south façade	119
72.	Burford Priory: east façade	119
73.	Hawling Manor	121
74.	Cruck house at Old Broadway	124
75.	Cruck house at Didbrook	124
76.	Taynton court rolls	125
77.	Map of Buckland	129
78.	Map of Stanton village	133
79.	Stanton: Warren House in 1905	134
80.	Stanton 'Rectory House' about 1804	135
81.	Stanton Court	137
82.	Stanton Court: doorway	137
83.	Little Rissington: Manor Cottages	140
84.	Wyck Rissington: College Farm	140
85.	Part of the map of open field strips in Hawling, 1748	141
86.	Northleach church, east end	145

LIST OF ILLUSTRATIONS

ix

87.	Northleach: former vicarage	150
88.	Bourton on the Water: former rectory	150
89.	Farmington: former rectory	151
90.	Buckland: former rectory	152
91.	Broad Campden Quaker Meeting House	154
92.	Burford Methodist chapel	155
93.	Northleach Congregational chapel	155
94.	Blockley church tower	157
95.	Campden House: Almonry	162
96.	Campden House: ruins	162
97.	Campden Court	163
98.	Bruern Abbey	164
99.	Northwick Park: west façade	166
100.	Northwick Park: east façade	166
101.	Rules for servants at Northwick Park about 1850	169
102.	Brockhampton Park	172
103.	Aston Subedge Manor House	173
104.	Bourton Manor	177
105.	Nether Swell Manor	177
106.	Sale particulars of Sezincote estate, 1880	179
107.	Map of hunts and gentlemen's residences, 1875	180
108.	Sale particulars for Stowell estate, 1923	182
109.	Moreton in Marsh market	186
110.	Burford: *Lamb Inn*	187
111.	'*Lamb and Flag*' sign	187
112.	Winchcombe: North Street	189
113.	Winchcombe: Hailes Street	189
114.	1832 Electoral Register	190
115.	Moreton in Marsh Curfew Tower	193
116.	Sundial at Naunton	194
117.	Sundial at Whittington	194
118.	Sevenhampton: cottage	195
119.	Model cottages Sherborne	196
120.	Hawling Elementary School and house	196
121.	Laverton model cottages	196
122.	Renewing a slate roof	197
123.	Repairing thatch	197
124.	Shipton Court in 1905	202
125.	Map of Condicote, 1797	204
126.	Map of Condicote, 1922	204
127.	Oxen yoked at Cotswold Farm Park, Guiting	206
128.	Wagon in Cotswold Countryside Collection, Northleach	206
129.	Tractor, 1927	207
130.	Broad Campden: Norman Chapel	208
131.	Winchcombe: Gloucester Street	209
132.	The *Lygon Arms*, Broadway	210
133.	Gordon Russell's premises, Broadway	210
134.	Stow on the Wold: Youth hostel	211
135.	Stone-walling	212
136.	Norman Hughes, making slates	212

List of Colour Illustrations

		between pages
I	Buckland church and manor house	68/69
II	Naunton church and village	68/69
III	Wooded slopes of Stanway Hill	68/69
IV	Open downland at Wontley	68/69
V	Farmcote chapel near a saltway above Hailes	68/69
VI	Condicote Lane	68/69
VII	Stanway church	68/69
VIII	Buckland Fields: Norman doorway	68/69
IX	Winchcombe: Bridge over the river Isbourne	84/85
X	Chipping Campden	84/85
XI	Poppies in the furrows	84/85
XII	The down at Fulbrook from Burford	84/85
XIII	Cross-bred 'mules' at Stanway	84/85
XIV	Sheep penned before shearing	84/85
XV	Sheep after shearing	84/85
XVI	Prize-winning 'Cotswold' sheep at Northleach, 1850	84/85
XVII	Prize-winning 'Cotswold' sheep, owner and shepherd, 1861	84/85
XVIII	The traditional 'Cotswold' breed of sheep at the Cotswold Farm Park	84/85
XIX	Stanway House	164/65
XX	Stanway House: Gatehouse	164/65
XXI	Whittington Court	164/65
XXII	Upper Slaughter Manor	164/65
XXIII	Yeoman's house in Stanton	164/65
XXIV	Sherborne: old farmhouse	164/65
XXV	Shipton under Wychwood church spire	164/65
XXVI	Coln St Denis church	164/65
XXVII	Sherborne church and west front of Sherborne House	164/65
XXVIII	Batsford Park	180/81
XXIX	Sezincote	180/81
XXX	Stow on the Wold market cross	180/81
XXXI	Guiting Power	180/81
XXXII	Bourton on the Water	180/81
XXXIII	Broadway Street	180/81
XXXIV	Snowshill Manor Cottages	180/81
XXXV	Condicote	180/81
XXXVI	Hailes	180/81

Acknowledgements

Photographs have been taken of many private houses and owners' permissions are gratefully acknowledged. Some open their gardens to the public under the National Gardens Scheme. The reader's courtesy is requested with respect to their privacy when and where not open to the public. Incumbents of churches are also thanked for permission to photograph on church premises. It is pleasing to be able to name the following for their help: Lady Ashcombe; Lady Dulverton; Lady Maureen Fellowes; Lord Neidpath; The Mother Prioress of The Priory of Our Lady at Burford; Mrs. V. Allen; Mr. P. Barclay; Bedford County Council; Mr. B. Berman; the Rev. Canon J. P. Brown; Mr. E. Burley; the Rev. C. D. J. G. Burslem; the Rev. G. G. B. Canning; Mr. and Mrs. R. J. Charleston; Mr. J. E. Clifford; Mr. A. Cooke; Cotswold District Council; the Rev. P. Draycott; Dr. D. G. Emery; Mr. and Mrs. M. Feller; Mrs. D. George; Mr. P. D. Granville-Edwards; the Rev. J. W. Hampton; Mr. Pip Handy; Mr. and Mrs. R. Handy; Mr. S. D. Harrison; Mr. J. Henson; the Rev. Canon P. B. Hobbs; Mr. N. Hughes; Mr. R. A. Hunter; Mr. Stuart C. Irby; Mr. P. Lee; the late Rev. C. H. Mc.Carter; the Rev. T. Thornton; Mr. D. H. Tongue; the Rev. R. N. Mann; Mrs. A. Martin; New Cavendish Estates plc; Mrs. M. O'Driscoll; Mr. R. Paice; Mrs. D. Peake; the Rev. F. Rothery; Mr. T. F. L. Royle; the owners of Stanton Court; Mr. J. S. Stover; Mrs. A. H. C. Voaden; Mrs. V. White; Mr. J. R. S. Whitehead for the Directors of Sherborne House; Mrs. M. Williams; the Rev. Dr. T. Williams.

Considerable help has been given by the following archive depositories and permissions to use illustrative material are also gratefully acknowledged: Bodleian Library, Oxford; Gloucester City Library; Gloucestershire Record Office; Oxfordshire Archives; Worcester Record Office. Quotations from documents at Longleat House are included by permission of the Marquess of Bath. Quotations from *The Diary of a Cotswold Parson* are made with the kind permission of Mr. F. E. B. Witts.

Specific acknowledgement for permission to use illustrations is gratefullly made to Davis & Co. Solicitors, Cheltenham, for Taynton 'Lots'; English Heritage for Hailes Abbey; Iona Antiques, PO Box 285, London W8 6 HZ for reproductions of two portraits of Cotswold sheep; Dr. Roger Leech for maps from *Historic Towns in Gloucestershire*; Russell and Hallmark, Solicitors, Worcester, for Northwick Park Servants Book; the Archivist of Gloucestershire County Council for an extract from the Electoral Register of 1832.

Photographic work has been expertly and cheerfully processed by Hamill Photo Services and more recently by The Darkroom and Michael Hall Photography, all of Cheltenham; particular thanks to Alistair, Rebecca and Jo, who continue a long-term collaboration.

Introduction

Themes in the History of the Cotswolds

The heartland of the Cotswolds is north of the Oxford to Cheltenham road, and includes such well-known places as Broadway, Chipping Campden and Burford, the Slaughters and the Swells, Stow on the Wold and Bourton on the Water. Most of the upland is in Gloucestershire. On the west the upland is defined with a sharp edge, and a series of settlements below have lands reaching up on to the hills. Here Broadway is a finger of Worcestershire, interrupting the sequence of Gloucestershire parishes. Meon Hill is the end of the upland to the north, like a full stop. On top of the hill there is an Iron-Age hill fort, built perhaps two and a half centuries before the birth of Christ, and from it there is a panorama of the Vale of Evesham. Gloucestershire used to include some of the Vale but the redrawing of county boundaries in the 20th century has separated Meon Hill from Mickleton, of which it had been a part, and Warwickshire now has this Cotswold vantage point. Ordnance Survey maps also draw a line a short way to the south of Meon Hill. To the east, the hills dip gradually down; Oxfordshire and Warwickshire are interwoven with Gloucestershire, but the core of the Cotswolds lies generally west of the Evenlode river and west of a line drawn northwards from Burford.

Division of the Midlands into shires was made sometime in the 10th century or very early in the 11th, because of the needs of military mobilisation against the Danes. Powerful men, bishops or abbots of the church as well as great secular landholders, were able to influence the placing of the boundaries, insisting that their lands should be within a particular shire to suit their own administrative convenience. Broadway, an estate of the powerful monastery of Pershore, was drawn into Worcestershire, despite the fact that the rest of the Cotswold edge was in Gloucestershire; so too were several small islands: Blockley, Cutsdean and half of Icomb, the estates of the Bishop of Worcester. The Four Shire Stone near Moreton in Marsh is a symbol of these arrangements; in Anglo-Saxon times four stones marked the four adjacent corners of separate estates, and when the shires were created, each estate was in a different county. There were four stones still when Defoe travelled the road. The creation of the first Ordnance Survey maps of England after 1801 must have contributed substantially to consciousness of such apparent irrationality, and so encouraged the transfer of lands from one county to another, a process which began in the 1840s, and has continued in the 20th century.

For a while in the Anglo-Saxon period the north Cotswold area looked to Winchcombe as its capital. There are references in later documents to Winchcombe-shire or 'Quarter'. Early in the 11th century Winchcombe Quarter was absorbed into Gloucestershire. Winchcombe was not really well-placed to control the uplands; it is at the foot of the main scarp slope, and roads up the edge are steep. Winchcombe's more natural lines of communication are to the north and west. Cheltenham, like Winchcombe, was also blocked from easy access to the upland by Dowdeswell Hill, a problem not overcome until the modern road was constructed in the early 19th century. The natural capital for the north Cotswolds was Bourton on the Water, especially in the period when Roman Buckle Street (or Ryknild Street) left the Fosse Way there, striking off north-westwards towards Weston Subedge and a crossing of the Avon at Bidford. Bourton is also at the confluence of three rivers, the Eye, the Dikler and the Windrush. There are many evidences of Roman occupation in the vicinity and the Anglo-Saxons probably had a minor capital here; a charter of 779 refers to a 'town' called Salmonsbury, a name still in use for the prehistoric encampment with earthen walls to the north of the modern settlement. The Fosse Way has been in continuous use since Roman times and provided the Anglo-Saxons with a good and direct route through the upland, as it does today's motorist, and Bourton is recapturing some of its past pre-eminence in the north Cotswolds.

Four main themes in Cotswold history are also the themes of the history of the English landscape: the patterns of the farmed countryside, of the fields and woods; the influence of the church; the division into manors and the power of manorial lords; and the relationships between settlements, the hamlets, villages and towns.

The Open Fields

The whole Cotswold area is notable for the former existence of 'open fields' or 'common fields'—a method of organising agriculture which emphasised co-operation and diminished the sense of ownership. In nearly every parish there were large arable fields divided into narrow strips; rippling contours across grassland are clearly visible in many places, where the ridges and furrows, made by ploughing the open-field strips, were not flattened before the land was converted to pasture after enclosure. The open-field system was widespread throughout Europe and its origins are mysterious. It has been dated to the Roman or early Saxon period, or placed much further back in prehistoric times; alternatively its origins may have been in medieval advances in cultivation, when newly-cleared land won from the waste was divided between the farmers of the area. Cotswold evidence points to the origins of the fields before Domesday Book and perhaps even before the Roman period. Roman roads in the area seem to slice through the pattern of fields like modern motorways, which also suggests that some field boundaries are even older.

There is much evidence of how the open-field system worked in the Cotswolds, and of its co-operative and intricate nature even in the late 18th century before it was finally swept away under acts of parliament. The open-field system served best when there were many smallholders of 'yardlands' or 'virgates'—each consisting of up to 30 acres of arable land and appropriate grazing rights; it made less sense when one farmer controlled many strips in each great field. Even before parliamentary enclosure, however, the number of farmers participating in the interlocking mesh of common rights and practices had been declining; enclosure merely encouraged still further the decline of smallholders. Each farmer now had separate hedged or walled fields, and sometimes in their midst a newly-built farmhouse. Isolated 18th-century farmhouses are witness to this vast reorganisation of the countryside.

While extensive sweeps of arable were once characteristic of the area, even in open-field parishes there was usually some enclosed land, and there were also areas of wood. It would not be true to imagine a landscape with no hedges or trees, though there were certainly fewer than there are today. In removing walls and hedgerows, modern tractor-based farming is tending to restore the appearance of the countryside as it would have been in medieval times.

INTRODUCTION

The prosperity of farmers has fluctuated since enclosure—in mid-Victorian times arable was the great profit-maker but since about 1870 foreign imports, particularly of wheat, have altered the structure of the agricultural communities.

Churches and Parishes

Our sense of place has been moulded by the church. 'Places' are parishes, groups of settlements clustered round a church building. Earliest written documents relating to the Cotswolds are records of the gifts of land in Anglo-Saxon times to endow churches which became major landowners until the dissolution of the monasteries in the reign of Henry VIII. The modern network of bishoprics and parishes was only gradually evolved. Worcester diocese was created in the seventh century; Gloucester diocese was split from it after Gloucester Abbey had been dissolved in 1540 and Oxford diocese was taken from Lincoln in 1542. The establishment of a parish involved the provision of a 'living' or glebe-land for the maintenance of the parson, and also the assignment of tithes, which were taxes on the inhabitants' actual produce. Where evidence about glebes has survived, it throws light on the agricultural and social system of the area, and the parson's glebe may have been a major factor in the long continuance of the open-field system. There are records of the operation of the tithe system and of the disputes caused by its intricacies. Tithes were a source of irritation in farming communities until the Commutation Act of 1836; in the Cotswolds tithes had mainly been abolished when the open-fields were enclosed in the 18th and 19th centuries.

Churches provide the visible focus for many village scenes, especially since so many towers were built, and in a few cases, spires as well. Domesday records few priests and very few Saxon churches have survived, but the Normans quickly established their presence by building stone churches, and there is a remarkable number of surviving Norman doorways and arches in this area. A second major phase of church building is well-known because of its connection with the wool trade: Burford, Chipping Campden and Northleach are famous examples of wool churches. Less well-known is the Victorian restoration movement which rescued many churches from severe decay, although provoking in the process the protests of those who saw the historical record being substantially altered.

Manors, Manor-houses and Lords

Domesday Book shows a network of a hundred or so manors in the Cotswolds. The manor was a practical means of organising petty sessions of the peace within a small area, in view of the difficulties of travelling. Manors were grouped together into larger units called 'Hundreds' and in each the King normally had one manor as the administrative centre, especially for tax-collecting. The manor was also a social system, making the lord of superior wealth and position and the villagers of subordinate status; it was closely integrated with the open-field system. The gradual transformation of manorial holdings or 'copyholds' into rented farms took many centuries to accomplish and in this area was particularly slow.

Each lord of the manor normally had a house or hall as the centre of his own farm, or 'demesne', and of the organisation of the area. A few manor houses are earlier than the Elizabethan period, notably Icomb Place and Sudeley Castle. The enormous release of land which took place when the monasteries were closed led to many families becoming owners where they had previously rented farms and manor houses from the abbots. This no doubt encouraged much building and rebuilding, as at Sherborne House and Stanway House. There were many minor gentry but few greater gentry or aristocrats. The Cotswolds are notable for small manor houses but only Sherborne was truly a mansion before the 18th century, judging

1 & 2. *(left)* The Four Shire Stone near Moreton in Marsh and *(right)* the Norman doorway in the former chapel at Broad Campden before restoration are two of the illustrations by Frederick L. Griggs in *Highways and Byways in Oxford and the Cotswolds* by Herbert Evans, published in 1905.

from the number of chimneys recorded in the hearth tax of 1671. Other big houses, like Brockhampton Park, Burford Priory, Stanway House or Northwick Park, were rebuilt or much enlarged in the 18th or the early 19th centuries. In the 20th century most manor houses have been separated from the farms for which they were the centres, while the problems of upkeep have become nearly insuperable for the mansions.

Hamlet, Village and Town

Cotswold settlements are mainly compact villages, clusters of stone houses, often sited in surprisingly steep-sided valleys. Much of the character of the area is the result of building in local stone. The uplands are pitted with old quarry workings, which were sufficiently numerous in Saxon times for several to mark the boundaries of estates. Taynton stone is the most famous of the Cotswold stones, supplied in the 20th century for the inside of the New Bodleian Library in Oxford, as it had been used in the construction of many of the colleges in the past; the Taynton quarries have the distinction of being listed in the Domesday account of the manor. Water in the area is not abundant but there are enough springs to supply the villagers and to water the animals. Place-names with the element 'well', meaning spring indicate the Anglo-Saxons' keen awareness of where water was to be found, and 'Broadwell' may indicate a better than average spring.

Nearly all the major place-names on the modern map have Anglo-Saxon origins; yet many settlements may be much older. Naunton, meaning 'new town', probably was established in the mid-Anglo-Saxon period, but hill-forts and burial mounds point to prehistoric estates not dissimilar to later manorial ones and so also do Roman villas. It seems that existing estates may have been given new names by the Anglo-Saxons, while settlements were moved to different sites. At some later date, estates were sometimes split into several manors and

INTRODUCTION

parishes: in Shipton five Domesday manors became Shipton Oliffe and Shipton Solers; in Barrington four manors became Great and Little Barrington; in Slaughter the two manors became Upper and Lower Slaughter. The division of such estates led to anomalies in the arrangement of the open-fields.

The Cotswolds are notable for deserted village sites. The characteristic humps and dips of house sites and roads are tantalising. Why were they deserted? Many answers are possible. The most well-known one is that they were closed to people in order to make way for sheep—the great source of wealth in the middle ages. It is more likely, however, that these sites were abandoned because the villagers moved to a more favourable site, to a site planned by an improving landlord, or to a site where they could escape from the tight control of the lord of the manor.

Winchcombe was the one Cotswold market-town at the time of Domesday, and had a special status, following the county town at the beginning of the Gloucestershire survey. In the years immediately following the Norman Conquest several more markets were licensed—they provided useful income to the alert manorial lord, and monasteries were particularly notable entrepreneurs. The upland area is ringed with these market towns: Burford, Northleach, Broadway, Blockley, Chipping Campden, Moreton in Marsh and Stow on the Wold, and all but Burford and Chipping Campden were monastic estates.

Evidence of occupations in the early 17th century reveals the essentially urban nature of the small towns, although they were mainly concerned with local trade, once wool ceased to be the most important English export; Stow was perhaps the exception, attracting purchasers from further afield to the horse market. In the 18th and early 19th centuries, turnpike travellers stopped the night in the coaching inns, but the rural quietness of the north Cotswolds was little affected by the increasing industrial bustle to the south in the Stroud area, or more notably in regions to the north. A railway was constructed through the area between 1855 and 1875 from Andoversford to Bourton on the Water, Stow on the Wold and Chipping Norton. It was expected to have profound effects; but its life was short and its effect far from dramatic.

By the end of the 19th century the Cotswolds were experiencing agricultural depression but fashionable discovery. The bicycle was surprisingly the first means of discovery, giving Herbert Evans, for example, the chance to travel from Oxford in 1905 through the whole Cotswold area. His book marks the start of the tourist industry. New occupants moved into the area in search of its traditional rural style as English towns became increasingly industrialised. Until the end of the Second World War, tours by car were still relatively uncommon; more recently the towns have faced a conflict between modest size and attractiveness to tourists, but so far modernisation has been successfully absorbed. Burford, Chipping Campden, Stow on the Wold and Winchcombe were all included in the list of historic towns drawn up by the Council for British Archaeology; their ancient town plans were well-preserved, they had a number of buildings dating from before 1800 worth preserving, and in Winchcombe's case had a well-preserved major ecclesiastical precinct. Burford and Chipping Campden were two of the forty English towns picked out as of national importance. However unlikely, an idyll of a past golden age of rural England can still seem close in the Cotswolds.

Chapter One

The Cotswold Scene in Domesday Book

A good starting point for a history of the Cotswolds is the Domesday Survey of 1086; however elliptical its testimony, it shows the main characteristics of the Cotswolds already established. Domesday Book is unique because it provides evidence for nearly the whole country, at a date earlier than any comparable European document, though it is possible to take the story back much earlier for a few places, particularly through the Worcester collection of Saxon charters. Domesday Book names over 13,000 places, including nearly all the main place-names of the north Cotswolds, as well as many minor ones. Some names may not be easy to recognise, but with the studies carried out over the last hundred years, nearly all have been identified. Most have hardly changed at all in the intervening nine centuries: Campadene, Bradeweia, Wincelcumbe, Bortune, Bureford for instance, or Swelle, Bradewelle, Hodecote, Colne, Icumbe, Turchedene or Turghedene, Colesburne and Dodeswelle.

Collecting Information in 1086
King William ordered the Inquisition or survey of his new country just 20 years after he had defeated Harold at Hastings and claimed the English throne. That such an undertaking could be organised at all says much for the administrative framework already existing in the country; that it was completed within a year is a further tribute to the Anglo-Saxon state which King William had inherited. The basic framework of enquiry was the county; the Royal Commissioners and their clerks probably met in the county town, or perhaps at a few other convenient centres as well, and collected the data together. The commission for Gloucestershire also covered Herefordshire, Worcestershire, Shropshire, Cheshire and south Lancashire. Much of the work must have been done beforehand, so that in the short time available the commissioners simply gathered confirmation of what they had been told and tried to resolve problems.

Within each county, the framework for the enquiry was the smaller territorial unit called a 'hundred'. A panel of jurors was called together in each hundred to submit information and to confirm the truth of what others had said. Hundreds were small enough geographical areas to allow men holding land to meet at regular monthly intervals to settle questions concerning law and order, property and taxation. In the north Cotswolds, there were 10 main Domesday hundreds. In later times they were reorganised and most of the north Cotswolds came into the hundreds of Bradley, Upper Slaughter, Lower Slaughter, Upper Kiftsgate and Lower Kiftsgate, which reached from Northleach and Withington to Campden and Ebrington. A few places were in Oswaldslow, a triple hundred in the jurisdiction of the Bishop of Worcester, who administered all his properties together, and Broadway was in Pershore hundred. Burford,

Fifield, Fulbrook, Idbury and Taynton were in Oxfordshire hundreds. This administrative framework was still used in the 19th century for the much more detailed surveys of the kingdom in the national Census.

The Domesday enquiry was designed to establish precisely who held the land; it was also possible to find out who held it 'on the day on which King Edward was alive and dead', as draft Domesday instructions said, so giving insight into late Anglo-Saxon England as well as into early Norman England. Information from each hundred was arranged to give a full county holding for each landholder, and has to be rearranged to give information on any particular area. It is surprising that so little double counting seems to have occurred—boundaries must have been generally well known. There was one double entry in the north Cotswold area, of land in Windrush said to be held by Winchcombe Abbey and also by Alfsi of Faringdon but this estate had recently been given to Winchcombe and may have been Alfsi's for his lifetime.

The word 'manor' was used to describe a landholding not under the control of another man. A manor was a well-recognised unit, with a fixed assessment for taxation purposes. The Domesday commissioners required written information from each manor and a representative attended the enquiry. In very few instances this did not happen—at Woodchester, for example, 'Nobody has rendered acccount of this manor to the King's Commissioners, nor has any of them come to this survey'. The jurymen of the hundred were still able to supply the manor's valuation, though not other details, showing that some records were available to them. Several manors were located by reference to the same place-name, for example Barrington, Guiting, Rissington or Slaughter, which seem to have been clearly defined districts, and no other identification was given for each manor. Some estates crossed district boundaries, like the land holdings of William Goizenboded in Aylworth and Caldicote, later known as Westfield. In Domesday this appears as two manors. As a result, although there were over a hundred Domesday manors in the north Cotswolds, this exaggerates the number of actual estates.

The size of each manor was described in units called 'hides', which were approximate measures of area, about 120 acres of arable land. The hide was of considerable antiquity; a document of possibly seventh- or eighth-century date, known as the Tribal Hidage, gives totals of hidages for early Anglo-Saxon kingdoms and similar information was used by Bede in the early eighth century in his *Ecclesiastical History of the English People*. In the early 10th century, one man from each hide had to do military service and supply a fixed quantity of money, food and services to the king. Taxes or 'geld' were still levied at a rate per hide in the 12th century; in 1083-84 William's geld was six shillings (30p) per hide and was considered very stiff.

The hide has had a long-lasting influence. A group of settlements assessed at one hundred hides was the basis of the administrative area of the hundred. The hide underlay the customary land holdings in each village or manor: it was divided into quarters, called 'virgata' in Latin, 'yardlands' in English, and these units, too, lasted in some places into the 19th century; each land holding was usually described as a whole or a fraction of a yardland, but sometimes the term 'quarter' was used. A yardland was approximately thirty acres of arable land, but varied from manor to manor. Some places were named from the hide. To the south of Stow on the Wold there is a farm and water mill in Maugersbury called The Hide; there was a mill here in Domesday, and the whole compact block of land which was described in an Anglo-Saxon land charter of 1016 was still called The Hide in descriptions of the fields of Maugersbury seven centuries later. Other places, like The Hide in Guiting, must have originated in the same way, though there is no early documentary evidence. One-hide estates were rare in the Cotswolds

THE COTSWOLD SCENE IN DOMESDAY BOOK

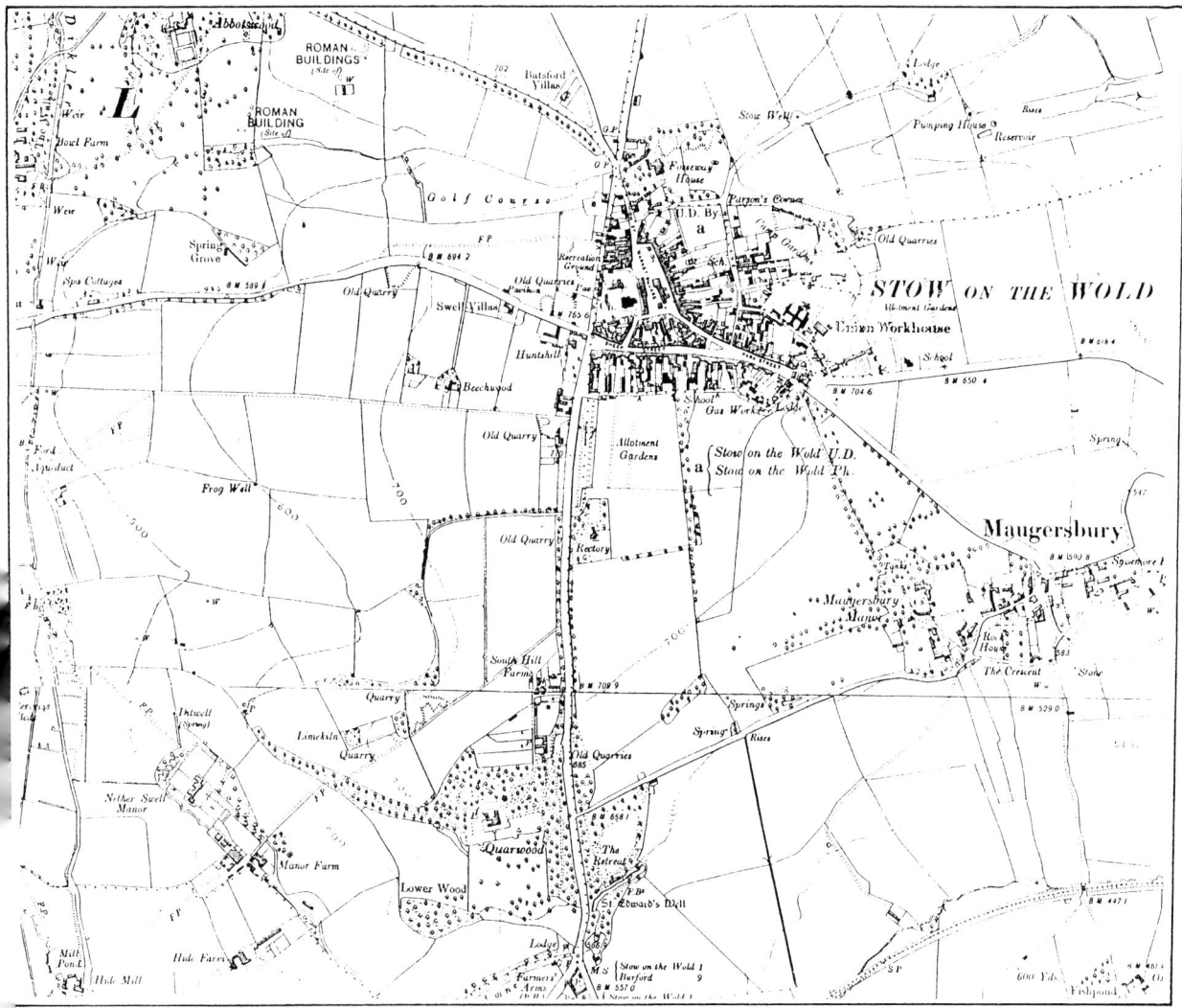

3. Stow on the Wold and Maugersbury from the Ordnance Survey map of 1923: Hide Farm and Hide Mill are in the south-west corner of the map.

in Domesday Book; most commonly estates were five or ten hides, large enough to include a small village or several hamlets. Fifield, in Oxfordshire, gained its name because it was a five-hide block of land, and in Domesday the name is 'Fifhyde'.

Norman landowners

The Anglo-Saxon landowners in the north Cotswolds had been displaced in the 20 years between the Conquest and the Domesday Survey, and replaced by Normans, as they had been throughout England; only four Cotswold manors, three of them very small, remained in Anglo-Saxon hands. Sometimes Saxon landholders may have been tenants to a Norman lord, but where Domesday mentions sub-tenants, they too have Norman names. Many Anglo-Saxon landholders, known as thegns, were killed in the two great battles Harold had fought in 1066, first against the Danes at Stamford Bridge, then against the Normans at Hastings; others had subsequently been involved in plots and rebellions. Their lands were forfeited and Norman lords stepped into the thegns' position. Sometimes several Saxons' holdings were amalgamated, as at Winson near Bibury and also at Weston Subedge, where five Saxons were replaced by one Norman, or at Longborough and Rissington where in each case four small manors were combined into one. All these land transfers were apparently well-known, and the sweeping reallocations carried out by the Conqueror were recorded generally without comment; where there were doubts or disputes, the King could give judgement. Within a short time, the record of the survey was accepted as final, hence its name; no appeal was possible against the verdict at the Day of Judgement or Doom. The name itself was certainly in use by 1179, and perhaps earlier.

No great baron dominated the Cotswold area; only William Goizenboded had a sizeable estate, consisting of Caldicote, Castlett, Ebrington, Farmcote, and parts of Aylworth, Barrington and Guiting, and he was the largest landowner in the county. His name may indicate some physical misfortune and contain reference to a witch. There had been no dominant Anglo-Saxon thegn in the area either; the largest had been Countess Goda, the sister of King Edward the Confessor, with four sizeable manors. Goda had died about 1065; three of her estates, Hawling, Hazleton and Yanworth, went to the Norman Sigar from Chocques in the Pas-de-Calais. Two

4. The church at Stow (which means a holy place) was mentioned in the Domesday Book entry for Maugersbury. The tower and the clerestorey windows are 15th century; the very splendid west window is 14th century.

5. Withington church was an Anglo-Saxon 'minster'. In Domesday Book a priest with half a hide of land is mentioned, but the very large manor was in the possession of the Bishop of Worcester.

THE COTSWOLD SCENE IN DOMESDAY BOOK

6. In 1086 there was a priest in Hazleton and a saltway runs through the parish. Together with Hawling and Yanworth, the manor had belonged to the sister of Edward the Confessor and by 1086 had passed to a Norman. The former rectory with its barns and dovecote is next to the church; it was always and remains a farmhouse.

other Saxons had had three manors each; one was possibly living on a very small manor at Ampney in 1086, and the other had been made an outlaw. The Godwin family had been very large landowners throughout the south of England, but had only one Cotswold manor, though it was an important one. Domesday scribes were not allowed to refer to Harold as King, so Earl Harold's estate at Campden was recorded, by 1086 transferred to a nephew of King William, created Earl of Chester; Earl Harold had also drawn a third of the revenues of the borough of Winchcombe.

It was not the case in the Cotswolds that a few Normans displaced a large number of small, independent Saxon landholders or 'free peasants'. Where there had been small Saxon estates, each had been transferred to a different Norman lord. In Sezincote, for example, six Anglo-Saxons, two of them possibly brothers, were replaced by five Normans; in Windrush and Condicote several small estates continued to be separate. In part of Swell, one Saxon was replaced by two Normans. After the Norman Conquest, a lord's estates remained as dispersed as they had been before; no doubt it was royal policy to avoid creating mini-kingdoms, as might happen if one man was given authority over several contiguous estates.

Half the land in the north Cotswolds was held by religious houses and bishoprics, an even greater proportion than in Gloucestershire generally, where the church held about a third. In this respect there was a large measure of continuity from Anglo-Saxon to Norman times, even though abbots, bishops and archbishops were Normans. The bishop of Worcester was by far the largest baron; he had two very large manors: Blockley, in the hundred of Oswaldslow and Withington, which included Aston Blank, parts of Colesborne and Compton, Dowdeswell, Hilcot, Foxcote, Notgrove and Pegglesworth. The church of Winchcombe was nearly as important, having a large manor at Sherborne, and a number of smaller ones: Bledington, Charlton Abbots, Stanton, Snowshill, parts of Hidcote and Windrush, and Frampton and Naunton near Winchcombe.

Other churches controlled considerable Cotswold estates. Evesham Abbey had Willersey, Upper Swell, Broadwell, Maugersbury and Bourton on the Water; the bishop of Hereford had Prestbury and Sevenhampton; Eynsham Abbey had Mickleton; Tewkesbury had Stanway and Taddington; Gloucester had Buckland, Pershore had Broadway. The roll of ecclesiastical properties is very long, and only two estates had been given to the church since 1066: Aston Subedge was given to St Mary's, Lambeth and Roel was held under the King by the French church of St Evroult-Notre-Dame-du-Bois. All the other manors had been in church hands in Saxon times. Edward the Confessor had given his new foundation of Westminster Abbey, consecrated just before his death, much of Deerhurst Priory's land, including Bourton on the Hill and Moreton in Marsh. Other Deerhurst estates at Taynton and at Coln had been transferred to St Denis, or St Dionysius, in Paris, which accounts for the place-name of Coln St Denis. The Archbishop of York had acquired Compton, part of Condicote, Northleach and Oddington as a result of Gloucester Abbey mortgaging these manors. The substitution of a new Norman bishop or abbot for a Saxon one made little difference to Cotswold farmers. In any case the holdings of the church, too, were extremely scattered, so that personal attention to each manor all the year round could hardly be expected. In the 12th century, the church's landholdings were enlarged still further, and its enormous importance lasted for another 400 years, until the monasteries were closed by Henry VIII.

Arable Land, Pasture and Woods
'Ploughs' were new Norman units of land assessment used in Domesday Book and intended to replace the older hides. A plough was a long and cumbersome implement, often pulled by eight oxen yoked together. It needed two men to control it, one leading the oxen and one guiding the plough. The oxen needed a rest after they had dragged the plough about 220 yards or a furrow length—a furlong; they only worked in the morning and in the afternoon went out to pasture. One plough and team cultivated at maximum one acre a day but more likely only half an acre. Even in the 18th century, when animals were larger and probably stronger, Arthur Young noted that from Northleach, through Gloucestershire, Monmouthshire and Glamorganshire, land was being ploughed at the rate of half an acre to one acre per day 'by teams of eight oxen, never less than six, or by four oxen and two horses'. No farmer would keep more oxen than he needed to draw the plough; they ate food which could otherwise feed people. Ploughs were therefore a good guide to the extent of arable, and were still being used in the *Valor Ecclesiasticus*, the survey of the resources of the church made in 1535. Later in the 16th century, the churchwardens of Whittington estimated their rector's income in the same way: he 'hath the tithe of our small parish, wherein are kept three ploughs wherefore we think his glebe and tithes worth 20 marks or thereabouts'.

Arable cultivation was widespread over a great part of the Cotswolds; there were very few manors where there were no ploughs at work. If the modern acreage of the area is related to the number of Domesday ploughs, the ratio is approximately 168 acres per plough, so that

THE COTSWOLD SCENE IN DOMESDAY BOOK

7. A team of four oxen, led (or prodded) by Charles Martell, pulls a wooden plough similar to one seen in medieval illustrations. The ox-bow links the animals to the traditional wooden yoke. The team moves quite fast, but at the end of a furlong the oxen are panting with effort.

up to two thirds of the land was arable. Pasture, meadow, wood, gardens, parks, quarries, ponds, roads and wasteland made up the other third. This did not mean that the Cotswold scene in the summer was an expanse of yellow and gold as it is now, because each year up to half the arable land had to be left uncultivated, that is fallow, and was grazed by the villagers' animals, mostly sheep, to restore the soil's fertility. A small part of the land would be used to grow peas and beans, though more than half of each year's crop was probably wheat and barley, and a small amount rye and oats. The summer scene would have been an extensive patchwork of brown and green with some wide sweeps of yellow where an arable field of corn was ripening, except when the whole scene was bleached by drought.

There were 30 per cent more ploughs than hides in the north Cotswolds, which was not untypical of England generally, and certainly suggests why ploughs were to provide a new base for taxation. Either more land was under cultivation than had been the case when hides were first assessed, or land had been reorganised and less was fallow each year. Estimates were made in some parts of the country of cultivable land lying waste, but not in Gloucestershire, probably because there had been little loss of arable land since the conquest. At the end of Domesday's account of the Bishop of Worcester's estates it says: 'in all these manors it would not be possible to have more ploughs than stated'—*in omnibus his maneriis non possunt esse plus carrucae quam dictum est*. Perhaps the Bishop of Worcester made sure that there was no scope for his tax to be increased in the future, as Maitland suggested; however, his Gloucestershire assessments had already been upgraded, because there were more ploughs on his manors than hides.

Each manor was valued in money terms in Domesday, and values were closely related to the number of ploughs on the lord's own demesne, generally £2 to £3 per plough, though the Archbishop of York's ploughs at Oddington were unusually valuable at £5 each. Oddington is still considered very good barley land. It is is odd that most ecclesiastical manors had increased in value between 1066 and 1086, whereas many lay estates had apparently fallen in value. Church manors like Blockley had risen from £16 to £20, Buckland from £3 to £9, Broadwell and Bourton on the Water from £8 to £12 each, Oddington from £6 to £10, and largest of all, Northleach, from £18 to £27; only Sherborne and Withington had declined a little. Why was the church apparently able to increase its income while the new Norman lords were not? Had the Norman abbots reorganised their lands and perhaps increased the amount cultivated each year? Or had Norman lords settled their followers on their demesne lands? In Campden, which had fallen in value from £30 to £20, the Norman Earl Hugh of Chester was well-known for his attachment to falconers and huntsmen; in his enthusiasm for the chase arable land was made forest. This attitude could have explained some cases where land values had apparently fallen.

Pasture was essential in the economy of an arable area, for the support of the oxen, but Domesday very rarely mentions it in Gloucestershire. In adjacent places in Oxfordshire, pasture is frequently noted and its amount estimated by length and breadth, expressed in 'leagues'. A league was one and a half miles. In both Burford and Fifield the pastures were one league long and one league wide, in Taynton one league long and half a league wide; yet in the neighbouring Gloucestershire places along the Windrush, for example Barrington or Windrush itself, no pasture is recorded. There was 'woodland and pasture for 40 hens' in Guiting, '15 hides in both woodland and open land and meadow' in Chedworth, and 'meadow and woodland in certain places, but not much' in Withington, but these are the only indications of pasture land, and even here it was apparently dotted with trees. Pastures and woods attached to a manor were not necessarily within its immediate boundaries. A description in Anglo-Saxon of Taynton manor, which included both wood and pasture, and was made when the estate was transferred from Deerhurst Abbey to St Denis in Paris in 1059, shows that the wood was a few miles east of Taynton, near Widford in the Wychwood; Faws Grove and Widley Copse were on its boundaries. The pasture, or 'moor', was at the confluence of the Windrush and the Thames, and was some seven miles south-east of Taynton, now called Northmoor. The manor was later called 'Taynton and More'. Taynton controlled a ferry over the Thames at Northmoor, which must have been of value in transporting stone from the quarries which were mentioned in Domesday Book. Eels provided an exceptionally good income to the lord and were no doubt trapped along Taynton's reach of the Thames.

Meadow similarly is not mentioned very much in Gloucestershire but was apparently much more extensive in Oxfordshire. Meadow was more valuable than pasture, because it could be mowed for hay. Meadows were mentioned along the flood plains of the rivers: in Barrington there were 26 acres, in both Bledington and Sherborne 30 acres and in Windrush 18 acres, and Blockley, too, had 28 acres of meadow. In the Oxfordshire places bordering the same rivers there were 170 acres of meadow in Taynton, 63 in Fulbrook and 60 in Idbury. The Oxfordshire manors were in the Wychwood; grazing was perhaps controlled by the king and not so easily lost to the plough as elsewhere.

The absence of pasture in Gloucestershire Domesday means that there is little indication of where the famous Cotswold sheep might have been found. Even at Shipton in Gloucestershire, where the place-name refers to sheep, there is no mention of pasture, though Shipton was fragmented into several small manors which may hint at sheep pastures once shared between several manors. For example, Pinswell in Colesborne had been a sheep pasture in the mid-seventh century but by the time of Domesday had been split between several manors.

In later centuries, sheep downs were common land, shared by the villagers; they did not provide the lord of the manor with income, and this may be the reason that the sheep downs were ignored by Domesday.

There were few large woods in the north Cotswolds, except on the steep, uncultivable slopes along the western edge of the hills, in Postlip, Sudeley, Hailes and Stanway; this is another indication of the widespread arable cultivation. Sudeley's woods were the most extensive, an area three leagues by two leagues, or about 8,500 acres; together with Hailes and Postlip, this was a large wooded sweep of land as it is today. There were smaller woods also in Whittington and Withington, and in Taynton in Oxfordshire. Other places where woods were referred to were Blockley, Hawling, Pinnock and Yanworth, and in Fulbrook, which like Taynton was within the forest of Wychwood. Small copses and bands of wood must have existed in every area, but Domesday was not concerned with them if they were not an economic asset to the lord of the manor.

Where a mill existed, this too was the lord's and provided income; for this reason the lord of Sudeley had retained all six mills along the Isbourne, and pushed Winchcombe town boundary back from the river. Extensive engineering effort before the time of Domesday had created water power for grinding corn, and possibly also for fulling cloth; it seems likely that some of Blockley's 12 Domesday mills might have been utilised for fulling. The earliest specific written record of a fulling mill is in 1185, in Barton in Guiting, belonging to the Knights Templars; there were three mills in Guiting in Domesday. A fulling mill at Bourton on the Water is mentioned in the early 13th century. Many of the Domesday mills were along the course of the Windrush, which is the most considerable river in the north Cotswolds, and there were a number along the Coln and the Leach, but a good spring, as at Syreford, was all that was necessary to provide water power. Domesday mills were mainly water mills; windmills had not yet been developed in England, but a few could have been treadmills powered by the feet of men or of animals. A mill at Campden and another at Paxford were both later called 'Pie Mill'; 'pied', meaning 'foot', would be in keeping as the origin of these names.

Mills were the lord of the manor's partly because he must have been the only person with the capital for the often extensive works: a canal to bring water to the mill at a higher level than the natural stream in order to create a fall over the water wheel, and a long tail race to draw the water away from the mill until it would flow back into the stream. As manors were reorganised, a mill might be shared between several lords. In Barrington there were four manors before the Norman Conquest, all the same size, and each had a mill valued at the same amount; it seems unlikely that there were four separate buildings with associated earth works, though there may have been four sets of grindstones. A pair of stones may be the 'mill' of Domesday rather than a building.

Townsmen and Villagers
Winchcombe was the only town in the north Cotswolds. Domesday does not state how many free inhabitants or 'burgesses' there were, nor how many plots of land or 'burgages', but an Evesham Abbey manuscript which was prepared in connection with the Domesday Survey shows Winchcombe with 100 burgesses, compared with 300 in Gloucester. The king held 60 burgages and the abbot of Winchcombe held forty. The king's burgages were let to ordinary townsfolk, the abbot's were let to major landowners in the area, who gained the advantage of free access to the market; they probably in turn rented their houses to local craftsmen and tradesmen. The lord of Hampnett had 10 burgages in Winchcombe, and the lords of the manors of Alderton, Broadwell, Childswickham, Clopton, Deerhurst, Guiting, Lechlade,

Oxenton, Prestbury, Pinnock and Withington also had one or more Winchcombe burgages. When King Alfred had first organised a new series of defensive towns to resist the Danish attacks, the area surrounding each town was probably required to supply men and money to keep watch and build the walls; a burgage in the town seems to have been a return for the obligation. In the same way, the lords of Burford and of Taynton had houses in Oxford. Baldwin, the abbot of Bury St Edmund's in 1086, had Taynton's Oxford house; he had been a monk at St Denis, and also physician to King Edward the Confessor.

The shire once centred on Winchcombe some eighty years previously was remembered by the monks of Evesham Abbey in 1086 even though it no longer existed. After detailing the Gloucestershire estates of the abbey: Adlestrop, Bourton on the Water, Broadwell, parts of Hidcote, Stoke and Weston on Avon, Maugersbury, Upper Swell, and Willersey, the comment is added that 'in the quarter of Winchcombe St Mary's of Evesham had 56 hides in the time of King Edward'—*In Ferdingo de Wicelcombe habuit Sancta Maria de Evesham LVI hidas T.R.E..* About the same date, a monk of Worcester called Hemming, who copied down all the church's existing land charters, noted that the amalgamation of the shires of Winchcombe and of Gloucester had occurred at the beginning of the 11th century. The existence of the shire is further confirmed in an earlier collection of Worcester charters, which were grouped under the names of the chief towns of their areas, Oxford, Gloucester, Worcester, Warwick and Winchcombe; the word 'scire' was added to the headings Oxford, Gloucester and Winchcombe. The estates listed under Winchcombe were at Andoversford, Aston Blank, Beckford, Bishops Cleeve, Cheltenham, Dowdeswell, Notgrove and Withington. Winchcombeshire therefore seems to have covered the north Cotswold area. It has been suggested that Winchcombeshire was half of Gloucestershire, but this ignores the Evesham Abbey comment about a 'quarter'. Moreover Gloucester had three times as many burgesses as Winchcombe, which seems to point to the relative sizes of the areas related to the two towns.

Apart from the burgesses of Winchcombe, there were few who had the status of freemen and were not under close control by the lords of the manors. It is surprising that only 18 priests were mentioned in the north Cotswolds, considering that the church as landholder was so dominant. It is quite likely that church buildings and priests went unrecorded; Domesday was concerned with land and resources for taxation, and a church with no specific endowment was not relevant to the enquiry. Priests, though they were freemen, were usually included with the villagers on the manor. A few 'riding-men', who were better-off independent cultivators of the land, were scattered through the area; in several of the abbot of Westminster's manors attached to Deerhurst, and including Bourton on the Hill, there were riding men, 'that is, free men, who all, however, ploughed, harrowed, scythed, and reaped for the lord's work'. Although technically free men, in practice they were little different from all the other villagers.

Most inhabitants in the area were unfree, called 'villani', 'bordarii' and 'servi' in Domesday, translated as 'villagers', 'smallholders' and 'slaves'. Villagers were the majority of the cultivators of the land. 'Farmer' would be the modern word, but 'firma' is 'rent' and a 'farmer' was a rent-payer, a rather different position from the majority of cultivators at the time of Domesday and for some centuries afterwards; 'villager' is a neutral term and more familiar than 'villein'. Similarly, 'cottager' might be an equivalent to 'bordar', but some of Domesday's bordars may have had more than a cottage garden, so 'smallholder' is a term which does not imply any particular size of land-holding. Eventually slaves, smallholders and villagers became merged into one class of unfree cultivators, and were all called 'serfs'.

The Cotswolds are notable for the many slaves. Slavery could have continued uninterrupted from the Roman period, or in the Anglo-Saxon period have been the consequence of defeat and capture in battle. There were certainly slaves in Anglo-Saxon England. The fair-haired Angles in the market-place in Rome waiting to be sold were supposed to have prompted Pope Gregory to send Christian missionaries to England in 594, and an Anglo-Saxon law code of the 10th century made provision for the punishment of runaway slaves who were living in bandit gangs. Nearly every lord of the manor had two slaves for each of his ploughs, one to guide the plough and one to drive the oxen. On the Bishop of Worcester's large manor of Blockley there were 16 slaves and eight demesne ploughs; the bishop also had 49 slaves for the 19 demesne ploughs in Withington manor. Other large ecclesiastical manors, too, relied on slaves; at Northleach the Archbishop of York and at Sherborne the monastery of Winchcombe each had twelve. Two large lay estates nearly matched these; at Campden, Earl Hugh had 12 slaves and at Guiting, Roger de Lacy had eighteen. There were a few manors without slaves, including Bourton on the Water, Cutsdean, Coln St Dennis, Oddington, and Whittington. Under the Normans, slavery gradually died out. Domesday records that the Norman William Leofric at Hailes had freed 12 slaves, but it does not say what became of them. Had Leofric provided them with land in Hailes, where 11 smallholders were noted?

The characteristics of the Cotswolds are therefore traceable in Domesday Book, and continuity from Anglo-Saxon England seems more striking than the changes made by the Norman Conquest. There were many small manors already in existence, though transferred into the hands of Norman lords. The church had a very large share of land. No fiefdoms had been created, either lay or ecclesiastical, and each man's manors were scattered throughout the area. The Cotswolds were thinly populated, if numbers of inhabitants are related to the amount of cultivated land, even compared with Gloucestershire overall, which was one of the least populous counties in Domesday. Much of the area was under arable cultivation, so the small population may point to low yields of grain, but it may also reflect tight manorial control, where sub-division of holdings had not been permitted; the monastic landlords certainly needed to produce surplus food from their estates to feed their communities. The situation also suggests that there were labourers who were not recorded. There is perhaps a hint of this in Sevenhampton where Domesday said there were three free men having seven ploughs 'with their men', *cum suis hominibus*. There were very few freemen in the north Cotswolds, though many slaves. Manorial organisation was a very important influence on the later development of agriculture and the pattern of settlement.

Chapter Two

Anglo-Saxon Estates and Settlements

Over six hundred years separated the Norman Conquest from the Anglo-Saxon invasions. The period appears foreshortened because there are few written records, especially for the first two centuries. About 446, the British faced renewed waves of invaders with no hope of help from Rome. The invaders did not take over the Cotswold area until the end of the sixth century; three British kings ruled small kingdoms from Bath, Cirencester and Gloucester before the battle of Dyrham in 577. The customs and practices of Romanised inhabitants of the area could more easily have survived here than in other areas of England after formal Roman control of the country was abandoned. The Anglo-Saxons, however, fixed a very large number of Cotswold place-names; many contain Anglo-Saxon 'ton', which is the most common place-name element. The divisions of territory used by the Anglo-Saxons have also had long-lasting effects, determining particularly the development of manors and parishes. Icomb, Naunton, The Slaughters, The Barringtons and the Shiptons are all illuminating examples. Traces of Anglo-Saxon territorial organisation often remained even in the 20th century.

Wychwood, Saltways and Wolds
Bede, writing at the beginning of the eighth century in a monastery in Northumberland, said that the people inhabiting the area stretching from Bath to Worcester were called the Hwicce and that they controlled 7,000 hides. Their kingdom corresponded approximately with the counties of Gloucestershire and Worcestershire. The Cotswolds was an important part and Winchcombe may have been the original nucleus of the Hwicce's territory. Later in the century, about 770, the Hwicce were absorbed into the large neighbouring kingdom of Mercia, and their name was almost forgotten. Before the name 'Cotswold' was in general use, the upland was identified with the Hwicce. Cutsdean was said to be *in monte quem nominant incola mons Huuicciorum*, 'the hill which the inhabitants call the hill of the Hwicce'; estates at Northwick and Dorn in Blockley, Evenlode, Daylesford and Icomb were all in the area 'monte Wiccisca' in 964. Even at the end of the 16th century, Habington, a Worcestershire antiquarian, noted that Broadway was at the foot of 'Monte Wiccesi', 'now called Broadway hills'.

The Wychwood was the wood of the Hwicce, yet it was not in the Cotswolds but in Oxfordshire. By the time of Domesday, Wychwood was one of five woods within a great royal forest stretching all the way across northern Oxfordshire. It was then nine leagues by nine leagues, about 182 square miles or 120,000 acres. It was bounded to the south and east by the Windrush and the Evenlode rivers, and it reached from Taynton to Woodstock, hence Ascot under Wychwood, Milton under Wychwood and Shipton under Wychwood. Shipton, the sheep town, shows that there was pasture-land within the forest boundaries. A forest was

ANGLO-SAXON ESTATES AND SETTLEMENTS

a carefully managed tract of land, with pasture, coppice and game resources within its area; traditionally the Wychwood was divided into 18 sections, one cut each year.

In the Anglo-Saxon period, the Wychwood probably helped supply the fuel for the Droitwich salt industry. The princes of the Hwicce had a monopoly of the salt pans and salt houses of Droitwich, and their rights were later absorbed by the kings of Mercia and then of England. A great deal of wood was needed in the form of charcoal, to boil off water from the brine which welled up there. Saltways radiated from Droitwich to carry the salt around the kingdom, but also to bring the wood or charcoal to the salt houses where the brine was processed. It is hard to imagine trees, or loads of wood, being dragged by oxen over the distances involved, and often wood must have been reduced to charcoal first, though it is fragile and difficult to transport. Shares in the Wychwood were given to early minster churches in the Hwicce's area: Gloucester had a tradition of a Wychwood estate, Deerhurst had Taynton manor, and Winchcombe's share of forest was at Enstone. It used to be thought that the curious name of the Hwicce was related to their reputation for salt production; 'Wich' was the Saxon name of Droitwich, to which 'droit' was added by the Normans. On the other hand, 'wic', and then 'wich', derived from the Latin word *vicus*, which was the smallest administrative unit in the provinces of the Roman empire. The Hwicce's name may have reflected the Roman organisation of the *vicus* which still existed in their kingdom. Roman

8. Parts of the church of Ascot under Wychwood date from the 11th century, in particular the lower two stages of the tower. The name refers to the early Saxon 'Hwicce', but a Neolithic chambered tomb on Ascot parish boundary shows much earlier occupation in the area.

organisation could also underlie later arrangements in Wychwood. The name remains puzzling and no derivation is really satisfactory.

Saltways, the main roads of the period, cross the Cotswolds in all directions. They are identifiable particularly from place-names: Saltersford, Salterswell, Salters Lane, Salt Street, Salt Way and Saltersway. Early churches seem to have been sited near saltways, and Domesday priests are noted in manors along their routes. Churches provided hospitality for travellers and especially for the king. The chief saltway entered Gloucestershire from Evesham, where the Abbey had early been endowed with property in Droitwich and with woodland. It passed through Hinton on the Green (now in Worcestershire) and climbed the Cotswold edge at Stanway, where there was a monastery recorded in Domesday. Stanway was one of the original endowments of Tewkesbury church and Domesday Book records that both Stanway and Tewkesbury had salt houses at Droitwich and significant amounts of wood. From Stanway, the saltway ran south along the top of the Cotswolds, with many salt place-names being noted in Hailes, Pinnock, Sudeley, Sevenhampton, Salperton, Eastington in Northleach, Coln St Denis and Bibury. Bibury, too, was an old minster church site. Domesday noted priests at Cutsdean, Salperton, Hazleton, Hampnett and Coln, and two in Guiting, all astride this route.

A second saltway climbed the Cotswold edge at Mickleton, whose Domesday lord was entitled to 24 measures of salt. It passed through Campden, Blockley, Longborough, Donnington, Upper Swell, Broadwell, Stow on the Wold, Icomb, Wyck Rissington and Windrush to Southrop. Blockley was another early minster, but this route is not so marked by Domesday priests, though there was one at Blockley, at Swell and at Broadwell and the church of St Edward was mentioned at Stow, where several routeways converged. A saltway going eastwards from Stow crossed the Evenlode at Daylesford, where another early minster church was established. There were ways up the Cotswold edge at Weston Subedge and Broadway, and Broadway had a Domesday priest. A north-south routeway following the edge is considered to be prehistoric. Starting from Mickleton and proceeding due south, it passed through Weston Subedge, Saintbury, Broadway, Buckland, Stanton, Hailes, Sudeley and Sevenhampton to cross the river Coln at Andoversford in Dowdeswell and thence on through Withington. This road is less marked by salt place-names or by Domesday priests, but there was a priest at Shipton and another at Withington where there was also an early minster church, and there had briefly been a minster in Dowdeswell.

The possession of forest by the Hwicce may suggest that Cotswold woodland was limited by the seventh century. Even before the Roman period, the upland had been substantially cleared; the number of Iron Age monuments suggests a large population and considerable cultivation of the land. After the end of the Roman period tree cover may have increased, for Roman villa sites like Spoonley in Sudeley were named 'ley', originally 'leah', signifying a wood or clearing. Even so, there is no major Anglo-Saxon place-name with 'wold', derived from 'wald', 'forest', and only two minor names, Upton Wold and Swell Wold. These two places were within a wood which in the early Anglo-Saxon period gave rise to the name 'Cotswold'. A stretch of country from the edge above Stanway to Blockley and Swell was apparently controlled by an Anglo-Saxon named Cod. He lived before the end of the seventh century, by which time his land was being divided up between different churches. His 'dean' or valley became Cutsdean, and 'Codeswellan' and 'Codestune' were both mentioned in early documents; he also had a hill-fort, 'codesbyrig', on the northern boundary of Swell, which was a landmark in 1055. 'Cod's wold' became Cotswold. Early in the Anglo-Saxon period, the word 'wold' changed its meaning and came to describe treeless upland pasture. As woodland was cleared it was grazed principally by sheep, because the land was generally too

9. Shipton under Wychwood was a royal manor in 1086 with jurisdiction over three hundreds which seem to have included the arable areas of western Wychwood. About 1000, the townships sharing the Wychwood were separated from other Hwiccian territory and placed in the shire based on Oxford. The manor house of Shipton Court was built about 1603.

high for cattle; sheep prevented the regeneration of woodland. Cotswold was then a name appropriate to these hills and the people of the Hwicce were a distant memory.

The earliest use of 'Cotswold' is when Giraldus Cambrensis, who died in 1223, wrote of travelling between Blockley and Evesham through 'montana de Codesuualt'; at a similar date 'Coddeswold' was described as 'towards Clapley', a place adjoining Bourton on the Hill and close to Upton Wold. In the 13th century and subsequently the name is variously written Coteswaud, Coteswold, Cottyswolde and in the 16th century a plural form Cottiswoldes. By this date, certain places in the area were being identified by the addition of Cotswold as a 'surname'—Westington (in Campden) is first named 'super waldas' in 1273, Naunton 'in Cotswold', 1289, and 'super Cotswold', 1303, Withington 'super le wolde', 1329, and finally Stow on the Wold in 1557. These places define the true Cotswolds, described in this book. Since then, the name has been applied to an increasingly wide area.

Anglo-Saxon Town and Borough
Although the Anglo-Saxons did not control the Cotswolds until the late sixth century, Celtic place-names thereafter almost all disappeared. 'Ton' is the most common place-name element. It seems to have indicated a place where the farmers' homesteads were grouped together, surrounded by their fields, pastures and woods. The characteristic of compact settlement has led to the modern usage of 'town', paradoxically describing non-agricultural settlements. The early 'tons', therefore, have to be distinguished from later 'market-towns' and could perhaps be described as 'farming-towns'. The Saxon 'tons' in the north Cotswolds are many: Aston,

Barrington, Berrington, Bledington, Brockhampton, Bourton, Charlton, Clapton, Compton, Donnington, Eastington, Ebrington, Farmington, Gretton, Hazleton, Laverton, Mickleton, Moreton, Naunton, Oddington, Salperton, Sevenhampton, Shipton, Stanton, Taddington, Taynton, Upton, Westington and Whittington. On the other hand, Rissington and Withington were not 'tons' but originally 'duns' or downs, while Hampnett was a 'ton', originally Hamton or Heam-ton and then with a diminutive added after the Norman conquest, Hamptonet.

'Village' was a later word describing an area going with a vill. 'Vill' was a Norman-French word derived from Latin, and described a distinct area used for the collection of taxes. A list of the vills which paid tax in 1316 for the prosecution of the war against Scotland is known as the *Nomina Villarum*. In the 19th century, places which had never been drawn into the church's organisation of parishes continued to be called vills, like the part of Icomb in Gloucestershire which contained Icomb Place. Village is a more general descriptive word than the originally specific Saxon 'ton'.

Towns in the modern sense of the word were very few in Anglo-Saxon England; the market-towns of the area were founded in the two centuries following the Norman conquest. If any Roman towns survived into the sixth century, like Cirencester and Gloucester, they might have been described as 'burhs'. A 'burh' was a defended site with earthen banks and ditches. Hill forts were called 'burhs' by the Anglo-Saxons; there are many in the Cotswolds, like Burhill in Buckland. More commonly, 'burh' has become 'bury', as in Idbury and Maugersbury. Salmonsbury in Bourton on the Water was also a burh, though it is not a hill-fort but a low-lying enclosure with earthen banks and ditches. 'Borough', too, derives from 'burh', and 'borough' or 'burry' is an Oxfordshire term for a sheltered position. 'Borough' eventually became a technical term, which applied to a well-defined urban community. Unfortunately 'burh' in place-names has over the centuries become confused with 'beorg', a barrow; Ganborough in Upper Swell is probably the 'green barrow' which marked the boundary in 779 and Wagborough Bush in Upper Slaughter and Longborough were barrows.

Early Estates and Manors
There is little doubt that there were coherent land units with definite boundaries long before the Anglo-Saxon period. A surprising number of later parishes have hill-forts, burial mounds or long barrows on their borders. Icomb and Maugersbury are interesting examples, with hill-forts on both northern and southern boundaries. It is difficult to know what word is appropriate to describe early land units but 'estate' gives the sense of coherence and also suggests that it could contain smaller subordinate units, by the time of the Normans known as 'manors'. A considerable number of descriptions of estate boundaries in Anglo-Saxon still survive, from which some larger estates and their later sub-divisions can be reconstructed.

One early organisation of estates seems to have been based on rivers, and resulted in settlement names and river names being identical. An area straddling the Leach was called 'Leche' in Domesday, later Northleach. Three Domesday manors of Coln were sited on the river of the same name. Windrush, which was linked with the Barringtons, formed a coherent estate spanning the river, and Sherborne spanned the Sherborne brook. Guiting was formerly the name for the river Windrush above Bourton on the Water, and Slaughter was also a river name, as a reference to Slaughter-ford shows, but the river was also called simply 'ea', 'water', and is now the Eye. It was not unusual for river and stream names to change, and there are other examples in the area. Taynton, at the centre of a large estate in the Wychwood, was the town on the 'teign', meaning stream. North of the village, and at the edge of the quarries, there was a ford with hazel trees growing round; eventually Hazelford became the name of the stream. Swell was probably the name for the upper part of the river Dikler; a satisfactory explanation refers to the river running underground from Hinchwick and reappearing at Donnington, where it forms a lake. Several river estates may have been administrative centres; in Domesday Book each was in a different hundred: the king's manor of Barrington was in Barrington Hundred, Coln was in Bradley Hundred, Guiting was in Holford Hundred, and Slaughter was in Salmonsbury Hundred. Northleach, Sherborne, Swell and Taynton were church manors.

In the later Anglo-Saxon period, estates seem to have been sub-divided to create several smaller manors. In some cases, a clear physical separation was possible. Coln St Denis was divided from Coln Rogers, Upper Swell from Lower Swell. Naunton was both a new manor and a new town settlement created from parts of several estates on the upper Windrush. In other cases, division was effected by allocating a certain number of villagers and their landholdings to each manor; the arable lands remained intermingled in the open-fields, and the manors shared the same pastures. Upper and Lower Slaughter and Great and Little Barrington are examples; partial separation of the manors occurred in the medieval period but was not completed until the 18th-century enclosures. Hampen and the two Shipton manors were never physically separated, and may once have been parts of a river estate based on the upper Coln.

The boundaries of late Anglo-Saxon manors were preserved into the 19th century by the church's organisation of parishes, which were defined after a process of sub-division of estates had been proceeding for some centuries. As the Church collected a tax on the produce of a parish, it was logical to draw the boundary round agricultural units that already existed. Parish boundaries still largely reflect the decisions made centuries ago about which fields, hamlets and villages belonged together. On a modern map they may appear very intricate, but it was easy to walk round the fields. The histories of Icomb, Naunton, the Slaughters, Barringtons and Shiptons provide indications of the structures of early estates and the processes of fragmentation which resulted in these long-lasting parish divisions.

The development of some manors and parishes
Icomb

The area called Icomb in Domesday, nearly 3,000 acres, and including the modern parish of Westcote, was an estate of considerable antiquity; in the north is the partially fortified Icomb Hill, its ditches forming the boundary with Maugersbury, while to the south Idbury has a hill-fort close to its boundary with Icomb. Both hill-forts are visible in part although as early as 1803 some of Icomb's banks had been partly destroyed by ploughing, while Idbury's banks were said to be eight feet high in the mid-19th century but were being ploughed out before 1900. King Offa gave part of Icomb to the church of Worcester before the end of the eighth century. As a result, Church Icomb was in Worcestershire while the rest of Icomb was in Gloucestershire. In 1844 Church Icomb was transferred to Gloucestershire and the Saxon division was obliterated.

Church Icomb's boundaries were the same in 781, when Offa's charter was made, as they were about 1400, when a perambulation of the estate was described for the Prior of the monastery of Worcester, and in the 19th century when the lands of Church Icomb were enclosed. A simple description of boundaries was attached to Offa's charter, giving four compass points: on the east there was 'Wyhen's uphill path', on the south 'Icancomb and Icangate', on the north 'Wiles Well' and on the west 'Salters well'. To those who knew the area these were sufficient to define the whole estate. The southern landmark, 'Icancomb', was

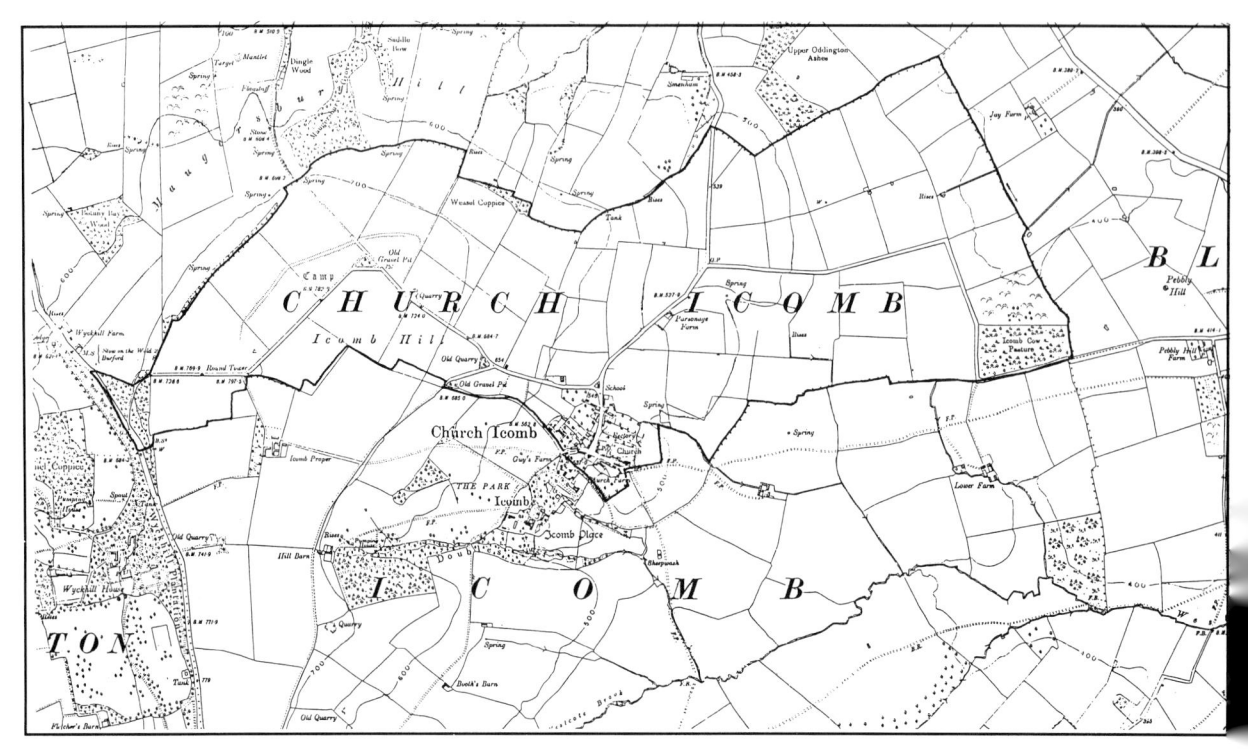

10. An Ordnance Survey map of 1923 shows the division of Church Icomb from Icomb in Gloucestershire, following the Anglo-Saxon boundaries. Weasel Hill, one of the boundary marks, is in the north.

the name of the village itself; the boundary was drawn closely round the churchyard and included the major part of the village in the church's estate, but excluded Icomb Place. 'Icangate' was the road leading up the hill away from the village; in the 18th century this road was called the Icomb and Gawcombe Turnpike Gate Road, and was still the boundary of Church Icomb. 'Gate' was the ancient road and unconnected with turnpike gates of the 18th century.

The perambulation of 1400 describes the boundaries in more detail. The two springs were still landmarks. Wiles Well gave its name to the field to the south of the spring, 'Wheeslye Hill' in the 17th century and in the early 19th century 'Weasle Hill Quarter'; Weasel Coppice is on the modern Ordnance Survey map. Salters Well on the west was called 'the Goodwell' in 1400 and was no doubt the spring near the main Stow to Burford road where parish boundaries still meet; the earlier name of the spring shows that the road was a saltway. 'Meer' or boundary stones were noted near Wiles Well, separating the bishop of Worcester's land in Icomb from the Archbishop of York's land of Oddington; no doubt they clarified the twists and turns evident in the present parish boundary. A 'meer ditch' separated Icomb from the Abbot of Winchcombe's land of Bledington; in the 19th century fields in this part of Icomb were still called Meer Ditch and Meer Ditch Ground. To the east, Wyhen's uphill path seems likely to have been the road to Pebbly Hill and Mickland's Hill which intersects the parish boundary and leads on to Bledington and was called Bledington Way in 1400. On the south-west the boundary went round furlongs in the open fields adjoining

ANGLO-SAXON ESTATES AND SETTLEMENTS

Icomb Place. At one point only the boundary touched the northernmost road into Icomb and in 1805 one of the landowners built a battlemented tower here. David Royce, the rector of Lower Swell in the later 19th century and a keen historian of Icomb and Gloucestershire, noted the story that in the tower you could boil water in Gloucestershire and drink tea in Worcestershire. The tower on the top of Icomb Hill has been replaced by a radio mast.

The later history of Icomb suggests that this estate already had a 'manorial' structure. Offa's charter had given the church of Worcester full criminal jurisdiction and so made Church Icomb an independent manor, but it was without a manor house; Icomb Place stood just outside the boundary in Gloucestershire. Consequently in the 13th century the villagers collectively owed the duty of hospitality to the Prior, together with provisions for five of his horses, when he made his annual visit. The monks, and subsequently the bishop of Worcester, claimed that the Normans had deprived them of Icomb Place.

The Gloucestershire part of Icomb was divided into two small manors and one large one at the time of Domesday. Royce thought Icomb Place was one of the small manors; Domesday scholar John Moore has concluded that both small manors were later combined in Icomb Place. The large manor was seen as the nucleus of the later parish of Westcote. Icomb Place, when it was built in the early 15th century, was obviously an important house and does not fit easily as the centre of a small manor. Royce lamented that so little could be established about its early history; 'the three-fold knot tied by the three Icombs or Combs in Gloucestershire is of three-fold perplexity', he wrote. Unfortunately, the two forms of the name, Icomb and Combe, are no help, as either form could be used for any one of the parts; Church Icomb in Worcestershire was 'alias Combe' in a 16th-century deed.

11. In Icomb village centre the war memorial in the form of a 'Saxon' cross is a thoughtful reminder of the village's documented Saxon history.

It may be suggested that the three manors were not discrete estates, but that the land was shared between Icomb Place and two small subsidiary manor houses, sited at Gawcombe and Westcote. Sometime before 1291, a separate parish was created of the area south of the Westcote brook and a church was built probably next to the small manor house of Westcote. The church became the focus of settlement and villagers at Gawcombe may have moved there; about 1700 the remains of houses could be seen in Gawcombe woods. The new parish was identified as Combe Baskerville from the name of its manorial lord, the Norman family who held the manor for about four hundred years, but who lived at Icomb Place. Within a short time the name Westcote was being used, and sometimes also Combe Westcote. In 1499 John Baskerville held Combe Baskerville, Over Westcote and Nether Westcote as one estate and in 1511 Thomas Hakluyt's will disposed of a lease of the whole of Icomb: Combe Baskerville, Over Westcote and Nether Westcote and also Icomb in Worcestershire. Stained glass in Icomb church used to contain a coat-of-arms of the Hakluyt family quartered with the Blaket family, who lived at Icomb Place *c.*1400. Icomb could be regarded as one manor in title deeds as late as the 17th century and Westcote never had a full manorial position, as was realised by purchasers of the estate in the early 19th century who tried to investigate and recreate the one-time manor of Combe Baskerville. Icomb Place was left in an anomalous position. Once the manor house for the whole of Icomb, it had its own chapel in Icomb church; the older church probably refused to allow Icomb Place to become part of the new parish of Westcote, but had no manorial authority over it, so Icomb Place gradually came to be regarded as extra-parochial.

Naunton
Naunton demonstrates the general antiquity of estates of the north Cotswolds. The name was written 'Niweton' in Domesday Book, 'the new town'. It was probably founded in the ninth or tenth century; the first written reference to Naunton is in 963. There are not many place-names of this sort in the area, and the jagged nature of the parish boundary suggests Naunton was carved out of pre-existing estates. There were two Domesday manors of Naunton, one of which may have been the small enclosed area of Little Worth near the church, but the later parish also included one or two manors called Aylworth and one called Harford. The main village street, running along the side of a hill parallel with the river Windrush, is the core of the new town. It consists of a set of regular plots running between the street and the river. To the north were open arable fields carved out of Guiting and divided by a ditch which subsequently became Sheepwell Lane. Arable land which had once been in Harford and Aylworth also became part of the open fields of Naunton.

Several Saxon charters with boundary descriptions relate to the adjoining area, and help to show the development of a new estate. The earliest is attached to a charter concerning Notgrove and Aston Blank, dated 743. It shows that Upper Harford and Aylworth were part of Notgrove and Aston Blank at this time; the western limits of the estate were the head of the Turkdean valley, near Slade Barn, and a ridgeway leading to the ford where Harford Bridge is, from where the boundary followed the river Windrush. Harford, which was on both sides of the Windrush, was split into two by this charter; both parts were later reunited in the parish of Naunton. The part of Harford east of the Windrush, called Lower Harford and Harford Hill, later consisted of only one homestead; this estate passed into the hands of the Templars and subsequently Corpus Christi College, Oxford.

A charter of 963 relates to an area of Harford west of the Windrush, now called Upper Harford, which was said to be 'in Naunton', thus showing that by this date Naunton had been

12. The ford at Lower Harford Farm was on the boundary of an estate recorded in 743. Nearby was a mill, already old in Saxon times, and a small leat and weir still exist. The road has recently been moved away from the farm, and this has involved the construction of a new ford.

created. When Grundy considered the boundaries accompanying this charter, he attempted to show that they related to Lower Harford east of the Windrush, but the Saxon landmarks do not easily fit the later parish boundary here. On the other hand, one landmark was 'Coldmore' and a similar name is found in Coldmoor Coppice and in the former Coldmoor furlong in Aston Blank, west of the Windrush in Upper Harford. The small, one-hide estate of the charter was still in existence at the time of the Domesday Survey, and included a mill. A small mill exists today on the Windrush at Lower Harford farm.

Both Aylworth and Harford are the sites of 'lost villages'. Characteristic raised house platforms and sunken lanes remain under the grass on the slope near Aylworth Manor and on the west bank of the Windrush in Upper Harford. One possible reason for desertion of both sites could be the removal of villagers to the new town. There is a tradition in Naunton that the original site of the village was at Harford. Some families might have remained in Aylworth and Harford working on the land which remained attached to those manors, but they were not part of a farming-town with an open-field system. Before the end of the 14th century both settlements contained only one or two families. At the time of Naunton's enclosure in 1778 by act of parliament, there were no open fields in Aylworth nor Harford, but tithe was paid to the rector of Naunton.

The Slaughters

The probable limits of a large river estate which included Slaughter and several other surrounding parishes can be reconstructed from much later historical evidence. Upper and Lower Slaughter are obviously linked by their names, but also by the intermingling of their

13. The view over Naunton shows in the centre of the picture the hedged and deep-sunk Sheepwell Lane, which was the Anglo-Saxon boundary with Guiting Power.

14. Clapton Bridge over the Windrush is on the site of a ford amidst willows mentioned in an Anglo-Saxon charter of 779; Clapton Lane formed part of the boundary of Bourton on the Water and of the separate chapelry of Clapton. The road is no longer used for motor traffic.

fields and pastures until enclosure in 1731. The Slaughters were also linked with Eyford and Bourton on the Water. Eyford was generally included with Upper Slaughter in administrative records until the 18th century and was also linked with Bourton on the Water, through that manor's traditional manorial control of quarries in Eyford, documented in 1542. Lower Slaughter's church was subordinate to Bourton on the Water, which is good evidence that the manors were once linked.

The Saxon estate of Bourton included Clapton, Aston Blank and Notgrove, Aylworth and Upper Harford. The bounds associated with the charter of 779 describe a long, thin tract of land stretching approximately westwards from the present village of Bourton. As with Icomb, four compass points were given: to the south a withy or willow ford and a barrow; to the west Turkdean; to the east the river Windrush; to the north the Slaughter ford. A bridge which was new in 1482 was built on the site of the withy ford and is now known as Clapton Bridge and part of the Bourton boundary followed Clapton Lane. The western mark, Turkdean, matches the Notgrove boundary of 743 and also a Hawling boundary mark, and so probably refers to Turk Down rather than the village. Slaughter was already separated from Bourton by the Fosse Way though Roman settlements were on both sides of the road. Similarly, the Fosse Way was the dividing line used to separate Aston Blank and Notgrove from Bourton before 949. A Roman road seems quite often to have served this purpose.

Several settlements within the Slaughter and Bourton estate became separate parishes, but only Upper and Lower Slaughter had the same name. A possible reason is that there was only one settlement until at least the 11th century. This solves the puzzle concerning which of the two Slaughter manors in Domesday Book became Upper Slaughter and which Lower Slaughter. An early Norman lord constructed a castle mound at Upper Slaughter, near a large church with Norman decorated arches and doorway. It would be expected that the church on the King's manor would be the superior one, but Lower Slaughter with its subordinate church was later the King's

15. A sketch of Bourton on the Water church about 1780 shows the old tower with a saddle-back roof. Popular tradition held that the tower was Roman.

manor. The difficulty disappears if it is assumed that both manors were located in one settlement at Upper Slaughter and a second settlement was founded lower down the river before the end of the 11th century, at first called 'Little' Slaughter. 'Over' and 'Nether' or 'Upper' and 'Lower' were being used to describe the two settlements towards the end of the 13th century, though the plural 'Slaughters' was also used. Slaughter mill was attached to the King's Lower Slaughter manor and Upper Slaughter had to lease Little Aston mill. Little Aston is another deserted village site; in 1340 surveyors for the taxation of a ninth of sheaves, fleeces and lambs were told that, before the tax had been granted by Parliament, seven of the inhabitants had 'relinquished their holdings and withdrew from the parish'. Had they been attracted to the new settlement at Lower Slaughter? Once the king's manor was at Lower Slaughter, the regular three-weekly court met there; though the hundred occasionally met in Salmonsbury in Bourton on the Water, it became known as Slaughter Hundred.

The Barringtons

Great and Little Barrington may have a somewhat similar history to the Slaughters. One of the four Barrington manors in Domesday Book was the King's and Great Barrington church is larger than many in the area and has fine Norman decoration. It was the superior church to both Little Barrington and Windrush. Barrington had a large Domesday population, 31 villagers, 10 smallholders, a priest and 25 slaves. It may be significant that there are two Roman villa sites in Great Barrington, on the south-facing slopes above the Windrush. Near each villa there was a water mill; a long canal carried the Windrush close to the rising ground on which the villas were built. Within fifty years of the Domesday Survey, three of the four manors had been given to the newly founded Llanthony Priory, but their former ownership continued to be reflected in the names of tithings: King's Hold, Canons' Hold and Sickman's

16. Farmhouses and cottages at Little Barrington above the Tight brook were part of Great Barrington parish. The main spring forming the brook rises in the bank below the houses. Great Barrington lies to the north, across the Windrush.

Hold. King's Hold, the King's manor, had been attached to the royal manor of Faringdon; consequently it was in Berkshire. Twenty-three houses in Great Barrington were part of Berkshire in the later 18th century and were not transferred to Gloucestershire until 1844. King's Hold and Canon's Hold were given to Llanthony by the Empress Maud, who claimed the English throne in opposition to the Norman King Stephen. Sickman's Hold was the most populous of the Domesday manors and the one with the priest; it was given to Llanthony for the support of 13 lepers, hence its name.

The manor not in Llanthony Priory's hands became the separate parish of Little Barrington. By 1291 the church's income in the Barrington estate had been divided, half going to Great Barrington

17. 'Beakheads' decorate the south doorway of Windrush church and are also found at Burford and Sherborne. Could the source for this motif have been a mysterious demon or a stylised representation of an ox's curved horns and head with a ring through the nose?

and the other half shared between Little Barrington and Windrush. The boundary between Great and Little Barrington followed the river Windrush, but only part of the open fields south of the river were Little Barrington's and part were in Great Barrington manor and parish. When was the settlement of Little Barrington founded? It would not have been very convenient to cross the river daily and plough the fields of Little Barrington, so there may have been a hamlet there before it became a separate manor. Even after the parish had been defined, the settlement remained very small, with only five taxpayers in 1327. The carving on the outside north wall of Little Barrington church is considered to be 11th century and is a semi-circular tympanum which once filled the arched part of an entrance way. A deeply-cut south doorway is a little later in date and Norman in style, and could date from an enlargement of the church about 1150, perhaps in celebration of separate parish status. Windrush church has a carved south doorway of the same period. A date in the first half of the 12th century is therefore likely for the physical subdivision of the Barrington manors, allowing a hamlet with its own church and manor house to have its own open fields. Great Barrington manor still regulated Little Barrington's fields. When Little Barrington was enclosed in 1759, the very picturesque row of farmhouses and cottages on the west bank of the Tight brook, and a compact block of land, was allocated to Lady Talbot, the owner of Barrington Park; Great Barrington's boundary then physically encircled the whole parish. Not until 1820 did Little Barrington manor escape from Great Barrington's overlordship.

The Shiptons
The relationship between manors and parishes in Shipton points to the existence at one time of a large estate based on the upper part of the river Coln. Lower down the river, by about 700, was the Saxon minster estate of Withington. Finberg argued that it is logical to assume that the original eighth-century boundaries of the minster were also the divisions between the Roman villa estates of Withington, Chedworth, Compton and Whittington. If so, Roman land divisions were later obscured, perhaps intentionally. Some half-century after its foundation,

Withington minster acquired land in Dowdeswell and Andoversford, where there also had been for a short period a minster; it thereby gained the sites of Whittington Roman villa and the Roman town whose existence is reflected in the field name 'Wycomb', written 'Wickham' into the 18th century. The Roman town had been sited near exceptionally strong springs of water at Syreford, which feed the mill-pond noted as a boundary mark to Withington minster estate about 1000.

Shipton manor boundary in mid-18th century matched the adjacent Withington minster estate as described some 750 years earlier, but did not correspond with parish boundaries. Parts of Shipton manor were in the parishes of Dowdeswell, Sevenhampton, Withington and Whittington. The river Coln formed part of Withington's late Saxon boundary, which meant that the agricultural land of Owdeswell was divided; some of its meadow and arable were in Shipton manor and Dowdeswell parish. In 1801 Shipton villagers were still entitled to pasture their animals in this part of Dowdeswell. There was a chapel at Owdeswell, disused by 1712, showing that it had once been a significant settlement. Andoversford, too, was divided by the minster boundary, but united in the parish of Dowdeswell. Onnanforda, which became Andoversford, and Onnanduun, the down whose name became Hannington, were both landmarks on the minster boundary; Andoversford was in Dowdeswell but Hannington Hill was in Shipton manor but Dowdeswell parish. Ancient links which Withington minster estate had apparently broken were still reflected as late as the 17th century in Shipton's claim that the hamlets of Owdeswell and Foxcote in Withington, Pegglesworth in Dowdeswell and Clopley, a lost settlement in Sevenhampton, were all subordinate members of Shipton manor.

There were five Domesday manors in Shipton, one rather larger than the rest; a century or so later, they had been consolidated to form two manors and parishes. The larger was associated with the Solers family by 1285 and there was a church next to the manor house. The Oliffe family held the smaller manor by 1285, and this also had its own church, which was probably the older one, dedicated to the Saxon St Oswald. Like Slaughter and Barrington, the two Shipton manors were not physically separated. The central part of Shipton village was allocated to the Oliffe manor, but the arable lands and the pastures were intermingled with the Solers lands; this remained the situation until enclosure in the 19th century. A deserted village site near Shipton Solers manor house and the Frogmill might relate to a short-lived attempt to divide the manors more completely. Eventually both were owned by the Peachey family, which facilitated the amalgamation of the two parishes in 1776. Shipton Oliffe church became the parish church and Shipton Solers was disused.

Shipton manor in the 18th century also included both Upper and Lower Hampen manor houses and Hampen's two common arable fields, though Upper Hampen manor house was in the parish of Sevenhampton. The villagers of Shipton had rights of common in Hampen until enclosure in 1801 and, conversely, Hampen shared lands in some but not all of Shipton's fields. The name Hampen suggests an enclosure or 'pen'. Between the two open arable fields in the 18th century there was a grass area, still called 'the Hitching', which contains lynchets made by the cultivation of small terraces of land in prehistoric times. This could be the 'pen' of the name, and relate directly to an enclosure for sheep husbandry; one Hampen manor in Domesday Book had no ploughland and its Saxon holder was called Pin, the name suggesting a shepherd.

In the 18th century, Shipton had a very complicated open-field system, with rights of pasture for different animals in particular parts of the manor. It may have resulted from ancient reorganisation of Shipton's fields, and hints of this may be the two open fields called 'Horsington' and 'Cowlington'; these names seem to indicate 'towns' or 'downs' reserved for specialised animal pasturing, just as Shipton itself was the sheep town. On enclosure in 1801, calculations

18 & 19. Syreford Mill in Whittington is likely to be on the site of a mill listed in Domesday Book. Syreford springs are exceptionally strong, and explain the location of a Roman town nearby. The building on the left houses the mill machinery and was once also the miller's house.

of how to make compensation for these rights required 80 columns of figures for 15 separate categories of common grazing rights.

An untidy and intricate network of common rights, which crossed manor and parish boundaries, may have been the product of adjustments to open-field systems as new settlements and manors were created and old ones decayed. It points to the antiquity of the basic pattern of farming and settlement, rather than suggesting that there was wild, untamed land in the north Cotswolds in the Anglo-Saxon period, where small communities competed for ownership as they pushed their boundaries outwards. The deserted village sites, too, could be the result of reorganisations of settlements, and of the open fields associated with them. While there were many such changes, the basic open-field system seems to have been a pre-existing and fundamental feature.

Chapter Three

Minsters, Rectories and Churches

The earliest written materials for a history of the Cotswolds are the many deeds or 'charters' from the eighth century onwards recording grants of land to the Christian Church. Bishops and monks were literate where many, even kings, were not, and they took care to preserve title deeds which were copied and recopied into 'cartularies'. In particular, the monks of Worcester made a collection in the early 11th century, the *Liber Wigornensis*, and later in the century a monk called Hemming added to it; his name has been attached to the whole cartulary. Histories of monasteries also preserved traditions about the earliest period of the church's organisation. The church continued to receive generous endowments of land over several centuries, and at the time when the monasteries were abolished held as much as a third of the land of England. Eight hundred or more years of church ownership had a great effect on the Cotswolds. Clerical landlords were rather unwilling to sell off part of an estate for temporary advantage; consequently church estates remained integral units. The church's organisation of parishes was also very important. By the end of the 13th century the whole country was largely included within a network of rectories or vicarages, and village farmers supported parish priests with their payments of tithe. The church building, and particularly the tower, symbolised its importance to the community.

The Parish and the Sense of Place
Roman Christian Church organisation had been based on an urban *parochia*, presided over by a bishop; the Greek word *parochia* described all the people in a church community. As missionary work was carried on, country churches were established in districts each subject to a bishop's authority and called a 'diocese'. Country churches might have a permanent staff of clergy, with the duty of ministering to the people and preaching to them, or they might be visited by the bishop and staff of the urban church. The 'minster' churches which were established in Anglo-Saxon England were on the pattern of the independent country churches of Roman times. 'Minster' was the Anglo-Saxon translation of *monasterium*; in the early centuries of the Anglo-Saxon church it did not imply a community of monks. A minster was often a 'college' of secular clerks.

The origins of most English parish churches, however, were the many chapels or oratories built on the estates of landowners. In Roman times, and in the Anglo-Saxon period too, these chapels were often served by priests from amongst the inhabitants; they were the landowner's property to dispose of as he wished. Such proprietary chapels, or *eigenkirche*, were much more numerous than minster churches both on the continent and in Anglo-Saxon England. A chapel could be up-graded to the status of a full church if the lord of the manor gave up his ownership, dedicated the church to a saint, and endowed it with land. In many cases this was done, though traces of the former ownership persisted; in particular the landowner retained the advowson, or right to nominate the priest. At the same time, many churches were built which never became the centres of parishes.

In a simple but basic way the church has defined the concept of place. The organisation of parishes encouraged the formation of place-names which are part of the Cotswolds' character: Upper and Lower Slaughter, Upper and Lower Swell, Little Rissington, Wyck Rissington, Great Rissington, Little Barrington and Great Barrington, Coln Rogers and Coln St Denis, Shipton Oliffe and Shipton Solers. These are all parishes defined sometime between about 1000 and 1300. On the other hand, some places appear infrequently in historical records because they were not parishes, like Hidcote, part of which was in Mickleton, and part in Ebrington, Calcot in Coln St Denis, Castlett and Farmcote in Guiting Power, Hampen in Shipton, Taddington in Stanway, Pegglesworth in Dowdeswell, Foxcote and Hilcot in Withington, Aylworth and Harford in Naunton.

When parishes were defined, the parson was established as a farmer amongst the village's other farmers; his land-holding was his 'glebe', from a Latin word meaning soil or land. Farms called Church Farm, Rectory Farm, Parsonage Farm, Vicarage Farm and Glebe Farm are reminders of this involvement in agriculture, which lasted for a thousand years. The parson was also endowed with the right to collect a tax from the local farmers, the tithe, an Anglo-Saxon word meaning 'tenth'. In primitive times it was natural to take tax as a percentage of the harvest: corn, lambs, wool, apples, eggs, and any other produce of the land. Though money was substituted in secular taxes, in some places the church continued to collect its tax in kind until it was commuted by act of parliament in 1836. Because of the tithe, the boundaries of a parish were carefully defined and remembered.

From the mid-16th century, successive acts of parliament gave the parish civil functions, of repairing the roads and caring for poor people in its area. The boundaries acquired further importance, for no inhabitants laboured to repair roads a yard beyond them nor were they willing to pay for the support of a poor man, woman or child found in desperate circumstances on the far side of the line. The parish lost these functions when parliament created a structure of elected local bodies in the mid-19th century, and the significance of parish boundaries and of the parish itself declined.

Old Minsters

Christianity in the Cotswolds may have endured from the Roman period through to the Saxon period as an active religion. An important reason for supposing this is that, while Bede gives dates for the conversions of Anglo-Saxon kings, in the case of the Hwicce he simply refers to a daughter of the royal house, called Eabba, who had already been baptised 'amongst her own people'. A second reason is the coincidence of a number of later churches and Roman sites. The little, remote church of Widford, in the fields beside the Windrush, has a Roman tesselated pavement beneath the chancel; Widford formed an island of Gloucestershire in Oxfordshire, and was once attached to the royal manor of Great Barrington where there are two other Roman villa sites. A Roman burial was found close to a wall of Notgrove church in 1873; David Royce said that similar archaeological finds had been made in the churchyards of Condicote, Lower Swell and Wyck Rissington. There was a local tradition that the church tower in Bourton on the Water was Roman. Unfortunately it was demolished with the nave in 1784, but a tower could survive that long, like the pharos at Dover. Bourton on the Water was an extensive Roman settlement and Roman remains are said to have been found under

MINSTERS, RECTORIES AND CHURCHES

20. Two large manors of Guiting in 1086 each had a priest. Guiting Power church has a notable Norman south doorway, showing that a stone church was built about 1100. Farmcote and other chapels were in its parish.

21. Temple Guiting church has traces of Norman work but was substantially altered in 1740-42. The tower was rebuilt in the 17th century.

the Rector's vestry in 1880. If Christianity in the Cotswolds survived the Saxon invasions, this may in part explain why so much land was given to the church; Bourton on the Water, Notgrove and Swell, for instance, were given to Evesham Abbey. It would have made no sense to endow a monastery with empty lands which the clergy were too far away to cultivate; if there were already inhabitants and church buildings, then these estates would be well supervised by a religious institution.

The adoption of Christianity by an Anglo-Saxon king was much more than a decision about personal religious belief; it was also a well-considered action for the firmer establishment of the government of his kingdom. The Roman Christian Church as presented by St Augustine during his mission from 597 was a hierarchy of literate clerks who could help the king with all kinds of written administration, including tax collection. The first thrust of Christian conversion was carried out through minsters. In 679, Ethelred, King of the Mercians, gave a nobleman called Osric the land of 300 'tributarii' at Gloucester for the establishment of a minster, and Osric's brother, Oswald, was given 300 'cassatorum' at Pershore for the same purpose. Tributarii and cassati were both later translated by the Anglo-Saxon 'hides'. Pershore Abbey had the right to collect church scot or tax from its three hundreds at the time of Domesday, even though by then it had lost much of its endowment of land to a recent royal foundation, Westminster Abbey. Tewkesbury minster may have been founded at the same time as Gloucester and Pershore, as the monks' own account of their history said the foundation was in the time of King Ethelred; Domesday also gives some indication that three hundreds were linked together round Tewkesbury. The scale of Evesham's endowments places it, too, among the primary or 'old minster' foundations.

Gloucester and Pershore minsters pre-dated by a few years the division of the country into dioceses, when a bishop for the Hwicce was placed with a 'head minster' at Worcester. The bishop was in some ways less powerful than some of his subject minsters, and this fact possibly prompted Oswald, Bishop of Worcester in 964, to persuade King Edgar to create an artificial three hundred unit, known as Oswaldslow. Some of the bishopric's Cotswold manors, Blockley, Cutsdean and Icomb, formed part of this triple hundred, and consequently were included in Worcestershire.

Some important Cotswold manors were amongst the endowments of these first minsters: Broadway was given to Pershore, Buckland to Gloucester, Stanway to Tewkesbury; Northleach did not become Gloucester's until late in the eighth century. Broadway and Stanway were sited on important roads, as their names suggest, and minsters had the obligation of stabling the king's horses. Evesham's Cotswold estates were centred on the Fosse Way, at Bourton on the Water, Broadwell, Donnington, Maugersbury, and Swell. The association of the church with roads and in particular with saltways is strongly confirmed by the evidence of Domesday that priests were mainly present in manors through which these roads passed. Almost at once a second series of smaller minsters was founded, including Bredon, Daylesford, and Withington, each with a surrounding estate of substantial size. They were regarded as the property of the bishop; after the deaths of the men or women at their head, they reverted to him. At this stage, minsters were established in royal manors at the head of a hundred, the 'villa regalis', pointing to their administrative functions. The first minsters survived until the 1530s as monasteries while the smaller, secondary minsters eventually became simple parish churches, served by one priest.

Winchcombe Abbey, later so influential in the area, was not founded until about 811; like Pershore, it was linked with the jurisdiction of three hundreds in Domesday. It has been suggested that Winchcombe rose to prominence after Cirencester became unsafe because of attacks by the kingdom of Wessex from the south; it may have been easier to defend as it was surrounded by hills. Mercian kings were buried at Winchcombe and the archives of the royal house were being kept there in safe custody in 825. Winchcombe's estates, apart from adjacent rural areas, were Charlton Abbots in the valley above Sudeley, Stanton and Snowshill to the north, Sherborne to the south, and Bledington on the east side of the Cotswolds; the minster therefore had estates in all parts of the north Cotswolds, the 'quarter' of Winchcombe.

Rectories and Vicarages

The old minsters originally had the right to tithes within their large parishes; as more parish churches were founded, tithes were diverted from them. About 960, a code of laws was issued which tried to protect the old minsters.

> This is the ordinance which King Edgar determined with the advice of his councillors, for the praise of God and for his own royal dignity and for the benefit of all his people.
> First, namely, that God's churches are to be entitled to their rights.
> And all payment of tithe is to be made to the old minster to which the parish belongs, and it is to be rendered both from the thegn's demesne land and from the land of the tenants according as it is brought under the plough.

The thegn was a freeman, holding his land directly from the king; he needed an estate of at least five hides to sustain his status and enable him to leave the cultivation of the land to others while he served the king. Edgar's code suggests that some thegns had churches on their estates, and a third of the tithes of the demesne could be given to them provided there was a graveyard; a church without a graveyard was a private oratory. The code specified when tithes were to be paid, and promised the help of the king in securing their payment. From this date, the law of the country continued to enforce the payment of tithe for nearly ten centuries.

The establishment of independent parishes around estate churches proceeded on the basis that the lord of the manor gave the priest an endowment of land and the old minster gave him an income by surrendering its rights to tithe within that manor. All parishes were therefore at first 'rectories', because the rector was the one with the right to tithe. The bishop gained control of a community's priest, the landowner gained status. He may also have wanted to give the major part of his demesne tithes to a religious house of his choice, which would pray for his soul for ever, and this was possibly allowed in return for endowing a parish church with land.

A priest with one hide or four yardlands was superior to most villagers whose average holding was more likely to have been a quarter of this amount, or perhaps a half; most important, he was free of the menial or practical services which most villagers had to do for the lord, and so was a 'freeholder'. He had a share of the demesne tithes and all the villagers' tithes. In the careful social distinctions of Anglo-Saxon laws, bishops were equivalent to earls and archbishops to princes; the village priest was equivalent to the ceorl. The word has given the adjective 'churlish' but at this time it indicated a free man, not having to work on the land of the lord of the manor. A priest was an educated member of the village community, the keeper of the weights and measures, and on occasions a mediator between the lord and his villagers. Wherever a priest is mentioned in Domesday Book, it is likely that a parish with a rector had been created in that manor. As well as the 'monasterium' at Stanway, the church at Stow on the Wold and the important landowning church of Winchcombe, 16 priests were recorded in the north Cotswolds where later there were 75 parishes or oratories; no doubt many private churches were not recorded. Rectories had been created on several of Evesham Abbey's estates, in Bourton on the Water, Broadwell, Swell and Willersey. A priest had one hide on the bishop of Worcester's estate at Blockley and another had half a hide at Withington. Other Domesday manors with priests were Barrington, Broadway, Coln, Cutsdean, Guiting (where there were two), Hampnett, Hazleton, Salperton, and Shipton. Most of the parishes in the Cotswolds, therefore, were formed after 1086.

The old minsters were naturally unwilling to give up either responsibility or income and the network of parishes emerged only slowly. They were particularly reluctant to create parishes within their immediate area; instead, chapels served the communities, but remained subject to the minster church. Blockley, Withington and Winchcombe were all successful in maintaining control over several subordinate chapels. Winchcombe monastery had apparently to be denied food from the estate before allowing Hailes church to become independent, even though the tithes were part of Hailes Abbey's foundation endowment in 1226. Chapels with no endowments were not mentioned in tax lists, and only architectural evidence shows that they existed by mid-12th century, and probably by 1102, when the erection of further chapels was forbidden. In mid-14th century, in a clerical tax list, Batsford, Condicote, Fifield, Idbury, Sezincote, Snowshill, Sudeley and Whittington were the only chapels mentioned.

Where a rectory had been instituted in one of the church's own manors, the temptation to take over the tithes for the bishopric or monastery's own use was nearly irresistible. With the permission of the Pope, the tithes of the demesne were appropriated first, and then quite frequently the whole of the rector's tithe. It was called 'appropriating' the rectory because permission was given to take the tithes, in the Latin phrase, *ad proprios usus*—to their own use. The bishopric or monastery became the rector of the parish and a monk might serve the parish church. This was not very satisfactory, either from the point of view of the monk's particular religious duties or the parishioners who had only a part-time minister; in 1122 a central council of the church forbade monks to serve as parish priests, but required a substitute, or vicar, to be instituted, and in 1179, monasteries in the Province of Canterbury were again ordered to present fit priests to their churches.

A permanent and full-time vicar needed an endowment of land and income, just as a rector did, and so the tithes and glebe were split. Early in the 13th century, Winchcombe Abbey endowed vicarages in Sherborne and Winchcombe itself with one third of the tithes and drew two thirds for itself. A monastery usually claimed the 'great tithes' of corn, which were easier to collect and brought much larger financial benefit, in preference to the 'small tithes' which were all the other villagers' produce, like honey or apples. Small tithes which the monastery of Winchcombe was exempted from paying from its demesnes in Hawling, Roel, Spoonley and Cutsdean in the 15th century were hay, young animals bred on the parish's pastures, lambs, geese, pigs, flax, hemp, doves, milk, calves, eggs, apples, green vegetables, wood and underwood.

In 1291, a list of churches and monasteries in the province of Canterbury, with details of the income of each, was made in connection with a tax authorised by Pope Nicholas IV to help defray the cost of Edward I's crusade against the Turks in the Holy Land. The framework of parishes which was to last to the 20th century was substantially complete by this date; there were 51 parish churches in the north Cotswolds, instead of the 18 of Domesday. Already Aston Blank, Little Barrington, Burford, Hailes, Naunton, Sherborne and Winchcombe all had vicars, though more vicarages were instituted in the following centuries. The full scale of monastic appropriation is not revealed in 1291, because a vicar's stipend was noted but not a rectory served by monks. Many of the 44 rectors in 1291 did not draw the whole of

MINSTERS, RECTORIES AND CHURCHES

the tithes from their parishes, because 'portions' were paid to other religious institutions. Often this was the result of the lords of the manor giving part of the tithes to a monastery rather than to the parish church; sometimes it reflected the fact that manors and parishes were composite estates with several separate field systems within them, only one of which might be used for the endowment of the local church. Thus in Campden, where there were four agricultural units or field systems, as well as the borough, the tithes and estate of Combe had been given in 1153 to Bordesley Abbey near Redditch, the first Cistercian house in the area founded 15 years earlier. This portion of Campden's tithes was noted in 1291. The most valuable rectories were Burford, Blockley, Campden, Withington, and Winchcombe. The list is interesting because Burford and Campden are not known to be minsters, but the size of the rectory incomes suggests that they may have been well-endowed early foundations, and correspondingly attractive to impropriators. The income of Burford rectory was seven times larger than most in the area, and twice as much as Withington or Winchcombe. The rectories of Broadway, Stow, Hailes, Mickleton, Great Rissington, Taynton and Weston Subedge were better endowed than most. Appropriations continued for another two hundred years; the rectory of Taynton was appropriated by Tewkesbury Abbey in 1500. Winchcombe Abbey even took the vicarage of Winchcombe in 1398. There was obviously a tendency for the richer rectories to be taken over, like Campden, taken by the abbey of St Werburgh in 1332, and Burford together with the chapel of Fulbrook, which had been given by William, Earl of Gloucester to his new-founded abbey of Keynsham, near Bristol, about 1170. Blockley was appropriated by the bishop of Worcester in the same year as Campden; the vicars of Blockley and Campden were both allocated the former rectors' houses.

The Pope Nicholas Taxation gives parish churches grouped together in deaneries; in the north Cotswolds there were three, Campden, Stow and Winchcombe, and a few parishes in the south of the area were in Cirencester deanery. Campden deanery seems to predate the creation of the shires about 1000, because it included Broadway, though in Worcestershire; a relationship to Campden church had overridden Pershore Abbey's ownership. Adjoining Campden, Blockley, too, was in Worcestershire, but Blockley minster, founded before 855, was not in Campden deanery. Although there is little evidence earlier than 1291, the deaneries often seem to have been based on much older minster parishes. The choice of Campden and Stow as centres is a tantalising hint of one-time minsters. In the case of Stow, St Edward's church may be very early; it is next to the Fosse Way, and in the area of a hill-fort.

In the case of Campden, there is some evidence of a minster, also sited beside a Roman road. Cadanmynster, Cada's minster, is referred to in a description of Broadway of 972, located on the boundary of the estate, somewhere near the top of the hill; the boundary then proceeded to the 'edge' and the salt-way. Similarly, Cada's minster was also a boundary mark for Willersey estate in the 11th century. The later parishes of Willersey and Saintbury both have long, narrow fingers of land which reach to the top of the hill and make use of the converging Roman road and salt-way. Near this junction could have been the site of Cada's minster, in the area of Campden later called Combe. Was the powerful Godwin family, who were lords of Campden before 1066, responsible for taking over the minster and its lands? The name of Cada may also be preserved in the Catbrook in Campden, and in Cadley Hill in Batsford. If so, Cada would appear to have been an early warlord, as his British name suggests, with a small kingdom stretching from the Fosse Way all the way across the upland to the Cotswold edge.

The medieval history of Campden church would become more intelligible if there had been a minster there. Hugh de Gondeville, who founded the borough, also founded

St Katherine's chapel in 1180; it was unusually well-endowed with two priests and three hides. The land was identified by naming the villagers who farmed it, including the deacon, Herbert Salins who served an existing church. The new chaplains paid one pound of incense to a 'mother' church, which was also assigned tithes from the four mills in Campden in addition to those which it already collected. The lord of the manor chose the chaplains to the new chapel, and the bishop confirmed their appointments. The foundation certainly increased the status of the manor, and seems possibly to have enabled a church to be built close to the new town and the manor house. A survey of part of Campden in 1273 noted an 'old chapel' dedicated to St Katherine, but Gondeville's chapel was then less than a hundred years old. Could the old chapel have been the minster?

Between 1282 and 1284 there was a furious dispute between the abbot of St Werburgh and the bishop of Worcester about the presentation to Campden rectory. The bishop would have had the advowson if there had been an early minster church but part of Campden's tithes had been given to St Werburgh's in 1096 and the abbot claimed to have been given the advowson, too. It appeared that the chaplain of St Katherine's chapel was also the rector, on appointment by the abbot, but the bishop had appointed a rival rector. In the end, the bishop conceded, but not before houses and church had been forcibly occupied and corn, probably tithe corn, stolen from the intruding rector. A free chapel of St Katherine still existed in 1387, when the chaplain was described as a warden, but there is no further record of it after this. St Katherine's chantries in the church of Campden survived until all the chantries were dissolved in the 16th century.

There was still room for dispute about the rectory 200 years later, and Sir Baptist Hicks and Sir Lionel Cranfield, both rich Londoners with the King's ear, attempted to profit by the uncertainties. Baptist Hicks had the support of the vicar. Cranfield's agent

> went to set the tithe ...we began to level it up in the cart and there the Vicar with some 12 more came and took it out of the cart by force, having with him a great mastif dog and all his folk, pitchforks ... in their hands.

The corn was stored in a barn and locked away from both contestants. The vicar

> contrary to his honest agreement, did get the key of the barn of the woman that doth own the barn, under colour he would look whether the rain had done no harm. And George Taylor's cart with two of his boys, Richard Adams and the Vicar himself carried away two loads of corn.

Cranfield abandoned the action, after being paid some money by Hicks, which could have been his intention from the first.

Norman Doorways and Church Towers
Only Coln Rogers church has survived from the period before the Norman conquest; the building has not been fundamentally altered since it was erected, and the construction of the corners of the nave with oblong stones laid alternately vertically and horizontally, in 'long and short work', is characteristic of Saxon masonry. Other churches have fragments which may be pre-Norman, like the carved tympanum at Little Barrington. Dedications at Broadway and Ebrington to St Eadburga, a Saxon saint of Pershore, and possibly a sister of Osric, King of the Hwicce about 700, suggest pre-Norman origins, though dedications can be uncertain or be changed. Coln St Denis, an 11th-century building, is now dedicated to St James Major, but was once known as St Catherine's, while its feast day was 17 July, St Kenelm's day, which would link it with the Saxon martyr of Winchcombe.

At least thirty-four churches in the north Cotswolds have Norman carved doorways characteristic of the period 1050-1150, and three more similar doorways survive in houses. They are simple, round-headed arches, often deeply incised with elaborate motifs, each one having its own peculiar details of decoration. It is convenient to call these doorways 'Norman', although some, like the tall, narrow south entrance at Saintbury, which has a sundial above it at least as old, may be earlier than 1066. The style is also called 'romanesque'. Zig-zag, or chevron, is the most common form of decoration and there are three examples of the rather unusual 'beakhead' ornament, most strikingly at Windrush, but also at Burford and in a house at Sherborne. This style was popular in Oxfordshire, and is considered to show Viking influence. Norman doorways have been preserved even when the churches were substantially altered; a number have been moved and reset, like the notable archway at Guiting Power, while some have been rescued and incorporated in houses.

22. Great Barrington chancel arch has remarkably sharp Norman decoration. It would be interesting to know how much Norman carving in the Cotswolds is original. Barrington stone was similar to Taynton and inside the carving would not have been eroded as much as outside, but the church was restored in 1880.

The existence of so many Norman doorways may be explained in a number of ways. The period has been called 'the Great Rebuilding' in respect of churches, as the century 1550 to 1650 has for houses, and the conjunction of all these stone churches and new Norman lords of the manor seems to be more than coincidental. The Normans probably considered the wooden churches which they found too mean, and they brought continental ideas and styles with them. The number of Norman doorways is linked also with the fact that the Cotswolds had been divided into a large number of small manors; the period of the 'Great Rebuilding' coincided with the creation of many parishes. Each Norman lord of the manor wanted to establish his authority over his manor and have a parish church to which he had the right of presentation. Norman-style churches exist also in manors held by monasteries. Though carved Norman doorways were often protected by porches quite soon after the church was built, inevitably they have become weathered by time, and it is tantalising to wonder how many are really Norman work and how many have been remade during restoration, perhaps several times. The church at Little Barrington has a very well-preserved Norman south doorway, protected by a porch, but the writer of the church guide has found record of the restoration by a carpenter of Little Barrington in 1865, who enlarged the porch so that the doorway should be more clearly seen, and at the same time took down the archway, cleaned it and rebuilt it. On the other hand, similar carving found inside some churches, like the chancel arch of Great Barrington, may never have needed restoration. The Barringtons and also Windrush were noted

23. The font and pillars at Old Broadway church are Norman, but as the church is dedicated to the Saxon St Eadburgha, it is likely that a modest, possibly wooden church already existed. The church is used only in summertime.

24. Oddington church, too, was replaced in the 19th century by a building more conveniently sited near the residential centre and is only used occasionally. The 'wine-glass' pulpit with sound board above is early 17th century.

for fine stone; Windrush church much impressed the Royal Commission which investigated stone for the rebuilding of the Houses of Parliament after they were burnt down in 1839, but the exterior beakheads round the doorway are now considerably eroded.

The decorated south doorway greeted the congregation as it came into the church; opposite it there was a second, smaller and usually plain doorway. The congregation was drawn into active participation in the services by processing out of the north door, round the church and in again at the south door. The nature of the church services at this time is not really known, but it has been suggested that they were akin to the Eastern or Byzantine Christian churches, with the congregation standing in front of the chancel. The bright colouring of the plasterwork in some churches, traces of which have been found in restoration, as at Hailes, Notgrove, Oddington or Stowell, could have been an attempt to recreate in England the varied stone colours of Eastern Christian churches. Hampnett, although painted by a Victorian rector, may give a real impression of what the inside of a church looked like in the early medieval period. The churches were dark, with few windows and none in the east end, as is still the case at Aston Blank and Notgrove; Postlip chapel gives a good impression of a church with little more than the Norman provision of windows. There were no seats; against the walls stone or wooden benches might have been provided for the sick or elderly, as at Buckland where there are early 17th-century wooden benches against the south wall of the aisle with a canopy above. There seems to have been little preaching, as pulpits are generally

16th-or 17th-century, though a wooden one in Stanton has been dated to the late 14th century. The font, on the other hand, is often very old, and sometimes pre-Norman, like the one in the old church of St Eadburga at Broadway.

Soon after they were built some Norman churches were enlarged by adding one or two aisles, as at Farmington. Alternatively, the existing church was sometimes turned into an aisle, and a completely new nave and chancel built adjacent to it, as at Northleach, Oddington and probably at Little Barrington, where the Norman arch was reset in the new south wall. The parish owned the body of the church, and had the cost and responsibility of maintaining its fabric; sometimes the lord of the manor owned an aisle and the rector owned the chancel. A considerable change occurred in the 13th century, when chancels were generally lengthened. There are many examples, but clear ones are Hailes, Icomb, Shipton Oliffe and Little Rissington. Hampnett retains the original Norman vaulted chancel. Coln St Denis has a small Norman chancel with remains of former vaulting. The extension of the chancel seems to indicate a wish to distance the altar and

25. Hampnett church near Northleach is unusual for its Norman vaulted sanctuary. The decoration, though carried out by a rector about 1871, may have been based on traces of colour found when the church was restored a few years before, and could well represent its early appearance.

priest from the congregation, and perhaps to create a holier area, sometimes even locked from access from the nave by a door in a screen. The priest also had his own small doorway into the chancel from outside, further enhancing his complete separation from the body of the church. At this period, three tall, narrow windows were placed at the East End over the altar; Little Rissington provides a good example. Though conveniently labelled 'Early English', the pointed arch was spreading throughout the continent, and enabled much taller and more ambitious buildings to be constructed in 'Gothic' style.

In the 15th century, extensive rebuilding again took place in the particularly English style called 'perpendicular'; it has dominated church architecture ever since, as little church building was again undertaken until the Victorian period. Winchcombe parish church exemplifies the style, a completely new building dated c.1465; Sir Ralph Boteler, who helped finance the nave, was also responsible for a smaller perpendicular church at Sudeley. Considerable building in this style was undertaken at Burford, Chipping Campden and Northleach. Its most obvious characteristic was light, and much larger windows were inserted in nearly all churches; Bledington is a notable example, but Great Barrington, Bourton on the Hill and Idbury might also be mentioned, with the clerestory at Stow on the Wold, which has unusual concave mouldings similar to Campden and Northleach. The insertion of big windows necessitated the removal of steep-pitched medieval roofs, and substitution of flatter ones, because the walls were no longer strong enough to withstand the thrust. At this time there was also an increasing emphasis on preaching; there are a number of 15th-century stone pulpits, for example in Coln Rogers, Naunton, Northleach, and Turkdean; early wooden pulpits generally date from the 16th century, and exist at Oddington, Shipton Solers and Windrush.

Church towers are particularly striking evidence of 15th-century religious revival. High towers were obviously symbols of dominance to the surrounding community, they reached towards heaven and they housed bells, but it was not necessary to make them so large or high for this last purpose. Chipping Campden's tower is famous, but numerous towers were either raised in height or built anew at this time: Saintbury, Upper Slaughter, Stanway and Withington towers were obviously raised and the small church of Compton Abdale has an interesting tower with heraldic emblems at the corners instead of pinnacles. A tower was added at the west end of the mainly Norman church at Farmington, blocking a Norman west window. Other perpendicular towers exist at Aston Blank, Ebrington, Guiting Power, Hampnett, Hazleton, Naunton, Stow on the Wold and Weston Subedge, together with a tower and spire at Stanton. Where towers were built inside the naves, as at Bledington, Didbrook, Turkdean and Willersey, it has been suggested that they might have replaced wooden bell-towers; at Bledington, however, a small Norman stone bell-cote also exists.

The main evidence for the dating of church towers has to be architectural, but the perpendicular designs of windows and pinnacles may frequently mislead. A tower was expensive to build, and once the stonework was there, other building would be fitted to it. In a number of cases the base of the tower seems to be much older than the upper storey, and may even pre-date the rest of the church. The base of Withington's tower is wider than the rest of the church, a feature considered typical of Anglo-Saxon design; this dating would be likely, as Withington was a Saxon minster. Other towers with possibly ancient bases are Coln St Denis, Longborough, Saintbury, Sevenhampton and Wyck Rissington. Sevenhampton's narrow tower which is 15th-century in style disguises the wide base which is apparent from outside the church. Were these really 'peel towers', that is defensive houses, as in the border land between England with Scotland? Oddington's massive tower was well-sited as a look-out to the ford over the Evenlode at Daylesford. The walls at the base of Longborough, Saintbury and Wyck Rissington towers are extremely thick and the stairs are within the thickness of a wall as in the peel towers. If some of the oldest towers were defensive houses for the priest and perhaps for the congregation too, was the ground floor the church and the room upstairs the priest's dwelling? In Saintbury, several details point to this: inside the tower there is a piscina, the stone bowl for the priest to wash his hands before the sacrament, and in the centre there is an octagonal stone—this could have been an original 'mensa' or stone altar table. The tower is now linked to the Norman nave to form a transept. At Coln St Denis, similarly, architectural details, including the position of an outside door into the tower, point to it predating the Norman nave; openings had to be made in its east and west faces when the nave and chancel were built, which weakened the structure, and the addition of the upper storey at a later date finally caused its near collapse.

The Dominance of the Parish Church

As parishes were created, some churches became more important, and were extended or rebuilt, with towers emphasising their authority, while non-parochial chapels remained unaltered

MINSTERS, RECTORIES AND CHURCHES

26. The 14th-century tower at Cutsdean was all that was saved when the church was completely rebuilt in 1863, because it was so ruinous. Although Cutsdean was a rectory, it became subordinate to Bredon.

27. Great Barrington church has a very notable range of 15th-century windows. The chancel arch (number 22) shows that earlier it had been an important church, in a royal manor and superior to Little Barrington and Windrush.

28. Farmington church is a good example of a type of building erected between about 1050 and 1150 and called 'Norman'. The porch protects a carved south doorway. The cross over the chancel is possibly 13th century. New, larger windows were later inserted and a tower built at the west end.

and eventually became disused. Surviving chapels may give the best impression of what an 11th-century church was like. Farmcote, which was in the parish of Guiting Power, is a simple Norman church which may contain Saxon stonework. In Winchcombe parish three apparently three Norman chapels did not have parish status, at Greet, Gretton and Postlip. Postlip chapel has a Norman nave and chancel, and a carved doorway. An illustration of Greet chapel shows an even simpler structure, with no chancel but with signs of a Norman-arched entrance; converted to a house before 1712, it had chimneys at each end, but was demolished c.1815. Gretton chapel had a small tower which survives, and a chancel, nave and Norman porch demolished in the late 19th century after a new church had been built.

Three Norman doorways now incorporated in private houses, at Broad Campden, Buckland Fields and Sherborne, provide interesting evidence of the decline of non-parochial churches. Broad Campden's Norman chapel may have been earlier but the church next to the manor house at Berrington became the parish church of Campden. The parish church at Buckland was sited next to Gloucester Abbey's manor house, but an earlier Norman chapel at Laverton also existed. About 1700 it was being used as a school, 'but much decayed and ready to fall'; the Norman doorway was moved to Buckland Fields at the beginning of the 19th century, and the dimensions and form of the house suggest that much of the masonry of the former chapel was re-used. Similarly the parish church at Sherborne was next to Winchcombe Abbey's manor house at the west end of the village, but a Norman archway from an earlier church at the east end of the

MINSTERS, RECTORIES AND CHURCHES

29 & 30. Drawings of Greet chapel and Gretton church, both in Winchcombe parish, were published in Emma Dent's *Annals of Winchcombe and Sudeley* (1877). Greet chapel was sketched by E.T. Browne Esq. before it was demolished about 1815. The drawings suggest simple buildings of *c*.1100.

village is built into a house not far away. There has been argument about where this archway originally stood. An account was published in 1936.

> The late Mr. George Freeman told the author that more than a century ago an ancestor of his lived in the farmhouse nearly opposite. At that time the doorway was standing in the garden facing the main entrance to the village. It was afterwards moved to its present position.

The carved Norman doorways may indicate community initiative in building a church, but the lord of the manor's authority was eventually more important. In all three cases, the parish church was next to the manor house, emphasising the lord's control, while a church which seems to have served the villagers remained unaltered and eventually became disused.

With the dissolution of the chantries, an Act of 1545 allowed superfluous church buildings to be pulled down. Chantries were special funds created to pay a priest to pray, or 'chant', for the soul of the benefactor, and so were seen by Protestant reformers as similar to monasteries in their religious significance. The church at Aston Magna in Blockley was regarded as a chantry chapel and was sold in 1549 to be converted to a house which is still standing. Most chantries were incorporated within big churches; there were four chantry priests at Chipping Campden and at least as many at Burford. These chapels have often survived.

Architectural and literary evidence show the existence of many other churches in the north Cotswolds. Traces of church architecture survive in barns at Dorn in Blockley and Taddington in Stanway. Two chapels in Guiting Power, Farmcote and 'Oldchurch', were mentioned in the ecclesiastical taxation list of 1292. Oldchurch could be at Ford, once the likely meeting place of the hundred of Holford; in 1712 the church here was described as converted to an ale-house. The size and shape of the *Plough Inn* make it possible that this was the building. Alternatively, Oldchurch was the Trinity Chapel near Guiting Grange, demolished before 1700. It stood 'near the famous well', and left traces in place-names: Trinity Ford and Bierway Piece; remains were apparently visible in the field next to the house about 1905. There is literary evidence of churches at Little Aston in Aston Blank, Coscombe in Didbrook, Owdeswell in Withington, Banks Fee in Longborough, Eastington in Northleach, Donnington in Stow on the Wold, Eastington in Northleach, Lower Norton in Weston Subedge and

31. The south doorway in number 88, Sherborne village, has very worn beakhead carvings and other Norman decoration; it was rebuilt in the late 19th century. The church had once served the east end of the village but the parish church was established near the manor house.

St Nicholas in Winchcombe. There are also lost parish churches at Eyford, Pinnock, Roel and Sezincote. Many of these references come from the notebook of Dr. Parsons, chancellor of the diocese of Gloucester in the late 17th century. By the time he was collecting his material, Eyford and Roel churches were already demolished, though some masonry from Roel church may survive in the farm. Pinnock's church was demolished in 'the late civil wars', and Sezincote was then in ruins; it was drawn on a map of the early 18th century but was demolished shortly afterwards. Coscombe chapel was 'profaned'. It had probably survived from the hospital of Hailes monastery at Coscombe, where the last abbot retired after the Dissolution. The chapel of St Mary Magdalene in Eastington was also demolished before Dr. Parsons wrote his notes, but the churchyard was recorded as part of the vicar's glebe in 1682. Chapel Close in Laverton, too, was part of the rector's glebe. Chapel Land in Banks' Fee in Longborough was the site of a church dedicated to St Edmund. Chapel Yard in Donnington, which was part of the glebe of the rector of Stow, seems likely also to perpetuate a previous church building. Church Hey, later called Church Yard, indicates the church site in Little Aston.

MINSTERS, RECTORIES AND CHURCHES

There were once two parish churches in Winchcombe as well as the abbey church. Leland, who talked to the last prior of the abbey, and whose testimony is usually very reliable, noted, 'There was of ancient time a church of St Nicholas in the East part of the towne, decayed many years since'. Chandos Street was formerly St Nicholas Street, and the vicar of Winchcombe still recorded the inhabitants of 'St. Collines parish' in the 17th century. (The present Roman Catholic church of St. Nicholas occupies a former school). A second parish church in Winchcombe stood on a site close to the abbey and may have been the town's first church. In 1245, the parson, Master Henry, wanted to lengthen the chancel and enlarge the south aisle, but was refused permission because it was claimed it would hinder free passage of the abbot's carts and the carriage of timber; also the wall towards the highway would prevent two carts passing 'and this would be of the greatest harm on the market days'. The building subsequently became disused and was probably demolished and the townsmen used the abbey church until St Peter's was built in the mid-15th century.

A Winchcombe monk copied into the 'Landboc', the abbey's cartulary, the calculation that there were 45,011 parochial churches in England. It has been dismissed as a wild exaggeration, considering that there were less than 10,000 parishes. The statement appears less exaggerated in the light of the many lost churches which are being documented in different parts of the country, particularly if the word 'parochial' is interpreted as relating to the service of local inhabitants, rather than in a legal sense to the churches of superior status. In addition, there were chapels or oratories in private houses, such as in Abbot's Grange in Broadway and possibly Icomb Place, and within religious institutions like Winchcombe and Hailes Abbeys and the Priory in Burford. If it was sure that God was in Gloucestershire, the old saying was even more appropriate to the Cotswolds.

Chapter Four

Market Charters and Town Councils

The towns of the Cotswolds were deliberately planned. Although a medieval town was distinguished from the surrounding villages by its weekly market, that was not its primary characteristic. A town was founded by the lord of the manor planting a compact settlement of freeholders. Several Cotswold manors where market-towns were later established had more than average numbers of smallholdings at the time of Domesday, perhaps occupied by craftsmen, which may have formed the nucleus of the new town. The lord of the manor had to buy a charter from the king giving permission to hold a weekly market and perhaps also an annual fair. A market charter did not make the town self-governing; this required the agreement of the lord and the ability of the townsmen to buy a charter from the king. Lords of the manor were generally reluctant to give up control and only Campden of the North Cotswold boroughs became independent. Winchcombe, the earliest market town in the Cotswolds, remained the largest town into the 16th century, though not very wealthy, while Burford and Campden grew significantly in wealth and size. Stow on the Wold and Northleach were successful markets, but Moreton in Marsh and Broadway did not achieve comparable success.

A Speculative Enterprise
The lord of the manor defined the area of a town within his estate and set out regular plots of land called 'burgages' because they formed the 'burh' or borough. Unlike the rest of the holdings on his manor, the burgage plots did not carry the obligation of work on the lord's own farmland and so craftsmen and others providing services to the local community were encouraged to occupy them. The lord paid for a charter because it enabled him to charge traders for stalls or standings in the street, where horses and carts were placed and wares were sold; burgesses or townsmen were exempt from these tolls. Trade did occur outside the licensed markets, though there were determined efforts to prevent it. At Chedworth, Newport Farm and Portway field suggest a market, as 'port' was the Anglo-Saxon word for a trading centre, whether on a river or coast, or inland. Domesday indicated that salt was sold at Chedworth, but there was no market charter, though the market continued unofficially.

Market-towns were created all over the country in the 13th century, as shown by the dates of their charters, but Cotswold market charters are generally earlier than this. Burford was founded between 1088 and 1107, and Stow on the Wold about 1107. The lord of the manor of Burford was Robert FitzHamon, who also gave a market charter to Tewkesbury and the lord of Stow was the Abbey of Evesham. A second series of market charters included Chipping Campden in 1185, granted by the baron Hugh de Gondeville; Moreton in Marsh in 1226, under the patronage of the Abbey of Westminster; Northleach through Gloucester Abbey's initiative in 1227; and Broadway under the Abbey of Pershore in 1251. Market days were designated so that traders could travel from one to another and were quite often changed. Winchcombe had a Saturday market; a second market-day was moved from Sunday to Monday in 1221 and then to Tuesday in 1575 but did not apparently succeed. Burford's market was also on Saturday, and Moreton and Northleach markets were both moved to Saturdays. Stow market was on Thursday, Chipping Campden on Wednesday and Broadway on Friday.

Two more places were potential market-towns, Blockley and Guiting Power. The bishop of Worcester obtained the grant of an annual fair in Blockley in 1239, but for some reason never developed the town further, perhaps because Campden, which was very close, was already a trading centre. Although Blockley had 25 smallholders in Domesday, they were probably scattered widely through the numerous settlements within this large manor. There is little indication of burgages in a survey of 1299 and there were fewer tax payers in Blockley itself in 1327 than in Upton and Northwick. Guiting Power was about the same size as Blockley, with 15 taxpayers in 1327. Guiting had been divided into several manors by the time of Domesday, and the royal manor later called Guiting Power was potentially important; it had five salt-houses from which the King drew 20 packloads of salt and two burgages in Winchcombe belonged to the manor. The inhabitants included a priest, three Frenchmen and two knights, which was rather unusual. In 1330, Lord Pancius de Crotone obtained a charter for a Tuesday market and for a fair. Evidence of attempted development may be found in the layout of the village Square; as in Blockley, there do not seem to have been any burgage plots and the market does not seem to have prospered.

Something of the nature of the Cotswold towns in the early 14th century can be deduced from taxation lists. Surnames at this date were not yet fixed by inheritance and can indicate occupation. The list of taxpayers in 1327, the Lay Subsidy, is the only surviving complete return for Gloucestershire from the period when individual assessments were made in each vill; it was published in 1786 by Ralph Bigland and again in the late 19th century by Sir Thomas Phillipps. Parliament had granted Edward III a tax of one twentieth of the assessed value of 'moveable' wealth; this did not include rents nor assets defined as 'essential', like military accoutrements, jewels, clothing, ploughs and carts. Though poor households were not taxed, large numbers of names are recorded, and comparative information can be drawn across the whole area, as Oxfordshire and Worcestershire returns also exist. The Winchcombe list is damaged, but fortunately there is one from 1312/13. From this it is clear that Winchcombe was the largest town in the area; there were 78 taxpayers, excluding any inhabitants of Sudeley or Coates who may have lived just outside the borough boundary. Burford had two thirds of this number of taxpayers, and Broadway a few less. Campden, Northleach and Stow were all much smaller, while Moreton had only 10 taxpayers. Except for Broadway and Moreton, rural areas within these parishes were listed separately.

Medieval Successes and 17th-century Challenges
Winchcombe
The earliest written record of Winchcombe is of the establishment of a minster church by Coenwulf, king of Mercia (796-821); the dedication and foundation charter was dated 811. It seems likely that a settlement of some size already existed, to provide necessary services to the minster. Three Roman villas in the vicinity, at Spoonley, Wadfield and Millhampost, indicate that there had been a well-developed economy in the area four centuries earlier, although few Roman finds have been made in Winchcombe. A site for a Roman town might

WINCHCOMBE
EARLY FEATURES

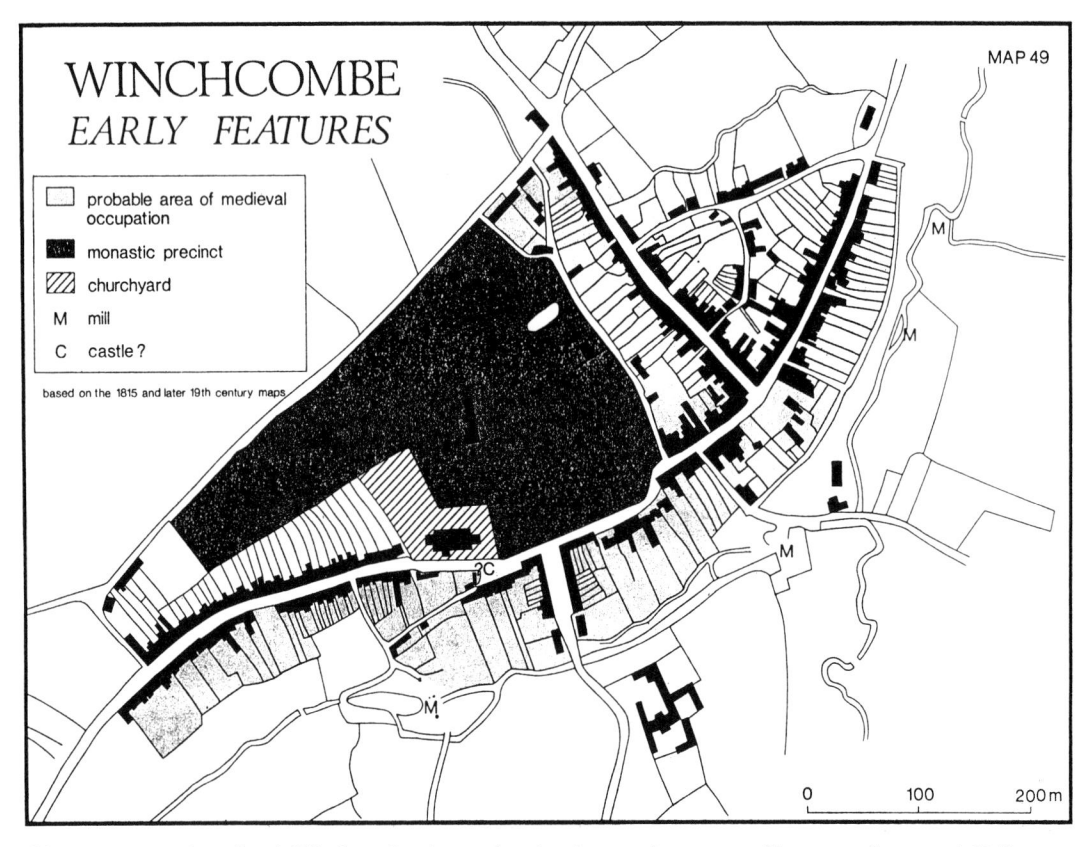

- probable area of medieval occupation
- monastic precinct
- churchyard
- M mill
- C castle?

based on the 1815 and later 19th century maps

MAP 49

32. The map of medieval Winchcombe shows that the three main streets—Gloucester Street and Hailes Street running east/west through the town and North Street at right angles—were established at least by the 13th century. The houses on the north side of Gloucester Street were probably built by the Abbey. The monastery precinct remains largely intact.

be Millhampost, two miles to the north-east, where extensive scatters of Roman pottery have been observed. This site is surrounded by the level arable fields of Hailes, where there was an exceptional amount of ploughland in Domesday. Winchcombe is on the side of a hill, facing rather easterly.

During the Saxon period and perhaps long before, the area round Winchcombe formed a large estate with a principal manor house in Sudeley; this estate was the basis of the minster's parish. Sudeley manor in the late 13th century contained Toddington, Stanley Pontlarge, Naunton near Winchcombe, Greet, Gretton, Piseley, Coates and Throp, which were called 'members'. Toddington became a separate parish but Winchcombe Abbey had some rights in all the other members of the manor. The lords of Sudeley were generous in their endowments to Winchcombe monastery but not until 1510 was the relationship reversed, when the Abbey itself became the lord of the manor and also had the advowson of Sudeley chapel. Common grazing for the men of Sudeley, Hailes, Piseley and Greet suggest that Hailes, too, once formed part of the same estate; about 1300 it required 12 men from Hailes and 12 men from Sudeley to establish and agree which fields were shared and which belonged to the lord. Hailes had become a separate manor by 1066, though the Cistercian monastery was not dedicated until 1251. The borough of Winchcombe was a small enclave within Sudeley. A number of houses in the borough, called Sudeley Tenements, were part of the manor, and the lord of Sudeley controlled the mills along the river.

Saxon Winchcombe was clearly defined by a defensive bank or wall to the west, now marked by Back Lane for some distance. Inhabitants of some of the burgage plots in the 14th century paid a small sum of money to the lord called 'walgavel', a relic of the obligation to contribute to the maintenance of the town's defences. Leland thought the town was walled on the other side of the river, too, towards Sudeley Castle, where he saw traces of a ditch and wall, but this seems more likely to have been associated with the castle. Burgage plots were probably laid out on both sides of a long main street, running east to west and parallel to the river Isbourne. Towards the west end the minster's grounds could have fronted the street, with housing being developed at a later date; on the north side of the abbey even in 1500 the gate opened onto the fields. The street plan also suggests that there was an older, less regular settlement nucleus around St Nicholas church on the north-east side of the town.

The names of High or Great Street and Hailes Street, which made up the east-west road through the town, and North Street, at right angles to it, were established at least by the 13th century; part of Great Street was renamed Gloucester Street, as development took place westwards. The Boothall or market hall was built at the junction of High Street and North Street and a market cross probably stood here. North Street was the horsemarket, for which Winchcombe was well known. At the end of the 19th century 'the horses stood on the footways, and were tethered to rings fixed in the walls of the houses, for which the occupiers claimed a small payment'. Medieval Winchcombe also contained a number of minor streets and lanes, most of whose names have changed, according to the principal inhabitants or trades for which they were noted. Ivy Castle Street, which is recorded later, could have been named from the castle described by Leland about 1540: 'There was a fortress or castle against the south side of the church of St Peter's in Winchcombe called Ivy Castle, now a place where are only a few old houses and gardens and ivy growing in the walls of it called Ivy Castle.' Ivy Castle street has disappeared and the position of the castle is uncertain. A reference in the middle of the 13th century to the Boothall as 'under the castle' seems to place it near the junction of North Street and High Street. When in 1837 a block of property was demolished near the church and between the abbey precinct wall and Abbey Terrace, one building was a 'turreted' hall.

Thirty-two of the 78 Winchcombe names in the Lay Subsidy of 1312 indicate occupation and show that its economy did not differ very much from that of other small towns. The largest occupational group was four millers. The cloth industry was not particularly evident, though there were two weavers, a dyer and a tailor. A maltster and wine merchant, a salter and a cook, showed some specialisation of service trades. The cook was probably a pastry-cook; pies and pasties were a well-established part of medieval town diet. There were workers in leather, iron and wood. A 'palfreyman' specialised in good quality riding horses. Three slaters were perhaps employed in construction work at the abbey, though roofing in stone appears to have been an unusual and costly project. A more complete survey of the town's occupations from the Poll Tax in 1381 shows that food processing and the textile industry involved rather over half the adult population. Two hundred and one people were listed, suggesting a population of about 350 or 400. Chipping Campden had a larger taxed population, but with a much smaller number of servants, Winchcombe had more households. About 20 monks lived in the monastery at this time, as well as at least 45 laymen. An undated list of wages of Winchcombe's 'family', which may have been prepared in connection with the Poll Tax, shows that the abbot of Winchcombe had a personal staff of 15, and the monks employed 30 servants. The abbot's butler was paid

33. Winchcombe parish church is notable because it dates entirely from the later 15th century, though the chancel roof was raised in the 19th century. There was an earlier parish church, perhaps adjoining the east end. Both were near the Abbey church which has been demolished.

twice as much as any other servant. The monastery employed cooks, a miller, bakers, a carpenter and tanner, a farrier and smith, and several stewards or sergeants were in charge of the Guest Hall, Church, Sacristy and Infirmary.

In the later 15th century Winchcombe built a new parish church, a mark of the town's prosperity and, even more, its wish for an identity apart from the famous abbey in its midst. During King Henry VI's time, Leland said:

> one William Winchecombe, Abbot of Winchcombe began with the Consent of the Town a Parish Church at the West End of the Abbey, where of old time had been and then was a little Chapel of St. Pancras. Abbot William made the East End of the Church. The Parishioners had gathered a 200L and began the Body of the Church; but that Sum being not able to perform so costly a Work Ralph Boteler Lord Sudeley helped them and finished the Work.

Because the town had its own church, the abbey church was destroyed when the monastery was closed.

Winchcombe Abbey was not one of the wealthiest monasteries in the country, nor even in Gloucestershire; when ecclesiastical income was reviewed in 1535, Winchcombe was valued at a little over £800 a year, about half as much as St Peter's, Gloucester. Fifteen monasteries in the country had more than £1,000 a year, amongst them Gloucester, Cirencester, Tewkesbury, Evesham and Worcester. On the other hand, Winchcombe's near neighbour at Hailes had only £408, while Bruern in Oxfordshire, another Cistercian house established in 1147, had £171; the hospital in Stow on the Wold had £25 and the hospital in Burford only

£16 a year. The abbot, the prior, and 16 monks were still resident in Winchcombe on 23 December 1539 when they surrendered the monastery to the King's commissioners; in Hailes the abbot and 21 monks surrendered the next day. At the height of a period of prosperity and fame under Richard Kidderminster, last abbot but one, about 1500, Winchcombe Abbey had no more than 27 monks. The pension given to the abbot of Winchcombe was very large, £140 a year and 40 loads of wood, but his prior was given £8 and the rest of the monks £6 each a year. Ninety laymen lived in Winchcombe Abbey, and 70 in Hailes; not far distant at Tewkesbury there were 39 monks and 144 laymen. Because of embarrassed financial circumstances, monasteries accepted money and in return provided the pensioner with a place in the monastery in old age. The monasteries also employed a number of administrators, 15 at Winchcombe, 7 at Hailes and 47 at Tewkesbury. The site of the monastery and the abbey's property were soon sold by the King. The conventual buildings at Winchcombe were immediatley demolished, except for the Abbot's House, which was demolished in 1815, but a few traces of the monastery remain, in buildings still sheltered behind the long wall which abbot Richard Kidderminster had built between the abbey and the town.

A survey of the former Winchcombe Abbey's property in the town, made for the Marquis of Northampton about 1550, lists 73 households; in 1563, according to an ecclesiastical census, Winchcombe had 146 households, so that the abbey had controlled about half the town. The main holding was in Gloucester Street; nine larger houses were scattered through the town but the two inns, the *Crown* and the *George*, were the only substantial properties. The rest of Winchcombe remained in the crown's hands, some 80 or 100 tenements in 1609 and five watermills; the divison between abbot and king had existed at least since the time of Domesday Book. A list of communicants made by the vicar in 1632 gives a good indication of the development of the town's streets. The population had increased since the mid-16th century, and the vicar noted 202 households but 338 families, as many households contained more than one family. Gloucester Street had 72 households, North Street 46, Hailes Street 36 and High Street sixteen. Four people lived in the remaining part of the abbey and 18 women and two men lived in the Almshouse. The lack of really wealthy householders can be gauged from the small number with servants, only 24 altogether, with seven households containing apprentices. More than a quarter of households were headed by women. Even so, the statement in the mid-17th century that 'near four thousand beggars of all sorts' inhabited the town seems rather exaggerated; the population probably did not exceed 1,500. Coates, Cockbury, Corndean, Greet, Postlip, Prescott and Sudeley were separately listed by the vicar. Even in the tight confines of the town, 28 households had farming interests and kept sheep, pigs and cows; the vicar kept careful note of the animals sold and the amount of tithe due to himself. He also noted tithe due on tobacco, hemp, hops and gardens. Tobacco was a special crop of the neighbourhood, and the vicar of Mickleton, too, was collecting tithe on tobacco early in the 17th century. Cultivation had only recently been introduced by a small group of local entrepreneurs including John Stratford of Farmcote and Sir John Tracy of Toddington.

Winchcombe had seemed like an independent chartered borough while the king controlled the town. A market court of 'pie poudre', pie powder, was held, so named from the dusty feet of itinerant traders who would use the court to claim their debts. There were two bailiffs, sometimes called 'portreeves', one chosen by the king and one by the townsmen and 10 assistants and constables. Unfortunately what was referred to as the 'charter' of 1588 was a limited agreement with the king's steward; it provided that burgesses were exempt from paying the fee to 'open any standing, stall or shop within the precincts or jurisdiction of this

Burgh'. The charter did not confirm the freehold status of the townsmen's burgages. In the early 17th century, James I sold his share of Winchcombe and a new owner tried to assert manorial rights. The borough and market were so ancient that there was little documentation confirming their constitution. Sir William Whitmore in 1637 demanded rents as on rural manors, and took his case to the Court of Exchequer. The inhabitants asserted that they had always bought and sold their houses freely, conveying ownership merely by the possession of the key, and they refused to pay any more—claims of extreme poverty in the town may be viewed slightly sceptically as a means of avoiding such payments. The Exchequer upheld the lord of the manor and the borough lost its legal functions to the manor court. Commissioners appointed to enquire into old municipal corporations in 1880 found

> no corporation in Winchcombe, but a body consisting of a high bailiff, a low bailiff and 10 burgesses, appointed at a court leet of the manor of Winchcombe, and in whom certain property in the town is supposed to be vested. There are no freemen. ... The corporation have no public duties and exercise no jurisdiction.

The Town Hall was the main item of property.

Burford

Traders probably congregated at Burford near the ford over the Windrush, and perhaps the 18 Domesday smallholders lived nearby. Burford's market charter was granted about 1100. The boundary of the borough was drawn round the new burgages separating them from the agricultural communities of Upton and Signet. The boundary crossed High Street above the Tolsey, skirted the back of Sheep Street's burgages and followed Priory Lane to the bridge. A section of Witney Street, with the mill, was in Upton, though the tannery next door was allocated to the borough. Behind Witney Street, a long thin piece of arable land called Burford Field was allocated to the borough to supplement the small garden plots. The inhabitants of Holwell continued to have a right to bring their sheep down a lane to the ford over the mill stream, which was now in the borough, into the 16th century. High Street and the south side of Sheep Street were probably laid out first, with the crossroads as the centre of the market. The Tolsey, where toll money was paid, was later built here. Sheep Street was the sheep market. At Michaelmas, the inhabitants had to pay a few pence to the town bailiff for their sheep pens; they agreed a rate with Simon Wisdom in 1562 which they intended 'to continue for ever and not to be raised'. At the end of Sheep street there was a pound for pigs.

The new market town of Burford flourished; in 1299 there were 105 freeholders, who altogether paid the lord £21 for their burgages. Market tolls were worth £12; with the water mill, 30 acres of meadow and other revenues from the law court, the lord's total income from Burford borough was £41. By 1322, a bridge which had replaced the ford was in need of repair; the lord of the manor gave up tolls on goods brought over the bridge for three years to finance the work. The items which could be taxed were listed in Latin. The number and variety was considerable. Corn, horses, oxen, cows and hides were listed first. Foodstuffs included bread, butter and cheese, garlic and onions, flour made of peas and beans, herrings, and other fish, bacon flitches and barrels of wine and cider. Honey was sold by the barrel. Wool and different cloths were mentioned, Welsh, Scotch or worsted and cloths with gold threads. Wood, charcoal, faggots and turves, nails and horseshoes, iron, copper, steel rod and lead, were all market goods. Unusual items like hand-mills for grinding corn and cauldrons and furnaces for brewing were listed. It was an impressive attempt by early bureaucracy to catch every conceivable item coming to market. Between the 13th and the 16th century the town did not expand further. In 1552, when a survey was made for Edward VI, there were

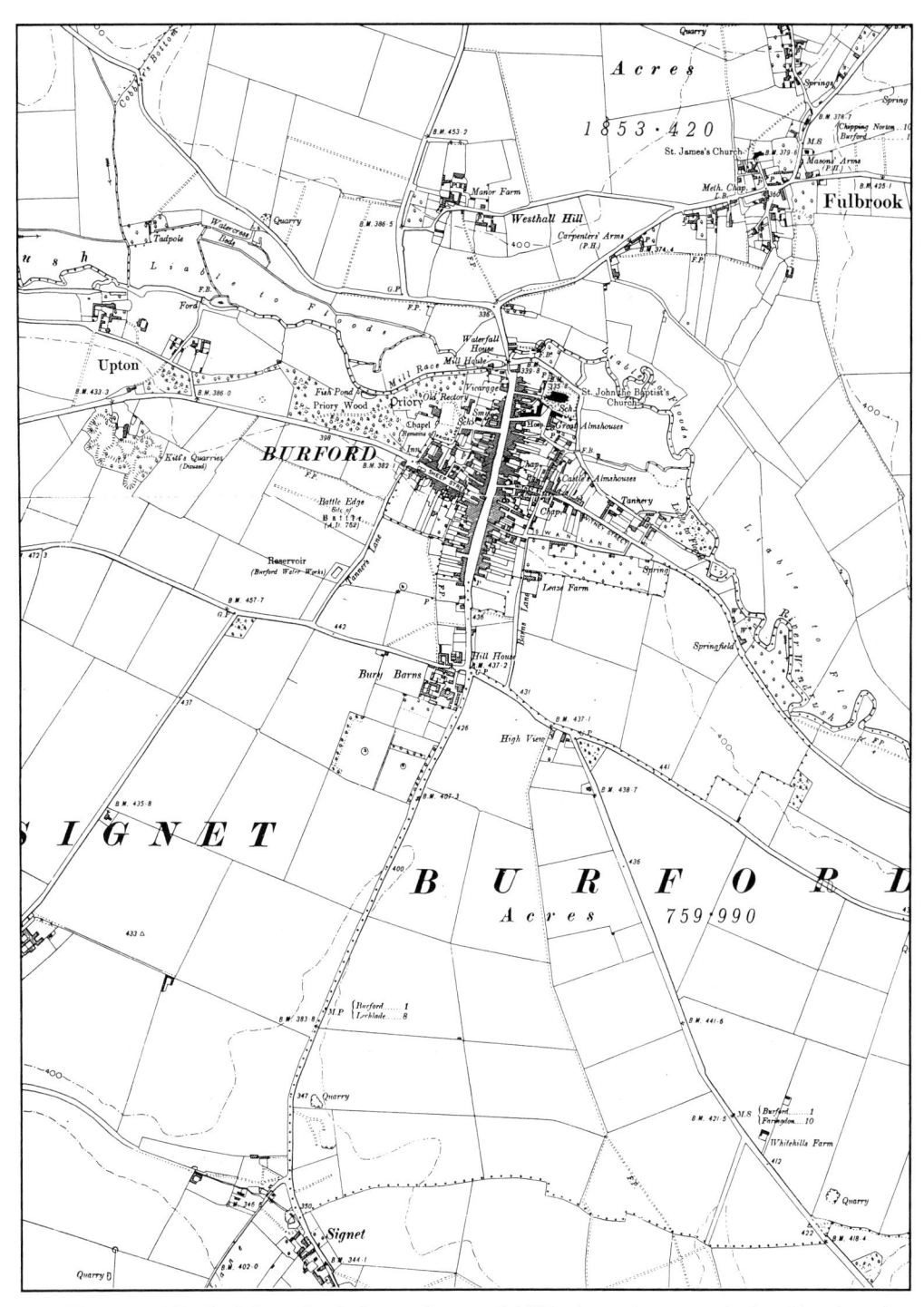

34. The map of Burford, from the Ordnance Survey of 1900, shows the two agricultural hamlets of Upton and Signet, and Fulbrook on the north side of the Windrush, which was a chapelry of Burford church. Cobblers Bottom in the north-west derives from 'Cobban broc', mentioned in an account of the boundaries of Taynton in 1059.

only 20 more burgages than there had been freeholders in 1299. Some few burgages may have been added at the end of Witney Street and there were some in Church Lane and Priory Lane, but more than half were in High Street.

Did the creation of the market-town affect the existing villagers or smallholders? Were the fields of Burford reorganised at this time? By 1300 there were two open-field systems in the manor, one in Upton and one in Signet, which made up Burford Outward tithing or Burford 'Foreign'; the borough was the Inward tithing. The place-name Upton is first recorded in 1295, Signet in 1299; both hamlets could have been created to take villagers displaced by the new market town. A survey of the manor of Burford in 1299 named 15 village farmers with 10½ yardlands in Upton and 15 with 13½ yardlands in Signet. With the lord of the manor's eight yardlands in Upton, the total exactly matches the number of Domesday hides in Burford. Upton had an appropriate section of Windrush meadow to the west of the town and Signet to the east. The separation of land-holdings was complete, and this allowed Upton to be leased as a separate manor, but Signet was leased with the borough. In the 17th century, and possibly before, the lord of the manor concentrated his lands in Upton, which was almost entirely owned by the Lenthal family at the time of enclosure in 1773. Signet enclosure involved many more landowners.

The first part of Burford's name, 'burh', may indicate a defended manor house near the ford rather than a hill-fort. Fulbrook, on the rising ground on the north side of the Windrush, was part of the estate, giving control over both sides of the river crossing. There was no manor house in medieval Burford, but topography suggests that it was originally where Burford Priory is situated, on land rising quite steeply from the river meadows, and defended

35. Burford High Street was planned to lead to a ford over the Windrush. The junction with Sheep Street was the focus of the town, where the Tolsey was built, and the High Cross was opposite. The top of the hill was not developed until the Elizabethan period.

MARKET CHARTERS AND TOWN COUNCILS

on that side by a canal bringing water to the mill. A precinct stretched downstream beyond the church, where the meadow between the mill stream and the river is called 'Bury Orchard'. When High Street was planned, running straight down the hill to the ford, it cut this site in two, which may explain why the manor house was given by Burford's lords to found a Hospital of St John the Evangelist, later known as the Priory. The dedication is not the same as the parish church, which is to St John the Baptist. Other evidence indicates that the Priory was the successor to the manor house. It was customary for the lord of the manor to own an aisle in the church and in Burford the north aisle belonged to the hospital.

Robert FitzHamon's charter had allowed Burford to have a Merchant Guild of two bailiffs, an alderman and 10 burgesses, chosen from a few, better-off merchants. They themselves nominated successors in place of members who had died. The Guild acted as the town council. It had a strong sense of fellowship and members helped each other. Pride in its identity led in the 13th century to the erection of a chapel and meeting house in the churchyard.

36. The west end of Burford church is seen from Lawrence Lane; on the right is the former Guildhall, which was later joined to the church. The Norman decorated tower echoes Robert FitzHamon's tower at Tewkesbury.

Guilds were dissolved by the Chantries Act in 1547 because one of their functions was to pray for the souls of past fellows and benefactors; Protestant reformers had little sympathy with this practice. Some Burford townsmen reconstituted a corporate body similar to the former Guild by buying back most of the charity lands which had been confiscated, and the charity trustees continued to act as a town council. The lord of the manor was distant and forgotten, but the court of burgesses had no legal authority. The corporation was therefore dismayed to find itself taken to court in the early 17th century by an acute if avaricious lawyer, who had purchased the manor. He claimed that the corporation had no right to collect the tolls from market and fair, nor to make bye-laws for the town. Sir Lawrence Tanfield won his case. Tolls had to be paid to him, and the town council's only function was to administer the charity property. Tanfield perhaps hoped Burford would buy its freedom and obtain a royal charter making it self-governing, but Burford's merchants did not follow this course. Until 1861 a corporation continued to administer the charities and to act in a ceremonial way as a town council but with frequent crises caused by inefficiency and lack of interest. An act of parliament regulating the charities abolished the council. At this date uniform rural district councils were created for the whole country. A few years after this the last markets were held.

Stow on the Wold

Stow on the Wold was also an early Norman market, founded by Evesham Abbey in its manor of Maugersbury though on the border with Broadwell; the houses on one side of High Street were in Broadwell. Maugersbury and Broadwell were granted to Evesham Abbey before 714, together with Donnington, Swell and Bourton on the Water. Inter-relationships persisted for centuries; for example, while Donnington was in the parish of Stow, it was part of Broadwell manor. Stow became the administrative centre of this group of manors and also of a church deanery. 'Stow' is a holy place; Domesday recorded that there was a church dedicated to St Edward, and for centuries the town was called Edwardstow or Stow St Edward's. King Edward was martyred in 979, a victim of political rivalries, and his murder allowed Ethelred to become king, though not yet ten years old. Ethelred the Unready subsequently tried to atone for his involvement in the murder by canonising Edward and dedicating churches to him, and Stow seems to be one of them.

Stow has the most inhospitable site of any of the market towns in the area; not only is it on top of a hill, but water had to be carried up the hill in carts until the mid-19th century; the so-called Stow well was not far away but was in the parish of Broadwell and in 1700 it was reported that 'there is no well or pump of water in all the town but they fetch it generally at the bottom of the hill from Lower Swell'. For a short while in the mid-19th century water was pumped from Upper Swell, but did not give the town an adequate supply. In 1871 the lord of the manor, Joseph Chamberlayne Chamberlayne, gave the money to dig a very deep well which served until 1937. Despite this disadvantage, the abbot of Evesham was right in thinking that the junction of the Fosse Way with several major routeways, including a salt way, would sustain a market town. As with Burford, trade was probably already established before the market charter was obtained about 1107. A strong oral tradition recorded that a hospital in the town was founded in the late tenth century by a nobleman called Aethelmaer and this supports the idea that there was more than an isolated hill-top church at Stow at that time. The name Maugersbury may tell us something of the history of the area. 'Maethelgar' might have been a personal name, but 'maethel' meant 'speech' or

37. A number of buildings encroached on the market place in Stow on the Wold; St Edward's Hall replaced some in 1878. From the church tower, the closeness of the countryside can be appreciated.

'council'; at a junction of so many roads, Stow would have been a natural meeting-place. The town was built within a 'byrig' or hill-fort, pointing to an importance before the Saxon period.

Although close to the Fosse Way, the town's development was based on a salt way, the winding road along the modern line of High Street, Market Square, Digbeth Street and Park Street, which continued on to Icomb. The site was as an approximate rectangle, bounded by Well Lane and Back Walls on the east and south and the Fosse Way on the west, with a thin projection to the north along High Street as far as the junction with the Fosse Way. The layout was adapted to the existing position of the church which formed the west side of Market Square; burgage plots were laid out on the east side of the Square. There is no record of the number of burgages but there were only 27 taxpayers in 1327. Sheep Street was a straight cut between the Fosse Way and the salt way. A sheep market may have been one of Stow's most important functions; Dr. Parsons noted that 'the sheep cubbs and other standings are a great advantage to the lord of the manor, John Chamberlayne Esq., being worth for standings at the fairs especially for sheep near £80'. Broadwell manor also profited from the sheep market, as it included land 'whereupon sheep folds were heretofore used to be set and placed at the fairs holden within the said town of Stow'. Evesham Abbey gave the government of the town and supervision of the market and fairs in 1539 to two bailiffs for life; following this, the townsmen appeared to be independent of a lord of the manor. They elected two town bailiffs, two constables, two sergeants-at-mace, two ale-tasters and two leather-sealers. In 1603, Edmund Chamberlayne purchased the manor of Stow with the right to the tolls from markets and fairs. Like Tanfield in Burford a few years later, he asserted his manorial rights. The townsmen hurried to obtain a charter, incorporating two bailiffs and 12 burgesses and a clerk and affirming all the town's former rights and liberties. Chamberlayne challenged the charter, arguing that there were no former rights and liberties to be affirmed, and Stow argued that there was no manor of Stow which Chamberlayne could have purchased. Unfortunately for the townsmen, the court found for Chamberlayne. As lord of the manor of Maugersbury, Chamberlayne's case was stronger; Evesham Abbey had not given its town a charter. A corporation continued to act, as in Burford, in a ceremonial way, but only for a few years. The Thursday market continued to be successful until about 1900.

Chipping Campden
Of the 13th-century market-towns, Chipping Campden was the most successful and the only one to become a borough by royal charter, and so become independent of the lord of the manor. Hugh de Gondeville obtained the first charter in 1185; he was one of the knights implicated in the murder of Thomas à Becket. The new town was not sited at an important cross-roads, but was laid out along a natural routeway governed by the river and low-lying ground, giving High Street the curve which adds much to Chipping Campden's attractiveness. The houses of the eight smallholders of Domesday and the 12 slaves were probably already here, near the manor house. The burgages seem fairly uniform on the west side of High Street and a lane called Back Ends gave access to the rear of the plots; on the other side of High Street, the plots are shorter and less regular. Sheep Street now appears too narrow to have had sheep pens along it. Farm stock was probably less significant in Campden than in Burford or Stow, but wool sales were important. The new borough was known simply as Campden; Chipping, meaning market, was added later. In 1247 Campden was allowed a three-day fair as well as a market; the lord of the manor collected fair tolls, but the town collected market tolls. A survey, made in 1273 following the death of the lord, Roger de Somery, lists 75¾ burgages, 21 houses not classed as burgages, and at least 106 inhabitants.

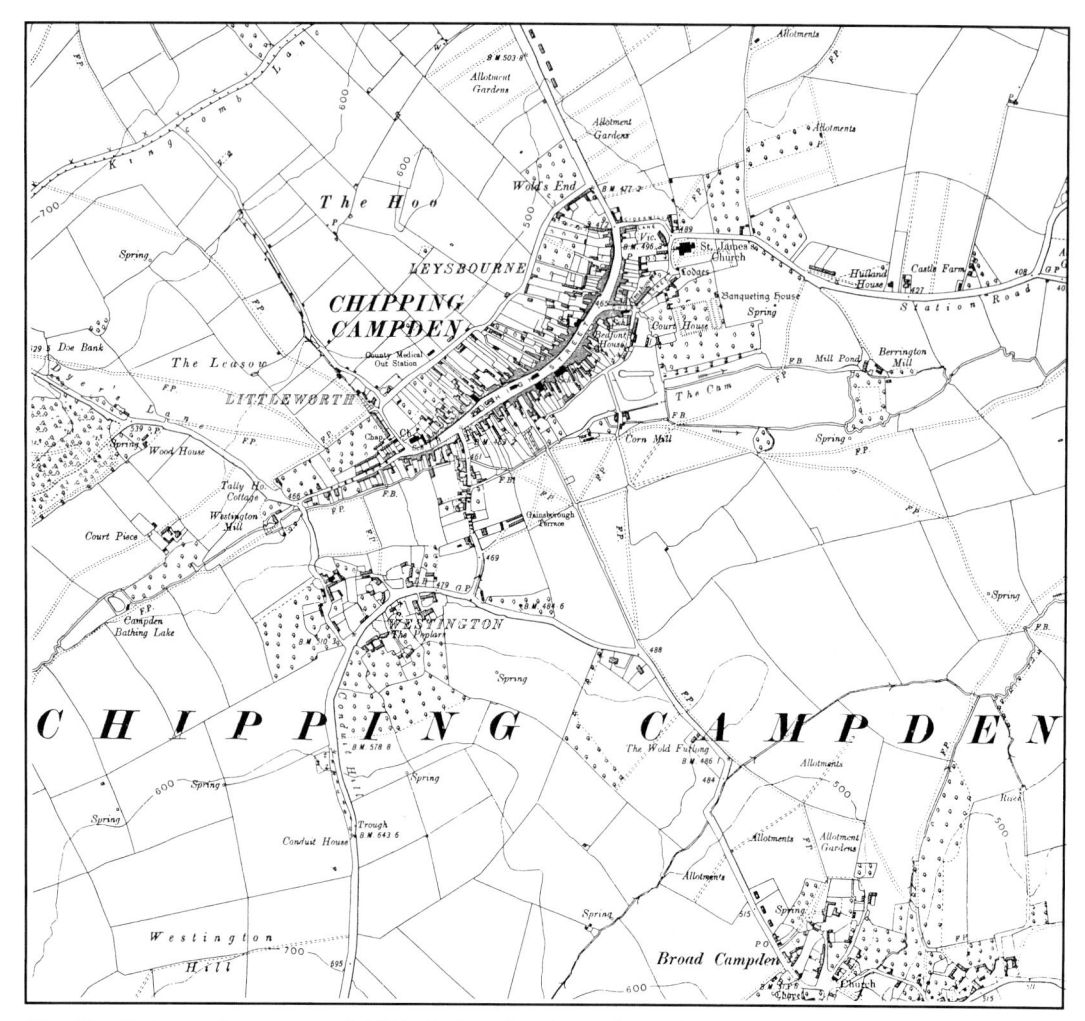

38. The Ordnance Survey map of 1924 of Campden shows the market town of Chipping Campden, Berrington to the east, Westington to the west and Broad Campden to the south; the Norman Chapel site is indicated here.

Surprisingly, in 1327 there were only 25 taxpayers, two less than at Stow, though some prosperous townsmen may have lived outside the borough boundary, in Berrington and Westington. One man paid three times as much tax as anyone else, and was probably the occupant of Campden manor. Later in the 14th century, more than a third of the households in Chipping Campden had resident servants, an indication of the relative prosperity of the town. William Grevil, the wool merchant and builder of the house which is known by his name, had six servants, and so did Robert Mors, a smith; Walter Ebyrton, innkeeper, had five, and three families had four servants each. Altogether servants formed 60 per cent of the poll tax payers in the town.

Campden manor was probably already divided into two nearly equal parts before the market town was established, the western half centred on the manor house and the eastern half on Broad Campden. The boundary between the two followed the road from Seven Wells and then the Catbrook. The western half of Campden included Combe, a deep valley, as its British name implies, which was detached from the rest of the manor at an early date to form a separate monastic estate. The western half also included the manor house, situated near the present church, with a mill conveniently nearby, and some enclosed land round it. A conygree or rabbit warren was made about the mid-13th century. The 'conieberries' or earthen burrows which were provided for the delicate rabbits when they were first imported into England were still there in the early 17th century when Sir Baptist Hicks bought the manor and rebuilt the manor house. After the borough had been created, the manor house was in the agricultural tithing of Berrington. Thomas Ludlow, one of the Gloucestershire gentry entitled to bear arms in 1381, was described as of Berrington, confirming the position of the manor house. Edward Ludlow held Campden manor in 1402 and was buried in Campden church. Both were likely to have been related to the notable Shropshire family of wool merchants.

The new borough cut the western part of Campden into two, and two farming settlements were therefore created : one called Westington, where the farmers who tilled the fields on the western side lived, and the other Berrington, named because adjacent to the manor house or 'bury'. Neither name is recorded until the early 13th century. The 1273 survey shows that the landholdings had been systematically divided as they had in Burford; two thirds of the holdings and two thirds of the tenants were in Westington and one third was in Berrington. The manor's own farm land was in strips scattered in the fields of both. The inhabitants of the borough and of Berrington were often listed together, though Berrington was called a vill in the survey of 1273 and was a separate tithing in the parish. Sometimes it was named Berrington in the Marsh, as it reached into the Henmarsh, also shared by Moreton in Marsh. The eastern half of Campden manor became known as Broad Campden. Like Upton in Burford, Broad Campden was made into an independent manor, and so remained until the early 17th century. Broad Campden was the 'foreign' or outside part of Campden, suggesting that Broad is equivalent to 'abroad'; it must have been named while the town was known simply as Campden. Broad Campden had its own church before 1150, and in 1327 there was a well-to-do chaplain living there. His land may eventually have passed to Tewkesbury Abbey, which had 6¾ yardlands in Broad Campden in 1540.

After the dissolution of the monasteries, the different parts of Campden manor were gradually brought together by Thomas Smith, and Anthony Smith his son completed the process in 1602 with the purchase of Broad Campden manor. This was a prelude to an attack on the privileges of the town's burgesses as at Burford and Stow. Hastily, the townsmen applied to the king and in 1605 secured a royal charter allowing them to have a council of 14 capital burgesses, from whom two bailiffs were to be chosen each year, and 12 inferior burgesses, all holding their positions for life. The council was empowered to make bye-laws and hold a court for actions concerning small debts; the tolls from two fair-days were to go to the corporation and from two more fair days to the lord of the manor. Anthony Smith accused the town of acting by stealth, and tried to get the charter revoked. During the course of the legal proceedings he sold the manor to two men acting for Sir Baptist Hicks. Campden kept its charter. Despite his defeat, Hicks built a market hall in the Square to provide shelter for some of the traders. The corporation continued to exist until the later 19th century, though after 1785 no longer tried to control the town very closely, and no more freemen were admitted after this date. The Commission in 1880 found that the income from tolls had nearly disappeared, apart from a few small payments for standings in the Square; the borough had no corporate seal and the burgesses did not take an oath on assuming office. The corporation was dissolved by the Municipal Corporations Act of 1883 and its property was taken over by the Charity Commissioners in 1890. The Town Hall, which has 14th-century fabric, was rebuilt in the 18th century; a new porch was added to celebrate Queen Victoria's Diamond Jubilee and the hall was completely restored in 1897.

Northleach

The Domesday manor called 'Leche' was divided into two sections in the same way as Campden. Northleach's name is usually thought to distinguish this manor from Eastleach and Lechlade on the lower reaches of the river, but could relate specifically to the position of the town in the northern part of the manor. Gloucester Abbey's demesne was here, described in later records as 'the Farm', showing that in the early days this was the only land 'let to farm', that is for rent. Northleach Farm was large; in the 13th century the abbey had five plough teams of oxen and one of horses. Although the land was divided into strips with the parson's land intermingled with the demesne, there were no common grazing rights for sheep, which later made enclosure easier. The villagers had their fields in the south and east of the estate, in Eastington. Their settlement probably existed before the creation of the market-town and Eastington had its own chapel. The agricultural area outside the town, both Eastington and 'the Farm', was called 'Northleach Foreign'.

The abbot of Gloucester obtained a charter for a market and a three-day fair for Northleach in 1227. The market-place was triangular, with one side adjoining the churchyard which was also part of the town's boundary. The burgages were set out on either side of the road to Burford and parallel to the river Leach. As at Stow, the Fosse Way was near, but was not part of the town plan. There is no Sheep Street in Northleach; the abbot built his hopes of success on wool from his own flocks in the manor and from neighbouring monastic estates at Barrington and Sherborne. A survey was made about forty years after the market charter; occupational surnames were common but were turned into Latin which is not always easy to interpret. In the market-place there were nine permanent stalls. One was taken by the doctor; a weekly display of his remedies seems like a 'surgery' for the country-folk of the time. A cook also had a stall, and so did a chapman or travelling salesman and a corn merchant; two stall-holders came from Bibury. A shop had already encroached on the market-place but most craftsmen had their workshops in their houses. Food was provided by two bakers, a cook and a corn-merchant. As well as the doctor there was a barber, a clerk and a beadle. Metal-workers included three smiths, a nailor and an ironmonger. There were two masons, a cobbler, rein-maker, sieve-maker, saddler and maker of winnowing fans for separating the corn from the husks, and a hay-ward. Two dyers, a mercer, a weaver, a tailor and a tailor's widow indicate that there was an active cloth industry.

With 64 burgages, Northleach had a few less than Chipping Campden, though only a third of these households were wealthy enough to pay the subsidy in 1327. Only one burgage had been divided into two half-burgages and a few people owned more than one. The standard payment for a burgage was 12 pence a year; there was also a toll on ale brewed and sold and on horses bought or sold in the town. The parson's burgage was one acre but most burgages must have been smaller than this, or there would not have been room for 64 within the 43 acres of the town. There were also 16 small closes where the townsmen could pasture horses or cattle, one occupied by a farrier. Four larger burgages paid up to six times as much as the standard amount of tax. They were probably in the east end of the town, where much larger plots are still evident and where the 'Great House' stood. This was once the lord of the manor's own burgage; the Great House was given to the town after the manor was bought

MARKET CHARTERS AND TOWN COUNCILS

NORTHLEACH
EARLY FEATURES

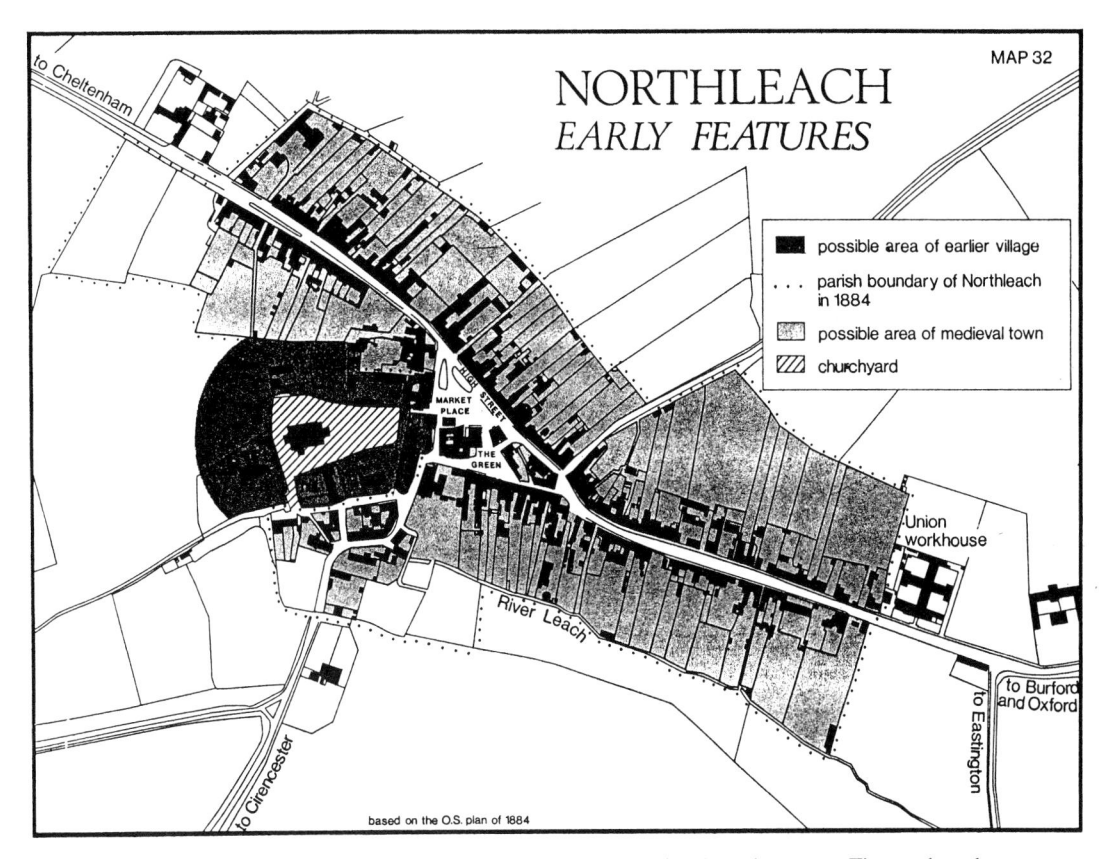

MAP 32

- possible area of earlier village
- ... parish boundary of Northleach in 1884
- possible area of medieval town
- churchyard

based on the O.S. plan of 1884

39. Map of Northleach, showing the probable extent of the medieval market-town. The market-place was a triangle, but permanent stalls early encroached on the open space.

by William Dutton of Sherborne in 1599, and part remains in Dover House. Three of these larger burgages were occupied by a doctor, a dyer, and a cook. The parson's burgage was empty, though there was another man 'said to be a priest' sharing a burgage with Alice the weaver. A few houses within the town boundaries were not classed as burgages and may have been there before the town was planned, possibly in the area of the mill.

The abbot of Gloucester agreed to pay the abbot of Cirencester £8 a year in order to be allowed to hold a court in the town to deal with petty offenders against law and order. The abbot of Cirencester retained the right to visit the court once a year, as he had supervisory powers over a group of seven hundreds round Cirencester. This responsibility was sold with part of the estate after Cirencester Abbey was closed, and has descended to the present Lord Bathurst. Northleach court acted as a town government, but the prosperous wool merchants were neither wealthy nor numerous enough to buy a royal charter. The abbot's steward, and later the lessee of the manor, presided over the court and was the town bailiff. When Gloucester Abbey was closed, Michael Ashfielde, gentleman, was leasing Northleach; he lived in the town, perhaps in the Great House, and kept 1,000 sheep on the Farm. He also had at least 60 tods of wool in store and at his death was owed money by two clothiers, one William Bushe of Northleach, the other from Leonard Stanley. The manor then passed to Thomas Parker, gentleman, a nephew of the last abbot of Gloucester. In 1576, Thomas Parker summoned a town court and regularised its constitution. The court's members were himself or his under-bailiff, and six men chosen by him as 'arbitrators'—men who could give judgement. He also chose the town clerk. They agreed to wear gowns as a mark of their status. Other officials of the court were two constables, two wardsmen for the East and West Ends, two 'sealers and searchers' who checked the length and width of cloth, and a sergeant. The sergeant's duty was to ring the bell to summon the court; he also had the duty of 'doling the downs', that is arranging for lots to be drawn by the burgesses for their shares of pasture on Northleach Downs. Tradesmen living in Northleach were asked to attend the court and in 1576 four innholders, seven brewers, two bakers, two butchers and two fishmongers and chandlers met in the Town House or Boothall. The importance of the cloth industry at the time is indicated by the two sealers amongst the court's officers, and the number of inns shows the busy nature of the cloth and wool market, as inns were places of business. By the end of the 18th century the town was 'much decayed' and the bailiff had few duties. The court continued to meet, even after the 19th-century provision of local councils, its one function as in Burford to administer the town charities.

Moreton in Marsh and Broadway
The markets at Moreton in Marsh and Broadway did not achieve the success of Burford, Campden or Northleach. Neither had a clearly defined urban status as neither had a town council separate from the manor court; the town was simply a tithing within the manor. Yet both places reveal their histories as planned towns, because the houses lining the main streets were of some size and pretensions, being built by men who owned their burgage plots.

Moreton in Marsh was part of the Deerhurst Priory estate centred on Bourton on the Hill and transferred to Westminster Abbey just before the Conquest. The Dean and Chapter of Westminster succeeded the abbot as owner after the Dissolution. When the estate was sold in 1856, there had been a thousand years of ecclesiastical ownership. Moreton, as a 'ton' or farming town, seems to have been a relatively new settlement, its open fields drawn out of the Henmarsh. The 'Henmarsh' was once common grazing land for a group of manors which included Bourton on the Hill, Batsford and probably Blockley, too, which was the superior church. This estate may have had a Roman origin. The site of the Roman settlement of Dorn is near Moreton in Marsh and was in Blockley parish; unusually, Dorn has a British name, not an Anglo-Saxon one. After the new town was planned, the Old Town remained a small settlement of cottage plots on two sides of the churchyard. A burgage in Moreton New Town entitled the holder to keep two cows or a cow and a horse on the Heath, but the town-dwellers were generally excluded from common rights in the open fields. Batsford farmers were given pasture-land in Bourton on the Hill to compensate for loss of pasture in Moreton in Marsh, and the smaller of the two manors in Bourton on the Hill was allocated a share of the New Town.

The abbot of Westminster's charter for Moreton in Marsh was 1226, nearly the same date as that for Northleach, but Moreton had to compete with an already established market town at Stow on the Wold, only a few miles along the Fosse Way. The market was the Fosse Way itself; regular burgage plots were laid out on either side. Back Ends, now Hospital Road, gave access to the rear of the plots on the western side. Medieval Moreton was small and not very wealthy; only 12 people were taxed in 1337, rather fewer than the parent manor of Bourton on the Hill, and most may have been farmers rather than traders. The 'portmote', a meeting of the town tithing, appointed a 'catchpole', a collector of manorial taxes who 'caught' every 'poll' or head; the portmote continued to meet at least until the end of the 18th

I and II Buckland *(above)* and Naunton *(below)* are characteristic Cotswold villages. At Buckland, church and manor house are side by side and the village originally consisted of cottagers providing services to the manor. Naunton was a setttlement of small farmers surrounded by its open fields, and church and rectory (the square house to the right of the church, were the dominant buildings.

III   The old road climbing Stanway hill through Lidcomb wood was shown on Ogilby's map of 1675 and is a public footpath. Woods are particularly prominent on the western edge of the Cotswolds.

IV   Open upland at Wontley: the barns mark the site of a deserted village. The unfenced road over West Down is typical of the countryside before enclosure and tarmacadam.

V   Priests are often mentioned in Domesday Book in manors traversed by a saltway. Between Hailes and Farmcote a saltway climbs the Cotswold edge; masonry in Farmcote chapel suggests that there was a stone church here in the 11th century. The chancel arch is visible and originally led to a round-ended apse.

VI   This section of the Roman Ryknild Street, which ran from Bourton on the Water to Templeborough near Sheffield, is known as Condicote Lane, but in the Anglo-Saxon period was Buggilde Street. The road is also called Buckle Street (*see* page 71). Short sections were used to demarcate parish boundaries.

VII Stanway church is probably on the same site as the 'monasterium' mentioned in Domesday Book and parts of the building are 12th century. The upper part of the tower was added in the 15th century and its ashlar facing is distinct.

VIII The doorway of the one-time Laverton chapel has strong Norman decoration. The chapel was rebuilt at Buckland Fields in the early 19th century.

MARKET CHARTERS AND TOWN COUNCILS

40. A town might have been planned on the east/west road at Bourton on the Hill; there was a large number of cottagers there in the 13th century, contributing to the later shape of the village, but Westminster Abbey created a new market town on the Fosse Way at Moreton in Marsh.

41. The basis of Moreton in Marsh's market-town development was the Fosse Way and a wide street was planned for the market stalls. The Redesdale Hall was built in 1887. The 16th-century curfew tower can be seen on the right.

MORETON IN MARSH
EARLY FEATURES

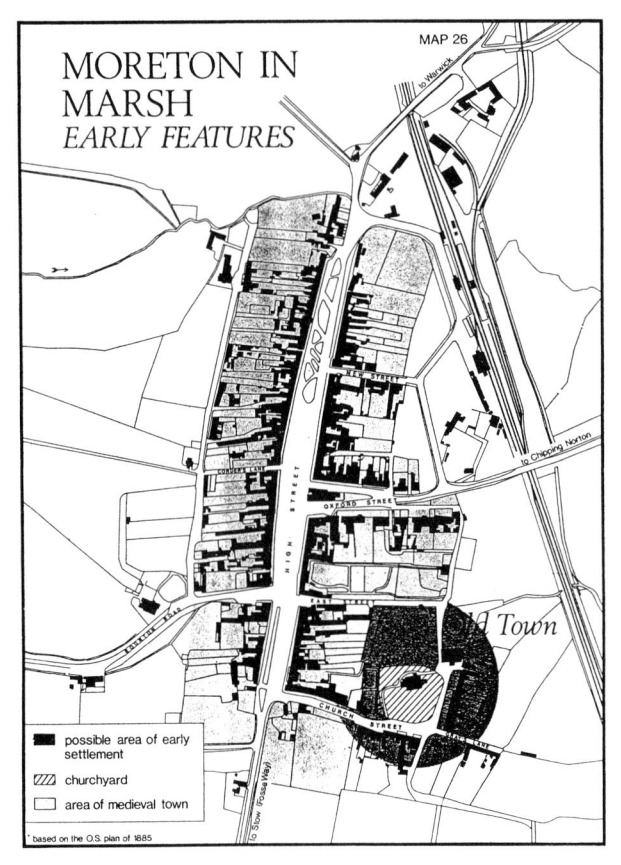

MAP 26

- possible area of early settlement
- churchyard
- area of medieval town

based on the O.S. plan of 1885

42. The map shows the burgage plots along the wide High Street of Moreton in Marsh which are a typical feature of a planned medieval town. The original farming settlement was probably in 'Old Town'.

century. Markets were revived temporarily only to lapse again. When Lord Redesdale became the owner of the manor the market was started again and this has proved more successful.

Broadway was perhaps founded too late; the abbot of Pershore obtained a charter in 1251, the last of the north Cotswold market grants, though a market had been licensed previously, between 1196 and 1198. Broadway was much wealthier than Moreton in 1327, and was comparable with Northleach and Stow, with 10 larger and 32 smaller taxpayers. Its boundaries are not known, and there is no record of how many burgages there were; they were not itemised in the valuation of Pershore Abbey's estate in 1535, but the term 'burgage' was used in medieval deeds. The area north of the main street leading up the hill has typical regular plots, with a back lane which separated them from the open fields and so appears to have been planned; on the south side the plots are less regular. The market failed to attract merchants and craftsmen and by the end of the 14th century Broadway's burgage holders were all engaged in agriculture. The reason may have been the reluctance of Pershore Abbey to make burgages full freeholds; as well as paying a rent of 12 pence, as other townsmen did, burgage-holders in Broadway also paid the abbot customary manorial dues, like 'heriot', a death duty. The portmote or borough court was a tithing in the manor court in 1379 and there were two agricultural tithings, Upend and Westend. Pershore's steward presided over the court. For a while two bailiffs or portreeves were assisted by two ale-tasters and 12 jurymen. Twelve men continued to act for the town tithing; another 12 acted for Upend and Westend together, as the 'foreign' of the manor. Markets had fallen into disuse before 1600 but a fair survived into the 20th century.

There has been argument about whether the 'broad way' of the name was the road climbing the hill where the town was sited or whether it was the road towards Snowshill, passing Broadway old church and going up Conygree Lane. The strongest evidence points to the road up the hill as the 'broad way'. There was an ancient trackway approaching from the Worcester direction; the arable fields beside the Worcester road were called the Ridgeway in 1771. This track then climbed the hill in a fairly straight line, where a footpath now shows the start of a worn hollow way. Habington's description at the end of the 16th century implies that this was the 'broadway':

43. Broadway street was an ancient 'ridgeway' and the main road from Worcester to London; it gave Broadway its name and remains a wide street, though the route up the hill has been altered to make it less steep.

> Broadway, the Broad and high way from the shepherds' cotes ... down to the most fruitful vale of Evesham ... is a town extended in a street tedious in length, especially in winter. This parish, though now obscured as a village, hath in ancient times been graced with a market and fair.

Habington also described the 'large pastures for sheep which are about and above the broadway and ascent to those hills'. The road up the hill is clearly shown on Ogilby's map of 1675 as part of the route from Aberystwyth to London. Ogilby also drew a route from Gloucester to Warwick, passing from Winchcombe through Didbrook, up Stanway Hill through the woods to Snowshill, and then across the high ground in the east of Broadway. Near the intersection of the Ridgeway or east-west road he noted 'pasture on both sides called Broadway Hill or Down', and at Snowshill he marked an alternative road which wound along the side of the hill through Middle Hill, joining Conygree Lane, but this was of secondary importance. As part of the enclosure in 1771, the Turnpike commissioners for the Worcester to London road insisted on 'a serpentine alteration up the said Hill' and the course of their zig-zag route may be traced in the fields at the side of the present road, where a larger serpentine loop was made in 1820. Though referred to as a 'new road', the turnpike road was an alteration of an ancient trackway.

Broadway manor shows even more clearly than Campden or Northleach a two-part structure, and there is evidence to suggest that it existed by the seventh century. When Broadway was given to Pershore Abbey about 679 it was an estate of 20 hides. In the enclosure award Upend was said to be 80 yardlands—exactly 20 hides. The boundaries of Pershore's 20-hide estate were described in Anglo-Saxon about 972. Grundy, who identified many Saxon boundary marks in the 1930s, was always inclined to start from later parish boundaries as his guide and there often is a close parallel. In Broadway's case, the estate had been considerably enlarged before parish boundaries were drawn, and was 30 hides by the time of Domesday Book. It is not easy to be sure of the location of the Saxon boundary marks, but it is possible that they describe the area of Upend rather than the later parish. 'Wad borough', the hill fort of the charter boundary, has been identified as Burhill in Buckland, where the county and parish boundary now is, but Barrow Hill could be an alternative identification, shown on the enclosure map and crossed by the Gloucester to Warwick road, so placing Westend as the later addition to Pershore's Broadway estate.

The manor house with its demesne lands was in Westend, with Broadway old church, a large, mainly 12th-century building, nearby. The land of Westend reached from Childswickham to Middle Hill, Spring Hill and Seven Wells; 'west meadow' was named in 972 and on the Enclosure map is located by the Childswickham road. There were open fields in Westend, but it was not too difficult to enclose them as the manor itself controlled so much of the land. Probably this process had started well before the Dissolution but afterwards the

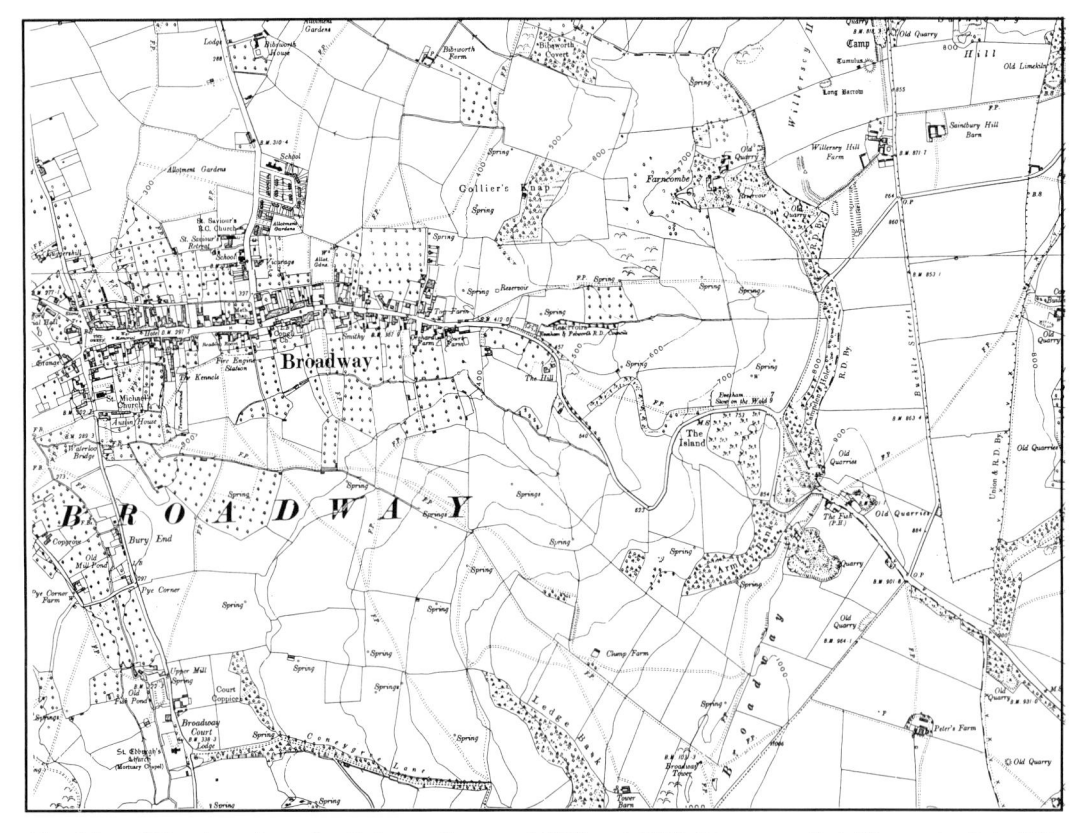

44. Map of Broadway from the Ordnance Survey of 1923 and 1924. The area called 'Nomansland' in 972 is on the eastern boundary, between Roman Buckle Street and the saltway. Close to Buckle Street is Combe in Campden parish, a possible site for the Anglo-Saxon 'Cada's minster'. Broadway's old church is to the south, and Conygree Lane was the road to Snowshill.

new owners made a number of farmers into freeholders which helped achieve further consolidation. Enclosure by act of parliament in 1771 concerned the open fields of Upend or Upper End.

Upend was a long thin slice of territory stretching from the top of the hill down into the vale towards Badsey, on either side of the main road. The new town was laid out here, surrounded by Upend's open fields. A chapel of St James existed in Upend at least by the 14th century, and perhaps centuries before; in the early 18th century, the manor court met in the chapel. It was situated near the Green, on the Snowshill road, where an early Victorian church now stands. Here was the original nucleus of Upend, with the Vicarage occupying a site called 'The Crofts', the name itself suggestive of an early settlement of farmers. As in other places, the church beside the manor house became the parish church, but in this case it may have been the older foundation, as it was dedicated to the same Anglo-Saxon saint as Pershore Abbey. In Broadway, however, the new town was planned away from the manor house, so that the parish church was distant from the main community. When the town chapel became the parish church, it was regarded as 'deficient in beauty' and early in the Victorian period was demolished and replaced by a church dedicated to St Michael and All Angels. A bell dated 1608 was probably taken from the old chapel and has given rise to the idea that it had been built then. The old parish church was saved from demolition and is used occasionally.

The history of each of the Cotswold market towns has many similarities. The pattern of streets and the regular nature of the house plots in each still displays the way in which it was originally planned. Once established, the town sites were firmly fixed because they consisted of freehold plots which gave considerable independence to their owners. Village sites were less stable; under the control of the lords of the manor they were liable to be moved and replanned. There are also interesting parallels in the history of the towns in the 17th century, when they battled with lords of the manor who tried, often successfully, to reassert the privileges of the medieval manor. The small size of the Cotswold towns would have led eventually to loss of urban status, but their medieval history has left notable architectural legacies for the 20th century.

Chapter Five

Sheep Downs and Common Fields

The Cotswolds once had many acres of upland pastures or Downs grazed largely by sheep. Apart from the unique value of wool for clothing, sheep also provided food, though as a by-product; when lambs were born milk was available for a few months, made into butter and cheese to be stored for less bountiful times of the year, and when their useful lives were over sheep were eaten. Most important, sheep were essential to arable farming. They manured the land while they grazed it, from the time that the corn harvest had been gathered until the next ploughing. The arrangements for sheep pastures fitted naturally into the common-field system, a carefully regulated sharing of the resources of the manor between its inhabitants and the lord. There is some evidence that common fields existed in the Cotswolds in the Anglo-Saxon period. For early medieval villagers, the common-field system involved working on the lord's land, but once this servile labour was no longer demanded, the system had many practical advantages for small farmers.

Downs and Husbandry
The three principal varieties of farm livestock, sheep, cattle and pigs, already had a history of 5,000 years of domestic use before the Anglo-Saxon period. Archaeological evidence suggests that sheep became more important in England from the eighth century, which coincides with the establishment of a settled pattern of Christian churches. The vocabulary of sheep husbandry is largely Anglo-Saxon: the word sheep itself, and the specialised words like ewe, lamb, teg, wether and ram; so too are the words cow, calf and ox, horse, mare and colt, pig, sow, boar, hog and swine. Our words for the meat, however, mutton, together with beef, veal, pork and bacon, are all Norman-French in origin. It used to be thought that 'Cotswold' was directly related to sheep husbandry, and was derived from the many 'cotes', or sheep shelters, to be found; in his notes on Broadway, Habington wrote about the road from the 'shepherds' cotes' down to the vale. This seems to have been a rationalisation of the Cotswold name which tells us more about the area in the 16th century than in the Anglo-Saxon period.

    The downs are the most important indication of the prevalence of sheep husbandry; the Anglo-Saxon 'dun' meant hill pasture rather than simply hill. Many Cotswold places had their downs, which were unfenced uplands shared by the farmers of the village: Hawling Down, Northleach Down, Campden Down, Naunton Downs, Blockley Downs, the Downs in Farmington, Salperton, Great Barrington, Upper Slaughter, Hampnett Down, Puesdown in Hazelton and Shipton, Little Barrington Downs, Bourton on the Water, Compton and Coln Downs—all listed in the county volumes published by the English Place-Names Society.

SHEEP DOWNS AND COMMON FIELDS

45. A typical view of open wold and down in the Cotswolds, looking eastwards from Wontley towards the high ground near Belas Knap. Much of the downland is ploughed, but there are still steep banks where thorn and rough pasture show how the downs would have looked in the past.

Downs in Aldsworth and Upton in Burford provided ideal open countryside for horse-racing and deer-coursing. Many more downs are to be found in estate maps or enclosure documents. Today these downs are unrecognisable, having been ploughed up for arable cultivation in the late 18th or early 19th centuries. The *Puesdown Inn* on the Cheltenham to Oxford road is surrounded by corn fields, and only the name is a reminder that the farmers of Shipton and Hazleton had their animals grazing here perhaps for over a thousand years.

'Dun' was used for the formation of place-names in the earliest years of the English settlements. Sometimes 'dun' has become 'ton', as in Rissington, a down noted for brushwood cover, 'hrisen', and therefore probably neglected when the name was coined; the whole long ridge which has the Windrush flowing along its base can be appreciated from Clapton, across the Windrush valley. Withington was Widia's 'dun' and Oxenton was a 'dun' distinguished by its use as a pasture for oxen. There were downs reserved for horses, as in Longborough where there was a 'horsendun' in 779, now Horsington Covert. Bredon is 'dun' added to an earlier British name for hill. Onnanduun and Onnandune in the eighth century in Dowdeswell's boundaries have become the field-name Hannington; there was a 'lang dune' in Evenlode in 775 and a 'heortdune' in 949. A reference to the 'ealdan dune', or old down, on the boundary of Hawling in 816 shows that new downs were being created. In her study of place-names, Gelling suggests that 'dun' was used for a hill with a settlement on top, but this is not appropriate for the Cotswolds. Bredon, Oxenton, Wyck, Great and Little Rissington, and Withington have all been established on the side or at the foot of their downs.

Because sheep were found everywhere, they did not usually provide a distinctive basis for place-names; Shipton, or Yanworth, the 'worth' or farm where ewes were 'yeaned', that is delivered of lambs, must have been unusually specialised manors. 'Pin', a fold or enclosure, in a place-name may be indicative of sheep farming; it is unfortunately easily confused with 'pen', the older British word for a hill. In the mid-eighth century Pinswell in Colesborne was bought by Eafe, abbess of St Peter's Abbey, Gloucester, so that she could conduct her sheep there; Professor Finberg imagined the sheep being driven along the Green Lane leading to this upland pasture from another St Peter's Abbey estate at Badgeworth, to enjoy the summer grass. Pinswell was known as the place where there was a well or spring perhaps serving the sheep fold. Hampen was a pen belonging to a man named Hagena, and nearby is Pen Hill, with an ancient earthwork enclosure on it, so that the name here may refer to the enclosure rather than to the hill. Pinnock was perhaps a 'small pen'.

46. The inn sign portrays an early period of motoring but Puesdown was downland shared between the farmers of Hazleton and Shipton Solers and Oliffe for perhaps a thousand years. 'Peulesdon' is first recorded in the early 13th century and derives from an Anglo-Saxon personal name.

Many minor place-names and field names, on the other hand, are connected with sheep farming in the Anglo-Saxon period. A sheep-edge in Dowdeswell is mentioned in a charter of 800 and a sheep-bank in Cutsdean in 974. Ramescumbe and Ramforde, in Hawling and Roel, are mentioned in a charter of 816; Raming Hill and Raming's Well perpetuate the Anglo-Saxon name for this area more than a thousand years later. Tagmoor Farm in Bourton on the Water and Tagmore Pool in Temple Guiting include the Anglo-Saxon word 'tagga', which described a young sheep before it was first sheared. Field names referring to sheep houses, sheep hills, sleights or slaits (pastures), hays (enclosures) and pens are widely recorded. The Slate Barn in Bourton on the Hill was originally a 'slait', and shows how the spelling of a name, though not the pronunciation, has been changed to make it apparently more reasonable.

There is little written evidence about farming practice until the beginnning of the 11th century, when a monastic schoolbook describes the shepherd's work in the form of an imaginary dialogue with a schoolmaster. Aelfric's description was no doubt based on knowledge of the farming scene in which all monasteries were engaged; it is also likely that his family were landowners and that he was kinsman of Earl Aethelmaer who founded the two monasteries, Cerne in Dorset and then Eynsham in Oxfordshire, of which Aelfric was abbot. He had gone from Eynsham before 1066. Is he the Aelfric buried at Deerhurst in 1052? Amongst the shepherd's tasks was milking the ewes twice a day and making cheese and butter. The shepherd drove the sheep out to the pasture very early in the morning, during the day guarded them from wolves, and returned them in the evening to the folds. He also moved the folds each day. Night-time folding on the arable fields ensured they were manured systematically, and it also helped to consolidate light soils, which are found in parts of the Cotswolds. The folds were probably made of wattles or hurdles. Farmers in Taynton all agreed in 1630 that their sheep be penned in a fold every night, after grazing the Downs, and a farmer, born and brought up on Hampen Manor, remembers the toil of moving the folds regularly, but this centuries-old practice has been abandoned because of the availability of artificial fertiliser.

Two documents of the 11th century take for granted the essential place of sheep in agricultural practice. One is a list of the duties of a reeve or steward of a large estate; it includes 'knowing about the matters that concern a homestead, both in the farmyard and on the down ... in field and fold'. It lists shearing, setting up sheep-hurdles and making folds amongst summer tasks and assumes that a household needed 'all the many spinning implements', in which the writer included weaving. The second document is the *Rectitudines Singularum Personarum*, a guide to the different types of person holding land in an Anglo-Saxon village. It was apparently prepared for an administrator with responsibility for a very large estate, and it emphasised the considerable variation to be expected from one locality to another. The reeve must 'know what are the ancient arrangements about the estate and what is the custom of the district'. The farmer (boor or 'gebur') 'ought to be given for his occupation of the land two oxen, one cow, six sheep and seven acres sown on his rood of land'. A 'rood' was a yardland. The farmer was also to be equipped with tools for his work and utensils for his house. The shepherd was differentiated from the other villagers by particular privileges: his land had the benefit of 'twelve nights' dung at Christmas' and he had a lamb from the year's young ones, one leading wether's fleece, and the milk of his flock 'for one week after the equinox' (22 or 23 September); all summer he could have a daily bowlful of whey or buttermilk.

The shepherd was not a 'Little Boy Blue', asleep while the sheep trampled the hay in the meadow, but a skilled and specialist farmer. He had the opportunity to build up his own flock from lambs selected from the lord's each year. Eleven shepherds and one shepherdess were assessed to the Lay Subsidy in 1327, some for very substantial sums exceeding those of many gentlemen and lords of the manor, like John Appelheved of Little Rissington and Walter of Upper Slaughter. Agnete was a shepherdess in Dorn and there were two shepherds in Winchcombe. Other shepherds paying tax in 1327 were in the Northleach area, at Owdeswell and Dowdeswell, Farmington, Salperton, Stowell, Clapton and Shipton or Hampen. They were flock masters of note.

The six sheep which an Anglo-Saxon farmer may have been given were enough to start a flock, which could potentially double in size every year, but numbers were severely limited by the need for winter feed. In the 13th century, at the time when the wool trade was expanding, the farmers collectively in the manor court began to impose limits on the number of sheep to be put on the common pastures. The allowance or 'stint' was expressed as so many 'per yardland'. Early records of stints most commonly permitted two oxen and 60 sheep per yardland; on the Bishop of Worcester's estates in the 15th and early 16th centuries, stints varied from 30 to 120 sheep per yardland but were largest on Cotswold manors. The variation is partly explainable by differing acreages of yardlands from manor to manor, but two sheep per acre seems often to have been the basis. This was twice the normal stocking rate of the best farms in the mid-19th century, though the animals then were larger and the weight of the fleece had trebled. The practice of stinting 'by the yardland' survived as long as the open fields

47. The farmer and owner of Hampen Manor, Mr. Robert Handy, drives sheep past the farmhouse for the annual shearing, nowadays carried out by a team of two shearers from Australia. There may have been a sheep farm here in the Anglo-Saxon period. Hampen Manor is listed in Domesday Book.

in the Cotswolds, and much surprised Marshall, an experienced agricultural writer at the end of the 18th century. The amount of the stints was sometimes reduced by agreement in the manor court, possibly in response to the increased size of the animals.

Villagers did not all individually own their full allowance of sheep. Nearly half the farmers who were tenants of three religious houses in south Wiltshire in the 13th century had none at all, but in some manor courts farmers were accused of putting too many sheep on the common pastures. It is difficult to understand why a farmer would 'overstock' the commons. The animals could only suffer from poor and disease-ridden pasture. Some sheep masters were possibly refusing to pay yardlanders for use of their pastures rights. There is record in 1340 of the Abbot of Tewkesbury complaining that 1,000 sheep had been stolen, which sounds implausible unless it refers to a loss of pasture rights or payment for them. Extra sheep also meant winter feed of peas and beans or hay which were being grown on arable land instead of corn. Another problem was that farmers were persuaded to put animals from a neighbouring grazier's stock on the downs in summer but when the sheep should have been manuring the arable in winter-time they were removed to the grazier's home manor. Profits of the wool trade were breaking down the local self-sufficiency of small-scale farms.

Lords sometimes retained pasture rights and did not give village farmers a share; they also retained the pasture rights when leasing their arable land, or gave them as endowments for religious houses. The rectory of Stanton was endowed with 400 sheep pastures in the common fields of Snowshill, for which the rector was compensated when they were enclosed. Hugh of Caldecote in the mid-13th century gave Winchcombe Abbey one yardland but 200

48. The abbot of Tewkesbury collected tithe from a large estate at Stanway, and the tithe barn would have allowed him to store grain and fleeces until the best conditions for marketing. The barn was erected in the 14th century and has seven bays. The roof is strongly constructed and probably from the first supported stone tiles; slaters were working in nearby Winchcombe in 1312.

sheep pastures over all his land. Thomas Bleke leased 2,500 sheep from the Bishop of Worcester in 1454 with pastures in Bibury, Blockley and Withington; four years later he bought the sheep. The *Valor Ecclesiasticus*, the general survey of all church wealth made in 1535, lists numbers of sheep pastures which appear to relate to common land. Gloucester Abbey had 400 sheep pastures in Eastington in Northleach; Bruern Abbey had 500 sheep pastures in Hinchwick, and 400 in summer but 300 in winter in Guiting Power; Llanthony Priory had 400 pastures in the Barringtons and 200 in Windrush; in Aylworth in Naunton the number was not stated but was probably 600, as a later farmer had this number; Winchcombe Abbey had 1,000 sheep pastures in summer in Snowshill but 500 in winter; 500 in Charlton Abbots in summer but 300 in winter; and 600 in Hawling all the year round; Hailes had 600 in Lower Swell and 300 in Longborough. These pasture rights were extremely long-lasting, often not extinguished until enclosure by act of parliament in the 18th and 19th centuries.

The Common Fields

It is necessary to talk of an open-field system rather than simply of open fields, because, as well as the physical arrangement of the cultivated land, a concept of shared ownership was involved which is quite foreign to modern notions of property. Arable was the largest element in the system, but pastures, meadows and woods were also included. In the simplest form of open-field system, the arable land was divided into two areas or fields, usually described by geographical position: land to the north or east of the village constituted one field and to the south or west a second field. Smaller sub-divisions within a field, called furlongs, might have banks, bushes or ditches round them, but would be subject to the same overall rotation of cropping one year and fallow the next. The year that crops were sown in the south field, for example, the north field would be 'open' or 'in common' for grazing by all the villagers' animals; when under crops, the several villagers had their own particular strips of land and harvested them individually, so that the field was then 'in severalty'. The most usual arrangement in the north Cotswolds was two fields, though later they were sometimes subdivided. For example, the rector of Stanton in the mid-17th century had lands in the North field, Middle North, Middle South and South fields.

Each villager's arable land was dispersed in strips throughout the two or more fields. A set of arable strips, together with an appropriate share of hay and grazing for the animals, was called a 'yardland' or virgate; the Latin virga meant 'rod', perhaps a measuring rod or a ploughman's goad for urging-on his team of oxen. The traditional method of conveying land to a new holder was by the symbolic act of handing a rod to him, a ceremony still in use in Burford in 1694 and as late as 1744 in Guiting Power. It is interesting that in Bourton on the Water in 1584 holdings are listed as 'eardlands', which links a yardland with 'earth' and with 'ard', the early plough. Most villagers in the north Cotswolds in the 13th century had one-yardland holdings. A yardland varied in size from one manor to another, and century to century, because it was a share of village lands and shares could be reorganised. A strip was an 'acre', and often approximated to a modern statute acre. An acre was earthed up into four ridges or 'lands', with furrows between the ridges; sometimes the lands were called 'selions' from the French word for furrow. Eight oxen yoked in pairs drawing a plough needed room to turn; consequently at one end of a set of strips there was a headland, in Gloucestershire called a 'hade', which was ploughed last. Each villager seems to have had his share of hades as well as ridges. A furlong contained strips running in the direction that suited the lie of the land, the furrows running down the hill or into a larger drainage ditch

49. Where the ridge and furrow of arable cultivation was put down to grass immediately after enclosure it escaped levelling by modern ploughing. This example is at Broad Campden but similar examples may be found generally in the area. Campden was enclosed in 1799.

or stream. A furlong was sometimes too small for everyone to have a strip in it, so the villagers' yardlands did not all have similar constituents, and also were not all the same size.

Patterns of ridge and furrow are visible in many places where open-field has become permanent pasture, usually after enclosure in the 18th century. The fossilised ridges often curve in an inverted S shape, which probably developed to help the ploughman turn his cumbersome team. The pattern is frequently seen on the lower slopes below the Cotswold edge and in the valley, but is less common on the hills, though it does occur, for example at Roel; on the upland, arable cultivation continued after enclosure and the ridges were ploughed out. The enormous height of ridges in Gloucestershire was commented on by Marshall in 1796 and by Cobbett in 1821. Marshall said that the high lands in the vale of Evesham 'have long been proverbial'; he doubted the story that men on horseback riding in the furrows could not see each other, but he wrote of how in the vale of Gloucester:

> I have myself stood in the furrows of a wheat stubble; the tips of which, upon the ridges, rose to the eye : a man, somewhat below the middle size, accidentally crossing them, sunk below the sight, in every furrow he descended into ... I afterwards measured a furrow near four feet deep.

Marshall regarded the ridges as 'extraordinary monuments of human industry', but 'one of those secrets which antiquity may call its own'. He discounted the popular notion that the soil was thrown up to increase the surface area, as far as arable cultivation was concerned, though it might have been appropriate to the fields when they were fallow and grazed by the villagers' animals. The ridges may have been preserved after enclosure because of their value in keeping some part of a pasture field from water-logging. Both Marshall and Cobbett described the ridges as like 'roofs', triangular in shape and, in Cobbett's description 'pretty nearly as sharp as that of some slated roofs of houses'; both thought that drainage of the land might have been one object in making them. Neither writer considered the idea that ridge and furrow had once made it easy to reorganise a village's landholdings. Farmers may have had a different set of strips in the fields year by year. Winchcombe Abbey's bailiff in Hazleton, John de Stanton, made an agreement with the abbey in 1317 by which he was allowed first choice of acres before the other abbey servants.

Some of the village's land was not suitable for arable cultivation; there are banks too steep for the plough, and these provided common grazing and often furze for firewood. Woods were generally not extensive, but could provide common grazing and firewood, though timber—that is oak, ash and elm—was reserved to the lord of the manor. Ralph of Sudeley in the 12th century was probably trying to stop this common right when he obstructed the people of Coates from using 'ways and paths' to the woods; the Abbot of Winchcombe protected them and secured a declaration of their rights from the King. Meadow was scarce and much more valuable; if shared by villagers it was mown individually, and was only available for grazing after the hay was taken. Often lots were drawn each year to determine which area of meadow each villager was to mow, and such a meadow might be called the Lot Meadow or Dole Meadow.

A document of 1729 preserved amongst Burford's archives sets out a complicated system of lots in the meadow called Highmead, which was by the river Windrush on the east side of the town. It was divided into four areas, called 'hides', each containing ten acres. Two acres in each hide were called 'laynes', and were allocated without drawing lots; the name implies that they were fenced and not open to commoner's animals after the hay had been cut. The remaining acres were indicated by symbols; these were a single cross and a double

50. Campden Hill Farm was built after the enclosure of Campden's open fields in 1799. It is unusual because it is built in brick. Such isolated farms usually post-date enclosure.

51. The isolated Lots Barn, Bemborough, in Temple Guiting, is an example of a traditional Cotswold arrangement with a sheltered area for stock. 'Bembro' or Bemborough probably refers to one of the numerous barrows in the district. The name Lots Farm may indicate that former Lot meadows were allocated to the farm at enclosure in 1804.

SHEEP DOWNS AND COMMON FIELDS

cross, which were church shares, one, two or three 'pitts', which sound like the spots on a dice, and a pitt combined with another symbol, called dock, dockseed, stone or thorn. When a property was bought and sold, the appropriate share of meadow was identified by reference to one of these symbols. The position of shares in the meadow was presumably determined afresh each year by the order in which marked pieces of wood or balls were drawn out of a bag; thus 'Memorandum. The Serjeant and Reeve's Acre was at the Upper End of the Meade this present year 1729'. Each symbol indicated an acre in each of the four hides. Some held all four, like John Pearse who had all Pitt and Dock, but in most cases, four different people held them, and lots were also drawn to determine who had which. For example, Martin Turner had the first lot of Pitt and Stone, without drawing; the remaining three acres were drawn for by three different occupiers. The rector chose which of the two crosses he would have. Drawing lots was the custom at least from the late 14th century, as a title deed refers to a holding of meadow *sicut per sortem acciderit*, 'as the lot will fall'.

Lords of the manor had strips in the open fields and participated in the routines of husbandry which the common fields imposed. When John de Sudeley died in 1336, 300 acres

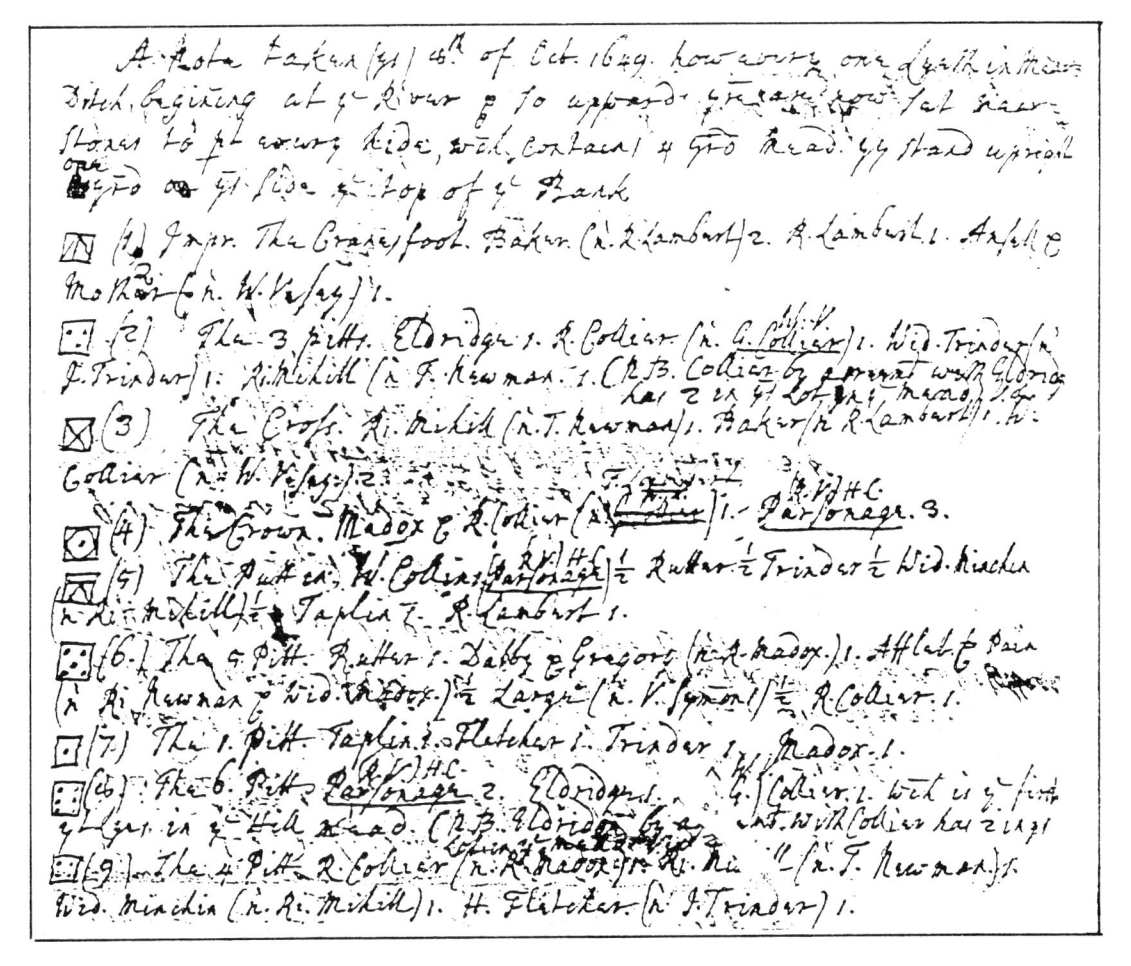

52. A graphic explanation of the symbols used by the farmers of Taynton to determine which share of the lot meadows each should have. The document describes the shares drawn in 1649.

in the manor of Sudeley were said to be worth nearly £4 an acre 'when they are sown, and nothing when they are not sown, because they lie in common'. The 12 men giving evidence about this estate went on to say that 140 acres had been sown before John's death 'at the winter sowing' and 80 acres 'at the Lent sowing ... and the rest lie fallow and in the common field'. John de Sudeley had 20 acres of pasture and 10 acres of much more valuable meadow which were not in common. He also had 100 acres of wood, of which 10 acres were felled every seventh year. Lords usually had some pasture and meadow which was theirs alone. Similarly the Bishop of Worcester in 1299 had oxen, cows, horses, bullocks and calves on the common pastures of Blockley, but also 'several' pastures for more than 1,300 sheep. Although the open-field system was very widespread, there were estates and areas within a manor in the early medieval period which were not part of the open-field system.

The Antiquity of the Open Fields
The countryside of open fields, of ridge and furrow and of unfenced common pastures, was described as 'champaigne' land and was very different from enclosed areas, categorised by William Harrison as 'woodland' countryside. The problem of how and when these basic differences in landscape developed, involving farming practice and patterns of ownership, has tantalised many researchers. The open-field system was once widespread on the Continent and was found in Scotland and Wales as well as throughout the Midland counties of England. A late-Victorian historian thought that it derived from a common Indo-European heritage, and Gomme described many parallels on the Indian sub-continent; modern historians are less confident about attributing ancient origins to the system. It does seem difficult to envisage large, co-operative estates being established at a time when the land was first being cleared for the plough. Eighteenth-century maps of open fields show numerous small furlongs, as though strips had been created within already-existing small fields.

Population pressure on limited resources could have led to the open-field system, which had some economic advantages. It maximised each villager's chances, when subsistence was threatened by weather and disease. The system was also flexible; it was easy to reallocate lands as population grew or shrank, or to meet a family's changing circumstances. It was impartial; each yardlander contributed two oxen to a plough and ploughmen presumably traversed the strips systematically, one after another. The system was also practical where little money was used; the only way a lord could pay men working on his land was by granting them a holding, but there was the danger that they would pay more attention to their own holdings than the lord's. Intermingled strips helped encourage cultivation of all the land. This was the popular explanation in the Cotswolds, reported by Marshall at the end of the 18th century; 'this intermixture was made, intentionally; to prevent the inclosure of the fields; and the crime is laid to the charge of the "Barons" '. Marshall added that he thought Abbots, not Barons, were responsible, but he agreed that as soon as land was enclosed it was converted to grass. The open-field system was also a recognition that land was essential to everyone's livelihood. No one had absolute ownership but there were various claims on the land: the king drew men and food for himself and his army; the lord drew food and labour from his villagers, so that he had leisure to serve the king as a soldier; the villagers drew subsistence. In time, the lord was classed as a freeholder, entitled to a voice in the government of the kingdom, while the villager was a copyholder, with no voice except within the manor. The inter-dependence of all became less obvious.

There is evidence that open fields existed in the Cotswolds at least as early as the Anglo-Saxon period and perhaps in Roman times. Campden's name is derived from 'campi',

IX *(above left)* The bridge over the river Isbourne carries the road from Winchcombe to Guiting Power; the buildings nearby were not in the borough but in Sudeley. Winchcombe main street was laid out parallel to the river. Though small, the Isbourne powered several flour and fulling mills *(see* illustration 32).

X *(above right and below)* The wide high street of Chipping Campden was the market place; the Town Hall was built within the street in the 14th century and the Market Hall in 1627. This is one of the best known buildings in the Cotswolds, built by Baptist Hicks in 1627 at a cost of £90 for the sale of butter, cheese and poultry.

XI The ridges and furrows made by ancient ploughing methods in the open fields are often seen best when the sun is low, but here poppies are growing in the furrows; the seed seems to have been brought to the surface by recent ploughing.

XII Downs seen from Burford hill are now used for arable cultivation but were once the common pastures of farmers in Fulbrook, Milton and Shipton under Wychwood. Fulbrook was enclosed in 1817, but Milton not until 1849 and Shipton under Wychwood in 1852, both very late.

XIII, XIV and XV The traditional husbandry of the Cotswolds was sheep and corn and this is still the case, but the sheep are generally no longer the famous 'Cotswold Lion' breed of the middle ages but cross-bred 'mules'.

XVI, XVII, XVIII   Two portraits of Cotswold sheep, prize winners at the Royal Shows of 1850 and 1861, by W. H. Davies and R. Whitford, in the collection of Iona Antiques of London. They were commissioned by William Lane of Broadfield Farm, Northleach; the owner and his shepherd are included in the later picture. Both emphasise the long, straight backs characteristic of the breed and may be compared with sheep at the Cotswold Farm Park.

SHEEP DOWNS AND COMMON FIELDS

53 & 54. Giles Coates of Chedworth surveyed the estate of William Peachey Esq. of Shipton Oliffe and Shipton Solers in 1764. He enlivened his map with little sketches. The extract on the right has Shipton Oliffe church and below Hampton (Hampen) Manor. The farmers or owners of each strip are indicated with capital letters.

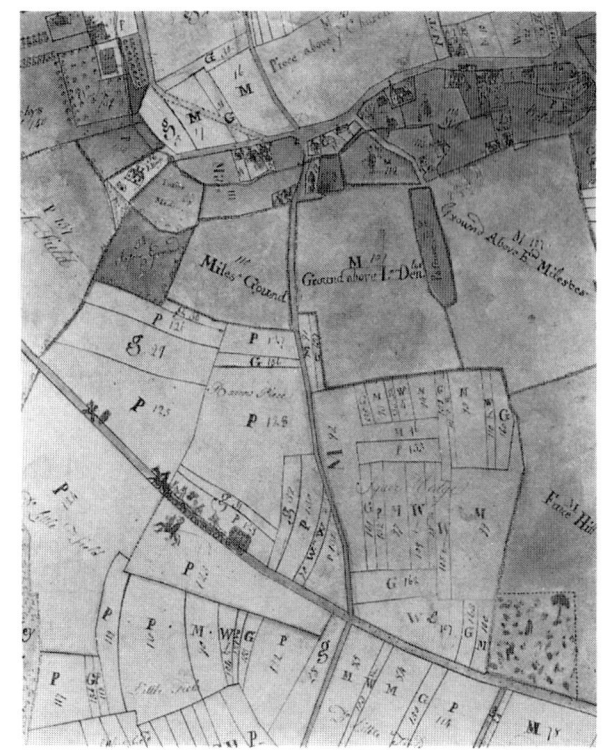

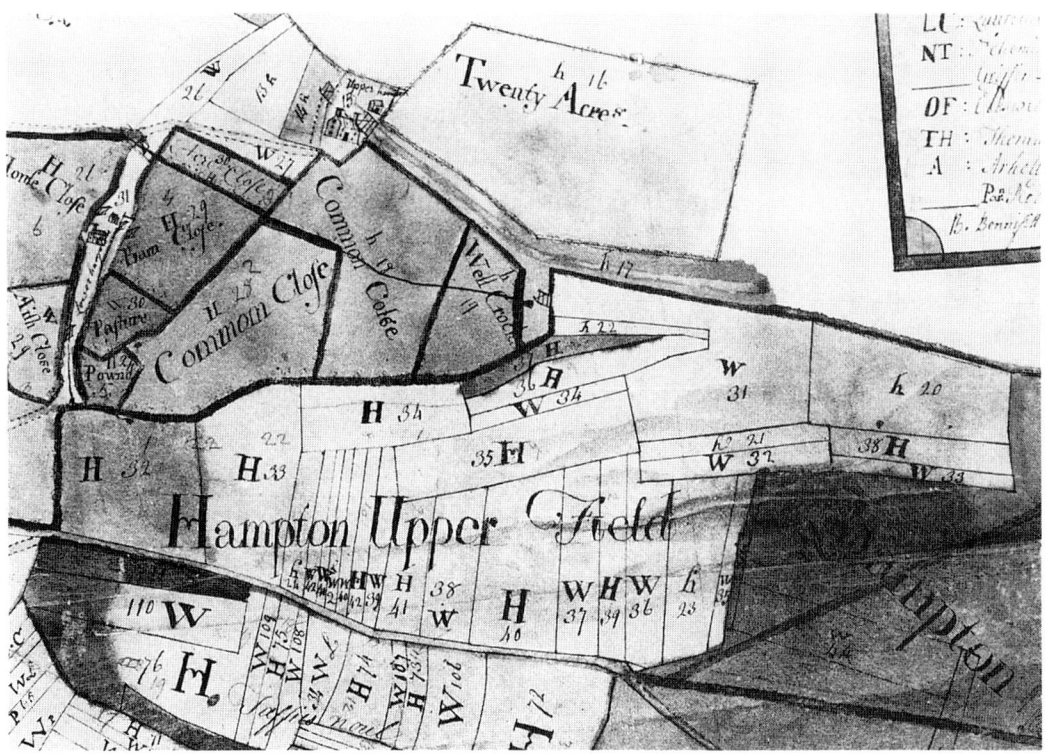

'fields' and 'den', 'valley'; the valley, ringed by hills, can be appreciated from the old road which climbs Broad Campden hill. The boundaries of the 'people of the fields', the *campsaetena*, are referred to in a charter of 1005. The survival of a Latin word in a place-name is rare and here the open fields could have survived from the Roman period. In a number of places, Anglo-Saxon descriptions of estate boundaries refer to open-field features. At Broadway, a furrow marked Pershore Abbey's land on the northern side, as would be natural in an open field. The Anglo-Saxon description could date from the late seventh century when Broadway became a Pershore estate and a ninth-century description of the adjoining estate of Willersey also refers to a furrow in the same area. In the late 18th century Broadway parish boundary followed an irregular course round an open field called 'Shearfield'. This field name may have arisen because the estate boundary was also the county or shire boundary, but it might also reflect the fact that the Anglo-Saxons had sheared an arable field in two. If a name such as Shearfield could last for a thousand years then it raises the question of how long open fields might have existed before any written references can be found. Furrows also marked the boundaries of Donnington, Maugersbury and Harford in Naunton. In the flat valley land near Broadway, headlands provided several Saxon boundary marks and are also mentioned on the boundaries of Broadwell, Cutsdean, Donnington, Swell and Withington. A 'felden way' was mentioned in Swell and land to the south of Hawling was the 'feld'; 'feld' was an Anglo-Saxon word which described open-field, not hedged enclosures.

The names of two manors which existed in the Anglo-Saxon period, Southfield and Westfield, suggest open fields were used to create small enclosed estates. The name Southfield was not recorded in Domesday, but the manor existed and was located in Longborough; later it became known as Bank's Fee, from a 13th-century family of le Blanck. Similarly, Westfield was not named in Domesday but the manor was located in Aylworth. In Saxon times points on the boundary were marked with a 'hoar stone', 'Scobba's stone' and a little barrow. Most of Aylworth was absorbed in Naunton parish, but Westfield formed a detached portion of Guiting Power, transferred to Hawling in 1883. Domesday recorded that Westfield was held by the same man as Caldicote Down in Guiting. There is no sign of a village in either—there were only slaves looking after the plough teams. For a long time, both names were used for this estate, showing that two separate areas had been amalgamated. Later the main farmhouse was located at Westfield and Caldicote gradually dropped out of use. In the early 19th century it proved difficult for a new owner to establish his title; after 'diligent enquiry of aged persons and others long acquainted with the Estate', it was said to be well-known in the neighbourhood and had always been called Westfield. No one knew where Caldicote had been located.

In the medieval period, the open fields were whittled away to create enclosures within which a lord could do as he pleased. Provided there were enough villagers involved in a field-system, custom protected them and their rights of common grazing. Where there were few villagers, or they were settled on areas of demesne like Icomb Place or The Farms in Broadway and Northleach, it was relatively easy to enclose. In Yanworth and Roel there seem to be documented examples. In 1312, Winchcombe Abbey made an agreement with the rector of Hazleton that he would not claim any great tithes of corn in the chapelry of Yanworth which was in his parish, nor his yardland there but only the house in which the chaplain lived. In compensation the rector accepted land in Hazleton. This agreement removed an obstruction to enclosure. Similarly, enclosure in Roel required the agreement of the rector of Hawling, since it was a chapelry in his parish. Roel manor was freed from tithe payments in 1404 though the rector had Hawling villagers' tithes. In 1464 the rector was paid a small sum to receive Roel's parishioners in his church. Was this when Roel village and chapel were deserted? Only a farm remains with traces of masonry possibly from the chapel. A settlement in Hawling seems to have been planned to accommodate Roel's inhabitants. Earthworks show that regular crofts were laid out on either side of the small stream, whereas the modern village is near the manor house and church. According to local tradition in the 19th century, these houses were 'destroyed by the Parliamentarians on their way to Sudeley Castle. The foundations of many houses are still to be seen'. More likely they were deserted centuries before, as a result of the reorganisation of the demesne lands of Roel and Hawling and the redefinition of their parish boundaries.

Lords and Villagers
The villagers within a manor were in many ways as much owners of their village lands as the lord was, for both were governed by custom, but the villagers' status was depressed because their farms were modest in size, and they had a burdensome obligation to work on the lord's land. Instead of paying a money rent, holdings were *ad opus*, 'for work'. Villagers were also tied to the land, as 'bondmen', and were not able to move elsewhere if they wished. Their lands were variously described as 'in villeinage', 'customary lands', 'servile lands' or 'bondlands'. Twenty-two yardlands in Broadwell were called 'Bondlands' in 1450 and 15 yardlands 'Freehold'. Information on the customs and labour services on open-field manors was collected in surveys or 'extents'. There are several for manors belonging to Gloucester Abbey, to the bishop of Worcester and to Worcester Priory. There are also surveys made for the king after the death of a chief landholder, called *Inquisitions Post Mortem*, and for Oxfordshire, records survive of a general enquiry into land tenure made in 1279 and known as the 'Hundred Rolls'. At their most detailed, every person holding land within the area of the manor, whether freeholder, yardlander or cottager, was named. The surveys reveal many basic similarities between manors but also interesting variations. Local custom was all-important.

The Prior of Worcester had his estates of Cutsdean and Icomb surveyed about 1249. Both had been granted to the church of Worcester in the late eighth century and were consequently in Worcestershire; this arrangement lasted until 1844 for Icomb and 1931 for Cutsdean, when they were transferred to Gloucestershire. Both estates had open fields before enclosure in the early 19th century. The income from Cutsdean had been assigned to the Priory's Chamberlain, who was responsible for the administration of the monastery itself, and from Icomb to the Almoner.

Cutsdean is a typical example of labour services. The farming year was marked by church feasts. It began and ended with the feast of St Michael on 29 September. Between this date and St John's day, 27 December, the villagers worked two days per week for the lord; for the rest of the year they worked on Mondays, Tuesdays and Wednesdays. During the winter months, between St Martin's day, 11 November, and the Annunciation, 25 March, they were expected to plough half an acre a week. The Priory Chamberlain might also require them to drive his horses and carts to Worcester, but he paid them a small fee if they took cartloads to Gloucester, Evesham or any other markets. On Mondays, each yardlander also supplied three men, but one man on the other two days. They were therefore expected to employ labourers, some of whom were no doubt the tenants of the six 'cotlands', which were holdings of a few acres. Each cottager had to work for the lord of the manor for one day a week between St Martin's and St John's days, and the rest of the year two days a week. It would be unreasonable to expect such men to do more work without wages because they needed paid employment to earn their living. The cottager could be asked to carry messages, but on foot not on horseback. Like the other villagers, he owed the lord the dues of 'merchet', when his

55. Cutsdean is a typical 'nucleated' village of farms grouped together round a green and surrounded by its open fields. The green belonged to the rector. The straight lines of hedges and walls dividing rectangular fields were created by enclosure in 1777.

daughter was married, and on his death 'heriot', his best beast; heriot was a survival of an Anglo-Saxon custom, designed to meet the military obligation of the villager. At Michaelmas, when the harvest was in and the farming year completed, all paid 'tallage' or tax to the lord. Other taxes were paid if a horse or an ox was sold and if a pig was kept. A new landholder also had to pay a sum of money or 'fine' when the lord registered his title in the manor court.

Eight yardlands in Cutsdean were described as 'servile' lands, and the villagers holding them should have performed the works described, but in fact they were no longer required. Money payments in lieu were recorded. The scribe noted down the duties, adding several times 'as they say', so that it seems as though services had been discontinued within living memory. The Priory owned nine yardlands; eight were said to be traditionally 'village' lands and were rented out to the village farmers. The ninth yardland was the Chamberlain's and was cultivated for him by the villagers: they ploughed, sowed with the Chamberlain's seed, harrowed, reaped and stooked his corn. They also scythed the meadow and raked the hay together; the chamberlain then claimed half. The villagers farming the Priory's eight yardlands had to pay the usual manorial taxes, of merchet and heriot. The distinction between farmers renting demesne lands and villagers holding customary lands was blurred in Cutsdean, especially as rents also covered payments made in lieu of services.

In Icomb, labour services had long been discontinued, and at the time of the survey it was not even known whether they had once existed; a note was made *Inquiriendum de operibus villanorum, si fuerint ad operationem*, 'ask about villagers' works, if they should hold by work'. The size and structure of this estate was similar to Cutsdean: it contained 16 yardlands, of which half belonged to the Priory; a 15-year lease of the demesne had been given to the villagers shortly before the survey. The distinction between village lands and demesne was not relevant in practical terms in Icomb either. Had the grant of these estates to the church turned villagers' lands into demesne and villagers themselves into rent-payers? Is this the reason that the Priory leased the demesne? The original Icomb manor demesne was probably in Gloucestershire and Cutsdean demesne may have been Hinchwick, significantly sometimes called Cutsdean Manor. Both areas were enclosed without recourse to acts of parliament.

Details of labour services varied from manor to manor. On some manors, villagers owed special services of washing and shearing the lord's sheep. Harvest-time was when most work was required and it was worth more than other services, as the lord ensured that his crops should be garnered first. The 13th-century villagers on John de Ludlow's Campden manor worked Monday, Tuesday, Wednesday and Thursday 'unless feast days interfere' during the three summer months; during the rest of the year they had to accomplish a certain amount of ploughing. At Sevenhampton in the harvest season, the villagers worked all day on Monday and Wednesday and half a day on Tuesday and Thursday, but only two half-days a week during the rest of the year.

The three manors of Fifield, Idbury and Taynton in Oxfordshire, surveyed in 1279, illustrate by their variations how the development of each manor was very individualistic. In Fifield, only six villagers owed very light labour services to the lord. They ploughed his land twice in the year, they carried one load of hay and one of corn, and at the lord's request they worked one more time on condition that he provided food for them and the 12 men they had to bring to do the allotted task. The services appear to be no more than tokens of the villagers' status, and otherwise money was collected in place of works. The rest of the manor was held in small parcels by 23 free men and two larger blocks belonged to Bruern Abbey and the Hospital in Burford. There is no indication of the labourers' cottages which must have existed; they were probably regarded as part of the yardlander's holding, the 'tied' cottages of the time. In contrast, a classic example of labour services is seen on the adjacent manor of Idbury. Twenty-four villagers ploughed, harrowed, mowed, made hay, washed and sheared sheep, carted hay and corn, and on three occasions did whatever was required of them, the 'boon' services. They paid for pasturing their pigs and were taxed by the lord. The structure of Idbury seems almost exactly the same as in 1086. Domesday Book recorded an unusual amount of pasture in the manor, and the Hundred Rolls add the information that the lord had to serve the King for 40 days with 20 horses in any war against the north Welsh. Taynton was a more populous manor, where works for the 22 yardlanders had generally been commuted for money payments; mowing and making and carrying hay were specifically stated to be included in the money payments but 12 half-yardlanders had to do some of these works. The quarries are not mentioned, apart from the name of Thomas the Quarrier. One yardlander held his land for his lifetime for a small money rent but he had to make the iron for the lord's two iron ploughs which were unusual at this date. Six yardlanders were free of services, one called Robert the Franklin, his name indicating his status as a freeman. Another free man was the warden of Taynton's wood within the forest of Wychwood.

There may once have been a relationship between the amount of work and the size of the lord's own demesne, but many alterations in estates eventually made the services inappropriate. By the mid-14th century, money had been substituted for services in all Winchcombe Abbey's estates and the change was proceeding everywhere. With labour services commuted, the open-field system served small farmers well, giving them access to large pastures which their animals could graze in a method of cooperative rotation which was not at all feasible if each man had his own small enclosed pastures. It was lords who favoured enclosure.

Chapter Six

Wool, Wool Churches and Cotswold Sheep

Wool production took precedence over meat throughout the medieval period. Although some young lamb was eaten by wealthy households and town dwellers, the household servants of the Bishop of Worcester were provided with elderly wethers, and the poorer countryman ate more tough mutton than any other meat. In an archaeological excavation at Upton in Blockley, sheep bones from the 12th and 13th centuries were almost all from mature animals, over two years old; 70 per cent of all teeth and bones came from sheep. On monastic and town sites which have been excavated, on the other hand, young sheep seem to have been eaten as often as cows and pigs. A system of stock breeding and wool production in the countryside and fattening closer to the towns seems already to have existed.

The Cotswolds, just one of the English regions which produced and exported wool in the medieval period, are specially famous because of the chance survival of the letters of the Cely family, who were wool merchants buying in the area. Some of the profits made by woolmen and merchants were directed into rebuilding their home churches, for which towards the end of the 15th century there is documentary evidence; there are also monumental brasses in the churches recording their lives. Several Northleach brasses portray the woolmen's sheep under their feet.

The Monasteries and Wool Production
Cotswold wool was certainly being exported in significant quantities in the late 13th century. *La pratica della Mercatura*, a guide book for merchants compiled by Francesco Balducci Pegolotti about 1315, included a list of English and Scottish wool production which probably dates from the previous century. Cotswold wool is listed at 11 marks per sack, a similar price to wool from several town markets and from districts like Elmet in Yorkshire and the Derbyshire Peak. These were areas where many local farmers' fleeces would be collected, and the wool was not of high grade. A mark was two thirds of a pound (66p) and a sack was 26 stone (166 kg); the average weight of a fleece varied around two pounds (about 1 kg), so that each sack contained at least 150 fleeces. Most of the Guide, however, is concerned with more than 200 monastic producers, classified by their religious orders. The Cistercian houses of Bruern and Hailes are included, also Winchcombe, Evesham, Pershore and Tewkesbury, four Benedictine houses with Cotswold estates. Bruern and Evesham are described as *in Chondisgualdo*—'in Cotswold'—and so too is Osney near Oxford.

Eight classifications of wool were used, according to how the fleeces were prepared and presented for sale. There is no indication of variation in staple length or fineness. Some small producers graded while larger ones did not. The Cistercians' fame as wool producers is well-supported by the Pegolotti list—nearly all their monasteries produced graded wool, whereas the houses of the other religious orders rarely did; as wool was the Cistercians' main source of revenue, the higher prices paid for the best quality were important to them. For others, wool was a by-product of their agriculture; Worcester Cathedral Priory, for example, received less than twenty per cent of its income from wool sales around 1300.

The best price, 28 marks per sack, was quoted for good quality wool from Tintern, Monmouthshire, Abbey Dore, Herefordshire, and Stanfield, Lincolnshire; next came Thame in Oxfordshire at 27 marks and Kingswood in Wiltshire at 26 marks. Bruern received 25 marks for good quality, 16 marks for middle quality and 13 marks for third quality wool, and had 12 sacks a year for sale. Hailes produced 20 sacks, the best grade worth 19 marks. All were Cistercian houses except Stanfield. Winchcombe produced 40 sacks of cleaned but otherwise ungraded wool, each sack worth 13 marks. Evesham produced 10 sacks and Pershore and Tewkesbury 12 sacks and these three sold their wool just as it was sheared, at 12 marks per sack.

Winchcombe's 40 sacks represented the fleeces of at least 6,000 sheep, and this sort of figure for Cotswold monastic flocks is confirmed by other evidence. The *Gloucester Abbey Chronicle*, for example, says that 10,000 sheep were being kept at this period, producing 46 sacks of wool sold for 12 marks per sack; the Priory estates of the Bishop of Worcester, when surveyed about 1290, included 5,650 sheep. Ely Abbey which had 13,400 sheep in 1086 or Winchester which had 29,000 in 1259, far exceeded these numbers. Even so, the monasteries' flocks provided a relatively small proportion of the estimated eight million fleeces or 30,000 sacks exported in late 13th century. Some landed magnates had similar numbers of sheep. Roger de Somery could put 1,000 sheep on the common pastures of 'the Wold' in Campden in the 13th century and Lord Berkeley with his estates in south Gloucestershire sheared 6,000 sheep early in the 14th century.

The ordinary village farmer's stock rarely exceeded a hundred sheep and was probably usually much less, but home-produced cloth necessarily used all these fleeces. In Cleeve in the 14th century, there were at least 1,000 lambs born to the villagers' ewes every year, and their wool production of 14 sacks equalled the total of the Bishop of Worcester's from all his estates together. The monasteries often acted as collectors for local production, and occasionally used it to make up the required quantities of their own wool, though only for the lower grades. A Cirencester merchant who bought wool at Barrington in 1319 from Llanthony Priory specified that it should be 'good, dry and well-cleaned' and from the Priory's own sheep, though if there was not enough he agreed it should be made up from other sources. Winchcombe Abbey also purchased fleeces in the mid-15th century from the Sherborne farmers, with money that the farmers had just paid in rent.

The Master Shepherd employed by a monastery organised the sheep into small flocks and moved them around the estates; on the Worcester estates individual manor's flocks varied in size from 120 to 800. Breeding ewes were placed in some manors and the main wool-producing wethers (castrated rams) in others. The sheep were put on hill pastures in the summer and in winter they were kept in the valleys, where stocks of hay, peas and beans were available. This was a traditional system of 'transhumance'. The monasteries had been endowed with estates in the valleys and on the wolds from the beginning and transhumance was the practice on Winchcombe Abbey's Cotswold estate and also on Westminster Abbey's; Westminster's sheep spent the summer at Bourton on the Hill but were moved for the winter down the road to Moreton in Marsh. A thousand sheep could be maintained on Cleeve Hill in summertime but only 200 in the winter. By the end of the 14th century the practice of transhumance was being given up and the hay was carried to the sheep. It was perhaps to enable more sheep to be overwintered that a second large, tiled sheepcote of eight bays was built in Blockley in 1383-84.

Once a year the sheep were collected together for shearing. Worcester flocks came to Blockley, which had been a centre for shearing since at least the middle of the 13th century. The manor itself specialised in wethers, which yielded the best fleeces, and wethers were also hardier and better able to withstand the winter on the Cotswold hills. In 1299, there was pasture in Blockley for nearly 500 ewes and 1,120 wethers and yearling sheep. Two substantial landholders in the manor were required to be present at the shearing and look after the wool as part of their manorial services. In 1389, 4,000 sheep were sheared in Blockley. William Grevil, the wool merchant of Chipping Campden, may customarily have bought the whole clip, because he owed money for 14¼ sacks from the previous year, which represented about 3,400 fleeces. There was another collecting point for wool at Cropthorne in the Avon valley; John of Burford, a pepperer and London alderman, was recorded as buying Worcester wool here.

Barrington was a centre for Llanthony Priory's wool clip and in the early 16th century 2,000 sheep were sheared there, supervised by the Prior. Winchcombe's central shearing at Sherborne is recorded in the 15th century; the Abbot and his servants moved there every Easter, and 12 sheep were allotted for a feast for those who helped. In 1485 it apparently took four days to deal with the flock, and 14 sacks of wool were packed. Fourteen cottagers in Sherborne were customarily required to help in the washing and shearing and two larger landholders were required for three days, probably as supervisors as in Blockley; it was apparently the only Winchcombe estate where these services existed. It seems likely that Gloucester Abbey's flocks were sheared at Northleach, because on this manor 42 tenants were

56. Sherborne Brook was used in the Middle Ages for washing sheep before they were sheared; the fleece dried on the sheep's back, which was the traditional though not the modern method. In the 13th century, the farmers had to give up their time to wash and shear the flocks belonging to the lord of the manor. The brook flows through the 16th-century park and joins the Windrush.

obliged to supply a man for one day at the lord's shearing, helped perhaps by the services of men in the neighbouring manor of Coln Rogers. Gloucester Abbey also had Buckland manor where the same services were customary. Though first recorded in the 13th century, shearing services were an ancient obligation; one of the earliest surviving statements of manorial customs, for Hurstbourne Priors in Hampshire, written just before the Norman Conquest, says that the farmers there 'must wash the sheep and shear them in their own time'. It is notable that the manors with which the early minster church of Gloucester was first endowed specialised in sheep husbandry.

All the places chosen for shearing the monasteries' sheep had ample pasture and, most important, good water supplies for washing the sheep. Blockley and Northleach both had good springs. At Northleach the river Leach has been canalised south of Eastington to make a sheep-wash; the parish boundary with Aldsworth has been carefully drawn to place the canalised section in Northleach. Barrington has the river Windrush which has also been canalised below Bourton on the Water, perhaps for the same purpose. Sherborne's name itself is the name of the stream, a compound of 'bourne' and 'scir' meaning bright or clean, an appropriate name for the river selected for the annual sheep-wash. Could the place-name have reflected the customary shearing there?

Northleach Woolmen

The Cely family's papers and correspondence, which concern the business of a father and his two sons between 1475 and 1488, were preserved through the chance of a law suit which Richard brought against his brother George's widow soon after George's death in 1489; the papers were required as evidence and were stored in the Tower of London where they remained until rediscovered some five hundred years later and transferred to the newly-created Public Record Office. Much of their wool was bought at Northleach. Richard Cely dealt with John Busshe and then his widow Alice, with John Perys or Peyrs, and with Jenkin Taylor of Farmington, but most wool was bought from William Midwinter, who later married the widow Alice Busshe. 'I have been in Cotswold this three weeks and packed with William Midwinter 22 sarplers and a poke', wrote Richard Cely junior to his brother in 1482. A sarpler was a bale of wool wrapped up in canvas and tied with ears at the corners, and is shown on several of the monumental brasses in Northleach church. Sarplers were stamped with the dealer's woolmark and also other information about the quality of the contents. It is estimated that a sarpler contained over 450 fleeces or up to three sacks. A poke was a smaller bale. Midwinter's wool was regarded as the best and other woolmen were rated according to whether their stock were as good. Fourteen sacks bought from John Perys were 'as good wool as Will Midwinter's'. On average in the years 1478 to 1488 the Celys shipped about seventy sacks of wool each year, amounting to the fleeces from between thirteen and seventeen thousand sheep. This may have represented about a twentieth of the Gloucester-shire production, on the basis of a later estimate of the numbers of sheep in the county.

The Northleach woolmen were middlemen, called 'broggers'; their function was to collect fleeces from local flock owners and store them in warehouses until the merchants could come and view them. There were storehouses in other Cotswold towns besides Northleach; Chipping Norton, Chipping Campden and Burford were visited by the Celys though they did not buy as much there. In 1482, for example, Richard Cely packed 22 sarplers at William Midwinter's and four at Campden. Merchants probably had regular links with particular woolmen. William Midwinter, indeed, tried to cement his relations with the Celys by proposing a wife for young Richard. In 1482 Richard Cely 'departed out of London into Cotswold-ward at three of the bell at afternoon'; 'I came to Northleach on a Sunday before matins, from Burford', he wrote to his brother. 'William Midwinter welcomed me. And in our communication he asked me if I were in any way of marriage'. The name of a local gentlewoman, Elizabeth Limerick, was put forward, the daughter of a Justice of the Peace in the county. Later she walked a mile to church in Northleach in order that Richard could meet her. Although she was found 'young, little, and very well-favoured and witty and the country speaks much good by her', the marriage did not materialise.

As well as buying fleece wool, the Cely family also dealt in fells—skins with the wool still attached. They were heavier and bulkier to transport, and obviously the flock-masters would not generally wish to kill their sheep. However, disease could be the reason that fells were for sale. 'There is like to be many fells, for sheep begins to die fast in divers country' (counties), Richard Cely reported in 1480. Fells were sold in 'long hundreds' of 120, that is, six score or ten dozen to each hundred. The Celys made purchases in Chipping Norton and Chipping Campden; Thomas Betson, whose correspondence has also survived, bought his fells from Whyte of Broadway and from Robert Turbot of 'Lamberton', probably Laverton.

The government first started to tax the wool trade heavily in the late 13th century; in their protests the barons claimed that wool was half the wealth of the country. The tax was continued despite their protests. In practice it was passed on to the growers who were paid less for the wool. In a case at Gloucester assizes in 1306, William of Combemartin, a London merchant and alderman, was accused of spreading a rumour at fairs at Northleach, Cirencester and Tetbury, that the king was going 'to take all wool'; as a result prices fell sharply. The king found it difficult to collect the wool taxes, particularly from foreign merchants; for this reason a single collecting point or Staple was designated. In the end the Staple was fixed at the English-held port of Calais, and a specific group of men were made responsible for the tax, the Company of the Staple. The Company had emerged in its final form by the end of the 14th century. About this time, the Woolstaplers' Hall was built in Chipping Campden. It seems to have been sponsored by the Merchants of the Staple: there was a clause in the title deeds of the property giving special exemption from any levy imposed by the company. The hall may represent the hopes of the wool merchants of the town to have Chipping Campden made an official Staple town, which they would have much preferred to Calais.

The Celys were members of the Company of the Staple, as was Thomas Busshe of Northleach. Wool staplers were mostly engaged in other merchanting ventures, too. As a Brotherhood, they helped each other and organised some aspects of the wool trade collectively. In 1505, there were 480 members of the Company, but not all were necessarily active in any one year. The staplers sold the wool to Flemish and north Italian clothiers who then financed the spinning and weaving. Italian buyers, from Lombardy, were sometimes found by-passing the Staple and coming direct to England for their wool. In 1480 Richard Cely wrote that 'I have not bought this year a lock of wool for the wool of Cotswold is bought by the Lombards', and his brother George in Calais reported 'there is but little Cotswold wool at Calais and I understand Lombards has bought it up in England'. Of 104 merchants shipping wool from London to Calais during the period 1478-79, the Celys were about eleventh in order of quantity shipped, and they were responsible for about 2 per cent of the country's exports; the largest individual merchant share was just over 3 per cent. The Northleach middlemen were smaller capitalists than the Merchants of the Staple. William Midwinter had to write a begging letter to the Celys on at least one occasion requesting earlier payment of moneys owed because of his losses; on the other side Richard could write about him when he was asking for his money, 'God rid us of him!'

Three memorial brasses in Northleach church relate to woolmen of the period of the Cely letters, John Taylor, William Midwinter and Thomas Busshe. At the bottom of John Taylor's memorial brass there is a woolsack with a sheep standing on top and his wool mark of two crossed crooks. There is also a crook underneath the wool sack, suggesting that he was a sheep master. The brass has been dated to $c.$1490. He lived in Farmington like Jenkin Taylor who did business with Richard Cely. A woolman who has his feet resting on a sheep and a woolsack, and has the letter M as part of the woolmark, is assumed to be Midwinter. William Midwinter's will was proved in 1501 and that of his wife, Alice, in 1502. He was Bailiff of Northleach in 1493. He also made bequests to 21 churches in the neighbourhood of Northleach, a roll call of sheep country: Farmington, Naunton, Great Rissington, Chedworth, Eastington, Hampnett, Turkdean, Notgrove, Guiting Power, Temple Guiting, Coln St Denis, Coln Rogers, Winson, Withington, Dowdeswell, Bishop's Cleeve, Hawling, Hazleton, Compton Abdale, Shipton Oliffe and Sherborne. He probably bought wool from the farmers there; his wife's bequests a year later were to 10 churches 'where I have been most accustomed to buy wools'.

Alice Midwinter's will refers to her two husbands and to her two sons, Thomas Busshe and Thomas Midwinter. Thomas Busshe and his wife Joan have the most elaborate brass memorial, reflecting his importance as a merchant of the Staple in Calais. The day and month of their deaths has not been engraved, only the years 1525 and 1526. Busshe's estates included lands and cattle in Wiltshire and Buckinghamshire, at Filkins, Kelmscott, Taynton and Upton in Oxfordshire, and Upton Wold and Whittington in Gloucestershire. He also leased the Bishop of Worcester's estate of Withington. Thomas Busshe left money to Northleach church and for the repair of the bells. The bushes in the canopies above Thomas and Joan's heads on their brass are a pun or 'rebus' on their surname; the sheep frolicking underneath show their farming interests. Joan Busshe has her feet on sheep and a woolpack; like Alice Busshe she must have engaged in the wool-dealing business on her own account.

Wool Churches
There is an obvious coincidence between the renewed interest in church building in the later 15th century and the unusual concentration of wealth which resulted from the monopoly of the Merchants of the Staple. Some wool merchants' bequests to their parish churches are recorded, as in Chipping Campden and Northleach, and these have particular claims to be called 'wool churches'; more generally the name is applied to churches in places like Burford associated with the wool trade. They all share the particular English perpendicular style, with large, square-headed windows with stone tracery dividing up the glass; battlemented parapets to naves, aisles and towers; and inside, tall, slender columns or clusters of columns, which in Chipping Campden and Northleach are concave.

John Fortey, woolman, paid for the central part of Northleach church, a wide hall with pillars on two sides and clerestory windows, now called the nave; the window above the chancel is unusual but characteristic of several Cotswold churches, including Campden. John Fortey's memorial brass shows him with his feet on a sheep and a woolpack. Part of the inscription has been lost, but Lysons recorded some missing words: '... prayeth God his soule to socoure, and after his disese the rofe made'; this seems to be the origin of the idea that he was only responsible for the clerestory. Fortey died in 1458. His major bequest was £300 'to finish and complete the work by me now begun'. He also left half a mark to each of 120 churches, 'the parishioners of the same to pray for my soul', and he asked to be buried in the 'new middle aisle' of St Peter's, Northleach. His brass is still there, though originally there was a canopy above it, resting on two supports built into the pillars. The middle aisle belonged to

57. The tower of Northleach church was built in the 14th century, but the top storey is clearly distinguishable as a later addition, from the period of the town's great prosperity created by the trade of its woolmen.

the impropriator of Northleach tithes; when John Fortey built it, he must have leased the tithes from Gloucester Abbey and this helps to explain his superior wealth. About 1520, a chancel was built onto the middle aisle. The chancel was the responsibility of the Abbot of Gloucester as rector of Northleach. It contains one brass of about 1530, commemorating William Lawnder, a cleric, who may have prompted the work.

The older nave and chancel of Northleach church are on the north side, and belonged to the parish. The place can be seen where a stairway once led to a rood loft, a wooden structure spanning the nave and supporting a cross, below which candles would be placed. William Midwinter left money in his will for the construction of the rood and was buried in 1501 'at the chancel door under the blessed crucifix of our Lord'. His brass, too, is still there. The former chancel, now a sacristy, contains a stone altar undisturbed at the Reformation when most were removed as idolatrous; the brasses also escaped destruction, so that the local citizens' respect for their church was stronger than their Protestant zeal.

WOOL, WOOL CHURCHES AND COTSWOLD SHEEP

William Grevil is probably the best known of all England's wool merchants and has been strongly associated with Campden church, though there are problems with dating. The Grevil family were established in Chipping Campden at least from the end of the 13th century, when two men with this surname were named in the survey of the estates of Roger de Somery. William Grevil bought property in the town in 1367 and then built a new stone house which still contributes distinctively to the frontage of the street. The bay window is an early example of the perpendicular style which was to be adopted in so many churches during the following century. Grevil was also a privileged member of the trading communities of Coventry and London; his status as a citizen of London was proudly recorded on his brass monument. He was able to lend King Richard II the sum of 300 marks in 1397 and, at his death in 1401 he left 100 marks to Campden church for 'the new work to be carried on there' and 300 marks for four chaplains to sing masses for his soul for 10 years. He owned 14 houses in the town and eight in Mickleton and some land, but his main purchase had been Milcote Manor near Stratford-on-Avon, where his family settled. It is unusual for a merchant to have both a wool mark and a coat-of-arms on his monumental brass, as William Grevil has, and this probably reflects his recent acquisition of arms. He was not a modest man; the brass inscription describes him as *flos m'cator' lanar' tocius Anglie* — 'the flower of wool merchants in all England'. In 1605, a descendant bought Warwick Castle and the title of Earl of Warwick was conferred in the 18th century.

58. Campden church seen from the garden of Campden Court: this is one of the most famous 'wool' churches. William Grevil, wool merchant, probably instigated and contributed largely to the rebuilding in the mid-15th century. There are striking similarities with Northleach church.

59. John Camber was buried in Sevenhampton in 1497 and his brass monument is in the chancel. He gave money to the parish in which he should happen to die, so it is surmised that he travelled and may have been a wool-merchant. Sevenhampton church was considerably altered as a result but retains evidence of Norman work. The tower and transepts were faced with ashlar and the porch has the characteristic Tudor flattened arch.

The nave and tower of Campden church were built sometime in the 15th century, and the whole church was unified with new windows and battlements. The difficulty of attributing the work to William Grevil is that the tall, fluted pillars and rather flat arches seem to belong to the Tudor period of the end rather than the beginning of the 15th century. There are striking similarities between Campden and Northleach and the style is so unusual, that it seems the same master mason was responsible, a man who was both architect and structural engineer in the medieval period. Northleach's rebuilding can be closely dated to the mid-15th century. Was Campden church before or after Northleach? It would be an interesting reflection on Northleach's importance if it set the style for its grander rival, but more likely a slightly simpler version of what was being built at Campden was commissioned for Northleach. The headdress of a lady on a window stop shows alterations to windows in the aisles were made about 1450. Grevil's money probably helped launch the rebuilding project, but much more had to be raised. William Bradway's gift in 1488 of 100 marks also contributed.

Burford's church suggests it was the wealthiest wool town in the Cotswolds. Some striking Norman parts remain, particularly the tower's main structure. Successive alterations culminated in the major rebuilding of the nave about 1420, dated from the costume on the headstops of the nave piers. John Pynnok, who died in 1486, and who was certainly involved in the wool trade, built the south transept chapel; other contributors' names in Burford are not known. A magnificent porch of three storeys was built a few years later. It is similar to Northleach's though larger and grander and also in all probability a little earlier. The chapel of the Merchant Guild was shortened and joined onto the main fabric of the church. The tower was also raised, unfortunately, because the extra weight of this and then of a spire caused its partial collapse.

Smaller churches also shared in the perpendicular architectural revival. Are churches like Naunton and Bledington wool churches? Both have the wide windows so characteristic of the period. At Naunton, a tower was built in the 15th century and most of the rest of the church was rebuilt in the 16th century. John Ayleworth, who was probably instrumental in at least some of this work, left sheep to the church in 1524 rather than money. Bledington has most striking perpendicular windows, and portraits of donors were painted on the glass, one dated 1476. This was an arable parish without any notable lords or richer merchants to finance the work. Is Sevenhampton a wool church? It has been assumed that John Camber was a wool merchant because he travelled the countryside. He died in 1497, and in his will left money for work on whichever church he happened to be buried in, according to where he was at the time of his death. A memorial brass records his name. It is assumed that the tower was inserted or perhaps raised substantially in height as a result. Its supports and flying buttresses are an interesting and unusual feature. It may be wondered how far all churches should really be called 'wool churches'. Where did the Norman lords draw the money from which led to so many stone churches being built in the Cotswolds? They had big estates, but it was hard to produce much surplus from the simple agriculture of the medieval period. Wool had been a main source of cash for a long time.

The Cotswold Sheep
The drawings of sheep on the woolmen's brasses in Northleach church are very special, as only two other examples are known. The drawings could be evidence for the nature of the Cotswold sheep around 1500; no written description exists as early as this. Although the brasses were engraved in London, standard patterns cannot have been used as the sheep on each is different. It seems quite plausible that the Northleach woolmen were so proud of their flocks that they provided the engraver with drawings, especially as they probably commissioned the brasses during their lifetimes.

The Northleach brasses show perhaps three variations in breeds, and two have similarities to the modern Cotswold. The earliest is John Fortey's, who died in 1458; his right foot is resting on a long-wooled and curly-fleeced animal, with wool on the top of its head, a very long, thin face and no horns. The modern Cotswold breed is long-wooled and notable for the curly locks on the head; it is also 'polled' or without horns. Two somewhat similar sheep are portrayed on the Midwinter brass of about 1501. A sheep standing on a wool pack at the bottom of John and Joanne Taylor's brass, of about 1490, seems to have slightly shorter wool and a long tail and is also polled; on Thomas and Joan Bushe's brass, several sheep apparently have shorter wool and long tails, and one has a curved horn which could indicate a ram and like the crook underneath show that the Busshes were sheep breeders as well as woolmen.

In general, the drawings on the brasses correspond with the first literary descriptions of the Cotswold sheep, which date from Elizabeth I's reign or just after. Camden described the Cotswolds as 'long backed and square of bulk and bone' and Gervase Markham said they were long-wooled. Michael Drayton's *Polyolbion*, published in 1614, a description in verse form of 'all the Tracts, Rivers, mountains, forests, and other Parts of this Renowned Isle of Great Britain', reaches the Cotswolds in the 14th song. Drayton says the sheep are of the whitest, with no black or brown on legs or face; the brows woolly and the flank as well covered as the back; the staple deep and thick; the body long and large. As he came from Warwickshire, his knowledge of Cotswold flocks was probably based on personal observation. The staple is the length of the fibre in the fleece, but the word is not the origin of the name of the Company of the Staple, which refers to a post or marker showing where goods were to be sold. In the modern definition of the breed, the straight long back and large size of the sheep are important, and the wool is described as 'coarse', which Drayton's use of the word 'thick' also seems to imply.

There seem to be characteristics of the Cotswold sheep in the 16th century matching those of modern times, but there are problems in assuming continuity and the origins of the

60. The sheep portrayed on two monumental brasses in Northleach church present an historical problem. The thin-faced sheep on John Fortey's brass of 1458 *(left)* has been described as 'uncannily like a Cotswold'. On William Midwinter's brass of 1501 *(above)*, the sheep has a long, curly fleece. Could the engravers have worked from special drawings or even from life?

breed are uncertain; the factor which has given lustre as well as length to certain longwools, including Cotswold, is also a biological mystery. Primitive sheep were short-wooled, short tailed and small in size, like the Soay to be seen in the Cotswold Farm Park. There is a tradition that the Romans introduced the Cotswold breed, and archaeological evidence suggests that they did bring to England a larger-boned sheep, which was not confined to the Cotswolds. Cross-breeding could quite quickly have increased the size of indigenous sheep. Other invaders brought their sheep types with them; the Normans and the Cistercian monasteries possibly introduced variations. By the 14th century individual fleece characteristics had developed in particular counties and in regions like the Cotswolds; schedules of wool prices list 51 different grades of wool, identified by area of production. Cotswold wool was dearer than most grades and later was taken as the standard Staple quality. Shropshire and Herefordshire wools were exceptionally valuable, implying that the predecessor of the Ryland, with short staple but very fine wool, already existed. Drayton noted the superiority of Leominster wool, 'that wool the silkworm's web for smallness doth compare', and it retained its superiority; Rudder quoted figures for 1767 when Herefordshire fleece wool fetched three times as much as Cotswold.

By modern standards, medieval Cotswold sheep may have produced wool which was middle-length and of medium fineness. Even so, it is uncertain whether the wool which the Celys sold at Calais for the cloth manufactures in Flanders or Lombardy could have come from this breed. It is generally assumed short staple wool was used. The Celys' customers sometimes rejected wool if the staple was either too long, described as 'gruff' or coarse, or too short, 'rabbit stuff'. Did Flemish and Lombard buyers value Cotswold wool for purposes other than the standard woollen-spinning of their areas? or were the sheep on the Cotswold hills not the same as in the 18th century? In one of the first books about sheep husbandry, published in 1749, William Ellis of Little Gaddesden in Hertfordshire, said

> In Herefordshire, especially about Lempster and on those famous Hills called Cotswold Hills, sheep are fed that produce a singular good wool, which for Fineness comes very

near to that of Spain; for from it a thread may be drawn as fine as silk.

Yet 30 years later Rudder would not allow that the wool was fine. Many writers who followed Camden in commending the wool for whiteness and fineness, he said, 'had never seen, or seeing, had no judgement in that article. What kind of wool this may have been four or five hundred years ago I can have no knowledge of, except from history; but can speak with certainly as to the present condition of it'. The fleece was 'prodigious' but coarse, so that 'the Cotswold wool, which was never fine within the memory of any man I have conversed with on that subject, is now become still coarser'.

61. A 'Cotswold Lion': this name for a Cotswold sheep was in *Grose's Provincial Glossary* in 1790, so its origin is considerably earlier.

The arguments about the the nature of the traditional Cotswold had already begun. Marshall's opinion was that the Cotswold sheep was 'a polled long-woolled, middle-sized sheep; a breed which has been prevalent on these hills time immemorial; it has been improved but it has not been changed'. Observers were keenly aware that the nature of breeds had been altering as the result of techniques associated with the name of Robert Bakewell but pursued in different places by many less well-known breeders. Eileen Power lamented this change. 'Bakewell may have his meed of praise from the economist, but to the historian he is an arch-iconoclast who defaced an irreplaceable collection of walking documents'. She perhaps exaggerated the extent to which local varieties had remained unchanged over preceeding centuries, and the brasses are a warning against assuming that all the sheep of even one small area were exactly alike.

Nineteenth-century writers found difficulty in believing that the Cotswold could have existed in the medieval period on unenclosed farms and on dry upland pastures, and this may be a clue to the apparent contradictions. The Cotswold breed could have been a specialism of a few flock-masters and distinct from the generality of Cotswold sheep grazing the Downlands and folded on the open arable fields. In Pegolotti's list, wools 'from the fold' were given the lowest prices and in the 19th century the Cotswold was considered unsuitable for folding. On enclosed pastures like The Farm in Northleach in the medieval period, specialist flocks could have been carefully maintained by larger Cotswold flock-masters, like the Taylors of Farmington. Was William Midwinter's wool so prized for this reason? Was there an echo of the medieval sheep-masters in 18th-century Farmington? Rudder noted that 'the farmers give much attention to the breed of their sheep, for which they are deservedly famous'.

As a result of the 18th-century agricultural improvements, the general run of sheep in the Cotswolds may have changed more than the pure Cotswold of the specialist breeders. Cotswold wool certainly became coarser and the sheep became larger through cross-breeding, mainly with the Leicester. Rudder said rams were 'sometimes brought hither in little carriages made for that purpose'. Marshall also noted that the Leicestershire rams 'had gained a firm footing on the hills', and Rudge in 1807 said that the pure breed 'is become scarce, in consequence of the introduction of the New Leicester'; even the advocates of the old native breed in Sherborne, he said, allowed some crossing with the New Leicester. In Northleach, the local sheep were the same cross, but with the Cotswold more predominant. 'Pure Cotswolds are still found on several farms', he wrote. 'At Daglingworth and Hampnett are still to be found the largest and purest flocks of the old breed'. Sale particulars of Mrs. Arkell's livestock at Whittington Court in 1817 described the sheep as of 'mixed Leicester and Cotswold sort'. Cotswolds were mainly sold at Burford and Stow markets.

'The primary object of the Cotswold husbandry is SHEEP', Marshall wrote. He spent a year in Gloucester researching his account of the county's farming practices, but only a week in the centre of the Cotswolds. 'All I have to say farther is, that, since the account has received its present form, it has been seen and approved, by those who are best able to form an adequate judgement'. Marshall saw that a large change in sheep husbandry had recently taken place. Whereas the whole district had formerly been stocked with breeding flocks, and year-old lambs were sold to graziers in neighbouring counties for fattening, now new crops like turnips and better grass management were allowing the farmers to fat their own sheep and sell at three years old. The quality of the fleece had become less important than the size of the animals and the speed of fattening. The improvement was not altogether successful; within a relatively short period the very fat carcase was not acceptable to the market, and the fleece did not compete with much finer wools from merino sheep. The meat was said derogatorily to be 'so inferior as to limit the chief demand to our manufacturing districts'. The Cotswold was 'a poor man's sheep', though 'hardy, prolific, and a good mother'. The Oxford Down became the popular sheep of the area, a cross of the improved Cotswold and the Hampshire Down, and even specialist Cotswold breeders like W. G. Garne of Broadmoor Farm, near Bourton on the Water, kept Oxford Downs as well as Cotswolds.

The Cotswold Sheep Society was established in 1892. The impetus to start the Society would seem to have been a realisation that the breed was rapidly losing ground and the Society hoped to facilitate good practice despite the declining number of Cotswold rams, and to maintain the breed's characteristics. The Flock Book recorded 45 flocks and 645 ewes. Not all flocks were registered; Samuel Walker of Hawling, for example, registered 200 ewes in 1904 but the flock had been started by his father in 1855. Cotswolds were a small proportion of the sheep in the area, and flocks were very small. The formation of the Society did not arrest the decline; 10 years later the number of registered flocks had fallen to 15, with a total of 476 sheep altogether. The last book of 1922 recorded 660 ewes, nearly half in counties other than Gloucestershire.

More than half of the flocks registered in the first Flock Book were located in the area of Burford and Northleach. Some were near Cirencester, and one near Banbury, and a few were registered in Herefordshire and in Norfolk. The Flock Book indicates that six of the registered flocks existed in the 18th century. Robert Garne's was originally from Sherborne, which is interesting in view of Rudge's comment about the advocates of the old breed there. Only Frederick Craddock of Eastington near Northleach could claim that his flock had been on the same farm since its foundation in 1790, and he thought it was probably established many years previously. Another old-established flock was George Bagnall's at Westwell Manor, near Burford, established by the 'present owner's forefathers, and has been in the family without intermission for the last five or six generations'; this places its start probably in the early 18th century. Most important, Charles Barton's flock was from Coln Rogers near Northleach, where it had been for 200 years before being moved in 1828 to Fyfield near Lechlade. Records of this flock were said to exist from the early 17th century, and it was thus recorded on a former Gloucester Abbey manor within a hundred years of the Abbey's dissolution.

The pure-bred Cotswold seems to have been something of a gentleman's hobby in the later 19th century. Lord Eldon of Stowell Park created flocks of 500 at Compton Abdale in 1881 and 450 at Manor Farm, Chedworth in 1882; Thomas Walker had a flock in Stowell Park itself, which was dispersed in 1884 before Lord Eldon started on a big programme of restoration and enlargement of the house. James Taylor of Rendcomb Park created three flocks of 275, 350 and 400 in his three model farms in 1881 and 1882; these were only registered for a short time. Major the Honourable L. Byng at Sherborne Home Farm briefly maintained a small flock of less than a hundred and H. J. Elwes of Colesborne Park registered 200 at Southbury Farm for a short while; this flock had existed since 1843. Lieutenant-Colonel E. P. Brassey had a small flock at Manor Farm, Upper Slaughter, just before the First World War.

The Garne family have been very important in the modern story of the Cotswold sheep. Robert Garne of Aldsworth was the first president of the Cotswold Sheep Society, and the Aldsworth flock was one of only four to be registered both in the first Flock Book in 1892 and the last in 1922; by this time it had declined in size from 355 ewes to 75. The family had farmed in Gloucestershire since at least the 17th century, and at Chipping Norton Margaret Garnes had sold Richard Cely some fells in the late 15th century. William Garne went from Sherborne to Wall Farm, Aldsworth, in 1799 with a flock of Cotswolds 'at which time it was a Flock of considerable note'. The son of William Garne promoted the Cotswold very successfully in the Bakewell manner. He let his rams to other sheep breeders from at least 1829, held sheep sales on the farm from 1844 which continued until the end of the century,

62. Broadfield Farm, where prize-winning Cotswold sheep were bred, was built on the former open fields of Eastington in Northleach after enclosure in 1783. The farmhouse and barn have changed little since 1850 (see plate XVI) and the road has a natural stone surface. William Lane and later William Houlton who farmed here were related to the Garne family who bred Cotswolds in the neighbouring parish of Aldsworth.

and exported Cotswolds. He won the prizes at the Royal Agricultural Society's meetings four years running, between 1849 and 1852, and was still winning first prize in 1892. He was proud of his sheep and had oil paintings of some of them. A relative, William Houlton of Broadfield Farm, Northleach, also maintained a Cotswold flock through these years and John Garne had some at Filkins, to the south of Burford, where the Cotswold Woollen Weavers is reviving the use of the small amount of lustrous Cotswold wool now produced.

By the mid-1930s only William Garne's flock was well-known, though some writers were wrong to say it was the only one; a flock survived at Stowell owned by Dowager Lady Vesty and one at Crickley Barrow, formerly called Cottage Farm, near Northleach, owned by Mr. O. H. Colburn who had a family connection with the Garnes. William Garne of Aldsworth refused to abandon the Cotswold which his family had kept for so long. He lived long enough to see the Cotswold Sheep Society re-established in 1966 and to become the first President at the age of 86. Some of his sheep went to the Cotswold Farm Park where the Rare Breeds Survival Trust is endeavouring to ensure that breeds like this are not lost. Interest in the traditional Cotswold breed is now growing, and in 1986 there were 58 flocks containing 447 pure-bred ewes, though by no means all were in Gloucestershire.

Chapter Seven

Knights and Manor Houses

The Cotswolds had many manor houses in the medieval period but few were occupied by gentlemen, partly because more than a third were in ecclesiastical hands until the mid-16th century. Men of 'gentle' birth were fairly sharply distinguished from the rest of society and 'gentry' is a convenient term for both knights and esquires in the early medieval period, although later the word took on a wider connotation. Icomb Place, which dates from the 15th century, is a unique survival of a medieval knight's house, the crenellations over the entrance a symbol of status. The largest manor house in the Cotswolds in this period was Sudeley Castle, first built in the mid-15th century, and largely rebuilt in the following century. By the time of Edward VI's death in 1553, the destruction of the religious foundations, whether great or small monasteries, hospices or chantries, was complete. Queen Mary tried to reverse the Protestant establishment in England but, with Elizabeth I's accession in 1558 Protestantism was secure. Religious estates were gradually sold off by the crown, with the result that the number of gentlemen's manor houses in the Cotswolds doubled. The history of these houses reflects some of the history of the Cotswolds, the periods of prosperity and decay.

Cotswold Gentry in the Medieval Period
In the early medieval period, a knight had to provide himself with horse and armour to serve the king in war; one and a half hides of land was probably enough about the time of Domesday to equip him and pay for a couple of month's service, and this amount of land was known as a knight's fee. As armour became more elaborate and costly, a knight needed at least five hides. It became more usual to collect 'scutage' or shield money, instead of requiring service in person. Men with smaller amounts of land gradually dropped out of the knightly class, or had their obligations reduced to fractions of a knight's fee. John de Sudeley had two knights' fees in 1284 but Adam Martell of Stowell, Thomas Comyn of Salperton and William de Solers of Shipton, for example, each had half a knight's fee. The squire was a man of less landed wealth but similar status, perhaps the younger brother or son of a knight. Society gradually became more stratified and by the 15th century the word 'gentleman' was in use to describe all those of gentle birth who were not nobles or titled; this group merged into the rich freeholders, particularly when men with sufficient wealth ceased to take up the title and obligations of knighthood. The gentry became distinguished by the right to have a coat-of-arms.

Only one in 10 of the manors in the Cotswolds and the Avon valley was occupied by gentry according to the poll tax returns of 1381-82, and the rest were occupied by men of lesser status. The knights of Gloucestershire who took part in county government or represented the county in parliament in the 14th century lived mainly in the Severn valley or under the western edge of the Cotswolds, like Sir John Giffard at Weston Subedge, Sir Robert de Somerville at Aston Somerville or Sir William Tracy at Toddington. True Cotswold gentry were Sir John de Sudeley at Sudeley, Sir Richard de Croupes at Whittington and Sir Thomas Ludlow at Berrington in Campden. For de Croupes, Whittington was his only major possession; Sir John Giffard and Sir William Tracy each had three manors, an estate typical of two thirds of the Gloucestershire gentry. Sir John de Sudeley had five manors, of which only Sudeley was in Gloucestershire. He was the only magnate in the Cotswold area. Church land still owed military service to the king, so abbots and bishops created small 'free' estates whose holders did not have to perform the usual labour services of the villagers but instead served the king in the feudal army. Some of Winchcombe Abbey's knights' fees were recorded in Domesday: there were two knights in Naunton near Winchcombe, and one knight in Alderton. In the Landboc it was recorded about 1300 that scutage was paid by William le Dogge in Hawling on one yardland, Richard de la Sale in Hazleton on one and a quarter hides, Walter le Freeman and John le Freeman in Snowshill on one hide each, and John Umfrei in Sherborne. Returns of estates owing military service under the bishop of Worcester in the late 14th century included whole knights' fees at Aston Blank, Dowdeswell and Notgrove, a third of a knight's fee at Foxcote and one fifth of a fee at Hilcot and at Little Colesborne. At Sevenhampton, at the time of a survey of the bishop of Hereford's estate about 1275, William de Notteclive paid the bishop scutage for his one and a half hides of land.

A few of these knights' fees, like Whittington, became established as independent manors and provided the foundations of notable houses of later times. Whittington had become a separate manor before Domesday, but had been part of the great Worcester manor of Withington. The Court was built on a moated site, probably in mid-12th century when moats were fashionable; in 1284 Richard de Croupes held it as a whole knight's fee and the de Croupes family were prominent in county affairs. The house today is mainly 16th century or later. Other knights' fees within the church of Worcester's estate of Withington did not gain independence. The holders of the church's free estates did not usually qualify as members of the gentry. Thomas de Bradewell, who had lands and a house in Evesham Abbey's manor of Broadwell, was an exception. In the poll tax returns of 1379, he paid more than the knight Robert de Somerville. An important figure in county affairs, de Bradewell served three times as sheriff of Gloucestershire, marking his arrival amongst the upper gentry of the county. His lands in Broadwell were eventually recognised as the separate manor of Nethercourt.

Ecclesiastical manor houses might be the homes of bailiffs, who had responsibilities for more than one manor, or might be occupied by tenants of the manor's farmland. Occasionally they were occupied by the abbots or bishops on their journeys or when attending to the business of a manor. Abbot Norreys of Evesham had 'a noble house' in Broadwell where he retired in 1202; it was apparently burnt down and then replaced by a 'grange' or bailiff's house. He also had a favourite house at Bourton on the Water. The abbot of Winchcombe stayed at Sherborne for the annual sheep-shearing. In 1266, Gloucester Abbey's manor house at Buckland seems to have been occupied by two small farmers, Nicholas in the Hall holding one yardland and Thomas in the Hall holding one and a half yardlands. Neither was the reeve who was the manager of the manor but was also a local farmer and so had his own farmhouse. When the abbot leased the manor house to James Appery, his wife and two children in 1518, he specifically required that twice a year for three or four nights his chamberlain and steward with their men and horses should be hospitably entertained.

Two knights' houses
Icomb Place

The site of Icomb Place is secluded on the east by a small stream which in the past separated it from Worcestershire and on the south-west by the deep combe or dingle which perhaps is the origin of Icomb's name. Close to the south-west corner of the house is a spring described as 'never-failing'. A large proportion of the early 15th-century house survives today: the great hall, and other ranges of medieval buildings round a small court. A more westerly range, which closed a second court, was demolished during the 19th century. Inside there has been adaptation, renovation and modernisation, but no substantial alteration. On the east side is a crenellated porch with a wide, tudor-arched doorway and two 15th-century chimneys. The roof timbering is similar to the great hall, which is entered across the court to the west through another wide tudor-arched door. To the north is a first-floor room traditionally called the chapel. This building appears likely to have been an open hall, floored at the same time as the front was erected; it was an important building as an elaborate oriel window has been added to give light to the north end. To the south is a further early range of buildings, with an outside door at first-floor level. This suggests a first-floor hall with an undercroft below, which would make it perhaps the oldest part of the Place; the undercroft was converted into a sitting room in the early 20th century. The court is not a true rectangle, and the north and south buildings were probably already in existence when the entrance wing and great hall were built to link them. It was characteristic of larger, early medieval houses to consist of several separate buildings.

Sir John Blaket lived at Icomb Place in the early 15th century, about the time the house was built. The family had been a knightly one in the area for nearly a century, as Roger or Robert Blaket had a quarter of a knight's fee in Icomb in 1346. Sir John Blaket was killed while fighting in France in 1430 and was likely to have been the same Sir John Blaket who was a knight at the battle of Agincourt in 1415. His effigy may be found in Icomb church in the chapel which belonged to Icomb Place; although there is no name on the monument itself, the heraldry of the arms on the side link it quite certainly with his wife's tomb in Nosely church in Leicestershire, which is identified. Sir John Blaket's will referred to his wish to be buried in the chapel of the Blessed Mary in Icomb church.

After the death of Sir John Blaket, the Place then passed to his son Edmund and thereafter there was no male heir. Edmund's will, made in 1444, required that he be buried in the chapel of the Blessed Mary of Bruern. All his goods in the manor-house of Icomb, the hall, chambers, bakehouse and kitchen, were left to his sister Anne, who had married Ralph Baskerville. They were also given a wagon and six oxen, 200 sheep and six cows. There was no mention in the will of the house itself, which probably belonged to the Baskervilles. Before the restoration of Icomb church, David Royce said that there were two fine brasses in the chapel showing a lady in a horned headdress of *c*.1480, and a knight with a tilting helmet under his head and plate armour; he surmised that they were Ralph and Anne Baskerville.

Icomb Place was 'a fair, ancient house' about 1600. Habington, who writes as though he had seen it, observed that it was 'well set out with honourable worthy armoury, yet not agreeing with those in the church'. The coats-of-arms which he saw have since been destroyed, but perhaps related to the Baskervilles, lords of Icomb or Combe from the Norman Conquest; Habington traced the later history of Sir John Blaket's daughter Anne, who

> married to Baskerville, was mother of Jane, wife of Simon Milbourn, who had by her eleven daughters, from whom are descended (I think) a thousand knights, gentlemen and

63. Icomb Place is one of the oldest houses in the area, and may have been built by a descendant of Sir John Blaket, a knight who fought at Agincourt and is buried in Icomb church.

64. The drawing of the north front of Icomb Place, about 1869, suggests that the windows were mostly blocked or inserted when the house was renovated later in the century.

others, in the counties of Hereford, Gloucester and Worcester. They speak loud of their great blood, and there is no smoke without a fire, for they extract their line from a branch of Devereux, then Lord Ferrars and created since Viscount Hereford and after Earl of Essex.

One of these heiresses, Blanche, brought Icomb Place to her husband, James Whitney, and Robert Whitney of Icomb in his will in 1541 referred to his lands in Oxfordshire and Gloucestershire, 'the evidences of which remain in my casket at Icomb'. The ownership of Icomb Place then passed to the Cope family and was divided between two heirs in the early 18th century. It was perhaps this fate that saved it from being rebuilt at the time when this was happening to many manor houses. When Rudder wrote in 1770 he noted that 'the large mansion house of the Copes is now in decay and occupied by one of the farmers'. A hundred years later its condition had not improved. David Royce, reading a paper to the Bristol and Gloucestershire Archaeological Society on the occasion of their visit, said that 'the present desolate condition of this venerable pile causes a momentary pang. This, however, speedily yields to the intense satisfaction, that the Place has been spared in comparative integrity to our time'. Icomb Place is a unique survival of the period.

Sudeley Castle

The knightly family who held Sudeley at the time of Domesday was unusual, because Ralph came from France with Edward the Confessor in 1041, some twenty-five years before the Norman Conquest. He was connected with the Frankish royal family and his wife was Goda or Godgifa, sister of King Edward. Ralph was made Earl of Hereford, and was noted for building castles on the Welsh borders, at Hereford, Richard's Castle and Ewias Harold, but not apparently at Sudeley, which was less liable to be attacked. Earl Ralph died in 1057, and in 1066 his son Harold was a minor under the charge of Queen Edith, Edward the Confessor's widow. Despite Ralph's Norman origins, his son's status was much reduced by William the Conqueror, who left him with Sudeley and Toddington out of the extensive estates which his father had held. Harold proved an able politician, and regained some of his father's estates. One of his sons married an illegitimate but royal lady of the name of Tracy, and adopted that surname; Toddington eventually became the chief seat of the Tracys, by the gift of the mid-14th-century lords of Sudeley.

On this foundation, the Saxon and Norman manor house at Sudeley may have been large. In 1139, during the civil war between Stephen and Matilda, rival claimants to the English throne, the manor house was attacked by the Earl of Worcester who was on Stephen's side. He wanted to avenge the burning of Worcester by the forces of Matilda. A chronicle written at Worcester soon afterwards recorded that the Earl

> marched with an army to Sudeley, for he heard that John, the son of Harold, had deserted from the king...If it be enquired what the earl did there, the answer must be such as should hardly be handed down to memory; for he returned evil for evil, by seizing and carrying off from the men there great booty of their goods and cattle which on the morrow, he returned to Worcester.

This same Earl, according to the fragmentary chronicle of Hailes Abbey, built a small castle in Hailes and a church next to it, to enable him to hold the area more effectively. The next year Winchcombe was attacked, burned and plundered, and Sudeley was threatened by a commander on Matilda's side, but escaped because 'while he was in mind to attack it, the troops which were in the town made a stand and compelled him to retreat'.

The status of Sudeley's owners is obvious from their seals; Otuer de Sudeley in 1193 and Ralph de Sudeley in 1222 each had a man in armour on horseback, spurred, and obviously riding energetically with stirrups and brandishing sword aloft. The manor-house of Sudeley was surrounded by a park, another indication of status which also ensured a meat supply, one moreover which could be killed in the excitement of the chase. The Park was enlarged in 1252, when an agreement about common rights between the Abbot of Winchcombe and the lord of Sudeley allowed more land to be enclosed; compensation had to be made for taking Piseley Grove 'out of the common'. The inner and outer Park walls are marked on

65. The seals of knights of Sudeley: Otuer (1193) and Ralph (1222), are attached to grants of land; the documents are in the British Museum and the seals were engraved for the *Annals of Winchcombe and Sudeley* (1877). The ruins of the 15th-century Presence Chamber in the royal suite reveal what an elaborate and costly building it was. Lysons made the engraving for his *Antiquities of Gloucestershire* in 1803.

the modern Ordnance Survey map. When John de Sudeley died in 1336, his manor was assessed as one and a half knights' fees. There were 300 acres of arable land, 20 acres of pasture, 10 acres of meadow and 100 acres of wood.

In the mid-14th century, the Boteler family acquired Sudeley through marriage with the heiress. Ralph Boteler was a magnate of wider influence than most county gentry. He was Treasurer to Henry VI, and brought wealth from royal service to building the castle. 'When it was made it had the Price of all the Buildings in those Days', Leland wrote. Ralph Boteler was also an admiral and Leland reported that the 'Portmare' Tower was built with money from a ransom. Leland was very impressed with the richness of the castle, noting several times that the windows in the hall were made of translucent semi-precious stones; yet despite this, he also said that 'now it goeth to ruin, more pity'. His notes were written about a hundred years after the castle was built, and provide evidence that it was not on the former manor house site. It was built *a fundamentis* and 'There had been a manor place at Sudeley before the building of the Castle, and the plot is yet seen in Sudeley Park where it stood'. Archaeological investigations carried out in 1875 by Emma Dent, who lived at Sudeley, confirmed that there were buildings in the broken ground called the Hop Yard, visible from the east terrace. Oral tradition surviving over 400 years held this to be the site of the former manor house. She thought the remains were Saxon.

The castle is mainly the result of two major rebuildings during the hundred years following Ralph Boteler's work. The exterior of the north gateway remains from the early 15th century, and probably the general layout of the two courts, with the middle towers on the east and west sides; the church and ruined barn also date from this first period. In the later 15th century the inner court was built, of regal scale and fineness of detail, but now in ruins. Boteler was a Lancastrian in the Wars of the Roses, and forfeited Sudeley to the Yorkist Edward IV in 1469, who passed it to his brother Richard Duke of Gloucester, later King Richard III. It is suggested that Richard rebuilt the inner court. The outer court was reconstructed in the 16th century, and is the most tangible reminder of a great magnate's house. For a short while the castle was the property of Lord Admiral Seymour, who brought his wife there, the widow Queen Katherine Parr, last wife to Henry VIII, but she died shortly afterwards in childbed. On Seymour's execution Sudeley became a royal possession once more.

In 1537 Sir John Bridges was made constable or warden of the castle and probably lived there through most of the changes of ownership over the next 17 years. After the dissolution he was responsible for destroying Winchcombe Abbey's buildings, in accordance with royal policy not to allow the remains of the monasteries to attract more monks, and he leased the site together with monastic property in the town, Corndean Farm and part of Sudeley manor. He must have been a tactful man—he was created Lord Chandos by Queen Mary in 1554 'for good services to Henry VIII, Edward VI and to Queen Mary'. He was allowed to purchase the site of the monastery 'to sustain the dignity to which she had raised him', but not its urban property. He died in 1557. Salvaged building materials no doubt came in useful for the rebuilding of the outer court for which Edmund, the second Lord Chandos, was responsible, and which is still standing.

Lord Chandos also purchased three of the former Abbey's woods, Deepwood, 370 acres, Humley Hoe, 50 acres, and Farmcote woods. Deepwood was planted with oak, ash, sallow, hasel and thorn of various ages, and there was apparently an annual wood sale of timber of 30 years' growth; some of the wood was 'spoiled by the highways leading through many parts'. Humley Hoe, on the 'hoe' or rounded shoulder of land near Belas Knap, now called Humblebee Wood, did not contain any substantial timber. It was considered to be to the detriment of the town of Winchcombe that these woods were sold, as it meant there was no timber for repairing buildings or five watermills; accordingly Westwood, of 70 acres, was reserved to Queen Mary and King Philip. In purchasing the woods Lord Chandos was bringing together again some of the Domesday lands of Sudeley.

Sudeley Castle was destroyed as the result of the allegiance of the sixth Lord Chandos in the civil wars of the 17th century. He was only 22 when the wars began in 1642; he armed his tenants, garrisoned Sudeley with 60 men under his brother, Captain Bridges, and set off to raise a foot regiment for Charles I. The parliamentarian General Massey attacked Sudeley, smoke from hay and straw being apparently enough to make the garrison surrender; the men went home promising never to fight for the king again. Royalist propaganda included horrifying stories of the plundering of the castle and profaning of the chapel; the Chandos monuments were broken, pegs were fastened into the pulpit to hang the carcases of the slaughtered sheep, and the communion table used to cut up the meat. The zeal of Puritan reformers or the lack of provisioning for the soldiers could equally be to blame. Despite the fact that in October 1645 he had changed sides, and sworn to the Covenant which parliament used as the test of true Protestant sympathies, Lord Chandos was obliged to make a statement of his income in order that he could be taxed for the benefit of the winning parliamentarian side. Sudeley and Winchcombe properties, including Corndean and Rowell, were worth £1,800, properties in Middlesex and Buckinghamshire nearly as much. He was required to pay £4,976. Yet Sudeley was destroyed by order of parliament in 1649; there must have been some hint of royalist plots. A mere £1,000 was abated from the fine in compensation. The ruined castle remained in the Chandos family for the next 200 years. In 1666, it was charged in the Hearth Tax for 18 chimneys, and four chimneys were said to have been recently demolished—no doubt it was very annoying to pay a tax on uninhabited rooms with fireplaces.

Part of the castle continued to be occupied and in the early 18th century the large park was stocked with deer. The church was 'quite out of repair'; at the end of the century services were held once a fortnight. As a ruin, Sudeley was a tourist attraction. When George III stayed in Cheltenham in 1788, he visited Sudeley several times. A story of the King's visit was told to Emma Dent by Mr. Edward Downe, who, when a boy, said he frequently saw the King both at Sudeley and in Winchcombe.

> On one of these visits to the Castle, the King was so intent on exploring part of the ruins, that he incurred considerable danger of losing his life by being precipitated down the turret staircase, which was then in a most dilapidated state. But this catastrophe was prevented by the timely, though unceremonious, interference of Mrs Cox, who inhabited a part of the edifice, and was then in attendance on His Majesty.

He rewarded her by giving one of her relatives a commission in the Guards.

Joshua Gilpin, an American, visted Sudeley a few years later, on 28 July 1796. He found 'a fine ruin, part of which, however, is fitted up for a farmhouse, part for a barn and stables and part in a neat garden ...the church forms part of it, the walls of which are pretty entire, only well washed with pug'. Pug was a mixture of lime and clay. He followed the road over Cleeve Hill, being enchanted with the views, but found Winchcombe a 'mean little village', and 'noticeably decayed', there being no good house in the village. About this time, according to Emma Dent, the castle was inhabited by a tenant called Attwood; 'it was then a public house (the *Castle Arms*). He also kept a stud of horses ... So careless were the owners, that Attwood pulled down a great deal, and sold oak beams and lead, and other materials, which were used freely in the neighbourhood'. John Attwood's effects were sold

66. Two centuries of deterioration followed the damage intentionally inflicted on Sudeley Castle by the Parliamentarians in the Civil War. William and John Dent started the work of restoring and adapting the surviving buildings after 1830.

by the Tewkesbury auctioneers, Moore and Sons, in September 1832. A very small amount of the castle was inhabited: a kitchen, small parlour and large parlour and several bed-chambers. The kennels were a major feature. The same auctioneer sold the contents of Sudeley Lodge. This, too, was quite a modest house, with three bedrooms and a servants' room; in the hall was a view of Sudeley Castle.

The decline of the castle was dramatically reversed by John and William Dent, glove manufacturers in Worcester, who purchased the surrounding estate centred on the Lodge in 1830 from Lord Rivers, and the castle itself in 1837 from the Duke of Buckingham. They were gentlemen of 'archaeological tastes', said the *Cheltenham Examiner*. The wealth of their business was poured into Sudeley. Their work in restoring the castle, 'long before the present-day mania for restorations and collections came in', was not sufficiently appreciated, Emma Dent thought; 'they did all in such a conservative spirit'. After their deaths in 1857, Sudeley was bequeathed to a nephew and to Emma Dent, his wife, for her lifetime. It has since remained in this family. She too enjoyed the historical and archaeological opportunities of Sudeley; several excavations were conducted by her and Roman mosaic pavements were exposed, which had been discovered as land was ploughed for the first time for many centuries. The results of her researches were published in 1877 in the *Annals of Winchcombe and Sudeley*. She continued the work of restoration with the chapel. 'It was a beautiful ruin, with its walls quite perfect, covered with roses and ivy, the green grass for a floor, and the sky for painted windows', a friend said. Sir George Gilbert Scott prepared plans which involved scraping the 'pug' from the walls, and in 1863 the chapel was rededicated. The yew hedges and walks were planted, which were no more than a 'procession of melancholy poles' in 1857 but are now impressive in size. Furniture and pictures were collected for the interior. Emma Dent was widowed in 1885 but continued her work until her death in 1900. The vicar said that in Winchcombe the 'preservation of its picturesqueness is largely due to her loving care'; she rescued a number of tumble-down cottages and sold them cheaply to local families and she paid for the provision of a water supply. She also instigated restoration of Winchcombe church.

New men and monastic manor houses
Sherborne House and Stanway House

About twenty Cotswold gentlemen were amongst 96 in Gloucestershire responding to Queen Elizabeth I's call in 1588 for an 'extraordinary aid, by way of loan' to meet the threatened Spanish invasion, and 79 were listed by Atkyns as paying £10 or more to the parliamentary subsidy 20 years later. Paul Tracy of Stanway headed the Armada list, one of three men in the county able to pay £50. Sir William Hobby of Hailes and William Dutton of Sherborne, Henry Winchcombe of Northleach, Thomas Warne of Snowshill and Edmond Helmes of Oddington each contributed £25. All occupied former monastic properties. Three people had estates which had not been in the church's hands: widow Alice Stratford at Farmcote, John Cotton of Dowdeswell and Robert Rogers of Lower Dowdeswell. It is not certain whether Combe, held by Richard Bridges, was in Campden and had belonged to Bordesley Abbey, or was Combe alias Icomb. The 1607 subsidy list included six Cotswold gentry occupying former monastic manors: William Dutton at Sherborne and Paul Tracy at Stanway, Lady Lane at Broadwell, Edward Ayleworth at Notgrove, Mr. Henry Stratford at Hawling, and Sir Edward Fisher at Mickleton. Six other subsidy payers were Nicholas Overbury at Bourton on the Hill, Mr. George Stratford at Farmcote, Anthony Smith at Campden, Sir Hugh Brown at Saintbury, widow Thomasine Grevil at Sezincote and Mr. John Carter at Lower Slaughter. Atkyns observed how few families stayed in the county more than three generations; out of the 79 paying the subsidy, only 29 were there a hundred years later. Two centuries on, Susan Hicks Beach, in her history of *A Cotswold Family* published in 1909, took the 300 coats-of-arms which Atkyns placed at the front of his history and checked how many of the families had survived; 'today 28 of these possess part or all their residential estates', and her own family and the related Noel family of Campden are still successful survivors. She said that a small number traced their descent from Norman or even Saxon forbears, but few 'can make precise statements about anything previous to 1550 or 1600'. The sale of monastic property established most of the Cotswold gentry families.

Sherborne is the most impressive of the houses built on the foundations of a monastic manor house. The Abbot of Winchcombe had given a lease of Sherborne at a peppercorn rent to Sir John Alleyn in 1533, probably hoping eventually to regain possession of the estate. Alleyn purchased the estate in 1551 and the same year sold to Thomas Dutton, who was holding a royal appointment as surveyor of crown lands in Gloucestershire. Thomas Dutton was a younger son of a Chester gentry family; his royal appointments, however, brought him sufficient wealth to embark on building almost at once, and a 19th-century watercolour suggests that some at least of this house lasted until the more ambitious rebuilding of the years 1829 to 1839. He entertained Queen Elizabeth in the house in 1574, and his son, William, also entertained the Queen in 1592. William created the Old Park; a second park

KNIGHTS AND MANOR HOUSES

67. Bourton House was built about 1700 on older foundations and is the principal house in Bourton on the Hill.

68. Next to the house is a barn dated 1570, of seven bays, making it one of the largest in the county.

was made on Aldsworth Downs to the south in mid-17th century for coursing, or deer chasing, and a grand lodge was built from which to watch the races. At this time Sherborne House was substantially enlarged. In the 19th century it was apparently dismantled stone by stone and rebuilt in the same style and largely on the same plan. Ralph Dutton was made a baronet in 1678 and James Dutton became Lord Sherborne in 1785; though sometimes passing through nephews rather than sons, Sherborne remained the family home until 1940. In 1981 it was converted into 30 luxury apartments and much of the estate is owned by the National Trust.

Stanway, too, became the seat of a notable gentry family. Richard Tracy, like Thomas Dutton was a younger son, of the Gloucestershire family of Toddington. Again in advance of the dissolution of Tewkesbury Abbey, Richard Tracy obtained a lease of Stanway in 1533, 'though it had not been let to farm for the past 100 years'; later Tracy became the owner. It was obviously a most desirable property; Abbot Cheltenham had largely rebuilt and extended the house about forty years before, as Leland reported, and it was well situated under the Cotswold edge and facing west. In the four hundred years and more since the ending of Tewkesbury Abbey's long period of ownership, which itself may have lasted as much as eight hundred and fifty years, the house has not again been bought or sold.

Richard Tracy's Protestant sympathies helped him in his rise. He secured a seat in the Reformation parliament of 1529 which began the break from Rome, and had positions on several commissions dealing with monastic and chantry lands. 'He is always ready to serve the King in commissions and other ways with most hearty fashion, according to his duty, letting for no costs nor charges at any time'. During Mary's reign, although summoned to appear before the Privy Council, he 'showed a very earnest desire to be a conformable man from henceforth' and so he survived the changes of the next few years. Paul Tracy, Richard's son, was the main architect of Stanway House as it is today. In 1611 he was made a baronet, a new order of hereditary knighthood which James I sold to raise money. His building at Stanway included the great hall, gatehouse and south façade. A great hall is a medieval feature and Stanway's may be one of the last to be built; the very large bay window lighting the 'high end' was inserted towards the end of the 17th century. The gateway is probably also of this date. Two smaller gateways which reflect the design of the main gate were built about 1720. The new work on Stanway House was not finished when interrupted by the civil wars; it was said that part was still not completed in 1685, though the initials IT on rainwater heads on the south front, relating to John Tracy the fifth baronet and lord of Stanway from 1666 to 1677, seem to date the completion of the exterior of the façade. The new buildings adjoined the 'fair stone house at the east end of the church which was the abbot's house', and which still stood in the early 18th century.

At one time there was a park round the house, perhaps from medieval times, but by 1700 this was 'now all ploughed up', according to Dr. Parsons. The ridge and furrow of arable cultivation in the park is clear and might have been taken as evidence for medieval cultivation; Parson's comment makes it seem more likely that the ridges are later. In the late 18th century a landscape was designed, it has been said by Capability Brown, and the unfashionable Dutch garden and water cascade were removed; the pyramid was built over the top of the cascade in 1750 as a memorial to his father by Robert Tracy. The trees are a mid-19th-century planting. Kip's engraving in Atkyns' *History* shows the road to Stanton passing through the main gateway, along the front of the house and out of the yard under the second smaller archway, thence winding through the park to leave by a five-barred gate opposite the

69. The Abbot of Winchcombe stayed at Sherborne for the annual sheep-shearing and after the Abbey was closed the manor was purchased by Thomas Dutton and became the centre of one of Gloucestershire's largest estates. The house was reconstructed between 1829 and 1834.

70. The grand entrance to the stables of 1776: by this date, the Duttons owned the whole parish of Sherborne apart from the rector's holding.

cricket field. Anne Tracy's diary, written between 1723 and 1725, more than once describes watching travellers go through the yard : 'saw Lady Keyt's equipment pass through the yard on the way to Toddington'; 'nothing happened in the morning except seeing Sir John Packington's equipment pass through the yard on the way to London'. The construction of a road turning through two right-angled bends to skirt the churchyard and take it further away from the house was therefore late 18th century or even early 19th century, when the last open land in the parish was enclosed.

Burford Priory and Broadway Court
The histories of Burford Priory and Broadway Court, former monastic properties, have many similarities with Sherborne and Stanway. The wealth to purchase and then to build came from the profits of royal service. The new gentlemen were clearly Protestant in their sympathies and helped Henry VIII and then his son, Edward, in surveying monastic property. They leased properties first and then purchased. During the short reign of Edward VI a number of former monastic properties were sold, making it much harder for Mary to reverse the Protestant revolution. Extensive rebuilding, however, was often not risked for at least a hundred years.

Burford Priory rivalled Sherborne and Stanway by the end of the 16th century, though it replaced the modest Hospital of St John. The buildings lay behind the wall on the west side of the town, in Upton, the 'Outward' tithing of the parish of Burford. A master and a few brothers had once ministered to the sick and poor, but by the time of its dissolution, in 1538, the Hospital was providing a sinecure for the vicar. The Hospital had three yardlands in Burford's open fields, the manor of Fifield and five yardlands and there were some small properties at Asthall, Little Barrington, Great Rissington, Sherborne and Widford. Edmond Harman first leased this estate in 1543; at about the same time he was able to buy the much larger neighbouring estate of Taynton, which had been Tewkesbury Abbey's. Together these properties made a good estate for a newly arrived gentleman. Edmond Harman was one of Henry VIII's doctors, and the son of an Ipswich man; he perhaps owed his royal patronage to Henry's powerful minister, Thomas Wolsey, also from Ipswich. He lived at Taynton and his daughter married Edmond Bray of Great Barrington; as a result, Taynton became part of the Barrington Park estate until it was sold in 1920. Harman was the first man for several centuries to bring together all the main Burford properties: the Hospital estate, Burford Rectory, which had been the property of Keynsham Abbey and which he leased from the crown in 1545, and Burford manor and its six yardlands which he leased from the crown about 1552. His wife was the daughter of the Burford merchant and clothier, Edmond Sylvester; Harman secured permission from the King to sell part of the Hospital estate to Sylvester which enabled him to build Falkland Hall in 1558, an impressive house on the corner of Priory Lane and High Street.

The aggrandisement of Burford Priory was carried out by two subsequent owners, both lawyers. The property reverted to the crown after the death of Edmond Harman in 1577, and was purchased soon after by Sir Lawrence Tanfield, Lord Chief Baron of the Exchequer. He spent £5,000 making it into a magnificent mansion. Queen Elizabeth may well have stayed here; on a progress in 1592 she came from Sherborne to Burford. In 1603 James I was entertained here soon after he became King of England. Tanfield also leased the Rectory estate and in 1617 he bought Burford manor, which led to the clash with the town's officials. He also manoeuvred the vicar out of his hide of land in Burford's open fields, thus enlarging the Priory estate. A monument in the church confidently commemorates Tanfield and his wife.

KNIGHTS AND MANOR HOUSES

71. After the small priory or hospital in Burford was closed in 1538, it became one of the larger gentleman's residences in the area. The chapel was built by William Lenthal, who despite his Puritan past had it dedicated by the Bishop of Oxford in 1662, and the picture gallery, lit by six windows, is also mid-17th century.

72. The front of Burford Priory has been much altered and its appearance is the result of a major reconstruction of 1808. When the Bristol and Gloucestershire Archaeological Society visited in 1897 it was reported that the house was 'in a very bad state; most of the floors are gone and the chapel is in ruins'.

The second man to enlarge the Priory was William Lenthal, who bought it in 1637 from Tanfield's heirs; three years later he became speaker of the Long Parliament which challenged Charles I's methods of government and led the country into war against the King. Over the next 20 years considerable building work was carried out, including the erection of a chapel, a surprising adornment considering Lenthal was a Puritan and against church ostentation. Towards the end of the century a Long Gallery was built to display pictures, some brought from Charles I's collection at Windsor. The Priory had become one of the largest houses in Oxfordshire. The Lenthal family remained in possession for nearly two hundred years; the Vicar in 1738 reported that 'the only family of note here (though there are many who have pretty Estates) is John Lenthal's, Esq.'. The Lenthals were instrumental in the enclosures of Upton in 1773 and of Burford 20 years later, and they were allocated 700 out of 800 acres in Upton and 200 acres in Burford. The costs of enclosure were no doubt met in the hope of increasing income through higher rents, but the family was in severe financial difficulty by the early 19th century. In 1809 a section of the house was demolished and the top storey removed; in 1833 the picture collection was sold and finally four years later Burford Priory was sold to Charles Greenaway of Barrington Grove. He wanted the land but left the house untenanted, and it remained empty and decaying for the rest of the century. Restoration started in 1908 and continued when the tea merchant, E. J. Horniman, bought it. As well as reconstructing the collapsed Elizabethan wing and making some extensions, he was also responsible for restoring several houses in the town. After the Second World War, the Priory once again became a religious establishment, when it was bought by an Anglican closed order, the Community of the Salutation of our Lady.

Two families, of Sheldon and Daston, were involved in complicated manoeuvres concerning Pershore Abbey's Broadway estate. Ralph Sheldon was a major tenant from at least 1533, and in 1538 he was given a lease of part of Broadway, while Anthony Daston in 1535 leased the manor house, gate-house with two little houses within, stables, kitchen and bakehouse, shepherd's house and two sheephouses. In 1540, Philip Hoby, a gentleman of the King's household, disputed Daston's lease, saying that he possessed one made in 1534 to follow the expiry of Daston's. The abbot refused to attend the enquiry, making an excuse of 'infirmities of age', but admitted that there had been another lease, made by the Prior without the consent of the community of Pershore Abbey. Eventually Daston won the case and he then sold the lease to Ralph Sheldon. Meantime Broadway manor had been sold by Queen Mary to William Babington; as Mary was a Roman Catholic and the Babingtons were later implicated in plots against Elizabeth in favour of the deposed Roman Catholic Scots Queen Mary, it seems likely that this Babington was a Roman Catholic, too. Habington, the early historian of Worcestershire, was probably a relation. His name was sometimes written this way and he spent a considerable time in prison because of his Roman Catholic sympathies.

'The Abbot of Pershore was not only Lord of the Manor, but also had here a farm famous for the greatness', Habington wrote; he also said that Anne Daston was mistress of 'Broadway's great farm' throughout a long widowhood. Anne, who was William Sheldon's daughter, had married first Francis Savage, and then Anthony Daston. She was a widow when in 1574 she bought a major part of Broadway from Babington, 2,900 acres, out of 4,700 then in the parish. Three thousand acres in the 16th century was an impressive amount of land, and seems to have been all the southern end of Broadway near the old church. Her son, Walter Savage, lived at Broadway Court. Over the existing gateway are the arms of the three families thus tied together in Broadway's history, Daston, Savage and Sheldon. The rest of

KNIGHTS AND MANOR HOUSES 121

73. Hawling Manor was a Winchcombe Abbey estate and after the monastery was closed, it became a gentleman's residence; the main block is Elizabethan. The north wing (on the right) was added in the 18th century. By the 19th century Hawling Manor was simply a farmhouse and the south end (on the left) was a granary in 1911.

Broadway was bought from Babington in 1576 by Ralph Sheldon and his son-in-law. Sheldon lived in the Westend of Broadway at his death. He sold off a number of houses and plots of land, Habington said in order to create freeholders—there was certainly an unusually large number in Broadway in the 18th century—or it may have been to facilitate enclosure of his land in the Westend.

The 'coat of the monastery' was no longer over Broadway, Habington said, and he regretted that before his death in 1647 this great estate had been split first into two, and then into three. In 1628 the 'great farm' was divided and Spring Hill was sold to Lord Coventry. Broadway Court and Middle Hill remained in the Savage family for another hundred years. In 1724 Middle Hill was sold to William Taylor who built the first mansion there, not far from the old church. The estate returned to the Savage family. They demolished Broadway Court in 1777, by then a very decrepit but ancient house, with a vaulted undercroft probably dating from before the dissolution of Pershore Abbey; they used the materials to build a new mansion at Middle Hill. This was where the book collector Sir Thomas Phillipps lived in the early 19th century. Only the gatehouse next to the old church now remains as the reminder of the once 'great farm' of Broadway.

Spring Hill house is a long way from the centre of Broadway, and in a very secluded position. The house dates from the 18th century, and Capability Brown landscaped the grounds. Broadway Tower is nearby, built by Earl Coventry on the very top of the hill, from where reputedly it is possible to see 13 counties. The hill was called 'the Beacon' and also Barrow Hill, and is likely to have been a site for bonfires which transmitted news such as the sighting of the Spanish Armada. Various dates are given for the tower, 1797, 1798 and 1800; plans drawn up by the architect, James Wyatt, are dated 1794. It was said that the Countess wished to see whether the hilltop could be seen from Croome Court, the family seat near Worcester, and caused a bonfire to be lighted there. The fire being plainly visible, she persuaded the Earl to build the tower. In 1797 fireworks and a bonfire on the hill celebrated a hundred years since the Earldom of Coventry was created, for which the tower was probably planned as a memorial. It also asserted the Earl of Coventry's importance in Broadway. Later the tower housed Sir Thomas Phillipps' private printing press and, when Evans visited it in 1905, it was inhabited by a labouring man and his family. The Springhill estate was sold by Lord Coventry in 1826 to General Lygon. He is reputed to have planted woods 'to represent the positions occupied by the British troops at the Battle of Waterloo'. The largest building in Broadway's main street, the *Lygon Arms*, was part of the Spring Hill estate. The inn was called the *White Hart*, a name that had existed since at least 1532. It was almost cetainly Pershore Monastery's hospice, a fitting building for the reception of important travellers, perhaps even of kings.

Chapter Eight

The Disappearance of the Cotswold Peasant

The peasantry as a major class of small cultivators disappeared before the end of the 18th century and the unusual division of English rural society into landowners, tenant farmers and labourers had developed. The disappearance of the peasant involved also the disappearance of the copyholder. Copyhold, like tithe, is a forgotten institution, abolished by act of parliament in 1926, when surviving copyhold estates were converted into freeholds. In the Cotswolds, copyhold had a significant and long-lasting influence. It was a form of land tenure whose terms and conditions varied from manor to manor according to long-established custom. Early in the 17th century, lords of the manor began to remove copyholds from their estates. Sometimes they gave freehold status to copyholders, as a way of persuading them to agree to exchanges which enabled the lords to consolidate and enclose their lands. Sometimes copyholders were persuaded to accept leases. The open-field system gave copyholders interlocked holdings in the arable fields, and common rights in the meadows and pastures. Gradually holdings were amalgamated into larger farms, so making the open-field system increasingly irrelevant, but farmers were still tied to the cultivation of acre or half-acre strips and to common rights and customs. Enclosure disentangled one owner's land from another's, and allowed more compact farms to be created. It did not end copyhold but it revealed how little survived of the old farming system, though some manor courts still functioned effectively at the end of the 18th century.

Copyhold Tenure
A peasant was essentially a countryman, belonging to the countryside or 'pays'. He was a small farmer, typically cultivating up to thirty acres, a yardland. The peasant produced his own food and had a small surplus to sell in the local market. He also had a large measure of security during his lifetime, and probably his holding passed to his widow and then his heir. Although he was subject to the lord of the manor in some respects, he also had independence, provided he could survive economically. 'Villein' was the usual word decribing a peasant until the 14th century; he was a man belonging to the 'vill', a villager. Villeins had paid rent for their land in the form of labour services, but by 1500 these had been converted to money payments and very few men were still legally unfree. In Gloucestershire, villein status survived longer than in most counties; in Buckland in 1546 there was still one person who was described as 'the lord's bondman', and almost the last legal case of villeinage, tried in the law courts in 1567, concerned a Gloucestershire man. Queen Elizabeth required the remaining bondmen in Gloucestershire to be made free in 1574.

'Husbandmen' were the 16th- and 17th-century successors to the medieval villeins. The constables of Gloucestershire parishes, who in 1608 prepared lists of men able to do military service and stated their occupations, called most farmers 'husbandmen' and used the word 'yeoman' very sparingly. At the beginning of the 17th century, an expert in the common law estimated that a third of the land of England was occupied by 'a very large body of copyholders'; in the Cotswolds they probably occupied between half and two thirds of the land. By the end of the 18th century farms were much larger and husbandmen properly called 'farmers', as they had leases and paid rent for their lands. The term husbandman dropped out of use. A tenant farmer did not have the rootedness that characterised the peasant, but moved up or down the agricultural ladder; if successful, up to a better and larger farm. He was a small capitalist, not concerned with self-sufficiency but with the marketability of his produce.

The Cotswold peasant, villager or husbandman, was a copyholder. Copyhold was conveyed by the manor court. Transactions were recorded on the court rolls; as a skin of parchment was filled, another was stitched to it, and the record was literally rolled up. The rolls were kept safe, as the only record of land ownership for most of the inhabitants, so that both the lord and the manor's inhabitants could jointly consult them; many have been preserved. A copy of the entry on the court roll was the landholder's deed of possession. The

74 & 75. Houses at Old Broadway *(left)* and Didbrook *(right)* display ancient cruck timbers. Although almost all the buildings of the Cotswolds have stone facades, timber-framed construction was probably general until the 16th century. These were previously farmhouses.

Court of Ralph Norwood esquire held there [Taynton] 7 May in the 31st. year of the reign of our most illustrious and most dread prince Henry VIII by the grace of God King of England and France, Defender of the Faith, ruler of Ireland and of adjacent land under Christ, Supreme Head of the English church.

Names of the tenants   William Byrchall   Ralph Taylor etc.

All the above tenants in this full Court attorned and acknowledged themselves tenants of Ralph Norwood esquire, viz. each of them by the payment of one penny and each of them makes fealty to the lord.

To this Court comes Robert Shellvock and produces copy bearing date 4 December in the 30th year of the reign of King Henry VIII [1538] concerning one messuage and half a virgate of land with all appurtenances To hold to the said Robert and Robert his son to the end of their lives and by a heriot when it should arise: 5 shillings [25p]

To this Court ... Robert Stokes ... Copy [1535] concerning one messuage and one virgate of land called Rechynners And one other messuage and one virgate of land called Carters and one Toft and half a virgate of land called Panyers And one Curtilage and erected house and 5 acres of land and part of one virgate called Shawes and Shares To hold to himself and Alice his wife for life of both And a heriot when it shall arise 13 shillings and 4 pence [67p]

To this Court ... Robert Gun ... Copy [1538] concerning the Reversion of one messuage and one virgate of land with appurtenances called Prattes now held by Robert Frebury To hold to himself and Agnes his wife, Alice and Margaret their daughters for life And heriot ...

To this Court ... Richard Gun ... Copy [1538] concerning Reversion of 3 messuages 2 virgates and a half of land with appurtenances called Bankettes and Prattes now held by Clement Michell etc To hold to himself for life And heriot...

To this Court ... William Cowper ... Copy [1496] concerning one messuage and half a virgate of land called Hordes To hold to himself for life And heriot...

76. When Ralph Norwood was given a lease of Taynton in 1539, he immediately held a court at which the tenants of the manor had to accept his authority and also produce their copies of entries in the court rolls. These were then recorded in the new court rolls. The preamble reflects the new supremacy of the King over the Church of England; Tewkesbury Abbey, which controlled Taynton manor, was dissolved a few months later.

distinction between copyhold and freehold land was carefully maintained; in Stanton in the 16th century, a title deed distinguished a small parcel of demesne land from the copyhold. Until the 16th century, a copyholder could only look to the manor court for help in disputes, either between himself and another man in the manor, or between himself and the lord. About 1570, the common law courts began to deal with cases concerning copyhold land, while respecting the peculiarities of custom each manor might have. The copyholder seemed to be freed from control by the lord, but it perhaps gave lords the motive to remove copyhold status, as their authority over it was lessened.

Copyholds were gradually transmuted into 'lifeholds', which were leases naming the present and future holders of the land. The lifehold expired when all those named in the lease were dead. Before this happened, it was usual to negotiate a fresh lease with new 'lives' added to replace any who had died. Very early examples of the lease for lives are found in the Saxon records of the Bishop of Worcester. On Gloucester Abbey's estates in the 13th century men like the miller and the bailiff in Buckland had such leases; they were the first villagers able to pay cash rents because they sold goods or received wages. The number of landholders with these leases slowly expanded. William Marshall thought lifehold 'a remarkable circumstance belonging to the Cotswold townships'; land was 'occupied by tenants for three lives, under renewable leases. A species of tenancy I have not met with, before'. The practice was not quite as unusual as he suggested, since the church continued to use these leases into the 20th century, but there was a difference. Cotswold lifeholds were classed legally with copyholds, and an old 'servile' payment, the heriot, was still required; a lease for life without a heriot was classed as a freehold, and gave its owner the right to vote in parliamentary elections.

Freeholders whose lands were estimated to bring an income of at least two pounds a year had voted in parliamentary elections in the county constituencies since the 15th century. The Parliamentary Reform Act of 1832 gave copyholders the vote if they had land worth £10, so excluding copyhold owners of cottages. A few copyholders and lifeholders were on the first electoral register of 1832. In one third of the places in the Cotswolds there were one or two; in Farmington there were six, in Turkdean and Icomb five, in Sevenhampton and Whittington four. As far as enlarging the number of voters was concerned, the 1832 act had most impact in the Cotswolds by giving the vote to occupiers of property worth £50 a year, which enabled many tenant farmers to vote. The register, together with information about farmers and labourers in the 1831 census, makes clear the disappearance of the peasant and copyholder since the 16th century.

The Custom of the Manor

Seventeen men of Sevenhampton and Brockhampton agreed under oath in 1503 to a written statement of the customs of the manor 'whereof there is no memory to the contrary'. The manor belonged to the Bishop of Hereford; in 1562 it was surrendered to Queen Elizabeth and was subsequently sold. There were two distinct settlements, Sevenhampton and Brockhampton, which had existed at least since the 13th century. Each had two fields, one cultivated and one fallow, and neither could pasture animals on the fields of the other, except in Puckham Wood. Written 'Puccumbe' earlier, the steep sides of the long, narrow valley are wooded still. One horse, four rother beasts and 40 sheep to the yardland could be pastured on the common land. 'Rother' is the Anglo-Saxon word for ox, and the allowance suggests that a yardlander was expected to have four animals for his plough and a horse for carting. The custom of the manor was the same for both settlements.

Richard Wenman signed the statement of customs first; he was probably the bishop's largest tenant, as in 1553 William Wenman leased the manor from the bishop. The first and most important statement was that

> according to the customs of the manor...the lords of the said lordship hath always, no memory to the contrary, granted the copyhold messuages and lands by copy and court roll as well in reversion as possession... which words maketh the tenants an estate of inheritance.

'Reversion' was what happened to the estate after the death of the copyholder and the statement about inheritance was important. If a land-holding passed automatically from father to son, it was close to the modern notion of ownership, and the lord of the manor had little control over it. The Sevenhampton men said that their estates passed 'as at the common law' to the 'son and heir or daughter and heir or next heir in blood', a custom which maintained the integrity of the holding by preventing its division. When a copyhold estate passed to a new owner, the lord was paid a 'fine', which was limited to 'three years' Rent and twenty pence'. A freeholder had to pay 'relief' on taking over his land, which was negotiated anew each time. Heirs or successors to copyhold land also had to pay a heriot, which was the dead man's best beast. The custom known as 'freebench' allowed a widow to occupy a holding for her lifetime. If the lord was cheated of his heriot and fine by the holder selling or letting the holding for more than a year and not informing the lord in the manor court, the copyhold was forfeited. The copyhold was also forfeited if a house was left to decay, so that 'the great timber' was uncovered and 'open to wind and weather'. This custom apparently safeguarded holdings against the pressure of more prosperous farmers wishing to amalgamate them. The customs of the manor of Sevenhampton were very similar in the late 17th century.

The customs of Buckland manor were recorded about 1590. As in Sevenhampton, there were two settlements, Buckland and Laverton, with their own fields. Here the reversion after death was not automatic. It was said that the lord 'may grant' a holding for a man's lifetime, or a man and his son might agree with the lord to hold jointly. The child of a deceased tenant 'ought to have the preferment of the holding'. The fine was negotiated between the lord and his new tenant, so that Buckland's inhabitants seem to have been in a less favourable position than Sevenhampton's. Harrison in his *Description of England* of 1577 wrote about 'the daily oppression of copyholders, whose lords seek to bring their poor tenants almost into plain servitude and misery ... doubling, trebling and now and then seven times increasing their fines'. Harrison also complained that excuses were found to confiscate the copyholder's estate for infringments of manorial practice.

How far back did 'time beyond the memory of man' go? There is no doubt that the villagers of Domesday and the customary tenants of medieval manorial surveys became the copyholders of the 16th century, a transition which Professor Finberg called 'a commonplace of manorial history'. Finberg warned against 'exaggerating the tenacity of local usage'. Customs could change, yet it is surprising that the Bishop of Worcester, after 650 years, had not brought his manors to a common pattern. For example, in Blockley and Withington the custom was to name one copyholder as possessor of land but three 'in reversion'; in Icomb the practice was to name up to three joint possessors and three in reversion. Customs were transmitted orally; Norden in his advice on how to be a good steward of land in 1608 suggested that the manorial customs should be written down. Lords did not always live on their manors, and sometimes villagers may have had the advantage in defining the customs of the manor.

Copyhold to Leasehold
Gloucester Abbey's manor of Buckland was bought by Sir Richard Gresham in 1546, and inherited by his daughter, Christian, who married Sir John Thynne. Buckland remained in the Thynne family's hands until 1799. During these two and a half centuries, a number of surveys were made, the first immediately after Gresham's purchase, but part of the Laverton section is missing. Another survey was made about fifty years after, and a third in 1673. The arable was divided into four fields, described according to the crops growing in each: the barley field, the wheat field, the pulse field and the fallow field, and each farmer had lands in all four. A four-field system, leaving only a quarter of the arable fallow in each year, gave the farmers 50 per cent more land to cultivate than a two-field system. A change from two fields to four may have occurred between the dates when Anglo-Saxon hides and Domesday

ploughs were assessed, and would explain why the manor had 10 hides but 15 ploughs. The four-field system continued until enclosure in 1779.

The manor house was in Buckland itself, surrounded by enclosed lands, including hill pastures behind the house, and the park which an abbot had created for himself on the lower slopes of Burhill. Some of the manor's 204 acres of arable in 1546 was in the open fields, and there were 45 acres of pasture and 48 acres of meadow. James Appery or ap Harry had been Gloucester Abbey's bailiff; in 1546 he had a farmhouse and one yardland in Buckland. The manor had apparently been leased to him, but only to allow him to act as agent in letting it. Mr. Gwente, who had been one of the king's commissioners taking the surrender of the abbey in 1540, was the tenant. He was now obliged to supply Sir John Thynne with a fat boar and 30 capons for 'the capon feast', in the same way as the abbey's chamberlain had been supplied in the 13th century.

In 1546, nearly all the inhabitants of Buckland and Laverton were copyholders. In Buckland there were seven cottage holdings and six farms in 1546, all copyholds. Some cottages had a few strips of arable in the open fields, some had no land at all; these cottage plots were probably where the eight slaves of Domesday had been settled. The six farmers had quarter, half or whole yardland holdings. Burhill was a cow common, and inhabitants could also keep six horses there if farming a whole yardland. A thousand sheep grazed on the Sheephill, 120 to each yardland and the manor farm had 400. Three properties were leaseholds: the manor house itself with its farm; a yardland leased by the bailiff; and the mill. By 1590, the number of leaseholds had increased to five.

Laverton, on the other hand, was a settlement of 22 farmers and in 1590 there was only one cottage. Laverton's farms were generally bigger than Buckland's. Most farmers had 100 or 125 sheep on Laverton's hills, but one man had an extra 200 with a sheephouse—perhaps the village shepherd's holding—making a total of 2,500 sheep. Farmers in the 13th century had been obliged to help wash and shear the abbot's sheep; since then, the manor's flock had probably been divided between the farmers. Twenty-two Laverton farmers in 1590 claimed equal shares in Moormead and the leasow, an Anglo-Saxon word for meadow; it is a striking coincidence that there were 22 Domesday villagers. Moreover, twenty-second shares were still being noted in the 18th century. Apart from the 22 farms, there was one holding of a few acres and a cottage. In total 37 yardlands were accounted for in 1590 in Buckland and Laverton together, and there had been 37 in 1266. In 1590 there were five leaseholds in Laverton, one noted as formerly 'customary' land.

The rural community in Buckland and Laverton between 1590 and 1608 was quite stable. Eighteen of the 23 husbandmen and five of the seven craftsmen named in the 1608 muster list had the same surnames as copyholders in 1590. The five craftsmen lived in Buckland. John Hanks, carpenter, had probably succeeded Henry Hanks, cottager, and Ambrose Mansell, miller, had succeeded Thomas Mansell; Richard Walker, tailor, was the holder of a quarter yardland in 1590, and Thomas Hughes, slater, and John Wilson, labourer, were cottagers in 1590. The steward of Gloucester Abbey who surveyed Buckland in the 13th century would have found the social structure of the manor in 1608 familiar.

By 1673, a major change had occurred. Many of the former copyholds had become leaseholds, and most copyholders no longer lived in the manor; few of the inhabitants paying tax on a hearth in 1671 were in the survey of 1673. In the early 18th century, concentration of ownership is apparent, a change which would inevitably lead to the end of the open-field system. Joseph Gloucester *alias* Wakeman or Warkman leased five other tenements in 1731 in addition to his family holding; an ancestor, Richard Gloucester *alias* Warkman, had been

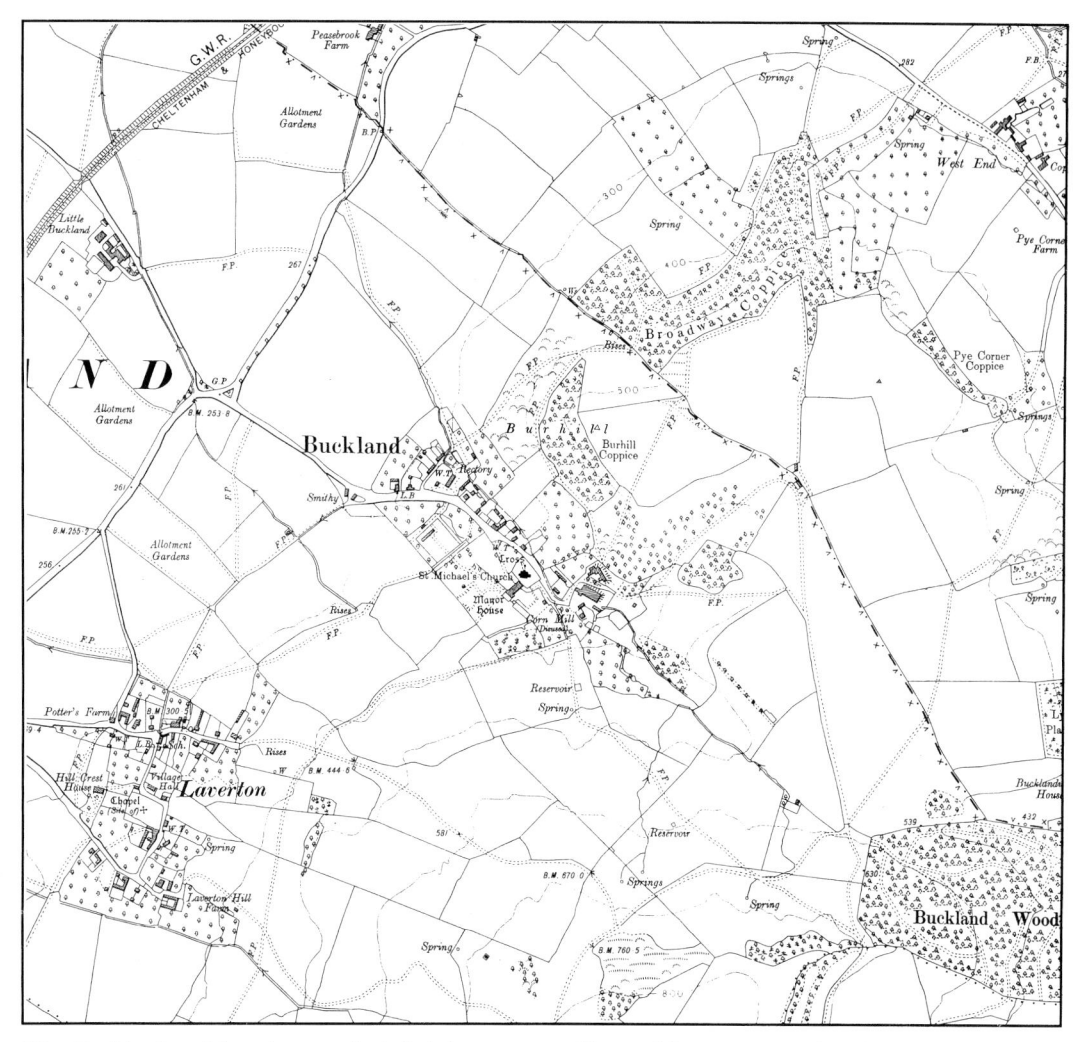

77. Buckland parish and manor included the separate village of Laverton; the site of the chapel was marked on the Ordnance Survey map of 1924. Peasebrook Farm on the boundary with Broadway in the north retains the name of a brook mentioned in a charter of 972.

a copyholder in Laverton in 1546, the *alias* perhaps indicating that Richard had been a monk of Gloucester. The advantage of leasehold over copyhold to the lord of the manor is obvious; Joseph Wakeman paid a fine of £1,890, and sums up to £550 were paid by other new leaseholders in the 18th century but the traditional copyholders paid less than £50 for new copies.

The act of parliament for the enclosure of all the common fields, some 1,800 acres out of the total of 2,200 acres, was passed in 1779. It stated that Lord Viscount Weymouth was the lord of the manor and owner of all the lands and grounds in the parish, apart from the rector's glebe. This was only true in a strict legal sense. The preamble continued: 'several other persons, by virtue of leases, are entitled to certain parts of the open common fields and common meadows, which are divided into, and together with the homestead thereto are called, Livings and parts of Livings.' Traditional copyholders were thus classed as leaseholders.

There were 13, and most did not live in Buckland. A number of the former farmhouses were now cottages for labourers. James Sperry had the Wakeman estate and was the largest landholder in Buckland after the lord of the manor; he was allotted about one-fifth of the land. Lord Viscount Weymouth's own share was over a third, and he had the old-enclosed lands of the manor in Great and Little Buckland Farms.

When the estate was sold in 1799 to Thomas Phillipps, there were 14 leaseholders and 23 copyhold cottages or houses. In 1831, there were 12 farmers, 10 of them tenants, employing 68 labourers. Three small-holdings survived, but in 1832 only two copyholders were entitled to vote. The Phillipps family bought up properties where possible and eventually owned almost the whole parish. Later in the 19th century, the family built new model cottages for the labourers. In 1952, about 1,400 acres and six farms were sold, including nearly all the village of Laverton and also Little Buckland. The biggest farm, Laverton Meadow, of 490 acres, had been built at some distance from the village after enclosure, and so had Bowmeadow Farm, 151 acres. Potter's Farm and Top Farm were the only two left out of the original 22 in Laverton village. Many of the tenants had the opportunity to become freeholders of their properties. The estate foreman and the stud groom, however, were given life tenancies, 'in appreciation of long service', thus showing an advantage of copyhold to a man with insufficient capital to buy a cottage and land.

On the other side of the Cotswolds, a parallel development to Buckland's took place in Icomb. After Worcester Priory was dissolved, Church Icomb was taken over by the crown but the Bishop of Worcester quickly acquired it again. The estate was surveyed in 1650 because, following the abolition of bishops by Parliament, their estates were to be sold. All the land was copyhold. Only a poor, ruinous cottage was held 'at the will of the lord'. The custom of Church Icomb was that copyholds were granted for two or three lives in possession and two or three in reversion. Only one copy in 1650 named three people as possessors, Thomas, Robert and Anthony Mathews, and their three young sons as the heirs. In most cases, two possessors are named, often a man and his wife, and two heirs. The reversion could be altered during the lifetime of the partners; Thomas Sandell's copy in 1593 had named two sons but in 1627 the sons surrendered the copy and another two were substituted. It was also the custom for widows to have freebench so long as they did not remarry. Fifteen separate holdings were recorded, which ranged from a few odd half acres to one of about 100 acres; nine of the copyholders or their families probably lived in Icomb 16 years later. With the Rector's glebe, there was a total of 16 yardlands, corresponding with the four ploughs of Domesday; there was no manor farm. Amalgamation of traditional holdings was already evident; the Mathews's had two while William Hodson 'in right of his wife Anne' had three.

The custom of the manor must have created great social cohesion in the small community of Church Icomb. It was natural for brothers, husband and wife, or children, to be named as the joint lives, but the possible connections of the six people who could be involved in one holding were extensive, and reached well beyond the nuclear family. One network in the village in 1650 linked together five separate holdings and three distinct families. George Bryan the elder held a yardland and house with his two sons Thomas and Richard. Thomas and another brother George held the copyhold of a second single yardland and house; George's two sons and a daughter were to inherit this. However, George together with John Roberts was co-heir to a yardland and a quarter held by George and Thomas Morrys, perhaps in-laws; George Bryan had married Margery Roberts in 1614. John Roberts and his brother held another half yardland and house, and living in Icomb also were Anthony and John Morrys with three-quarters of a yardland. Such a network of relationships must have made the farmers co-operative in attitude to each other. The ability to alter or add to the copies meant that there was rarely a complete break in the tenure of the copyholds.

After the Civil War, bishops were restored to the Church of England, and in 1662 the Bishop of Worcester recovered Church Icomb. Between this date and a survey of the manor in 1771, a great change had occurred. As in Buckland, farmhouses had become cottages, and there were fewer but larger farms. There were nine copyholders and the rector, but only three farmers. One man, Thomas Hambidge, with Widow Hambidge, had one third of the land; his family had lived in Icomb since 1666. Eight holdings were occupied by George Bryan, whose name is a familiar one from the 17th-century survey. There was one other small farm and six cottages. The Dean and Chapter of Worcester explicitly tried in 1771 to convert their copyholds to leases. 'Ordered that in Copyholds when three lives are dropped, fresh copies shall not be granted except in houses.' They decided that when Estates 'fell in', because all named heirs had died, they 'should be re-granted on Lease for 21 years'. The survival of copyhold then depended on whether there were heirs to carry it on. Heriots were used to maintain control of copyholds. Bailiffs were ordered to seize heriots and take them off the premises, and not to give them back until an agreement had been made with the lord. When estates were let, a pledge or bond was required for payment of heriots.

The Dean and Chapter did not enclose Church Icomb's open fields for another 40 years. The act of parliament was passed in 1809, dealing with 500 acres, virtually the whole parish, and the new enclosures were confirmed in 1813. Fifteen yardlands held by five men and the rector's glebe were still distinguishable. George Hambidge was allotted 145 acres; sometime later in the century a member of the family became the owner of Icomb Place. One other allotment was nearly as large and included 'Bryan's' holding; 70 acres were allotted to Thomas West for 'Mathew's', and there were two other small allotments. In the 1831 census, three farmers, all tenants, and 29 labourers, were living in Church Icomb. Two farmers and two labourers lived in Westward Icomb, in Gloucestershire. Copyholds had survived enclosure, as in Buckland, and five copyholders were on the electoral register in 1832 but they were neither farmers nor resident in Icomb.

The balance of advantage in the change to leases was with the lord, but there were reasons why some copyholders agreed to the change. The lease could specify to whom the holding should pass instead of being bound by the custom of the manor. A lease was also a legal document, recognised in the courts rather earlier than the copy, and might seem more reliable than manorial custom. For the lord, the lease gave opportunity for raising the fine paid on purchase of a holding. The tendency to increase the fine militated against a small copyholder and encouraged the transfer of the holding to someone with more capital, possibly no longer the occupier of the farm. What had once been effectively ownership was reduced to leasehold, and the ability of the lord to see himself as sole owner was encouraged, and so to ask the highest rent possible for the land. Maitland, a professor and historian of English law, wrote at the end of the 19th century that the legal concept of ownership of land had in recent times grown 'more intense', and his comment seems to be illustrated by the experience of the Cotswold copyholder.

Copyhold to Freehold
There is an interesting group of Cotswold villages where copyholds were converted into freeholds around 1600; it includes Great Barrington, Bledington, Bourton on the Water, Broadway, Mickleton, Naunton, Oddington, Stanton, Great, Little and Wyck Rissington, Donnington and Maugersbury in the parish of Stow on the Wold and Lower Swell. In all these places, the

lords of the manors gave up their rights to small payments from the copyholders of the area. It is notable that these were nearly all former monastic estates. The monasteries were conservative landlords; far from being rapacious, they probably maintained the bulk of their rural tenants on their small farms. Some of the new men, who bought manors from the crown after the dissolution of the monasteries, then made a quick financial return by dismembering the manors and selling the manorial rights. The government's campaign against enclosure in the 16th century also led to a search for an acceptable method of achieving it.

At Mickleton, the motive for turning the copyholders into freeholders was certainly to promote enclosure. Mickleton was a large and valuable manor, with parts of Clopton and Hidcote also within its jurisdiction. It had belonged to Eynsham Abbey, and the monastery's own farm was a third of the arable at the time of Domesday and by 1291 was larger still. In an enquiry made in 1572, it was stated that there were seven freehold properties, 29 holdings with 30½ yardlands held 'by copy of court roll for terms of lives according to the customs of the manor', 13 cottages, and four yardlands belonging to the rectory, a total of 50 landholders. Sir Edward Fisher purchased Mickleton in 1612; he immediately 'did greatly labour and much endeavour to enclose the manor'. He wanted to disentangle his own lands from the common fields, and they were sufficiently extensive to make it worth the sacrifice of the manorial rents. A draft deed of 1612 states that

> Sir Edward Fisher and the Tenants and inhabitants being landholders in Mickletom and Francis Welles vicar hath agreed and mutually consented to improve and inclose and to hold in severalty diverse parcels of the lands and tenements being in the manor of Mickleton now lying dispersed scattered here and there in the fields of Mickleton ...

The larger landholders were willing to agree to the reorganisation of their fields, particularly if they gained the status of freeholder, but smaller landholders were reluctant and were the cause of a battle between the vicar and Sir Edward Fisher in the Exchequer Court a few years later. The story was that Fisher

> did endeavour to inclose and improve the said manor, thereby to treble his own benefit, and did treat and deal with the tenants of the said manor to that purpose and finding that he could not effect the said inclosure without the consent of the vicar and of some other poor men who were to sustain loss by the said inclosure and who did oppose the same, the said Sir Edward Fisher began then to treat with Francis Welles for his good will...

Fisher offered to increase the amount of vicarage land, to raise the vicar's income, and to give 33 acres of land for the benefit of the poor, who were going to lose their common grazing for cows on the Upper Field as a result of enclosure, and more important their fuel from 'the great quantities of bushes and furzes' growing there. 'Upon which fair promises' the enclosure went ahead, and nine or ten people took possession of the former vicarage lands; even before the draft deed of 1612, the new lots 'were already appointed and marked out' and the vicarage lands were hedged with blackthorn at Sir Edward Fisher's expense.

Fisher then refused to honour his promises; he even turned the vicar's cattle off his promised meadow and let the land to two other men. Fisher's defence was that he now found the manor's lands were less than he had been told, and he would not honour his bargain unless his lands were increased; it seems he suspected, perhaps rightly, that the villagers had used the enclosure to enlarge their holdings and exploit areas of uncertainty. For his part, he said, 'he will be content if all were again cast abroad in common'. Eleven men gave evidence on the vicar's side, and suggested that Sir Edward Fisher had actually increased the value of

THE DISAPPEARANCE OF THE COTSWOLD PEASANT

his manor by 500 marks (£167) a year. It also emerged that 16 acres had been withheld from their allotments in order to provide for the poor, so Fisher's real contribution was actually only 17 acres. The poor did eventually get the promised 33 acres. A century later there were 54 freeholders in Mickleton, an unusually large number, which closely matches the total of landholders in 1572. At the same time, there were 72 households altogether, and by 1711 there were 83, so that there were landless inhabitants in Mickleton, whose numbers grew in the 17th century. Mickleton's specialisation as a market-gardening parish, already evident in the early 17th century, was probably encouraged by the creation of these many small freeholds.

At Stanton, there was a partial enclosure as a result of turning copyholds into freeholds. The former Winchcombe Abbey manor was bought by Thomas Dolman, a clothier of Newbury in Berkshire, in 1558; his will of 1571 left his 'lordship and manor of Stanton in the county of Gloucester' to his son, Mathias, who was a haberdasher and citizen of the City of London. Another son, John, had the advowson of Stanton and Snowshill. Soon after inheriting Stanton, Mathias Dolman sold off the manor in parcels; each copyholder bought a share of the manor's lands in proportion to his existing customary holding, and also the manorial jurisdiction over it, so creating mini-manors. No lord of the manor could therefore be named by John Smyth at the head of the village muster list in 1608. Parsons noted 'No court or Manor since Mathias Dolman sold his Right to the tenants, who having leases for lives were made freeholders by him in Queen Elizabeth's reign'. Documents exist relating to the purchase of a modest holding in 1584 by Richard Wright. He bought three small lots: the house in which his father lived, with a close, a quarter of a yardland, and meadow and pasture for one horse and 20 sheep; a second quarter yardland and pasture rights for two oxen; and a cottage, three more arable ridges and pasture for a horse, in all amounting to eight acres. He paid £9 on the sealing of the indenture, and then had to pay a further £40 in four instalments, over two years; the money was paid at Mathias Dolman's house in St Andrew's Undershaft in the City of London and two of the receipts still exist. Richard Wright had doubled his holding and now had a whole yardland. His history illustrates that a modest smallholder could find money to buy land. The sale of wool could have provided such cash.

Rudder named five men involved in the partition of the manor: William Jackson *alias* Booth, Nicholas Izod, Thomas Warren, Nicholas Kirkham and Humphrey Wright, and said there were also others. The five were presumably the larger farmers and copyholders. Eight estates at enclosure in 1774 had shares in the 'waste', the odd, unclaimed pieces of land in the manor, suggesting there had been at least eight purchasers of the

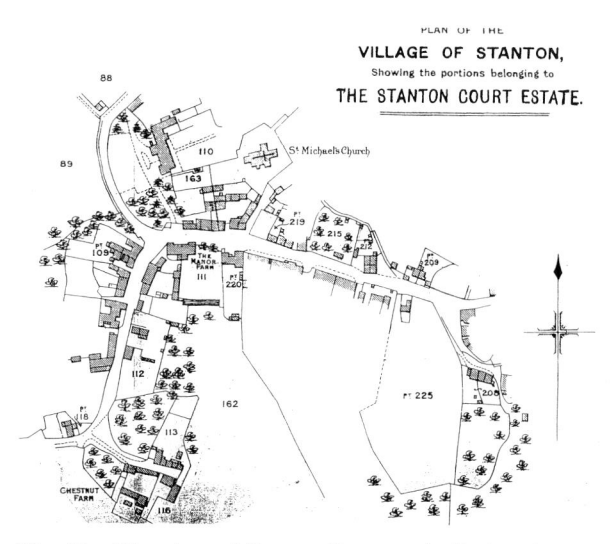

78. The Wynniatts of Stanton Court gradually bought farms and farmhouses in Stanton until they owned most of the village, as shown on this map prepared in 1906 when the estate was sold to Mr. Philip Stott. Number 109 is Warren House or Manor (illustrated on page 134) 110 is Stanton Court (illustrated on page 137), and the Manor Farm is number 111 (plate XXIII).

manorial rights. The list of able-bodied men in 1608 included several of the purchasers. Nicholas Izod and Thomas Warren were described as yeomen and Nicholas Kirkham as a husbandman. At least five men, called either Jackson or Booth, some described as yeomen and some as husbandmen, could have been related to William Jackson *alias* Booth, who had died in 1602. Three other yeomen lived in Stanton, two called Izod, and there were three more husbandmen, a total of 15 farmers. A smith, a weaver, three masons and three labourers were also listed in 1608.

Stone-masons were busy in Stanton about the turn of the 17th century; the new status of freeholder gave confidence to the former Stanton copyholders, and stimulated the rebuilding of their farmhouses along the village street. Some have date stones: Warren House or Manor is the earliest; the initials of Thomas Warne or Warren and the date 1577 are carved over the doorway and inside a ceiling incorporates the family coat-of-arms; it was built very soon after Dolman's sale of shares of the manor. Other houses are dated 1604, 1615 and 1618. The prosperity of the village can be gauged from the rector's list of households in 1623; 17 out of the total of 37 had female servants living in, and 12 households also had men servants, who mainly worked on the farms. The rector, Henry Izod, and his wife, had three female servants; four more households of Izods all had female servants, too. Thomas Warren and Thomas Booth shared a house, and had three men and two women servants; Richard Jackson father and son lived together with two adult sons and four daughters; this extended family was probably large enough to work the holding.

Thomas Jackson *alias* Booth sold his two yardland holding in 1658 to Richard Ingles of Dumbleton, gentleman. It consisted of 120 ridges or selions of arable land, with common grazing rights for six oxen and eight horses, a messuage and dovehouse, and 'pews, seats and kneeling places in the parish church now used by the said Thomas Jackson *alias* Booth, Elizabeth his wife or any of their servants'. Richard Ingles came to live in Stanton. His house had a hall, a parlour with some mahogany tables and chairs, a dairy, and buttery, pantry, brewhouse and kitchen; upstairs there was a bed-chamber with garrett above, servants' chamber and chambers over the brewhouse and pantry. The inventory, made in 1684 following his death, shows him actively concerned in husbandry, with corn and malt in the house, carts and ploughs, harrows and harness, seven horses, four pigs, 18 cows and 104 sheep. Significantly he had an income of £120 a year from rents, and this may have been the distinguishing mark

79. Warren House or Manor in Stanton with a wing endways to the street, is dated 1577 but is a medieval house; the decorated doorway is on the north side. It could be called a 'manor house' after Winchcombe Abbey's estate was dismembered in the Elizabethan period and the leaseholders each bought shares of the manor.

of the gentleman. The value of his possessions amounted to £407, quite a lot compared with many husbandmen but not extremely wealthy. The Ingles family continued in Stanton until the end of the 18th century, and on enclosure Mrs. Ingles received an allotment of 70 acres of land; she was also given 10 perches as compensation for the loss of her share in the 'waste'.

The Izod family were probably connected with Stanton Court from at least the mid-16th century, when John Izod was Winchcombe Abbey's bailiff in Stanton. This was the manor house. It has been suggested that Warren House was the original manor-house, but this misinterprets the history of the village; landholders could call their houses 'the manor' after Dolman's sales. The Izod family came from Ireland in the mid-15th century and quickly established themselves in Stanton, Buckland, Chipping Campden and Toddington. Maurice Izod, husbandman, who died in 1585, was a significant landowner; he left the main part of his estate to his son, Nicholas, whom Rudder named as a purchaser of part of Stanton manor. Some land was left to two sons, William the elder and William the younger; William the elder also lived at the Court and inherited a desk in the hall where it had to remain, and his land reverted to Nicholas after his death. William the younger shared a house with his brother, John, who had two yardlands; he was given 10 sheep 'taking them as they shall run out of the pen'. If John would not share his house then he was to endow his brother with the tithes which his father owned. Winchcombe Abbey had appropriated to its own use three quarters of the great tithes of Stanton, leaving only one quarter to the Rector; the Izod family, as the tithe owners after the dissolution would be wealthier than any other in the village. Stanton Court might consequently be called the 'Rectory'; it seems to be the building illustrated in Lysons' *Antiquities of Gloucestershire*, before the front was modernised in the 17th century. Both Francis and William Izod were taxed by Charles I in 1631 for ability to sustain knighthood.

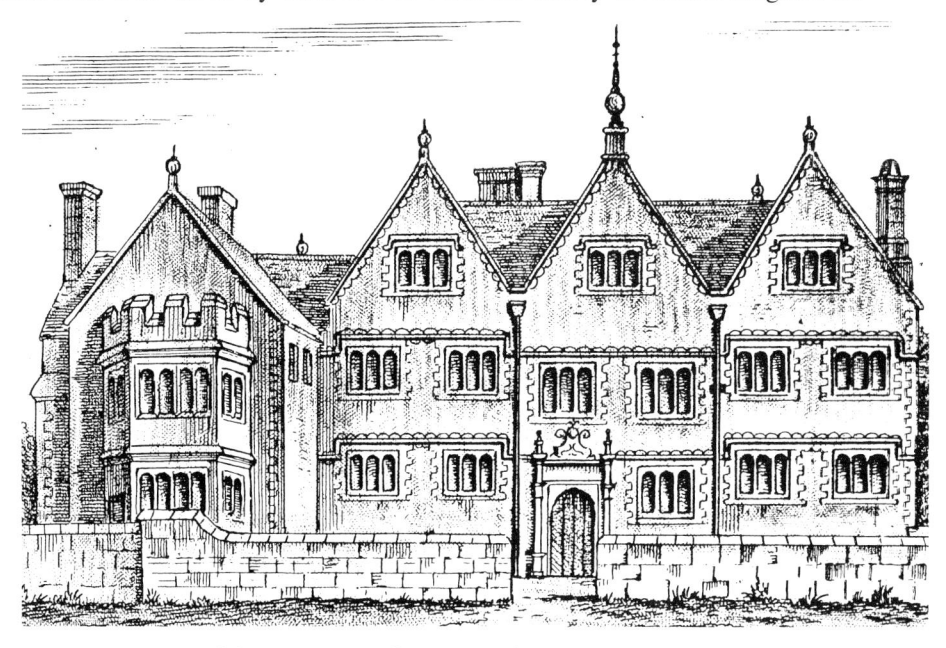

80. An etching of Stanton rectory from Lysons' *Antiquities of Gloucestershire* (1803). If the rectory is compared with Stanton Court (number 81) it appears to be the same house before the two square towers were added and the entrance moved. The drawing has an indication of the cartouche with Wynniatt's arms over the door (number 82). Lysons made the etchings himself, but might have worked from an existing drawing.

Henry Izod had the advowson of Stanton in 1623, and presented himself to the living, remaining there until his death in 1650. He was a meticulous recorder of his public and private affairs; he listed the parish's householders as soon as he became rector, in order to collect the pennies due from each at Easter. The volume he kept was bound in with one kept by a later rector, the two together giving many insights into Stanton life in the 17th century. Richard Parsons, chancellor of the diocese of Gloucester from 1677 to 1711, married Mary Izod, and so was particularly well-informed about Stanton. Dr. Parsons was called in on several occasions to give judgements in tithe disputes, and he gave a pulpit to the church. A notebook contains his collection of material for a history of the county, which he allowed Atkyns to use. He described Stanton as 'one of the neatest villages in the kingdom', consisting 'generally of good stone houses in a small street'; on the hill there were 'quarries of white stone fit for building'. There had obviously been a transformation since the mid-15th century when it was reported to Winchcombe Abbey that 'the village is in ill-condition owing to delapidations and neglect of repairs'.

Izods continued to live in Stanton for the rest of the 17th century. Subsequently Izod property was left to Wenman Wynniatt, whose coat-of-arms is now displayed over the entrance to Stanton Court. In the mid-18th century, Reginald Wynniatt inherited all the Izod estate and his son, who became rector of Stanton in 1771, 'has lately purchased several others in the same place, so that he is now possessed of the greater part of the parish'. The rector eventually acquired the advowson of his own living, exchanging one in Oxfordshire with a kinsman, and he owned the tithes, and at least seven holdings in addition to his 'patrimony'. This enabled him to pursue the enclosure of Stanton, for which he paid nearly two thirds of the costs. An act of parliament was passed in 1774. Reginald Wynniatt had 149 acres of enclosed but tithable land, including Shenborough Hill; 290 acres was allotted to him for common lands and pastures; and a further 150 acres was land in lieu of tithes. It was no burden to him to give up some land in order to end tithe payments. With the rectory lands, Wynniatt controlled nearly all the parish. There were 10 other small owners of land, with 172 acres between them, but only four actually lived in Stanton. The character of the village had changed significantly since the early 18th century, when more than half of the 49 households had been freeholders; in 1832 there were 11 freeholders but 60 families, and only three small, family farms survived, while seven farmers employed on average six labourers each. Stanton's character is largely the result of the two centuries when it was truly the village of independent yeomen farmers.

Abolition of the Open Fields

Agreements between landholders had whittled down the amount of common land in the Cotswolds, but at the beginning of the 18th century, three quarters of the parishes were still largely open. During the following 120 years, the authority of Parliament was used to enclose the fields. A private act was obtained for each parish, or occasionally for two parishes together. The act for the enclosure of Farmington, in 1713, was one of the first in the country. A few were passed in the following decades: Upper Swell in 1724, Little Rissington in 1726, Wyck Rissington in 1729, Upper and Lower Slaughter in 1731, Hawling in 1755, Little Barrington in 1759 and Snowshill in 1760. After 1760 the pace of parliamentary enclosure quickened; at least 28 acts for Cotswold parishes were passed in the next 40 years, and 11 more between 1800 and 1821. The number of acts is an indication of the enormous change which was accomplished in about seventy years. Enclosure made large changes in the countryside. Hundreds of stone walls were built and and hedges planted, to mark off the separate lots of land, and subsequently to divide them for more efficient management of

81. Stanton Court was a wealthy yeoman's house at the beginning of the 17th century; the Izod family could have accepted the status and obligations of knighthood but chose to remain farmers. In the following two centuries the house was enlarged and by 1800 it was recognised as a gentleman's residence.

82. The arms above the door of Stanton Court are of the Wynniatt and Phillipps families; the stone cartouche was found in the grounds in the early 20th century and was re-erected.

livestock. Sweeping changes in land-use also followed enclosure; the old downs were ploughed, but some arable became permanent grassland.

Parliament's authority was needed for three reasons. One was to extinguish common grazing rights over all the land concerned. A second reason was to overcome the customary rights of copyholders; they were not classed as owners, but they could not be ignored and Marshall considered them the main obstacle to enclosure. The acts also made void leases for limited terms of years and for 'rack rents'; sometimes the commissioners fixed the new rents. A third reason for requiring parliament's authority was to include church glebes in the reorganisation and to extinguish tithes.

It was expensive to get the lawyers to draft a bill, to ensure sufficient support for the bill in the House of Commons and the House of Lords, and to pay the commissioners. Commissioners were chosen who did not have direct interests in the place concerned. They were empowered to order surveys of the lands, they accepted or rejected claims to land, they altered the course of roads and water courses to make them more convenient, they created the new physical pattern of land-holding. It cost just over £500 to enclose 832 acres at Cutsdean in 1777, three fifths of which was paid by one principal landowner. Amongst the expenses itemised in the commissioners' accounts, the largest item, £177, was for securing the passing of the act itself; £77 was paid to a solicitor, £18 to a printer, £40 for a witness who attended parliament to prove that what the bill said was true, and £24 to a gentleman who lent money and arranged to alter the wording of the bill. The clerk who wrote the final award on seven skins of parchment received £1 11s. 5d. The rector's allotments were fenced at a cost of £44, paid by all the other landowners in the parish, as was usual. The two commissioners' own expenses were modest; £30 for their entertainment and fees of 17 and 18 guineas. The labourers who showed the commissioners round the lands earned 18s. 6d. (92½ p) and were given another four shillings (20p) for digging to find stone beds for use in making walls and roads. A farmer spent a day with his plough-team cutting a new road for 11 shillings (55p) and a carpenter put up signboards and supplied stakes to mark out roads and allotments for £2. Larger and more complicated enclosures naturally cost more.

Early enclosure acts were simply confirmations of arrangements already made. Farmington's act in 1713 for 'Parting and Enclosing two great open Common fields, the One called the North-Field, and the other the South-Field, and a large open Greensward Common Down', 1,985 acres in all, referred to the new blocks of land 'now Bounded and lately Set out'. The Right Honourable Richard, Earl of Scarborough, was lord of the manor, and owned two thirds of the common fields. There were only two other sizeable estates, one a freehold, allocated 453 acres, and the other a leasehold, allocated 174 acres. The origin of the second freehold was no doubt the division of Farmington into two knights' fees in the early medieval period, and one reason for obtaining an act of parliament was because the owner was an infant; his uncle and guardian was empowered to sell the estate and substitute for it the manor of Harnhill in the south of the county. The act does not say who owned Harnhill or to whom the Farmington freehold was to be sold, but it may be presumed it was the Earl of Scarborough. The leasehold estate of Thomas Bedwell was made freehold; Bedwell's Farm was one of six in Farmington in 1825 but by then it, too, belonged to the lord of the manor. Six cottages were the property of lifeholders, and their leases were specifically left undisturbed by the act. They were the predecessors of the six lifeholders on the electoral register in 1832. The two great arable fields were commented on by observers of the time; although divided into numerous furlongs, there seem to have been few hedges or walls. For the next 60 years the countryside retained an open, treeless character:

The face of this part of the country is turgid, uneven, and almost wholly destitute of plantations, in which last particular, there is certainly great room for improvements. The soil produces very good corn, to which the greater part is appropriated.

The 'Greensward Common Downs' had been ploughed, which was a common result of enclosure. The population of the parish doubled during the 18th century, and in 1825 there were 34 cottages. In 1831, five tenant farmers employed 46 labourers.

Upper Swell's enclosure act of 1724, and Wyck Rissington's of 1729, also confirmed previous agreements. At Swell, only the lady of the manor, Elizabeth Rushout, and the rector were said to have common grazing rights and the act confirmed the surrender by the rector of his lands and tithes. In 1695 there had been 11 copyholders in Upper Swell, but the act made no mention of them; the rector was the only freeholder in 1832, and there were three tenant farmers. At Wyck Rissington, the manor seems to have been divided between the farmers before 1712, allowing the manor's own land to be consolidated in the north of the parish round Wyck Hill; the act confirmed the enclosures already made in this area. Completion of the enclosure, of 30 yardlands out of 58, held by the village's 15 freeholders, was to be carried out by commissioners. Wyck Rissington is unusual in the Cotswolds, with cottages and houses round a wide green. The act referred to the common land in the village street, and transferred it to the village proprietors, but cottages on the common were given to the use of the poor. Seven smallholders of one yardland, and one of half a yardland, were protected by the act, which required that each should be given not more than three separate pieces of land, with one piece of at least eight acres near the house. There were also five larger holdings of two to three yardlands, the rector's three yardlands of glebe, and College Farm, owned by Oxford University, of six yardlands. Only two small farms survived to 1831, and six tenant farmers employed on average eight labourers each. The Hope family, holders of five and a half yardlands in 1729, still owned a house in Wyck Rissington in 1832, but by 1868 the Wyck Hill estate owned nearly all the parish.

The enclosure of Upper and Lower Slaughter in 1731 completed the physical separation of the two manors which had been created before the time of Domesday. Although there was a parish boundary, the lands of the manors were still partly intermingled, there were no hedges or walls separating them in the open fields, and the grazing rights were shared: the sheep of both manors grazed the fallows, and while Lower Slaughter's sheep spent the summer on Upper Slaughter's Downs—Wagborough Down towards Harford and Upper Down in the north of the parish—Upper Slaughter's horses and cows pastured on the Marsh in Lower Slaughter. Whereas half Upper Slaughter had been permanent pasture, the downs were ploughed after enclosure; 'arable far exceeds pasture and meadow', the Rector said in 1832. Until the mid-19th century the farms were in the village centre and only one, Kirkham Farm, was built on the eastern edge of the parish. Hill Farm and Wales Barn have since been built closer to their fields, and Manor Farm was built in order to remove the buildings from the vicinity of the Old Manor House. In Lower Slaughter, however, the opposite process took place and some of the open fields were put down to grass, while 50 acres were planted with woodland. Dairying became important here.

A very careful written schedule and map of Hawling were made for William Wyndham, lord of the manor, in 1748, seven years before the enclosure act. Ferdinando Stratford of London established ownership of all but three of the 1,281 strips of land which were distributed through 75 furlongs, grouped into three fields. Rather under half of the parish was in common field at that date. Even after enclosure, Hawling Scrubs and Hawling Downs

83. The farmhouse at Little Rissington, now called Manor Cottages, had seven hearths in 1672 and was the largest house in the village, after the manor house near the church had been demolished. It was probably built after the copyholder became a freeholder. The house was divided in the mid-19th century. Dawber used it as one of his examples of Cotswold vernacular architecture.

84. College Farm, Wyck Rissington, belonged to Oxford University and at enclosure was one of the larger farms in the parish; the substantial farmhouse reflects this.

remained common. The Scrubs was a detached, 43-acre piece of woodland in Roel, which supplied the commoners of Hawling with firewood. Wyndham took this 'in hand' soon after the enclosure and, until 1808 at least, a small sum of money was paid to three copyholders as compensation for their 'firebote'. The Downs, 125 acres, also remained common land at that time; four farmers, with 99-year leases in place of former copies, had rights of pasture but by 1821 the Downs, too, had become enclosed arable land. In 1808, the three principal farms were the manor itself, Middle Farm and The Lodge, all owned by William Wyndham; all were large, the Manor farm about 800 acres. New House Farm was created about 1821. Some copyholders existed in 1808 but there were none on the electoral register in 1832, though there were quite a large number of copyhold cottages in Hawling. Four tenants farmed the whole parish and manor, and each employed on average 11 labourers.

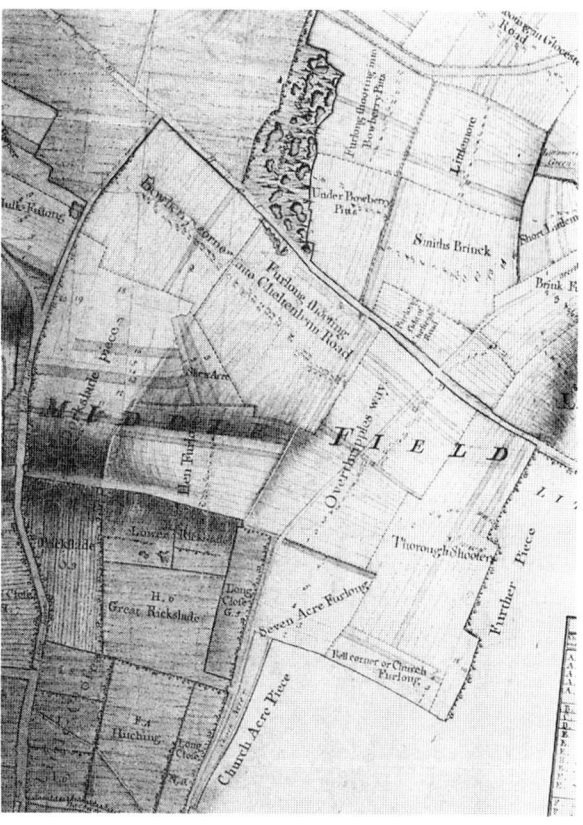

85. Ferdinando Stratford surveyed Hawling's open fields in 1748. The extract from his map shows the aptly-named Skew Acre, divided into three strips, and the grouping of numbers of furlongs and strips into the 'Middle Field'.

Campden Manor Courts

In Campden, three quarters of the parish was still 'in common' at the end of the 18th century. Records of courts for the three tithings of Broad Campden, Berrington, and Westington and Combe, held on 25 October 1782, were preserved by the Cotterell family, yeomen farmers of Broad Campden; Edward Cotterell was one of the few freeholders involved in its enclosure in 1799. A connection with Sir Thomas Phillipps contributed to their preservation, in Middle Hill bindings. Edward Cotterell kept similar records for Hidcote where he also owned land. All three courts reveal the essential cooperation which the open-field system demanded.

Meetings at Broad Campden, 'to settle business for the use of the town', could be called by the constable 'at three days' notice', and decisions were by 'a majority of voices'. A sequence of farming operations was set out, starting with 'haining the hill'. 'Hain' was an old Norse word, commonly used in Gloucestershire for fencing. Hurdles were set up to contain each man's livestock within his part of the pasture; cattle were not turned on to the hill until it was done; pigs could go up there one week later, but had to be ringed. Cows and horses could go up on St Andrew's Day, New Style (30 November); the fences were to be put onto Sedgecombe and the Clover Hill at Old Candlemas (14 February). The change in the calendar in 1752, bringing England into line with the Gregorian calendar of the continent, had meant that Lady Day (25 March), Michaelmas (29 September), Candlemas (2 February), and other church festivals were effectively 11 days earlier than they used to be; the English calendar had jumped from 2 September to 14 September in 1752. For the farming seasons, this often meant New Style festival dates were too early, hence the use of Old Style. At Old Lady Day each farmer was to mound from Upper Wall to Northwick Wall, according to the amount of land he held. 'Mounding' was another word common in Gloucestershire, for walling, hedging or banking. When Broad Campden farmers decided to mound Sedgecombe Plain by Old May Day or Westington and Combe's farmers to mound the West Hill within a fortnight, and that the mounds should stay until the wheat was sown, it must have meant temporary earth balks or ridges to mark each man's land.

Farmers agreed when fields were to be ploughed and what crops were to be sown: clover from Witherset Hedge to Sedgecombe Plain, peas from the top of Wheeler's Gore to Lower Hall, vetches on Staple Cop and Walk Edge. A farmer could grow different crops from the standard wheat, barley and pulse, but if so had 'to turn' on his own ground; in other words, he was required not to swing the plough or drill so as to spoil a neighbour's arable strips. Agreements also concerned the common grazing. In Berrington the sheep could graze or 'break' the pulse stubble three days after harvest, the barley stubble on 22 October and the wheat stubble on 2 November; the pulse stubble in Westington was broken at Stow Fair. Stow Fair (13 October) was a crucial date in the Cotswold farming year; in Westington, lambs counted as sheep for pasturing from then on and so were included in the stint or allowance. No one farmer was permitted to steal a march on the others and get better feed for his animals by being earlier onto a field. The number of animals was specified and varied at different times of the year. In Broad Campden a shepherd for the Low Field was employed by the village collectively, each man paying according to the size of his holding, and a bull or bulls was provided collectively in all three tithings. Furze was cut from the Bratches in Berrington by the tithing man but paid for by the farmers. 'Bratches' was a common field-name, an Anglo-Saxon word describing a brake or thicket. The meadow was managed similarly and hitching before a certain date forbidden; in Broad Campden and Westington, hitching and baiting on the highways was forbidden. 'Hitching' was tying horses to a post to graze and 'baiting' was feeding. Every village seems to have had a field called the Hitching or Hitchen, near the village centre, convenient for tethering horses or oxen. The Cotswold practice of hitching part of the fallow field and sowing it with crops, tying it temporarily to the cultivated field, is an alternative origin of the field-name.

Seventeen years after this series of tithing court records, Campden Enclosure Act was passed. Three Commissioners were named: Samuel Reeve from Rutland, where Campden's lord of the manor had his main estate, who was his land agent, Hugh Jackson from Lincolnshire and John Stone from Pull Court near Tewkesbury. The Act said that 'all Persons claiming any land, or any Right or interest whatsoever...shall lay their Claims, in writing, before the said Commissioners at some Meeting to be holden for that Purpose', 14 days' notice having been given in the Gloucester and Oxford newspapers. Notes from freeholders stating their claims, expressed for the last time in terms of yardlands, are preserved in one of the Commissioners' letter books. One, dated 16 July 1799, reads

> I, Samuel Reeve, of William in the county of Leicester, do claim for Gerard Noel Noel Esq., lord of the manor of Campden, as follows : In Broad Campden 22 3/8 yardlands and 6 yardlands In Westington 24 yardlands The whole of the hamlet of Berrington

Lord Northwick, whose Park bordered Broad Campden, claimed six-and-three-eighths yardlands; in the act he was guaranteed an allotment of 62 acres in Sedgecombe and other adjoining lands. Edward Cotterell claimed four yardlands. Three men, one from Broad Campden and two from Westington, claimed 1½ or 2 yardlands each. Two tiny claims were allowed. 'I claim on behalf of my father William Brain of Northwick in the parish of Blockley one messuage, garden close, two lays of furzeland on Broad Campden Hill and two sheep commons'. This man was allotted a quarter of an acre, and the other was given 18 perches. Apart from the vicar and the lord of the manor, there were only five significant freeholders in the whole of the agricultural area of Campden, but 20 people in Broad Campden and Westington had paid tithe to the vicar that same year. Of Gerard Noel Noel's allotment of 2,500 acres, about one tenth was for lifeholders in Campden manor; in 1832 there were no copyholders or lifeholders on the electoral register. The enclosure was completed within six months. Trees on the new allotments were valued, and the timber either bought by the new owner or cut and carted within six months. At a meeting at the *George Inn* in Chipping Campden, now the *Noel Arms*, a notice was drafted on 2 December 1799 to be put on the church door : the allotments had been made in Berrington, Broad Campden and Westington and 'rights of common in and over the same shall cease and be for ever extinguished'.

Chapter Nine

The Modernisation of the Church

Rectors and vicars were once amongst the larger farmers of their parishes; while the villagers had one or two yardlands, they might have three or four. They were also supported by tithes, the ancient tax on the produce of the land. The system was complicated and various, particularly the small tithes, which were collected on all the multifarious produce of farms and gardens, with the exception of corn and hay; each parish had its own particular customs. Criticism became more forceful as the Church of England lost the allegiance of a proportion of the population. Enclosure gave the opportunity to remove the tithes at the same time as the fields were reorganised. Tithe owners, many of whom were not rectors and vicars but landowners, were compensated generously. Awareness of the neglected condition of many churches grew because of late 18th-century and early 19th-century religious revival; they were also unsuited to the current ideas of their function. Some new churches were built, by Dissenters and by members of the Church of England, and many were restored. In the later 19th century the Society for the Preservation of Ancient Buildings helped to create an appreciation of the historical value of buildings which still remained unaltered, and conservation became the priority.

Glebe Terriers and the Custom of Tithing
Details of the land and buildings belonging to each parish priest were recorded by the churchwardens, in documents known as 'glebe terriers'. A large number of those prepared for Archbishop Whitgift's formal visitation to the diocese of Gloucester in 1584 have been preserved, with others made for subsequent visitations. A full return included the location of each of the parson's strips of arable land in the open-field furlongs, and even the names of those whose land abutted the sides of each strip. There could be hundreds of such names, and several parchment sheets used in writing them down; sympathy might be felt for the churchwardens of Willersey, 'to butt every land we are not able because we have not sufficient time and know it not'.

At the end of the 16th century, barns and other farm buildings usually stood alongside the parsonage house; a dovecot, too, was a privilege of the rector as well as of the lord of the manor. The rector of Bourton on the Water had one of the largest glebes in the area, five yardlands, and he also had land in Clapton and a house and land in Lower Slaughter. Near his new mansion or dwelling house in 1584 were two barns, a stable and cow house, sheep house and pigeon house. The rectory at Broadwell was probably an ancient building, with an undercroft beneath the hall; at one end of a range of buildings were a stable, sheephouse and large barn. The usual way of indicating the size of buildings was to describe the number of bays, each bay being the space between two sets of structural uprights. Hawling's rector had a five-bay house, four-bay barn and three-bay cow house. At Hazleton, there were said to be 18 bays of 'housing', which included farm buildings. The dwelling house and barns were in a long row, with a dovecote built into a barn. When a new rectory was built, in 1861, the former rectory became Glebe Farm and continued to be the farmhouse for the rector's land. Naunton's rector had 24 bays of housing, of which five were later said to be the dwelling house. He was not farming his glebe in 1584, but the land was leased by a Naunton farmer. Richard Olliffe was one of the churchwardens making the statement at Shipton Oliffe. The rectory house was divided into three; part was let to a local man, part, with the orchard, garden and two closes, was used by the rector, and the rest of the house with the yardland of glebe was occupied by a second Shipton man. Along the road, Shipton Solers' rector also had a house and barn. In Whittington, despite having 47 acres of 'barren, hilly land abutting on Walley furlong waste', the rector farmed the glebe himself, and had a barn, oxhouse and stable. His kitchen was separate from the house, which was still quite common in the 16th century. This rectory had been endowed after 1291, rather later than most, which perhaps explains its poor land.

Glebe terriers often included detailed descriptions of the 'custom and manner of tithing'. Great tithes were simple to collect; as set out in Upper Slaughter's terrier, the tenth sheaf of wheat and cock of grain and hay were 'due to the rector'. In Buckland, the rector had half the tithe corn and the patron and impropriator of the living had the other half; each appointed two men to gather the tithe. Small tithes were much more complicated. The statement by the churchwardens of Northleach in 1682, the only Northleach terrier which has been preserved, is particularly detailed. For the purposes of tithing, the parish contained three separate communities: there was the borough of Northleach, the 'Farm', which was the former Gloucester Abbey demesne, and Eastington. Parishioners of Northleach paid Easter offerings to the vicar, two pence each and one penny for a garden; men servants not born in Northleach paid six pence and women servants four pence. Easter offerings had originally been the parishioners' contribution to the cost of communion bread and wine. Two pence per horse and cow were also collected at Easter, and the week before Easter the vicar gathered his tithe eggs, two eggs

86. Gloucester Abbey, as rector of Northleach, was responsible for building a new chancel about 1520 with a roof so high that it partly obscured John Fortey's wide clerestory window. The church was restored in 1884, and could provide 500 'sittings'.

for every cock kept by an inhabitant and one for every hen. He had strips of arable in the Farm and could pasture three cows with the Farm's cows, wherever they should happen to be put. The Farm was tithe-free. He also had four yardlands with pasture rights in Eastington, which he farmed himself. Adjoining his house were nine bays of stable and barns and a dovecote.

The vicar of Northleach collected small tithes from Eastington's inhabitants. The customs were carefully described in the terrier and illustrate graphically the intricacy of the system. The tithes on animals were designed to enable the vicar to collect something no matter how small a man's herd or flock. The vicar was not bound to take his tithe on calves until they were five weeks. He claimed the tenth calf, but if the farmer had only seven, the vicar could take the seventh while paying the owner nine pence. A farmer with less than seven animals could either pay a tenth of the proceeds when they were sold, or leave the tithe over for another year. Flocks of sheep were expected to be larger, and tithe was based on 30 lambs, a probable reflection of the number of sheep allowed to each yardland; all lambs born in Eastington were tithable. From the first 10 lambs, the vicar chose the third, after the owner had picked two; from the next 10, the vicar chose the eighth; from the third 10, he had the tenth. For numbers less then 10 or more than 30, money payments adjusted the amount of the tithe or it could be postponed for a year. When a sheep was sold, if it had been pastured in Eastington for a whole year, the vicar collected two pence. If pastures were let to someone from outside the parish, tithe of one penny was still paid for each sheep, a due called 'agistment', from an old French word for 'lodging'; this ensured the church was not cheated of tithe. Sir Ralph Dutton of Sherborne House had to pay the vicar a small sum of money in compensation for land which had been enclosed to create the New Park, used for deer coursing or racing, as it no longer carried crops or animals on which tithe would once have been paid.

In harvesting each product of their land, the inhabitants of Eastington had first to remember the vicar's small tithes, and the churchwardens wrote down each item in the terrier. The vicar took second choice out of 10 pigs or geese. He could collect tithe milk in kind if he wished, but 'at present all that keep cows pay in lieu six pence per cow for the whole year in Eastington'. When a hive of bees was killed in order to take the honey, the vicar could choose either the tenth part of the unrefined honey or a tenth of the honey in the comb; the owner had to give notice of the intention to sell bees and pay the vicar a tenth of the proceeds.

> No Inhabitant is to gather any apples before notice is given to the minister to come and take his tithe.
>
> No hemp or flax is to be carried away by the owner before the Minister hath notice given him to come and take his tithe.
>
> No hops are to be gathered by any Inhabitant before the minister hath notice...
>
> No Inhabitant must gather any cherries before notice is first given...
>
> No sheep of what kind soever ought to be sold by the Inhabitants of Eastington out of the fields thereunto belonging before first notice is given...

Such customs were maintained because many people were involved—clergy did not want to lose their incomes and farmers did not want to see increases in tithable items. Though customs were similar in many places, there were also local particularities. Even the amount of Easter offering was not uniform; in Buckland, which like Northleach was a Gloucester Abbey manor, householders paid four pence, together with four pence for a maidservant, one penny for a garden and one penny for a chimney. This last payment may reflect the earliest form of church revenue, as the old minsters were entitled to a penny per house in their parishes. In Hampnett the Easter offering was two pence per person aged 16 and over, at Shipton Oliffe it was two pence for those aged 15 and over. In Shipton Oliffe, on the other hand, 'there is a custom due from our Minister to provide two wheat loaves and two hard cheeses and a barrell of strong beer at the Parsonage house of Shipton Oliffe every Christide date in the afternoon to be disposed of as formerly it hath been'. The rector of Buckland had tithes of lambs, calves, pigs, wool and apples; if a calf were killed for the family, the rector had the left shoulder. On Good Friday, one egg was paid for every hen and two for a cock. Hen-keepers in Upper Slaughter also paid eggs, but there the rector had two for every hen and three for a cock. Gardens in Hampnett were only tithable if 'more Ground is sowed or planted than serves the family'.

The rector of Stow on the Wold was entitled to tithe milk from Donnington but not from Stow or Maugersbury, which were also in his parish. The milk was to be taken on the evening of the second day in May and the morning of the third day, and on every tenth day until 1 August. The collection of tithe milk was described in similar terms in Lower Slaughter, where the terrier added that the rector had to pay the cost of milking. The rector of Stow was also entitled to 'the Clack of the Mill' in Donnington, a toll on the corn ground in the mill; the sum of six shillings and eight pence was paid in 1706, and the same amount was still being paid in 1807. The rector of Upper Swell had common pasture rights for a bull, and the Naunton terrier specified that the rector's common was for the 'town bull', which was provided for the benefit of the community. The rector usually owned the churchyard, and Naunton's terrier states this and continues:

> Parson holdeth himself grieved that there is a door out of the house of one Margery Townfield widow into the churchyard through which the swine and the cattle of the said Margery do oftentimes annoy the churchyard.

The rector of Stanton was entitled to the trees in the hedges round the lot meadows, and when enclosure took place, he was careful to value them before the land was taken by its new owner: round one meadow called Marelesow he had 48 ashes, 13 elms and an oak; round another, called Winsales, 75 ashes, 7 elms, and 15 oaks; and round the meadow next to Laverton, 7 elms and a hawthorn. The total value was £55. To keep track of so many details, rectors and vicars often made lists of their inhabitants and the tithable items which each had, down to a hen or two which some Winchcombe townsfolk had.

Disputes with parishioners usually arose over which lands were subject to tithes rather than which items were tithable. Monasteries had usually exempted their own demesnes from tithe, and after the dissolution those lands were regarded as tithe-free. In Winchcombe Abbey's manor of Stanton, the freeholders insisted that the demesnes which they had purchased at the end of the 16th century were tithe-free, despite the fact that the demesne strips were intermixed with their own in the open fields, and the chancellor of the diocese of Gloucester agreed. In a dispute about tithes in Broadwell in 1772, the evidence used went back to an agreement between the rector and Evesham Abbey in 1450. The case illuminates attitudes to custom. From time immemorial, the document of 1450 said, the abbey had been entitled to tithes of corn and hay on the village lands, and also tithe of lambs; however, certain freehold land in the parish paid one third of the tithe of corn and of lambs. These tithes were difficult to collect, the document continued, so the rector was to have them all. The real motive for this generosity was to persuade the rector to free the demesne of tithes. No doubt at that time every one knew which lands were referred to. By 1772, a farmer called Hodges was the holder of strips of land which he maintained were tithe-free, 'and in fact no tithe has within memory been taken of his Common Field lands'. On the other hand, an enclosed pasture had always paid tithe hay 'and there is not even any tradition when it was first enclosed', but the year before, Hodges 'broke it up and sowed and reaped a crop of corn, and carried off the crop without paying any Tithe insisting on the above Exemption'. The dispute was one of several with the tithe owner at the time. Changes in agricultural practice could obviously create dispute; tithes were suited to a static agricultural system.

Acres for Tithes
Although tithes were the main source of a rector's income, the system was fiercely criticised. Many tithes had been diverted from the parish priests into the hands of laymen, which seemed quite unjustifiable; this had happened when the crown sold former monastic property. Tithes were required from all producers, no matter how small, and took no account of ability to pay. Most important, the church lost its command of everyone's allegiance, particularly after the freedom of the Civil War period; those who were not members of the Church of England were increasingly hostile because forced to support it. In 1836, after centuries of agitation and complaint, all remaining tithes were commuted and money payments substituted, but in most Cotswold parishes tithes had already been abolished before 1836, in the course of the great re-organisation of land carried out with parliamentary authority under enclosure acts, and the parson had usually been compensated in land.

In early enclosure acts, the rector was given an annual money income in place of tithes. The rector of Farmington, on enclosure in 1713, accepted an annual income of £120 in place of both tithes and glebeland. The Earl of Scarborough owned nearly the whole parish and undertook to pay most of the rector's stipend, and only two other landowners were involved in the enclosure. The rector of Upper Swell in 1724 surrendered tithes and four yardlands, which he had been letting for £49 10s. a year, 'being the utmost improved yearly rent which can be gotten for the same' and accepted £80 a year from the only other landowner, the lord of the manor. The rector of Wyck Rissington accepted £84 a year in place of tithes in 1729 but in this case retained his glebeland. Tithes of the demesne at Hawling had already been commuted sometime in the 17th century, for 13s. 4d.; this exact sum was being paid to the rector in the early 19th century. Tithes on the 30 yardlands of the 'Towne' were commuted for 25s. for each yardland at enclosure in 1755. The lord of the manor paid the rector 10s. per acre in compensation for giving up his 63 acres of glebe, and the total sum of £69 was a charge on the manor estate when it was sold in 1808.

In the long run, the exchanges were not favourable to the rectors, whose income declined with inflation though, at a time of low prices, money payments no doubt seemed easier than having to let land. An alternative way of extinguishing tithes was generally adopted in later 18th-century enclosures, that of giving land to the rector or other tithe-owners. Thousands of acres in the Cotswolds were allocated to the church and many rectors of Cotswold parishes were changed from farmers into landed gentry. The change distanced them from the daily work of the villagers; the large new farms were leased and new farmhouses and barns were built away from the rectory itself. Enclosure therefore tended to be arranged latest in parishes where there were a number of proprietors who had to surrender significant quantities of land.

The amount required to buy permanent exoneration from tithes was often specified in the acts of parliament. Marshall thought the freedom was purchased dearly, but enclosure could not proceed without the agreement of the church, because of glebeland in the open fields.

> Under the Cotswold inclosures, the tithes of the respective townships were set out, in land...the proportion was unusually high : in some cases, one fifth of the arable and one ninth of the grasslands of the township: but the privilege of laying down so intolerable a burden as that of tithes, in an arable country, can scarcely be purchased too dear.

Naunton and the two Shiptons are examples of those proportions; in Withington the rector's allotment was two ninths of the arable, but this was in a limited part of the parish. Hazleton's rector, it was reported in 1807, was given enough land to increase his income by half as much again as it had been from tithes, presumably in recognition of the increased production to be expected from enclosed farms.

Some examples show the scale of the transfer. The rector of Hazleton had 82 acres of glebe, and 188 acres for tithes at enclosure in 1766. The rector of the small parish of Cutsdean had probably been non-resident for a long time, and at the time of enclosure in 1777 he lived in Bredon, but, in addition to his glebeland of nearly 80 acres, his compensation for loss of tithes was 224 acres. Naunton's rector in 1778 had 53 acres of glebe but 444 acres for tithes; in 1830 he had one farm of 230 acres at Summerhill, some distance from the village, with new farm buildings on the former open fields, and a second farm of 201 acres. The rector of the two Shiptons had about 60 acres already, but received six times as much for tithes in 1801, giving him 445 acres in all. Great Rissington's rector in 1816 was given 98 acres for glebe, but 411 acres for tithes.

Particularly wealthy rectories included Bourton on the Hill, Bourton on the Water and Withington, and enclosure, together with agricultural prosperity, seem to have provided income to rebuild the rectory houses. Bourton on the Hill's rector collected tithes from Moreton in Marsh too, and together these gave him on enclosure in 1821 a total of 450 acres; with the stimulus of this landed position, a new rectory was built. Part of the tithes was owned by Lord Redesdale, who was allotted 121 acres. Bourton on the Water's rector also had two sets of tithes: Lower Slaughter was enclosed first, in 1731, and the rector was allotted 259 acres which formed Lower Slaughter Farm. When Bourton on the Water was enclosed 40 years later, 209 acres were compensation for tithe, which together with glebe made the rector owner of a second farm of 282 acres. A new farm house, Bourton Hill Farm, was built there in 1804 and a new rectory house a few years later. Seven hundred acres still paid tithe. Thomas Ireland, rector in 1807, found difficulty in collecting it, particularly the levy on sheep pastured in the parish but not belonging to parishioners: 'the Inhabitants seem inclined to resist the payment of Agistment; for the present, to preserve peace a Money payment hath been accepted by way of composition for one year only'.

At Withington, 'a very great glebe of meadow, pasture and arable' had always belonged to the rector; he had four yardlands in the open fields of Withington itself and one in each of the six hamlets which had been included in the former minster's manor. The manor demesne may have been transferred to the rector, as the priest in Domesday had only two yardlands. In other minster parishes, parish priests were less fortunate; in both Blockley and Winchcombe, most of the tithes and the rectory lands were taken by the monasteries, leaving a poorly-endowed vicar to serve the inhabitants. Withington rectory had substantial farm buildings in 1680, 27 bays of barns, stables, hen-house, cart-house, sheep-house, cow-house and dovecot. Most of the parish was already enclosed before the enclosure act of 1813 reorganised the last remaining open fields. The rector's allotment was 214 acres, but altogether he had over a thousand acres, divided into four farms. The old part of the rectory was occupied by the farmer of the newly-enclosed north field, until relocated in a new farmhouse

87. The vicarage at Northleach was built in 1863. The house is possibly on the site of the medieval rectory or manor house.

88. Bourton on the Water was one of the wealthiest rectories in the area. The house was rebuilt after the rector's large acquisition of land at enclosure in 1773 and the removal of farm buildings to Bourton Hill Farm. The church tower is late 18th century and was retained when the church was largely rebuilt a century later.

THE MODERNISATION OF THE CHURCH

at Thornhill. Thorndale, Revenswell and Tickhill were the other three farms. The impressive rectory next to the church shows the wealth of the living in the late 18th century, when a new house was built adjacent to the old. It was described as a mansion, and had accommodation designed for a gentleman, including a vestibule, two parlours, servants' hall, butler's pantry, cellars and coach house.

Vicarages were not so well endowed, either with glebe or tithes, but their status improved considerably after enclosure. Burford's vicar had apparently given up his lands to Speaker Lenthal in the mid-17th century, but after enclosure had 100 acres instead of tithes, though the bishop of Oxford, who had acquired the major share of Burford's tithes in the mid-18th century, received 564 acres at enclosure. The bishop of Gloucester received 491 acres for Northleach tithes in 1783, and the vicar's glebe more than doubled to 137 acres. Blockley's vicar had only 20 acres of land but after enclosure in 1773 he had 92 acres in Blockley and Paxford. Richard Freeman and Sir John Rushout leased most of Blockley's tithes from the bishop of Worcester, including Aston Magna, which had been enclosed in 1733. The vicar of Campden had only four acres of glebe, but 257 acres at enclosure instead of tithes; the Noel family owned the larger part of Campden's tithes and was allotted 393 acres. A new vicarage house was built in Campden in the 18th century and enlarged in the early 19th century.

Once land was enclosed, higher rents could be charged. Thomas Scotman, Buckland's rector, wrote to his agent in Campden, George Cotterell, in 1812:

> I am informed that Mr Phillipps has doubled his Rents at Buckland—at which I am surprised if he has not raised them before, since they became his property. I am in

89. The rectory at Farmington was built about 1788. In 1811 it was considered small by a rector who lived in the family mansion of Farmington Lodge.

90. The north-west side of Buckland Rectory is almost unaltered since it was built in the late 15th century. It contains an open hall and inside there are angels carved on the two centre hammerbeams of the roof.

> possession of a document which says that the Rectory of Buckland produced £163 a year before it was inclosed—now, 30 or 40 years later, it ought to be worth almost three times as much.

This was over-optimistic, but in 1816 he did get £390. Scotman lived in Great Barton, near Bury St Edmunds, and a gift of Suffolk turkey quite often accompanied letters to his agent. He found 'many obstacles oppose my residing on my Living at Buckland' and he had a licence from the bishop for non-residence. He wanted to exchange his Suffolk rectory for one in Gloucestershire which would 'allow a proper place of abode'; exchanges, he said, were 'now common cases'. He was not successful in this, and his letters to Cotterell continued over the next decade. Buckland was served by a curate who did not live there either; he moved to a church which he could walk to more conveniently.

The Buckland rectory land allocated at enclosure in 1779 was 228 acres on the edge of the parish at Buckland Fields, and Cotterell was responsible for letting it. Scotman was conscientious in his attitude to his tenant; in 1812 he thought the times justified an increase in rent, but he did not want 'to strain it so high' as to deprive the tenant of a 'fair living Profit'. Corn prices were high because of the war against France, but as the defeat of Napoleon was achieved, he wrote in January 1814 that he hoped his new tenant was a 'very responsible man', as 'farming is not, and perhaps may not be, for some time, so profitable, as it has been of late years'. In January 1815, 'the very best wheat was sold in Bury market on Wednesday last for two guineas per Quarter; I really think the Farmers cannot grow it at that price'. Abatements of rent for Buckland Fields Farm were made and Scotman wondered what farms were let for, 'in the line of country in which my farm is placed. I should be sorry to have the farm thrown upon my hands and I should be equally sorry to let it at so high a price that the tenant would lose by the bargain'.

Buckland parsonage house was also difficult to let. It was a very old building, and the non-residence of the rector probably saved it from alteration or demolition in the 19th century.

> I almost wish we had kept the orchard and Buckland Green separate from the Farm, as they might have been the means of letting it with greater ease and with more advantage...I own I should be glad to hear that the House was occupied, not only as a means of emolument, but as a means of preserving it from decay.

When he heard that two families were living in the house, he feared 'they use the best chamber as a Sitting Room ... I do not think it right to convert the rectorial house into a poor House'. A tenant was found who took the house, orchard, and field 'once known by the name of Buckland Green', and also Chapel Close in Laverton. A terrier of 1808 refers to Chapel Close where there was 'a building called the Chapel', which was occupied as two cottages, though previously a school. Scotman took the building down sometime before 1828, as another terrier recorded, and re-erected it at his own expense on his land at Buckland Fields, still as two cottages. The carved Norman doorway was thus preserved, if not on its original site. A date stone over the doorway, 1622, may have been placed there when the chapel was converted to a school.

New Chapels and Churches
Non-residence was a serious problem for the Church of England, as it left village communities without any strong figure of authority; the lord of the manor also was likely to be resident only occasionally, if at all. This was the opportunity for some more rebellious spirits to withdraw from the church and set up their own group of 'hearers', usually of methodist preaching. One of the local farmers in Icomb described the progress of Methodism in this small village. About 1826 'we introduced a minister to preach to us at home ... Being very much persecuted, we met together in barns, attics, and a malt-house'. The first time that a Methodist meeting was held in a cottage, the village was in an uproar.

> There were shoutings, blowings of horns, beating of old pots and kettles; in short, everything was done that was calculated to hinder the preacher and annoy the hearers; and they were supported in their lawless proceedings by an opulent farmer, who sent them cider in buckets, and instructed them how to act.

This opulent farmer walked through the village the following day with his coat turned inside out, and a placard on his back which said—'I am a turncoat, but no Methodist'. Some poor people were deterred, but the house had been duly licensed and there was nothing authority could do to stop the meetings. The rector, who lived many miles off, visited Icomb only once a year. News of the Methodist incursion reached him with the rent for his parsonage land, and he hastened to the village to preach, pointing out how well-qualified and knowledgeable the ministers of the established church were, and emphasising the need for sound doctrine. The Methodist church nonetheless survived and two years later had a special thatched building for meetings, despite some continuing harassment, jeering and sneering. Carpenters were the mainstay of the little congregation, a group who were not quite so closely tied to the authority of farmers in Icomb.

By the mid-19th century the Methodists were challenging the Church of England's traditional hold on rural and urban communities alike. Before 1850, Methodists had built

91. The Meeting House at Broad Campden dates from 1663; it was abandoned in the later 19th century and put to various uses, but has now been returned to the Quakers. Its scale and simplicity as well as its doorway reflect early Norman churches.

chapels in the small towns of Broadway, Burford, Chipping Campden and Stow on the Wold, and also in Hawling. The Methodist chapel in Winchcombe is dated 1886. Old Dissent, particularly the Baptists and Congregationalists which had been established in the mid-17th century, also shared the revival. The Baptists had a strong presence in Bourton on the Water in the later 18th century, when a Baptist minister lived there; Rudder commented on the unreliability of the parish registers as a result of some dissenters being buried in the church but others at the meeting house burial ground. The meeting house was rebuilt several times, most recently in 1876. The Baptists also built in Burford, Blockley and Guiting Power in the early 19th century and in Naunton, where the chapel dominates the village very strikingly. Later in the century a Baptist chapel was built in Chipping Campden. A Congregational chapel was built in Broadway, and in 1860 in Moreton in Marsh. Other Nonconformist congregations no doubt met in private houses or other buildings, as in Icomb.

The Church of England felt the strength of the religious revival and landowners who benefited substantially from the ending of tithes perhaps felt a sense of public obligation to repair churches or build new ones. Lord Redesdale, for example, built a church at Aston Magna in Blockley in 1846, after he had inherited the land which had been allotted in place of tithes; there had formerly been a chapel there, closed with the chantries in 1547 and converted into two cottages. It is perhaps significant that a largely new church was built at Moreton in Marsh, 1858, and a new one at Batsford, 1861, also places where Lord Redesdale had been a tithe-owner. New churches were built at Broadway in 1839; Oddington, 1852; Snowshill, 1864; Gretton, 1865; and Paxford, 1866. In Broadway and Oddington, the new

THE MODERNISATION OF THE CHURCH

92. Burford Methodist chapel was created in 1849 in the shell of an early 18th-century house. A large congregation had heard Wesley preach in Burford in 1739.

93. Northleach Congregational chapel in Early English style was opened in 1860 and provided 260 seats.

churches were more conveniently sited for the inhabitants, while the old churches were left standing and used occasionally. At Fifield, 1840, Lower Swell, 1852 and 1870, Sherborne, 1859, Cutsdean, 1863 and Lower Slaughter, 1867, part or all of the old church was retained, although the scale of building was so extensive that in effect it was a new church. A wish to move the building a little further away from the big house was a major motive in the rebuilding at Sherborne. At Bourton on the Water, the nave and tower were rebuilt in 1784, but only the tower of that date remains, as the church was substantially rebuilt for a second time between 1875 and 1891; the 14th-century chancel was left undisturbed on both occasions.

Church Restoration

Interest in church restoration rather than rebuilding grew in the later Victorian period. Restoration meant two things: firstly an historical and archaeological interest in investigating the structure and in attempting to put the clock back to some imprecise date in the medieval period; secondly, a revival of interest in ritual and medieval forms of worship, and a wish to remove the work of two centuries of Puritanism. In the 17th and 18th centuries, churches had been fitted like lecture rooms with wooden galleries ranged round the pulpit, and with the communion table surrounded by benches. An arrangement of the chancel like this may still be seen at Hailes. Between 1847, when Stow on the Wold's church was first restored, and 1904, when Compton Abdale's was, 33 major architect-directed church restorations in the Cotswolds were financed and completed. The 1870s was the decade of maximum effort, and included restoration of three of the largest churches in the area, Burford, Chipping Campden and

Winchcombe. At Burford, the vicar and William Morris argued about the rectitude of the work being done and this contributed materially to Morris's later action in founding the Society for the Preservation of Ancient Buildings.

Winchcombe's decision to restore the church was taken in 1850, when the roof was found to be 'absolutely dangerous'; the west end also was propped up with timbers, but the work was not undertaken until 1872. Emma Dent, who was an archaeologist and historian, and had taken part in the restoration of Sudeley Castle and chapel, was instrumental. She described the inside of Winchcombe church prior to restoration, with galleries, seats surrounding the communion table and old, large pews. All were taken out. Typical of the decisions taken by church restorers was the rebuilding of the chancel battlements, which had fallen in 1690. The vicar defended the work to the Bristol and Gloucester Archaeological Society in 1910; he said that he 'dissented from the view that the parish church had been injured by its restoration'.

The three small Norman churches in Winchcombe parish still standing at the beginning of the 19th century, in Greet, Gretton and Postlip, all seem to have been disused. Greet chapel was demolished before 1815; Gretton chapel was replaced by a new church in 1868 and the old one by 1877 was very dilapidated indeed; only the tower still stands. Postlip chapel was rescued by the enthusiasm of the owner of the big house.

> Till the present owner took it in hand, had it put into repair, and restored to sacred uses, it was a mere cattle shed and sheep pen, and only the great thickness of the walls and its massive foundations had preserved it from going to ruin. It is now fitted up for regular services; there is a resident priest at the Hall, and after a silence of three centuries and a half, mass is once more celebrated at the altar.

Evans wrote this in 1905 and was probably right concerning the length of time since a Roman Catholic service had been held there, but Postlip's chapel was recognised in surveys of the diocese at least until 1712.

The foundation of the Bristol and Gloucester Archaeological Society in 1876 reflects the strong interest in the architectural history of parish churches and in local history, as well as in Roman archaeology. The older and larger manor houses engaged members' attention to a lesser extent, but appreciation of 'vernacular' architecture, of the ordinary houses of the area, had not yet developed. The Society held two field meetings a year; members listened to papers and went on tours. One of the first summer meetings was held at Stow on the Wold in 1882. Participants were transported in horse brakes to Icomb, Lower Swell, Oddington, Notgrove, Upper Slaughter, Bourton on the Water, Farmington and Hampnett, encouraged particularly by the enthusiasm of David Royce, who was vicar of Lower Swell, an archaeologist and historian and a frequent contributor of papers. Another meeting returned to Stow in 1897 and a spring meeting was held in Northleach and Chedworth in 1907 and in Toddington and Winchcombe in 1910. The accounts of these meetings give interesting information about the progress of restoration, and also show the strength of feeling which preserved buildings like the 'ancient and singularly interesting church' in Oddington, by 1882 'fast becoming a ruin', or Shipton Solers, which in 1883 had trees growing up through the roof. 'The church was found by the present rector in a very bad state being used as a shed for cattle etc. and a view of the building, dated 1888, depicts the windows all blocked up, and a general appearance of neglect and decay'. The church was disused because the near neighbour, Shipton Oliffe, was in the centre of the village, and the two livings were united.

J. E. K. Cutts, architect, presented papers to the Bristol and Gloucester Archaeological Society in 1882 on two churches which he had supervised, Notgrove, restored in 1873, and

THE MODERNISATION OF THE CHURCH

94. Blockley church tower is seen from the Square. The old tower was taken down in 1725 after at least a quarter of a century of worry because of the 'great cracke' in it. The new tower was constructed by a mason from Chipping Campden to a traditional design with echoes of Campden's. The church was generally restored in 1871.

Upper Slaughter, 1877. In 1875 he worked on Aston Blank, in 1879 on Wyck Rissington, in 1881 on Bledington and in 1884 on Temple Guiting; he was responsible for more restorations than any other architect in the area. Notgrove, he said, had

> suffered from some of the evil consequences of its out-of-the-world situation : one half of the manor-house was empty and falling to pieces, the other half only being used as a farm-house, the rectory also was used as a farm-house, the rector being non-resident; the church was forlorn and neglected, and there were no parish schools. The village has entered on happier times. The resident rector, the first for 90 years, has restored and added to the rectory house, and made it picturesque and charming; some years ago he planted the churchyard; and he has completed an artistic restoration of the chancel.

Meantime the nave was in a dangerous state. In the wall between the nave and the chancel the restorers found the remains of the original Norman arch, which had been enlarged at some later time 'quite out of the centre of the nave and chancel' and was in ruinous condition. It was removed and a larger chancel arch inserted. The south wall of the nave was much out of the perpendicular and when taken down was found to rest partly on the Norman foundations but partly on no foundations at all. Traces of the original decorations of the walls, including the windowless east end, were found, which perhaps inspired the vicar of Hampnett to undertake the decoration of that Norman chancel in 'authentic' style.

Cutts' work at Upper Slaughter was much more controversial as a 'restoration'.

> Many features of the old church, which had been hidden and removed, were, in the process, brought to light, rendering the restored church so unlike what it was previously, that it may be of interest, first, briefly to record its appearance when the restoration commenced, and then to describe the various points of interest as they were disclosed in the process of the work.

Such an admission of total change was what enraged the conservationists such as William Morris. The most striking feature of Upper Slaughter's church prior to restoration was that the Norman pillars separating the north aisle from the nave had been removed, and one large room had been created with a plaster ceiling. A lath and plaster partition hid the lofty carved arch leading from the nave into the tower. Cutts speculated that the alteration had been made in the late 18th century. Francis Witts' diary in fact describes the work being done in 1822; it was partly paid for by Vernon Dolphin of Eyford, and was intended to accommodate 70 more people, including Mr. Dolphin himself, who had 'with difficulty' been placed in the chancel up to this time. In 1877 Cutts removed this alteration completely, together with the high square pews 'with which our ancient churches were encumbered and disfigured until recently'. He found enough of the Norman pillars, used as seat supports, and of their capitals, to reconstruct one complete pillar, which was then copied. A copy of the tower arch was inserted between the chancel and the nave. The tower arch is itself somewhat puzzling, as it combines a pointed arch with earlier Norman chevron decoration; probably the arch had been reconstructed in the 15th century. The chancel arch is quite unauthentic. Upper Slaughter's two pointed arches with chevron decoration are a surprise for later observers.

When Herbert Evans wrote his guide to the area in 1905, the Victorians' energetic church restoration work was mainly finished; he frequently commented on the disaster which he considered had struck Cotswold churches. On the other hand, he wrote approvingly of the work at Guiting Power, where, until three years previously, the chancel had been boarded off and was falling into ruin. He found the restoration there as conservative as was possible in the circumstances, though very large alterations had been made in 1820 and 1844 which could not easily be removed. Morris's Society for the Preservation of Ancient Buildings was by this time having a noticeable effect; it prevented the crumbling tower of Coln St Denis being taken down, insisting that it could be propped up, as it still is, somewhat perilously. Churches had been altered and extended to suit the requirements of church usage throughout their history, and the danger was that they would become museums, albeit 'sacred monuments of the nation's growth and hope', as Morris wrote. Despite the criticisms of the conservationists, it is likely that, without the late 19th-century restorations, many churches might have become highly dilapidated.

The ancient relationship of the parson with the land largely ended in the 20th century. The money sums paid since 1836 in place of any still existing tithes were finally abolished.

THE MODERNISATION OF THE CHURCH

More important, the church farms were gradually sold, particularly after the First World War, as agricultural prices fell, and rents did not provide adequate incomes for the clergy. Hazleton glebe was sold in 1920, and Oddington and Shipton glebes were sold about the same time. This was the year of enormous numbers of land sales of all sorts. Naunton glebe was sold between 1935 and 1939, and the rectory house, too. Broadwell glebe was sold in 1937. Most of Westcote glebe was purchased for Little Rissington aerodrome from 1939. After the Second World War, the retreat from the large old rectory houses gathered momentum. Oddington rectory house was sold in 1946, and Bourton on the Hill glebe and rectory house in 1957. The trend has continued, and is symbolised by the removal of Bourton on the Water rectory in 1960 from the rather grand early 19th-century house into its stables.

Chapter Ten

Gentlemen and Country Houses

Gentlemen in the 17th century were lords of the manor, and were still powerful figures in their villages. A number paid dearly for their prominence and support of the King in the Civil War. After the restoration of Charles II in 1660, the Hearth Tax reveals the number of larger houses in the Cotswolds. As the concept of ownership of land strengthened, the manor court declined; status was conferred by wealth, not by the title 'lord of the manor'. By 1800, the title was rarely used, and instead 'gentlemen's seats' were simply substantial houses at the centres of landed estates. Northwick Park is a nice example of the style of life in a smaller country house in the 18th and early 19th centuries. The affluence of country estates in the later 18th century allowed considerable rebuilding and extension, but some old-fashioned houses slipped down the social scale. In the later 19th century, a number were upgraded and new ones built. After the First World War, the problems of the country house became serious, and even more so after the Second World War. The National Trust began to take some over from private owners.

The Civil War

According to John Smyth, who collected the 1608 muster lists of Gloucestershire, six men were lords of more than one Cotswold manor: Edmond Bray Esq., the ancestor of the Talbot and then Wingfield families, Lord of Great Barrington and Great Rissington; Sir John Tracy, ancestor of the Earl of Wemyss, Lord of Didbrook, Hailes and Stanway; Henry Stratford, gentleman, of Guiting Power and Hawling; Sir Anthony Culpepper of Hazleton and Yanworth; Edmond Chamberlayne, of Maugersbury and Oddington; and George Stratford Esq., of Farmcote and Wyck Rissington. These were amongst the greater county gentry of the area. Most Cotswold gentlemen had only one manor or estate. A few years later, Sir John Tracy put forward the names of 82 men in Gloucestershire, who had an estimated income of at least £40 a year but had not accepted the title of knight. They had to pay a special tax to Charles I. Thirteen were in the Cotswolds; they were Francis Heydon Esq. of Shipton Solers, Anthony and Robert Lawrence of Sevenhampton, John Golby of Chipping Campden and John Hopkins of Winchcombe, all called gentlemen, Thomas Harris of Broad Campden, Robert Hyron of Westington, Richard Freeman of Batsford, Thomas Fifeilde of Farmington, Anthony Hodges of Broadwell, Francis and William Izod of Stanton, and John Durham of Willersey. They were all lords of the manor, or principal landowners where a manor no longer formally existed. None seems to have been a committed Royalist in the civil wars a decade later.

Twelve gentlemen were recognised Royalists, and at the end of the first civil war in 1646 were made to pay for their allegiance to the defeated King; either they paid a cash sum or had their estates confiscated. The fine was anything between a tenth and a third of the value of the property, calculated from its estimated rental value over 20 years, which was described as 'at twenty years' purchase'. Five men in the Cotswolds were required to pay more than £1,000: Sir Edmond Bray of Great Barrington, John Chamberlayne of Maugersbury, Sir Humphrey Tracy of Stanway, John Dutton of Sherborne who paid more than £6,000, and Baptist Noel, the heir of Baptist Hicks of Campden, who had to pay the enormous sum of £9,000, despite the destruction of the new and magnificent mansion house at Campden. Baptist Hicks' fortunes had been built on merchanting in silk in the City of London and on lending large sums of money to James I, and he had purchased the manor and former monastic property in Campden. As he died in 1629, he was spared seeing his new mansion burned by a Royalist commander, 'wantonly', Clarendon thought, but some said to prevent it being held by the Parliamentarians. Lord Chandos of Sudeley was dead, too, by the time the list was published in 1655; his composition had been over £15,000. Another seven men compounded for amounts exceeding £100; these were the lords of Aston Subedge, Bourton on the Hill, Dowdeswell, Farmcote, Mickleton, Turkdean, and Winchcombe.

John Chamberlayne of Maugersbury put up a valiant rearguard action against his composition, preparing a detailed statement of his losses as a result of the war. Because his manor was near several main roads which meet at Stow, he found himself required to provide food and shelter for soldiers many times, sometimes for as many as 120 men.

> Imprimis quartered upon the coming up of the Marquis of Hertford with the welshmen 120 foot soldiers and 20 officers and their horses 5 days at £5 a day comes to ... £25
>
> When my Lord of Essex's army marched to the relief of Gloucester, they spent me in household provision of bread, beer, cheese, meat and provender £6
>
> I had corn upon the ground spoiled by the two armies, Prince Rupert facing my Lord of Essex at Stow, worth £40 at the least
>
> Quartered more of Sir William Vavasor's men, a major and 23 men and horses two days which comes to .... £3 1s. 4d.
>
> Upon their departure came Colonel Clarke, his major and 32 men and horses and continued two days and nights which comes to .... £4 5s. 4d.
>
> When Sir William Waller chased the King's army towards Worcester, I quartered of the King's men 43 men and horses one night which comes to .... £2 17s. 4d.
>
> The next day I quartered of Sir William Waller's army, Colonel Birch and 30 officers and 40 horses and 120 foot soldiers five days which comes to .... £27 10s. 0d.
>
> When Sir William Waller lay at Stow the carriage horses were turned in my corn and did me at the least £30 worth of hurt.
>
> The 4th of September three commanders and six troopers one night comes to .... 12s. 0d.
>
> In the same month came Captain Bowen and His lieutenant with them three men and horses. He was under the command of Major General Skippon. He stayed with me five weeks .... £11 13s. 4d.

95 & 96. Two banqueting houses and the Almonry of Campden House escaped the fire which destroyed Baptist Hicks' very expensive mansion in 1645. The fire may have been an accident or intended to prevent the house being acquired by the Parliamentarians in the Civil War. Materials have been salvaged from the ruins until little is left to show its grandeur.

97. After the destruction of Campden House, Baptist Hicks' daughter, Juliana Noel, lived at Campden Court, probably an older building on the edge of the manor house site; this has remained a Noel family home.

The toll continued, described in 56 separate entries, and culminating in the cry:

beside I have quartered many more which I have forgotten. I have lost seventeen plough horse, taken out of my teams upon that land, and many times paid great sums of money to stave off quartering and for post horses and to avoid carriage and other charges incident to war which I reckon not. I lost above a hundred sheep by soldiers, all which I leave to your considerations and refer myself wholly to your mercies.

As his services had been rendered to both sides impartially, the Committee for Sequestrations was inclined to reduce his final composition to £316. Alas for John Chamberlayne, eight months later the Committee summoned him to answer for his Churchdown estate; here he could not make the same pleas in mitigation and a much heavier fine was imposed. In the end it amounted in total to £1,246. Nonetheless, his descendants were still in Maugersbury two and a half centuries later. Experiences like John Chamberlayne's were probably typical. After the restoration of the monarchy in 1660, Charles II found himself unable to make any restitution to these men for their loyalties because of the much greater political need to avoid making enemies of the former Parliamentarians. Even so, legal stability for landowners returned with the Restoration, and many houses were either completely rebuilt or considerably extended.

In an attempt to solve the crown's financial problems, Parliament agreed in 1662 to a tax on chimneys or hearths; it was repealed in 1689. The more rooms that were heated, the larger the house was likely to be and the wealthier the occupant. Assessments for Gloucestershire have survived for 1672; there is a series for Worcestershire, and the Oxfordshire returns for

98. A country house at Bruern was built about 1720 on the site of a small Cistercian monastery. The house was damaged by fire and partly rebuilt in 1780.

1665 were printed in 1940. The Hearth Tax lists are not necessarily complete; at the bottom end of the scale, poor householders, who were excused payment for a number of reasons, were not always recorded. In Burford, for example, only three assessments for one hearth were recorded, while the total of 90 named heads of households is just over half of the number listed in a borough tax list of 1685. Thirty households in Taynton in Oxfordshire were recorded in the Hearth Tax list for 1662 and only 23 in 1665, but 48 households paid the Poll Tax in 1666. At the upper end of the social scale, the Hearth Tax is more reliable; as Sir William Petty, the probable author of the scheme, said, it was 'easy to tell the number of hearths, which remove not as heads or Polls do'.

A reasonable indicator of a gentleman's house may be 10 or more hearths. There were 54 such houses in the Cotswolds and nearly half were former monastic manors. Two could be called mansions: Queen Elizabeth, with all her court which accompanied her when she went on progress, had been able to stay at Sherborne, with its 56 hearths, and James I had stayed at Burford Priory, which had 36 hearths. Stanway House was next in size with 21 hearths. All the other large houses had between 10 and 18 hearths. In the north of the area these were Bourton on the Water, Broadwell, Campden, Idbury, Lower Slaughter, Maugersbury, Northwick in Blockley and Sezincote; at Bourton on the Hill two large houses reflected the two manors; on the western edge there was Buckland, Charlton Abbots, Farmcote and Mickleton, and four in Broadway; in the south there was Bruern and Tangley, Great Barrington, Great Rissington, Taynton, Hawling, Northleach, Shipton, Stowell, two in Withington and no less than seven in Burford, including Burford Priory.

XIX Stanway manor belonged to Tewkesbury Abbey and since the monastery was closed has been continuously owned by the same family. Stanway House was considerably extended early in the 17th century.

XX The Gatehouse was built about 1630 but the coat-of-arms on it is later, and reflects the marriage of John Tracy and Anne Atkyns about 1700.

XXI Whittington Court is mainly early Elizabethan. It is on the site of a medieval knight's house, and is within a moated enclosure and immediately beside the 12th-century church.

XXII The Manor House at Upper Slaughter was described by Herbert Evans in 1905 as 'one of the most beautiful examples of its kind in the whole Cotswolds'. Three front gables are 16th century and the fourth is modern, but there is an older, vaulted undercroft and massive ashlar blocks beneath the hall, which was approached by an external stone staircase. 'Gillyflowers' were being planted in the garden at Northwick Park in 1705.

XXIII Datestones on the front of one of the largest farmhouses in Stanton record the years 1615 and 1618 and initials which seem to refer to the Jackson *alias* Booth family, who bought a share of the manor and became yeomen. The house ceased to be a farmhouse in 1925, when the buildings at the rear were adapted.

XXIV An old farmhouse in Sherborne is probably more typical of a yardlander's or peasant's house than the handsome buildings erected by the new freeholders in Stanton, illustrated above.

XXV *(above left)* The architect inspects the leaning spire of Shipton under Wychwood church, added sometime after the tower was built about 1200. As at Burford, the structure has been damaged by the weight, necessitating frequent repairs. Shipton benefice is now combined with Fifield and Idbury, so recreating part of the large, early medieval parish.

XXVI *(above right)* Coln St Denis church retains much of the basic Norman plan. The Society for the Protection of Ancient Buildings has campaigned for the preservation of the tower, which was weakened by the addition of an extra storey.

XXVII Sherborne church was originally on the same axis as the late 13th-century tower and spire, but about 1850 it was rebuilt next to the tower in order to give more light to some of the rooms in the house. The church combines classical form with medieval details. Some of the Dutton family monuments were resited in the Victorian church.

Running a Country House
Northwick Park

The style of life in these modest-sized mansions of the Cotswolds did not change very much between 1700 and the mid-19th century. Northwick may be taken as an example. The Rushout family owned Northwick for 200 years, from 1683 to 1887. Twice the owner died intestate, in 1705 and 1859, with the result that inventories of all household possessions and livestock were made and 'appraised' or valued; the inventories give many indications of daily life and also provide an opportunity for comparison. After the death in 1887 of George Rushout, third Baron Northwick, and of his wife in 1911, the estate came to Captain Spencer-Churchill, who deposited all the Rushout family's accumulated papers in Worcestershire Record Office. Between 1937 and 1939, E. A. Barnard arranged and listed a collection of 3,200 documents.

The foundations of a gentleman's seat at Northwick were laid in the 12th century, or even before, in two freehold estates or knights' fees within the bishop of Worcester's manor of Blockley. Northwick has remained part of the parish of Blockley and so was in Worcestershire until transferred to Gloucestershire in 1933. The amalgamation of the two freehold estates through a fortunate marriage by William de Clipstone in 1346 may have provided the impetus for the first really substantial house on the site; in 1383 John Childe was the holder of both estates and in 1427 Thomas Childe of Northwick was the King's escheator, responsible for the King's property rights in the county, and so considered the 'most worthy bearer of arms in Worcestershire'. In 1666, Thomas Childe paid tax on 14 hearths. He sold Northwick to Sir James Rushout in 1683; overall the Childe family had held the estate for some three hundred years, though not continuously. Sir James Rushout immediately set about building a new block on the west side; the date 1686 is embossed on existing rainwater heads.

Sir James Rushout's family was of substantial wealth and social standing; he had been created a baronet in 1661. His father was a Flemish immigrant who had been naturalised in 1635, so that the gables of the 1686 house are an appropriate reflection of a traditional Flemish architectural style. Though built of Cotswold stone, the house is grander than the vernacular style of the area. Sir John Rushout enjoyed his new house for only a decade; he and his wife both died in February 1697, leaving two sons and three daughters out of nine children. The Rushout family has not been fortunate in this respect. The next heir, James, died in December 1705, two months after his wife; they were aged 29 and 25 respectively. The two young children were taken to London to be cared for by relatives, but the boy also died within a few years. The nurse's wages in January 1706 included £14 for 'wet nursing' or breast-feeding for a year. This was the first occasion for a careful inventory to be made, and accounts were also kept of the sale of stock and payment of wages.

The inventory shows that the main part of the house corresponds to the west side of the present building. There were three storeys: on the ground floor the principal rooms were the Great Hall, the little parlour and a 'veneered room', which sounds as if it was wainscotted, with a crimson damask bed and 14 chairs. There was a Great Staircase and a back stairs. Other rooms included the steward's parlour, the nursery, pantry and 'old' dining room. On the first floor my Lord had a dressing room and so did my Lady, and the principal bedroom was described as 'the white cloth bed chamber'; a white cloth bed trimmed with scarlet was expensively valued at £35. The floor above contained at least six more rooms and there were three garrets. The appraisers then moved to the extensive service area of the house, perhaps the old house of Thomas Childe. A 'Ploughman's Hall' suggests that farming was closely integrated with the big house. Gardeners and grooms also had their own rooms. Certain foods

99. Northwick Park was undergoing major renovation in the late 1980s to create apartments. This part of the house was built in 1686 by Sir James Rushout, the son of a Flemish immigrant connected with the textile trade, and there is Flemish influence on its style. His arms are above the west front entrance.

100. The east front was remodelled in 1730.

were separately prepared and stored; there were rooms for flour, cheese, meat, malt, milk and fruit. A great deal of silver and linen was listed, and a collection of 53 pictures, including four 'Dutch pieces'. The cellars contained two hogsheads of red wine and 36 hogsheads of beer. In a greenhouse or Orangery were 37 orange trees in tubs and pots, 21 pomegranates, five fig trees, and 54 glasses for the cultivation of melons. Fifteen dozen July flowers (gillyflowers or wallflowers) were awaiting planting out in the garden. In fact, Sir James seems to have been about to embark on a garden scheme, as there were 119 yew trees in pots in the lower garden. Several local gentlemen purchased these.

Farm stock included nearly two hundred sheep, but only 44 breeeding ewes; a shepherd was in the list of servants and two years' clip of wool was unsold. Some of the sheep were bought by John Dutton, of Sherborne, and it is tempting to think that they were the special Cotswold sheep which were maintained at Sherborne in the 19th century. Northwick sheep were still being sold at Chipping Norton Fair six months later. There was a small herd of bullocks, heifers, cows and bulls, and stacks of wheat, barley and pulses, a new wagon and two old ones and three ploughs. Sir James Rushout owned a coach and six black coach horses, and an old chariot.

The servants, 12 men and eight women, had to be discharged immediately. Ann Brabant's name seems to indicate that she shared the Rushouts' Flemish connections. It was decided to give them an additional three months' wages because of the suddenness of their departure, and because it was winter-time and they might suffer or complain. One woman, probably the housekeeper, had not been paid for nearly six years and most were owed more than a year's wages. Some servants bought materials or stock in the sales. The steward bought two pigs and an old cow and calf. Bacon flitches were sold, and hops and ale and farm stock of all sorts.

Sir James Rushout's brother, John, inherited Northwick; he made alterations to the house and moved there after his marriage in 1729, and died in 1775 at the age of ninety. Sir John seems to have been the architect of the Park. There is no mention of deer in 1705, but, when Nash visited Northwick about 1779, the Park was then stocked. Northwick is on the north side of the manor of Blockley and the parish boundary passes very close to the rear of the house itself. Half the Park is in Campden. In the mid-19th century there were 800 fallow deer, and a keeper and under-keeper were employed, and also a flock of 250 sheep and three Cotswold rams.

Alterations to Northwick Park were made in 1778, when the next John inherited it. 'The three best rooms have no fireplaces', Nash commented. The great bay windows on the south side were added at this time, perhaps an experiment in solar heating. John Rushout was created Baron Northwick in 1797. His daughter married Sir Charles Cockerell, first baron Sezincote. The curved iron staircase and round landing at Northwick Park suggest that George, the second Lord Northwick, carried out extensive rebuilding on the east side in the early 19th century. He was particularly known for his picture collection for which he built a gallery. He was a most hospitable man. His obituary in the *Morning Post* said that

> Not his pictures only, but his whole house and park were at the service of the public. They who have frequented that lovely spot for picnics or parties of pleasure know well the hospitality with which its noble owner would send out choice fruit or other refreshment by way of welcome to his often unknown visitors.

He lived until the age of 89, dying intestate in 1859. For a second time the estate was inventoried and appraised. On the ground floor was the saloon, the principal room and the most expensively furnished in the house, the dining room, drawing room, library and small library, and picture gallery. Four bedrooms and three attics were associated together as in the 1705 inventory, but the Victorian house contained a further 14 chambers, as well as the principal bedroom with two dressing rooms. There was one bathroom. Individual bedrooms were provided for four men servants and five maid servants, the butler and housekeeper both had separate bed and sitting rooms, and there was a Servants' Hall. The out-buildings were extensive: charcoal house, wood house, coal house, deer slaughtering house, bone house, knife house, wash house, brewhouse, bakehouse; the engine house contained Northwick Park's fire engine; dairy, cheese room, boot room, laundry, feather room and flour room. There were stables, coach house and harness room, a carpenters' department and all the buildings required for animal and poultry husbandry.

The contents of Northwick Park were valued at a little under £10,000. Silver plate accounted for nearly £1,300; the picture collection was worth only half as much. Seven smart equipages, painted in one of two liveries, were kept in the coach house. A yellow and black chariot was crested. Lord Northwick was famous for driving in a coach and four to and from Thirlestane House in Cheltenham, which he had purchased partly in order to house his ever-growing picture collection. A barouche was painted in the same colours. A dark green and white four-wheel phaeton, a dog-cart, a green phaeton and a green Irish car made up the complement. The 16 carriage horses were worth more than twice as much as the conveyances they pulled. Beer, ale and cider were generously stocked and a cellar of 45 bins contained 2,600 bottles of wine of all sorts: sherry, madeira, port, hock, light wines, liqueurs, brandy, rum, constantia, claret, French wine, champagne, white and red Hermitage, and one gallon of British Brandy, altogether valued at eight hundred pounds.

The regular establishment of servants was eight men and eight women. Five years before the inventory was made, in 1854, a wages book was started, recording the amount agreed with each servant for a year's service. The gradations of pay emphasised the gradations in status below stairs. A book of 'Rules to be observed at Northwick Park', written sometime in the 19th century, has also been preserved. Together these show that the house was run by the butler and the housekeeper; these were the only servants permitted to make purchases. For 34 years Louis Mayland had been employed as butler, at 50 guineas a year; when he died, his nephew Henry Mayland succeeded him and received six months' arrears of wages owing to his uncle. The housekeeper was paid 35 guineas. Under her were the cook, one laundry maid, who both washed and mended the linen, dairy maid, two house-maids, kitchen maid, and a still-room maid. Their wages ranged from 18 guineas for the cook to 6 guineas for the still-room maid. Men servants were a footman, coachman, gardener, who was married to the cook, two stable men or boys, and park keeper and under-keeper. In the 1880s, under the last Lord Northwick, a secretary, valet, school maid and nurse were also employed.

Life below stairs was carefully regulated. The major concern was to prevent the largesse of the kitchen being spread too freely amongst the servants and their friends. The housekeeper had strictly to keep the women servants out of the servants' hall except when at dinner and supper, and the men servants 'as much as possible out of the kitchen'. Only she was to carve the meat and she had to remove it from the hall when she left. She also had the keys to the food stores. Only she and the butler had cream in their tea. 'No victuals to be given to travelling beggars.' Another fear was of the men and women mixing freely. Female servants were not allowed to walk alone with any 'friend' without permission and their outings were few and strictly watched over; Sunday afternoon walks were allowed, provided they were not to Blockley, but the walkers had to return before dark. For the women servants, the day began at 6 a.m. and before breakfast they had to wash their own clothes. At the end of the day the

GENTLEMEN AND COUNTRY HOUSES

101. The duties of servants at Northwick Park were recorded in a notebook about the middle of the 19th century. The cook was expected to serve up a good dinner for 12 to 14 persons and was well paid at £18 a year, with 'tea and sugar found'. The groom, in addition to specific duties, had to do as Lord Northwick ordered! His wages were £2 a year.

housekeeper checked that everyone was in bed, the coal house locked, the windows fastened and the shutters shut before she could herself retire. Provided that she agreed the day's work had been accomplished by supper time, the women or girls could then work for themselves. On Sundays the most junior servants took it in turns to cook dinner for the other servants who were at church.

For one year, in 1853, Lord Northwick or his gardener used 'Samuel H. Webb's Practical Farmer's yearly account book' to note equipment, crops, wages and the tasks allotted on each day of the week throughout the year to the 16 men and boys employed weekly or quarterly for outside work. There was less need to keep a record of the terms of their employment, and no doubt there were casually employed men in the early 18th century too, of whom no record survives. Three men and a boy worked for the gardener, and also employed were three labourers, two carpenters, two bricklayers/masons and their labourers, two sawyers and a watchman. The Northwick estate was nonetheless relatively modest; it may be compared with the Duke of Beaufort's establishment at Badminton in the south of the county, where about the same time, 183 men and women were regularly employed, nearly half of whom were indoor servants in the house.

The Northwick garden establishment had charge of nearly one hundred pigs, five cows and a calf, 20 breeding ewes, and a poultry yard of chicken, ducks and drakes, pigeons, turkeys, guinea fowl and two peacocks and peahens. That year vetches, swedes, carrots, parsnips, mangolds and turnips were grown in about equal quantities and smaller amounts of potatoes and cabbages, wheat, oats and kohl rabbi, a popular vegetable. The work of the winter months comprised a great deal of wood cutting and carting, riddling coal and fagotting apple trees, killing pigs, setting quickthorn, ploughing the garden, digging, shifting dung, clearing the road of tumps and breaking stone. In the spring the meadows were rolled, the 'sally bed' ploughed and planted with carrots, docks got up, and time was spent carting and brewing. In the summer months the sheep were sheared, the yard cleaned, nettles pulled up, carpets beaten, swedes and cabbages hoed, potatoes earthed up, kohl rabbi set, hay made. Summer also brought hedge trimming, pumping water, carting lime, cleaning and stanking the pond in Sawpit Orchard, making a watering place in West Meadow, carting water for brewing, picking up windfall apples, cutting grass—but this job was not recorded very often. The spouting on the counting house was fixed one day, the windows were mended, also the pump in the stable yard. Autumn came, with apples to be picked and crushed in the cider mill, mangolds to be got up, the reservoir cleaned, and a boat to be launched and attended to—and so back to winter and wood cutting.

Two coppices were planted that autumn. Bebnal coppice contained 750 larches interspersed with spruce, scotch fir, oak, chestnut and beech, and a few black pine and black willow. Nash Bank was predominantly larch, nearly 1,500 of them, and 530 spruce with a few deciduous trees; the coppice was surrounded with 420 hawthorns. Coppices provided shelter, cover for game, and wood for fuel. Many of the trees round Northwick may therefore be about a hundred years old; Augusta Coppice, marked on the Ordnance Survey map, commemorates the last Lord Northwick's wife and was probably planted towards the end of the 19th century. Once agriculture began to experience severe depression towards the end of the century, more coppices were created on arable land which no longer brought an economic return, and the wooded nature of some parts of the Cotswolds is attributable to this.

Country House Society Observed
F. E. Witts, Rector of Upper Slaughter from 1808 until his death in 1854, was a member of the circle of Gloucestershire gentry through his grandmother, Anne Tracy of Stanway. Meticulously, throughout most of his life, Witts recorded in 90 neatly-written volumes his duties as churchman and J.P., his impressions and activities. The explanations of family connections and his descriptive style suggest he was writing for posterity, perhaps for his son. He was quick to note those with less impecccable social origins than his own, like Mr. Gist, 'the eldest son of the rich parvenue residing at Wormington Grange', or Sir Thomas Phillipps from Middle Hill, Broadway: 'He cannot boast of being an hereditary gentleman; his father raised himself from menial employments to considerable wealth by successful enterprise in the most money-making times of the cotton manufactory'.

Witts was unduly snobbish about Thomas Phillipps, the famous book and manuscript collector; he was educated at Rugby and Oxford, and made a baronet in 1821, and his collecting was inspired by a desire to save manuscripts which he saw were being thoughtlessly destroyed. He became a trustee of the British Museum and a fellow of the Royal Society; his daughter, Katherine Fenwick, inherited his collections with Thirlestane House in Cheltenham which he had bought from Lord Northwick to house them. On the other hand, Witts was pleased to meet Lord Redesdale of Batsford at a dance at Maugersbury and to dine with Lord Deerhurst of Bourton on the Hill at Northwick Park. Lord Deerhurst had married a daughter of Sir Charles Cockerell of Sezincote, who had married a daughter of the first Lord Northwick. Such family connections were typical.

Witts visited Northwick in 1838: 'We were sumptuously entertained on plate with an excellent dinner, good wines, and courteous and friendly reception. There was general conversation on politics, all being Conservatives ...' He slept at Northwick and next day was shown the picture gallery and the house. He admired the park with 'a large herd of deer, a fine sheet of water, a prospect over rich and fertile land', but his host was censured for not being prepared to give his time and effort to county affairs and the magistracy. Witts often called on his relatives at Stanway. In 1826 'a noisy but not unskilled band of musicians from Broadway played most of the evening in the hall, and a promiscuous dance among the gentry and domestics was kicked up'. He was invited to dinner quite often at Oddington House. Here he found 'well-lighted cheer' but bemoaned the journey of seven miles in the dark.

18 January 1833

> Dinner at half past six o'clock: lamps lighted in our carriage to go to Oddington: cold raw weather and thick fog: home at a quarter past one o'clock. Our fathers were more sensible, who kept earlier hours and visited when the moon was bright.

Witts was a keen sightseer, and his diary illustrates the growing interest in architecture and the restoration of old buildings. In 1828 he went to Sezincote and was shown round whilst the owners were abroad; he was critical of the house and of its site, though he admired the gardens and shrubberies. He described Buckland Manor before its extension and restoration:

> The church is on a bank, where the valley is contracted between two wooded hills. Close behind is the ancient gable-ended white-washed, half ruinous spacious old mansion, now occupied as a farm-house with a courtyard in front, and short avenue leading from the village road.

His diary spans the years of Sudeley Castle's first restoration; in 1839 he explored the 'ruins' but in 1851 recorded somewhat ruefully the lavish hospitality offered by Mr. Dent, the new High Sheriff of Gloucestershire, which he foresaw would be a difficult precedent for susbsequent holders of the office. At Snowshill he found 'a good old-fashioned mansion house where Mr. C. Marshall, Lord Wemyss's steward, resides'. At Farmington Lodge he saw a 'very comfortable residence, now that it is in good repair and well-fitted up' and he also noted its suitability for field sports; there was a complete set of kennels there for hounds. At Sandywell he observed the new owner in 1824 altering and modernising the house, and extending the park by planting up to the new road which was being cut between Sandywell and Whittington Court, to avoid the steepness of the direct ascent up Dowdeswell Hill.

Cotswold manor houses were left untenanted, Witts observed, because the gentry found it more pleasant to reside in Cheltenham, like the owners of Mickleton Manor, or Lady Elcho, who took a house for two months 'that she might enjoy more society than she could command at Stanway'. The Chamberlaynes of Maugersbury said their reason for moving to Cheltenham was 'the severity of the climate', but in truth, 'Mrs Chamberlayne sighs for the society to be enjoyed only in or near a public place, and is dreadfully ennuyee with the solitude of the old mansion near Stow, and the infrequency of social engagements in its vicinity'. The Talbot family resided in London for much of the year: 'so it is that fashionable people desert their country seats, their rich parks and lovely gardens in the finest season, and live there only in the gloomiest months of the year'. When he was nearly seventy, Witts was approached to become deputy lieutenant of Gloucestershire; modestly he noted 'country squires, well qualified and permanently resident, are few in this district'.

Gentlemen's Seats

In his survey of the agriculture of Gloucestershire in 1807, Rudge identified 24 'gentlemen's seats' in 69 north Cotswold parishes. In 13 of the 24 places there were large houses in the 17th century; these were Barrington, Bourton on the Hill, Bourton on the Water, Broadwell, Buckland, Campden, Maugersbury, Sezincote, Sherborne, Stanway, Stowell, Sudeley and

Weston Subedge. Northwick Park in Worcestershire was also in this category, with at least one of the big houses in Broadway, the Priory in Burford, and Bruern. The other houses in Rudge's list had been newly-built or enlarged to become gentlemen's seats; these were Batsford House, The Grove at Little Barrington, Eyford House, Farmington Lodge, Guiting Grange, Temple Guiting House, Saintbury, Salperton Park, Brockhampton Park in Sevenhampton and Stanton Court. Middle Hill and Spring Hill in Broadway, similarly, were newly-built. Rudge found only half the houses actually occupied by their owners.

> The residence of gentlemen at their mansions is a matter of not inconsiderable importance to the welfare of the public, and when they occupy a part of their estates with a view to its improved cultivation, highly favourable to the agricultural interests of the county.

Stanway, for example, was occupied only intermittently during the 19th century, especially after ownership passed to the Earl of Wemyss, whose main estates were in Scotland.

A number of former gentlemen's houses had declined in status to be simply farmhouses, and were not included in Rudge's list, like Banks Fee in Longborough, Charlton Abbots, Dowdeswell Court and Sandywell in Dowdeswell, Farmcote, Hailes, Hawling, Hinchwick, Icomb, Mickleton, Notgrove, Great Rissington, Shipton Solers, Lower and Upper Slaughter, Snowshill, Whittington and Withington. Within a few years Stowell, too, was described as 'an ancient mansion now a farm house'.

In 1870 Kelly's *Gloucestershire Directory* listed 26 'principal seats' in the Cotswold area, nearly the same number as Rudge had noted, but in 1914 the number had increased to

102. Brockhampton Park was built between 1639 and 1642 and was much enlarged in the mid-19th century to become a 'gentleman's seat'.

GENTLEMEN AND COUNTRY HOUSES

thirty-seven. Some quite new gentlemen's seats were built before 1914, many houses were up-graded, and nearly all Rudge's 24 houses were added to or altered. It is surprising to find that this activity continued unabated or even expanded after the onset of agricultural depression in the 1870s. Owners with new sources of wealth came into the Cotwolds and, while there were large numbers of manor houses for sale, it did not necessarily mean decline for the houses themselves.

Older houses restored and extended to become gentlemen's seats include Icomb Place, Eastington Manor in Northleach, Notgrove and Turkdean Manors and Leygore Farm, Postlip Hall, Stanton Court and Whittington Court. Early in the 19th century Dowdeswell Court and Sezincote were completely rebuilt, and Sherborne was taken down and re-erected. Oddington House, Salperton Park, Barrington Grove and Northwick Park were all enlarged. Sudeley Castle's restoration started after 1837. In the middle of the century Brockhampton Park, Buckland Manor, Campden House, Farmington Lodge and Stanway House were all substantially added to and new gentlemen's seats were created at Ebrington Manor and Great Rissington Manor. Towards the end of the century Stowell Park was greatly enlarged. Abbotswood in Lower Swell was built in 1867, followed by Batsford, Bourton on the Water and Eyford, together with new country houses at Copse Hill in Upper Slaughter and Nether Swell. Part of Mickleton Manor was taken down and rebuilt higher up the hill to form Kiftsgate Court; after 1918 a famous garden was created there, inspired and helped by Lawrence Johnston's garden at nearby Hidcote. Willersey Manor was also moved higher up the hill.

103. The Manor House at Aston Subedge was a notable early 17th-century building which has continued as a farmhouse and not been dramatically restored or altered.

New Architectural Enthusiasms

The most remarkable of the new country houses of the 19th century is Sezincote, built in 1805. During the Civil War the houses in the village and the church had been ruined, in an attack on Bishop Juxon, a well-known Royalist; he actually lived at Little Compton, where he was reputed to enjoy the hunting and kept a pack exceeding 'all other hounds in England for the pleasure and orderly hunting of them'. The destruction gave his nephew and heir, Sir William Juxon, a chance to rebuild the farmhouses at a distance from Sezincote House; the Home Farm is all that is left of the former village and the church was demolished in the 18th century. Sir William Juxon paid tax on 15 hearths in 1671. The old house was gabled in traditional style, according to a little sketch of 1705. Charles Cockerell became the owner of Sezincote in 1798; he had worked in India for the East India Company and, like the Rushouts at Northwick, brought new sources of wealth to the improvement of a Cotswold estate, and foreign influences on the building style. His brother, Samuel Pepys Cockerell, an architect and surveyor, drew the plans for Sezincote, although he seems not to have visited India himself. The Cockerells designed a house in Cotswold stone based on Indian styles, including the striking large onion dome on the top. Exotic gardens were developed round the house. Charles Cockerell was made a baronet soon after, and his son adopted the name of Rushout. The adjacent estate of Hinchwick was purchased in 1826 and the manor house immediately rebuilt, also to a design of Samuel Pepys Cockerell, but in the vernacular idiom.

In 1871, Sir Charles Rushout and his family were resident at Sezincote, with an establishment of 14 servants, and there was stabling for upwards of thirty horses. His death caused the estate to be sold in 1884 to James Dugdale from Lancashire. Since the beginning of the century, the estate had more than doubled, to 3,645 acres, divided into 11 farms. There were 400 acres of woodland and the house was situated in 'a beautifully timbered park', which the Cockerells had planted. Sezincote had not been particularly wooded when Rudder described it, as he commented on the lack of support for the theory that the name was derived from the French word 'chesne' meaning oak. In 1944 Mrs. Dugdale sold Sezincote to Sir Cyril Kleinwort, who restored the house while Lady Kleinwort restored the gardens, after a period of considerable neglect. Sezincote's exotic and colourful appearance today attracts many visitors.

Abbotswood in Lower Swell was built in 1867 by Alfred Sartoris, younger son of a Frenchman, though educated at Eton. The house perhaps reflected continental influence. He had bought part of the Lower Swell estate in 1865 and also owned a large part of Upper Swell; in the return of owners of land in 1873, he had nearly a thousand acres. Abbotswood was built a short distance away from the original manor house, which was known as 'The Bould' or 'Bowl'. The name is derived from the Saxon word for building; as there was a Roman villa near, this may have been the reason for the name. In 1881 the Bowl was lived in by the farm bailiff, but has since been demolished. The occupants of Abbotswood were the butler, housekeeper, two housemaids, footman and kitchen maid. Mark Fenwick, who was connected with Sir Thomas Phillipps, bought Abbotswood in about 1901 and had it remodelled and enlarged by Edwin Lutyens. Verey in his survey of Gloucestershire's buildings considered Abbotswood to be Lutyens' 'major work in the Cotswolds'. Lutyens also laid out the beautiful gardens which are now occasionally open to the public.

Eyford was a 'small, pleasant seat with delightful gardens and ponds' early in the 18th century. In 1840 the house was described as a 'well-arranged gentleman's Residence upon an inexpensive scale'. Sir Thomas Bazley bought Eyford in 1850. His wealth was made in cotton spinning and merchanting and he was notable for his important part in the Anti-Corn Law

League, and for being a commissioner for the Great Exhibition in 1851 and for the Paris Exhibition in 1855. He became one of the Members of Parliament for Manchester in 1858 and shortly afterwards retired from business in order to devote his time to 'his numerous public duties'. in 1870 he tried to sell Eyford with 1,127 acres, but then decided to rebuild on a new site further up the hill and away from the Cheltenham to Stow road. In 1873 he owned nearly 560 acres in Gloucestershire and in 1881 was resident in his new Cotswold house, with six servants. The coachman and his laundress wife lived in the Lodge. A new owner, John C. Cheetham, demolished Bazley's house in 1910 and built another, designed by Sir Guy Dawber, as well as a farmhouse at Eyford Knoll.

About the same time that Sir Thomas Bazley was building Eyford, Sir Thomas Brassey was also building a new house not far away at Copse Hill in Upper Slaughter. Copse Hill was an estate of 455 acres which had been separated from the rest of Upper Slaughter manor in 1852. Lord Sherborne had persuaded the vicar of Sherborne and Windrush to accept it in exchange for 330 acres in Windrush, so consolidating his estate round Sherborne. The old Manor House of Upper Slaughter was the farmhouse for the new estate. At the same date, the manorial rights were sold to the rector, the diarist F. E. Witts, and so the rectory became the manor house, hence its later name, the *Lords of the Manor Hotel*. Sir Thomas Brassey was the son of the well-known railway contractor, a small landowner and surveyor in Cheshire who, after meeting George Stephenson, became a contractor for railway works; another son established himself as a gentleman at Heythrop, not far away, with an estate of 4,000 acres. Sir Thomas Brassey only came to Copse Hill for eight or ten weeks 'on purpose to hunt with his Brother, and visit him at Heythrop Park', John Simpson Calvert wrote in his diary. Copse Hill was remodelled by Lutyens in 1900, some years before Abbotswood. Lutyens was also employed to restore eight cottages in the Square in Upper Slaughter known as Bagehotts Cottages, part of the Copse Hill estate. Sales particulars in 1913 said, 'it is needless to say more than that Copse Hill is typical of Mr. Lutyens at his best'. The house was lit by its own Acetylene Gas Works.

Perhaps fortunately, Brassey did not want to live in the old Manor House, which remained unaltered and occupied by the farmer. When Evans made his bicycle tour of the Cotswolds in 1905, he found it 'one of the most beautiful examples of its kind in the whole of the Cotswolds'. The house is built into the side of the hill above the river Eye, and consequently has four storeys at the back but three in the front. Underneath the back part of the house there is a 15th-century undercroft, and the corbelled chimneys also appear to be 15th century. On the south side, there may originally have been a cross-wing, which was brought into line with the rest of the house when a new, gabled front was erected about 1600. A porch was built later in the 17th century. On it are the arms of the Slaughter family, who may have owned the house from the 12th century. The last member of the Slaughter family died in 1741. Some time later, there was a complicated legal enquiry to establish who was the heir; none was found, so that in 1809 Lord Sherborne was able to establish his purchase of the house, and subsequently to divide up the estate.

Captain Brassey decided to sell Upper Slaughter Old Manor House in 1908, together with 628 acres. The valuer noted 'its front of three quaint old gables' and said it was an 'exceedingly picturesque and interesting stone-built house'. The farm manager was living there. There was a croquet lawn and an excellent kitchen garden, stables for eight horses, loose boxes and outbuildings:

> I do not think the Manor House should be regarded as part of a farm homestead but as an exceptionally attractive Cotswold Tudor House which would appeal very strongly to anyone seeking to purchase a fine old-fashioned residence which has escaped

restoration...The natural beauties and healthfulness of the Cotswolds are becoming year by year more widely appreciated, and old Manor Houses on the Hills invariably find ready purchasers.

At the same time, before it became a gentleman's residence it needed not only restoration but extension. The estate was considered unsuitable for hunting, because it was not compactly within a 'ring fence', but the Heythrop, Cotswold and Warwickshire hounds were all within easy distance, and there was good trout fishing in the Windrush. The valuer's hopes were not realised and no purchaser was found. Captain Brassey thereupon himself restored the house. In 1913 the whole Copse Hill estate was advertised, of 765 acres, and consisting of cottages in Lower Slaughter and the water mill and bakery as well as the Square in Upper Slaughter. Upper Slaughter Manor House was now described as 'thoroughly and lovingly restored in recent years, the innovations including Electric light, Hot Water Heating and up-to-date sanitation'. A subsequent owner enlarged the house with the addition of a fourth large gable on the front, very much in keeping with the original house.

The design of Batsford is considered traditional, based on Elizabethan models. It replaced an 18th-century house, of which the owner had been sufficiently proud to provide an illustration for Rudder's *History* in 1779. Rudder said that the Freeman family had been there for 300 years, but the last Freeman died in 1808, and John Mitford, who was a distant relation, acquired the estate and also added Freeman to his own name; he had been made Baron Redesdale a few years previously. It is said that he rebuilt Batsford church in 1822, but the church was demolished and rebuilt in the same style as the estate cottages near it in 1862. His son in 1873 owned more than 4,000 acres in Gloucestershire, and in 1877 was made Earl of Redesdale. On his death in 1888, a nephew somewhat unexpectedly inherited Batsford and 'a very considerable fortune'; he resigned his position as Secretary to the Board of Works, sold his house in Chelsea, and took possession of his Gloucestershire estate. He, too, added Freeman to his name. The new owner decided to build on a new site a short distance away from the old house. Algernon Bertram Freeman-Mitford had travelled widely, and brought to Batsford an interest in tropical gardening. He was also a writer, and *The Bamboo Garden*, published in 1896, was an *apologia pro Bambusis meis at Batsford,* 'an apology for my Bamboo at Batsford'. In 1902 he was created Baron Redesdale. Batsford was sold in 1920 to Gilbert Wills, President of the Imperial Tobacco Company. He became Baron Dulverton in 1929. His heir carried on the particular interest in Batsford's grounds and created an arboretum which is open to the public.

Sir Guy Dawber's first introduction to the Cotswolds was when he was sent as clerk of works by Sir Ernest George, the architect, to supervise the building of Batsford. He so enjoyed Cotswold vernacular architecture that he decided to stay in the area for a few years and opened a small office in the village institute building at Bourton on the Hill; his success enabled him to open a London office in 1891. Dawber designed a largely new manor house in Bourton on the Water in 1890, and in 1903 an entirely new house, Nether Swell Manor, with a model farm nearby, in a part of Lower Swell close to Stow. Eyford followed in 1910. By this time Dawber was well-known. His study of Cotswold architecture led to a book in 1905 on *Old Cottages, Farmhouses and other stone buildings in the Cotswold District*, which followed his study five years earlier of buildings in Kent and Sussex. Many of his examples of craftsmanship and design were drawn from Stanton, which he visited just before the village was restored. Dawber was impressed with the traditional materials and knowledge of local Cotswold stonemasons. He found the introduction of 'foreign' materials like Welsh slates for roofs 'unrestful'.

104. Bourton Manor is a 17th-century house at Bourton on the Water, remodelled in 1769, and named about 1900 when the owner purchased the 'lordship of the manor'. The original manor near the river was rebuilt to a design by Sir Guy Dawber.

105. Nether Swell Manor was designed by Sir Guy Dawber in 1904 and extended in 1908. The tower housed water tanks and the servants' stairs. Ashlar stone came from Milton under Wychwood and roof slates from Eyford. The name 'Nether Swell Manor' was a reflection of status rather than of history, as Lower Swell manor house was in the grounds of Abbotswood.

> New buildings should be designed in as modern a spirit as we wish, but using the materials at hand. The very fact that in so doing we shall be more or less governed by the same conditions and limitations as these old builders, will give our work to-day a continuity in design and feeling, in harmony with the old, and will help to carry on in a certain sense the spirit and tradition of bygone days, which surely in these times of change and hurry, will appeal to many.

It is not surprising, therefore, that Dawber's own Cotswold buildings echo vernacular styles, and that he was one of the founders in 1926 of the Council for the Preservation of Rural England. He was knighted in 1936, two years before his death.

Stanton was restored by Sir Philip Stott, one of a family of architects, based in Manchester and Oldham; he was particularly known for the design of cotton mills in all parts of the world. He bought Stanton Court in 1906 and settled there in 1913 and was made a baronet in 1920. His architectural interests were brought to bear on the restoration not just of the big house but of most of the village. At the Court, the inside was modernised, while outside, the front door was moved and the rake of the gables was 'altered to conform to the Cotswold style'. The stone cartouche was put over the front door, with the arms of Wynniatt and Phillipps, 'after lying about in the grounds for many years'. The Court, church, village hall, school and street were lit by electricity generated by a water turbine at the waterworks, which was built in 1906-7 to supply the village. The bathing pool was created in 1910. In the village, the farmhouses owned by Stott were adapted, the Manor Farm was made into a private house and the cottages opposite Warren House, once the old malthouse, were made into a farmhouse. His work included moving three timber-framed barns into the village. Stott also made the path up Shenberrow Hill, called the Ladies' Walk, which is said to have taken two men two years to complete, between 1921-23.

The Decline of the Country House

'It used to be considered that an estate of 10,000 acres was needed to maintain a country house.' Returns of owners of land in every county of the United Kingdom, made between 1872 and 1873, indicate that only Lord Sherborne in the Cotswolds then met this criterion, with nearly 16,000 acres. His rivals in the south of the county were Lord Fitzharding at Berkeley Castle, and the Duke of Beaufort at Badminton. There were 23 landowners based in the Cotswold area with more than 1,000 acres, of whom no less than 16 were eligible for inclusion in John Bateman's list of the Great Landowners of Great Britain; his criteria were 3,000 acres and £3,000 in income. Although the holdings of his 'great landowners' were spread over several counties, all 16 had at least 1,500 Cotswold acres. The largest landowner was the Earl of Wemyss at Stanway, who had nearly 5,000 acres in Gloucestershire, and 57,000 acres in Scotland. From the point of view of local influence, equally significant were Edward Rhys Wingfield at Barrington, with 6,000 acres in Gloucestershire and Oxfordshire, and 13,000 in Bedfordshire and Glamorgan, the Earl of Eldon at Stowell with 7,000 in Gloucestershire and 19,000 in other counties, Lord Redesdale of Batsford with 9,000 in Gloucestershire, Oxfordshire and Warwickshire, and another 17,000 in Northumberland, and Lord Northwick, who had 5,000 acres in Worcestershire and Gloucestershire and another 2,000 in Shropshire, where his other country house was situated at Tenbury. Great landowners with large interests outside the Cotswold area were Earl Harrowby of Weston Subedge, the Earl of Gainsborough of Campden and Lord Craven of Brockhampton, who each had two to three thousand acres locally and up to 29,000 acres elsewhere.

GENTLEMEN AND COUNTRY HOUSES

The other men in Bateman's list had more modest estates of between 3,000 and 5,000 acres which were mainly local: Sir Thomas Bazley at Eyford, John Coucher Dent at Sudeley, R. R.Coxwell Rogers at Dowdeswell, of whom Bateman noted that 'This family have held most of these lands continuously since Henry VII', Sir Charles Rushout at Sezincote and Mrs. Lawrence at Sevenhampton, though Thomas Beale Browne at Salperton and Edmund Waller at Farmington each had a second estate outside the area, the first in Ireland and the second in Yorkshire. A number of the Cotswold manor houses were sustained by smaller amounts of land; the owners were J. C. Chamberlayne at Maugersbury, Mrs. Greenaway at Little Barrington, Walter Lawrence at Whittington, W. F.Lawton at Wyck Rissington, J. C. Phillipps at Broadway, the Hon. and Rev. G. G. C. Talbot at Withington, though this estate included the very large rectorial lands, and Miss Jane Talbot at Temple Guiting. Alfred Sartoris at Lower Swell, Charles Whitmore at Lower Slaughter and T. W. Wynniatt at Stanton each had a little less than 1,000 acres.

The concentration of peers in the Cotswolds was notable and gave estate agents a useful selling point for properties. When Wyck Hill in Rissington was advertised in 1868, the brochure said, 'The Society in the Neighbourhood is of a very select character, the Seats of Lord Sherborne, Lord Redesdale, Lord Dynevor, Sir Charles Rushout, Lord Leigh, J. Grisewood Esq. and others being in the immediate vicinity'.

Estate agents also emphasised a property's suitability for sporting and hunting. For Wyck Hill, a map was produced showing where all the hunts met. When Springhill in Broadway was advertised in 1922, the estate particulars included details of 'the Game Bag' over the period 1908-11: over 2,000 pheasants and 3,000 rabbits, with a few partridge, woodcock and hares.

From 1868, so many big estates were offered for sale that it suggests that a depression in arable farming affected landowners' rents in the Cotswolds rather sooner than in other arable areas. In 1868, the 'manorial estate' of Upper Swell was advertised, 'compactly situated in a ring fence' and including the whole parish and village of Upper Swell. The Home Farm was 'formerly the manor house', and there were four other farms, Swell Mill Farm being 'recently erected'. The same year, the Wyck Estate was advertised, with 'a large part of Wyck Rissington

106. When the sale particulars for Sezincote estate were prepared in 1880, no mention was made of the unusual appearance of the house; on the other hand, the gentry residing in the neighbourhood were considered an important advantage.

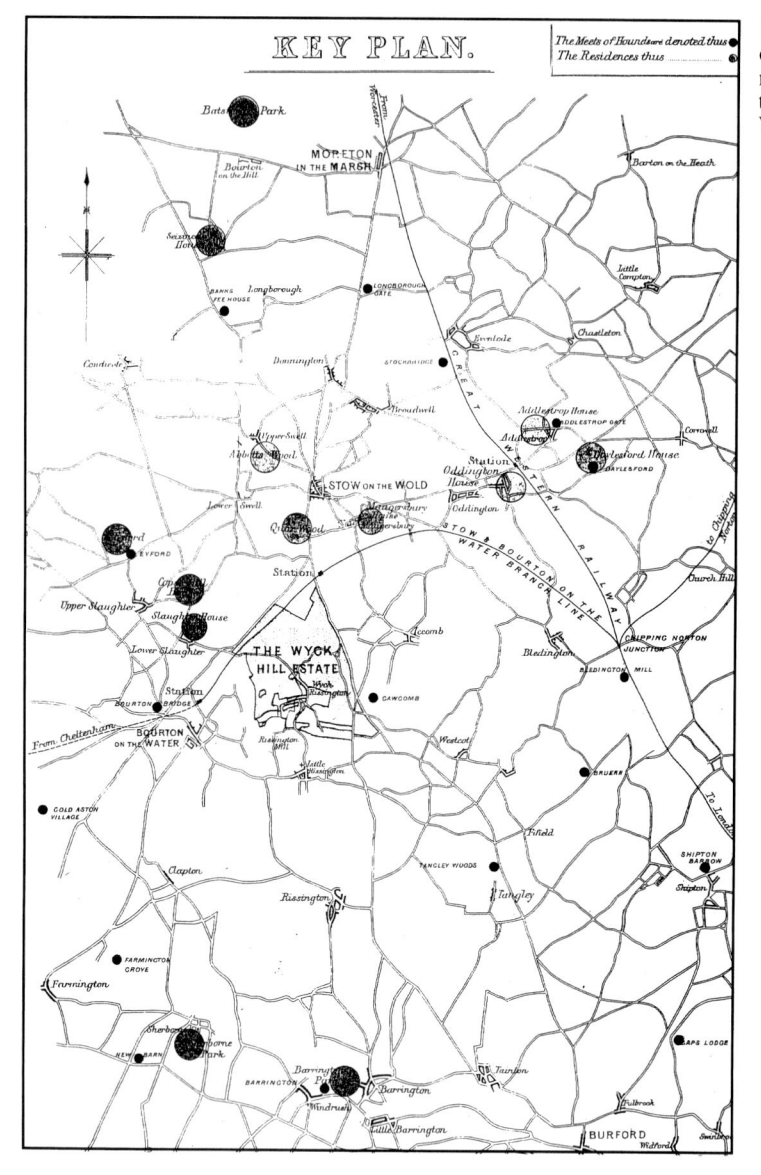

107. A map of the location of hunts and gentlemen's residences was provided with the sale particulars of the Wyck Hill estate in 1875.

village'. A prospective buyer in 1870 found the Eyford estate on the market, and the following year the whole parish of Notgrove, excluding only the rector's land, with all the village cottages and four farms, one of which was the old Manor House. Sezincote was offered for sale in 1880. Salperton Park and Upper Hampen were sold in 1890, with almost the entire parish of Salperton, and in 1900 Shipton Solers and the Waller's big estate of Farmington, Turkdean and Hazleton, 4,452 acres. These three manors had been owned by the Waller family since the mid-18th century. A large auction of Gloucestershire estates took place in 1911, comprising Cold Aston or Aston Blank, Hawling, 'one of the prettiest villages in the county', and some parts of the Stowell estate: Hampnett, including 'practically all the village' and the lordship of the manor, and Lower Farm, Compton Abdale.

XXVIII Batsford Park was rebuilt on a new site between 1888 and 1892. Sir Guy Dawber studied Cotswold vernacular style in the district while supervising the work.

XXIX Experience in the East India Company inspired this exotic house at Sezincote in Indian style but Cotswold stone. The earlier manor house was traditional and gabled.

XXX The market cross in Stow on the Wold was headless and used as a lamp standard until it was restored in 1878 in memory of J. C. Chamberlayne of Maugersbury.

XXXI The memorial cross of 1920 in the Square of Guiting Power is a reminder of the attempt to establish a market here in the early 14th century. It was placed where there were foundations of an ancient cross.

XXXII Bourton on the Water had been denied full town status by Evesham Abbey, but nonetheless developed many of the characteristics of a town; it was described as handsome in the 18th century and the canal of the river Eye was much admired.

XXXIII Broadway Street has an exceptional series of houses built by freeholders, and has something of an urban character.

XXXIV Manor Cottages in Snowshill are the oldest in the village. The taller one was a malthouse. In the background is Oat Hill; there was formerly a quarry on the top of the hill. Like the Manor House opposite, the cottages are now owned by the National Trust.

XXXV Condicote Cross stood by a pool and marked the division of the town between Slaughter and Kiftsgate Hundreds. Both pool and cross are marked on a map of 1797 (*see* page 204). The 14th-century cross was given a new head in 1864. About 1898, when visited by Arthur Gibbs, vegetables were being grown on the Green.

XXXVI The ruins of Hailes Abbey are maintained by English Heritage; modern tourists have replaced the medieval pilgrims. The Abbey was built in a sheltered and secluded spot and the atmosphere is still of peacefulness.

In the first five years after the First World War, as agricultural depression again set in, more estates changed hands, including Batsford, Spring Hill in Broadway, and Roel farm of 1,090 acres. Parts of the Barrington Park estate were sold: 1,105 acres in Great Rissington and land in Taynton which included the famous stone quarries, though some of the stone area was retained by the Barrington estate. In 1923 the Earl of Eldon sold Stowell. The estate was still 6,300 acres and comprised 10 large farms; Stowell Park with the Home Farm was nearly a thousand acres and the other farms were in Chedworth, Compton Abdale and Yanworth. The estate has continued to be an unusually large one in the Cotswolds. Five of the greater Cotswold landowners remained through the difficult years of the late 19th century and after the First World War, and were in possession of their estates in 1939, at Barrington Park, Sherborne, Stanway, Sudeley and Whittington. Three estates had not changed hands in four centuries but, after the Second World War, Sherborne, too, was given up.

One particular problem for landowners after the First World War was obtaining servants to run the houses which had been so ambitiously enlarged in the previous century. Colonel Wingfield of Barrington Park found that the financial crash of 1931 was mainly responsible for his difficulties. It sharply reduced the value of his investments and rents, while Americans, who had prior to this been keen to tenant English country houses, were removed from the market. He could look back to an establishment of 23 resident servants in 1881, and a French governess, looking after his family of nine. Though he had sold off part of his estate in 1920, it had not solved the financial problem of maintaining one of the larger Cotswold mansions.

In 1934, 16 owners of mansion houses in the Cirencester Assessment Committee's area decided to appeal against their local tax assessments, or rates. They were prepared to bring their case if need be to the Quarter Sessions and agreed to pay the costs in proportion to their existing assessments. The owners of Batsford, Northwick, Sezincote, Copse Hill, Barrington and Sherborne were among those appealing. Valuers were employed, and the initial appeal in November 1934 resulted in an offer to reduce the assessments, but not by as much as they all considered fair or necessary. Legal advice was obtained to help prepare the attack on the Assessment Committee, which eight owners now pursued.

The case was heard at Quarter Sessions two years later, and a report was published in the professional journal, *Rating and Income Tax*. A list of 57 mansions in the area was produced, from which it was calculated that the 'standard mansion' was rated on average at £280. Batsford's actual rate at £574 was the highest, Northwick was £425, Stowell £400, Brockhampton £370, Sherborne £350, Barrington £340. Also included were Dowdeswell and Sandywell, Ebrington, Farmington, Kiftsgate, Notgrove, Wyck Hill, Salperton, Sezincote, Shipton Oliffe, Copse Hill, Nether Swell, Abbotswood, Norton Hall in Weston Subedge and Willersey. Colonel Wingfield was called first, and was the only one required to give evidence. Naturally he tended to highlight the disadvantages of his situation, and he painted a gloomy picture of his family mansion.

> There were many rooms, and in particular servants' rooms, which were dilapidated and unfit for habitation. Water had to be pumped from a spring 1½ miles away. The nearest railway station was seven miles away and all goods sent there had to be carted, including 250 tons of coal and coke a year. Repairs were constant and expensive, the roof and water pipes were in a very bad state, and there were many outbuildings and large stabling which was expensive to keep up and exceeded the needs of the ordinary occupier. The domestic quarters were in a semi-basement, 19 steps below ground floor level and were dark, dreary and damp. Artificial light had to be used ...

He pointed out that he had to live somewhere, and must try to preserve furniture, fittings and fabric.

For the rating authority, it was argued that he had exaggerated. The house was 'a fine one', the servants' rooms were not in the main mansion and in any case had not been included in the valuation. The roof was not that bad, and anyway was irrelevant since it was the landlord's responsibility and the rating assessment was based on what a hypothetical tenant of the house would pay! Argument turned on whether the house could be let; it was alleged that the Cotswolds were well-known for sporting and social amenities. The competence of the valuer was questioned; under examination he admitted he had never let a mansion himself. An agent maintained that he had not let such a mansion for two years; the Assessment Committee said that four mansions had recently been let and 13 sold. The court reduced Barrington's assessment to £230 gross and the other seven cases were at once settled out of court.

In 1934, the same year that the Cotswold mansion owners were making their complaint, Lord Lothian addressed the National Trust and warned of the danger of the end of the country house. Before 1939, only two houses in England were taken over by the Trust, but the Second World War finally ended this way of life. No one any longer was called the squire of the village. Since 1945 a number of big houses have been demolished, some partly demolished, and some 100 in England have been acquired by the National Trust; institutions have also taken some over. In the Cotswolds, Brockhampton, Northwick and Sherborne have all been divided into apartments, which has maintained the external fabric, though not always the interior. Snowshill Manor has been given to the National Trust and is open to the public. Hidcote gardens were the first to be presented to the joint committee of the National Trust and the Royal Horticultural Society, formed in 1948 to preserve gardens of outstanding merit. Hailes was also presented to the National Trust, though the house created out of the ruins of the monastery had largely been demolished in the 18th century. The ruins were transferred to the Department of the Environment, and then to English Heritage.

108. The sale particulars of Stowell Park estate in 1923 drew attention to the sporting facilities in the neighbourhood, including the proximity of three packs of hounds.

Chapter Eleven

The Decline of the Village and Town

Cotswold villages were shaped by the open-field system. The groups of farmhouses, barns and outbuildings, and the cottages, were conveniently sited for access to both the arable and pasture. Copyhold tenure had helped to preserve the fabric of the villages, because it had discouraged sub-division or amalgamation of holdings. Although small, in 1608 the villages were well-balanced and thriving communities, and the market towns reflected their prosperity. Villages were changed completely by the end of the 18th century by two developments which were concurrent: the enclosure movement and the increasing concentration of land ownership in fewer hands. The result of both together was that most farms became much larger, and a number of old farmhouses were no longer required; a few new farms, or sometimes a barn and cottages, were built away from the villages. The whole social balance of the villages was altered, as labourers came to out-number all other inhabitants.

Contrasting Occupations in Village and Town
William Harrison suggested in his *Description of England* in 1577 that villages typically contained 40 to 60 households and 200 to 300 communicants. Clergymen were occasionally asked to report how many families or households there were in their parishes, and how many 'houseling people' or communicants, those aged about sixteen and over. Several returns for Gloucestershire survive and also for Cotswold parishes in Oxfordshire and Worcestershire. Few Cotswold villages reached Harrison's typical size; only Mickleton had 200 communicants in 1551, and Bourton on the Water and Sherborne in 1603; most villages had less than 100 communicants or perhaps 160 inhabitants. A more sophisticated analysis was made at the end of the 17th century by Gregory King. He tried to calculate how many settlements there were in each of eight or nine bands and he estimated that villages ranged from 150 to 400 inhabitants, the average being around two hundred. Again, Cotswold villages appear to have been small; only one village had as many as 400 inhabitants in 1712, and not even a quarter reached 200. Sixty years later, Bourton on the Water and Withington had populations of 500, but, despite general population growth, more than half of Cotswold villages still had less than 200 inhabitants.

Although small, Cotswold villages in the early 17th century had a surprising variety of craftsmen. The militia lists of men able to do military service in 1608 are likely to indicate a large proportion of all occupations; no women were mustered, but of the men only the old, the very young and the disabled were not eligible. In about half the villages there were tailors and carpenters though only one village had a joiner, who was a maker of better-quality jointed furniture. Smiths were listed in just under half of the places, and so were masons; one was a freemason. Millers were named in a third of the places; Lower Slaughter and Sherborne each had three millers. Weavers were concentrated in the Winchcombe area; nearby there were also three dyers in Didbrook and a fuller in Stanway, where Tewkesbury Abbey had had a fulling mill. Only five villages had a butcher and only one a baker; in this respect, the villages since 1945 have moved back to a traditional relationship with the nearby towns which supply such services. Some craftsmen may have been temporary residents, like the glazier in Coln Rogers, who seems likely to have been glazing the church or a big house. In Guiting Power one man was identified as a musician. Longborough and Bourton on the Water were amongst the larger Cotswold villages and had the most craftsmen, though the two villages of Mickleton and Sherborne were twice as large.

Bourton on the Water was perhaps more a town than a village in character, and significantly had a carrier living there, but this was one of the few places where occupations were not always stated. A census of households in 1771, preserved in a later local doctor's notebook, shows more clearly the urban character of this community of 125 households and 615 inhabitants, with a population of gentlemen and gentlewomen, a surgeon, and nearly as many tradesmen as farmers and labourers. 'This handsome village', Rudder called Bourton on the Water; it consisted then of houses arranged irregularly along the river or canal, whose banks were well-gravelled and made a 'delightful walk'.

> Nature has been lavish with her favours to this place, and with a little more of the assistance of her younger sister Art, it might vie in beauty and elegance with any Dutch village. Many topographers have made no mention of it, and none have done it justice; for though it has not a market, there are shops for the supply of goods, and the more necessary kinds of trades are carried on as in a market town.

Cotswold towns were also smaller than average. Harrison thought market towns contained 300 to 400 families and 2,000 communicants; King thought that only about 140 of the 800 or so towns in the country reached the level of 1,000 inhabitants. None of the Cotswold towns in 1551 or 1603 had anything like 2,000 communicants. Winchcombe in 1551 had 700 communicants, Campden 485, Northleach 400, Stow on the Wold 350 and Moreton in Marsh only 250. The minister in Burford in 1547 returned 544 communicants before Easter but 1,000 after Easter, illustrating how these figures can give only approximate estimates of populations; possibly the second return included Fulbrook, which was a chapelry of Burford, or perhaps it was simply the Easter communion which had brought everyone to church. Town parishes, of course, included agricultural hamlets within their boundaries; Blockley, for example, in 1551 had 400 communicants in the parish, which included six rural hamlets, but in 1563 only 87 families in Blockley itself. The muster list in 1608 named 153 men in Winchcombe and 123 in Chipping Campden; Northleach and Stow on the Wold each had just a few less and Moreton in Marsh only 44 able-bodied men. These numbers correspond to between a third and a fifth of the number of communicants five years previously.

In the early 18th century, Chipping Campden, Stow on the Wold and Winchcombe had more than 1,000 inhabitants, which places them amongst the larger towns in the country, though in no way to be compared with the five cities in Gregory King's calculations, which had over 20,0000 inhabitants each. Burford probably also had more than 1,000 inhabitants, with 409 houses counted in 1738, and Blockley with its hamlets, with 300 families in 1776. Northleach had nearly 1,000 inhabitants in 1712, but Moreton in Marsh, with a population of only 500, was still typical of the majority of places King reckoned as towns.

The market towns were quite different from the villages, not just because of denser building but because of the pattern of occupations. Most town inhabitants in 1608 were engaged in providing goods and services; farmers formed less than a tenth of the town populations. The majority of the townsmen were innkeepers, butchers, bakers, tailors, shoemakers, mercers, carpenters, masons, slaters and smiths. Coopers, wheelers, chandlers, tanners and curriers occur occasionally, and in all five market towns there was a rather small cloth industry, chiefly weavers but also one or two dyers and fullers, a shearman, tucker and cardmaker. In Winchcombe, there were 16 tailors, 11 butchers, six shoemakers, five smiths, four mercers, four carpenters and a joiner, four bakers, two slaters, a mason, an innkeeper and an ostler. The roads around Winchcombe were notoriously bad, and the town did not lie on a major route through the county, so there was little business for inns. Another 40 tradesmen came from a wide variety of trades, two men were musicians and one a drummer, and labourers made up most of the rest of the able-bodied men. Winchcombe was the only town to have two professional men, a physician and a barber, the latter closer to a surgeon than the name implies today. Gloving was significant in Winchcombe and Northleach, and malting in Chipping Campden. In Northleach two parchment-makers and a vintner were mentioned; in Chipping Campden a cutler and rope-maker; in Stow on the Wold an ironmonger and a cheese-monger. The variety makes the towns quite individual.

There is no muster list giving occupations for Burford, but between 1575 and 1630 many are incidentally recorded in the Burford charity records. The more prosperous were likely to become trustees of charity property; their trades may therefore give a fair indication of important employers in the town. There is clear evidence of the cloth industry in Burford. The trustees included four mercers, two haberdashers, two clothiers, two tailors and a broadweaver, and other cloth workers mentioned incidentally are six more clothiers, a coverlet-weaver, a dyer, a draper and a woollen-draper. However, a considerable range of trades occur amongst the trustees: three tanners, two chandlers, two shoemakers, a saddler, smith, innholder, ironmonger and clergyman, and there is incidental mention of a barber surgeon, cutler, glazier, slater, cooper, butcher, baker, currier, two glovers and five more chandlers.

The word 'yeoman' is quite often used to describe the Burford charity trustees; the word was obviously used in a general sense implying status, and does not necessarily imply farming interests, as a shoemaker, mercer, saddler, chandler and clothier were also called yeomen. However, many of Burford's inhabitants probably were farmers. Thirteen of the 50 owners of town burgages in the survey of the manor of 1552 owned quite large amounts of land, varying from 20 acres to 336 acres, and nine others had small-holdings. Edmund Sylvester, who built Falkland Hall in 1558, was a clothier who owned one and a half burgages but he also had a yardland in the open fields. At his death in 1568 he left money which was to be loaned to young craftsmen; another Edmund Sylvester, clothier, together with a glazier, dyer and draper, were the first recipients. Simon Wisdom had 143 acres of enclosed land as well as a large block of property in High Street and a smaller block in Sheep Street; he was variously described as clothier, mercer, yeoman, and fish merchant. His name is well known because his initials appear over a number of house doors in Burford, and he was an important instigator of the grammar school foundation. In the countryside, the yeoman was an owner of land, as is illustrated in Stanton, and was distinguished from tenants of land who were called husbandmen; probably this status of ownership applied in the towns, too.

Cotswold Towns in the *Universal British Directory*

Cotswold towns reflected closely the fortunes of the villages. As the numbers of small farmers fell, so did the prosperity of the market towns; the bulk of the labouring population had very little money to spend in their markets. Trade Directories began to be published in the late 18th century. Of the seven Cotswold towns included in the *Universal British Directory*, only Burford was apparently sharing something of the urban expansion being experienced in other regions of England.

Blockley, it was noted, had no market, though there were two fairs, and 'the silk manufacture employs a number of hands and meets with considerable success'. Campden had 'a tolerable market' every Wednesday and four annual fairs, the December fair being notable for sales of cattle; here too a 'silk mill and manufactory have been recently established in this town and neighbourhood, and which promise great advantage to the proprietor, Mr. John Franklin, and to the public, by the employment given to the great numbers of the poor'. Although on the London-Worcester road, only a waggon service started from Campden. Moreton in Marsh was 'a poor, inconsiderable town, coaches and waggons passed through, along the Fosse Way, from Bristol to Worcester. A market on Tuesdays had been granted by charter but it had 'long been discontinued'. Some decades later, following the opening in 1826 of the horse-drawn rail road between Moreton and Stratford on Avon, the market was refounded by Lord Redesdale, resident nearby at Batsford; he had leased the manor from the Dean and Chapter of Westminster Abbey a few years previously, thus illustrating the continuing relevance in the 19th century of the lord of the manor. Northleach, too, according to the *Universal British Directory*, was 'a small, ill-built town', and 'has now neither trade nor anything deserving notice except the church, which is a noble old Gothic structure, and a well-endowed grammar school in good reputation'. Nonetheless there was a large grain market on Wednesdays and three annual fairs, while coaches and waggons passed through daily. Stow on the Wold, in 'the high Cotswold country', was also an 'ill-built town of very little trade, the poor here being very numerous'. A variant of the common reference to Stow's position on the top of a hill was reported: 'This place stands so high, and is so exposed to the winds, that it is a common observation, that they have but one element, viz. air, there being neither wood, common, field, nor water, belonging to the town'. A

109. Moreton in Marsh market was revived by Lord Redesdale in the mid-19th century after he became lord of the manor. The town house in the background was the headquarters of the North Cotswold Rural District Council, established in 1935.

THE DECLINE OF VILLAGE AND TOWN

110 & 111. *(Above) The Lamb Inn,* Burford, with *(right)* its 'Lamb and Flag' sign, is a reminder that sheep were penned in front of the houses in Sheep Street on market day. The building is mainly 15th century and the inn may be at least as old as that. The sign is a traditional picture of the *agnus dei* carrying the flag of triumph.

Thursday market was held, and two fairs; Defoe's remark that 20,000 sheep were sold at one fair was repeated, some eighty years later. Coaches and waggons passed Stow along the Fosse Way and there were said to be three good inns in the town.

Winchcombe was described as 'populous', but carried on very little trade, 'owing in a great measure to the badness of the roads in its vicinity, which are by far the worst in the county', a charge repeated by other observers. A *Guide Book* of 1781 warned travellers that the road from Cheltenham

> is in some parts steep, rough and unpleasant. In its present state, which cries out for amendment, it will not do for wheel carriages of the genteeler sort; and even the farmers' draught horses are to be pitied, much more than the owners, for dragging through it! The avenues to the town of Winchcombe are neglected with an equal insensibility to convenience and obvious self-interest.

Market day was Saturday, and three fairs continued, two particularly noted for horses. One waggon a week went to London. Rudder also said that the market was 'very inconsiderable' and the town 'little frequented', he thought partly because it was not on any 'great road', though the two fairs on 6 May and 28 July were 'well-supplied with cattle and draught horses'. Winchcombe had actually declined in size quite significantly during the 18th century from 2,715 to 1,960 inhabitants.

A more encouraging account was given of Burford: 'a large market town', with excellent accommodation and two 'capital inns'; 'it attracts the attention of travellers'. Good turnpike roads connected Burford with a number of principal cities, London, Oxford, Worcester, Bath, Birmingham and Gloucester and the usual route between Oxford and Worcester went through the town. A coach from Gloucester to London called every evening at 7 o'clock at the *Bull*, and another London coach left at ten o'clock from the *Red Horse*; a weekly waggon to London left on Monday morning, and another to Bristol, Oxford and Bath. Gloucester waggons took up goods at the *Lamb* in Sheep Street. In 1812, shortly after the *Directory* was published, unhappily for Burford's innkeepers, the Turnpike Trustees built the bypass which is the present main road, and traffic no longer went along Witney Street and past the Tolsey into Sheep Street. A new coaching inn, the *Bird-in-Hand*, since renamed the *Cotswold Gateway*, was built at the top of the hill on the new road.

The Directory noted that in Burford 'are said to be sold the best rugs, and here is also a good manufacty of duffels ... Burford is famous for saddles, and lying near the downs, draws a great profit from the horse-races, which are frequent here'. Burford races enjoyed a late 18th-century period of popularity, though they were no longer held near Burford but at Aldsworth; the enclosure of Burford after 1795 and of neighbouring parishes about the same time must have contributed to the ending of the races in 1802. The Saturday market was noted for corn, as the town was 'situate in a fine corn country' and also for cattle; two fairs were held.

The occupations actually recorded in the *Directory* do not entirely bear out the descriptions of the Cotswold towns. In each one there were two or three doctors, at least one legal man in all except Winchcombe and a fair number of resident gentry, except in Northleach. The cloth trade was still represented, though not very strongly; Burford seems to have had the most businesses in this traditional area. A range of service trades was recorded, butchers, bakers, inn-keepers, grocers, malsters; Burford and Stow each had a distiller and Winchcombe two liquor and cider merchants. Paper-making was established at Postlip, in Winchcombe's rural parish, and in Burford there was a clock and watch-maker.

'Close' Parishes and Large Farms

Many Cotswold parishes would probably have been described by early Victorian commentators as 'close' or closed, where very few people owned the land, and tight control was kept on cottage building and on population. There had been a considerable reduction in the number of people who owned land during the 18th century, as is seen by a comparison of figures for 18th-century freeholders and parliamentary voters in 1832. Atkyns stated numbers of freeholders in his *History* in 1712 and printed lists are available for 1741 for Worcestershire and 1754 for Oxfordshire; they relate to those qualified either to serve on juries or to vote in parliamentary elections. The first statutory register of parliamentary electors was prepared following the 1832 Reform Act.

A parish usually had at least two freeholders, the lord of the manor and the parson. A rectory or vicarage was a freehold since the parson did not have any obligations to work for

112. North Street, Winchcombe, was the horse-market; horses were tethered to rings on the houses which at the end of the 19th century could still be seen.

113. Hailes Street shows intensive development of houses and cottages at this end of the town; timber-framing is still common, probably because not all the town's inhabitants were prosperous enough to refront them in the fashionable Cotswold stone.

the lord of the manor in return for his benefice. Many parishes also included within their boundaries one or two freehold estates, which may once have been knights' fees. Any parish with five freeholders or less could therefore be classed as a 'close' one. A third of Cotswold places came into this category in 1712: Buckland, Charlton Abbots, Compton Abdale, Cutsdean, Farmington, Hailes, Hampnett, Hazleton, Hawling, Icomb, Notgrove, Pinnock and Hyde, Salperton, Sherborne, Lower Swell and Upper Swell, Sezincote, Shipton Oliffe and Shipton Solers, Sudeley and Whittington; in Eyford, Roel, Stowell and Yanworth there were no registered freeholders. Not all were dominated by a big house, while parishes like Great Barrington and Stanway, where there were notable gentlemen's seats, were not closed at this date. Nor were all closed parishes small; Sherborne was one of the largest villages in the area, but was nonetheless owned by one family. There had been only five freeholders in Sherborne from at least 1661, and after this date the Dutton family consolidated their ownership; the last small freeholder sold his holding to James Dutton in 1766.

Thirteen agricultural parishes would have been called 'open' and had significant numbers of freeholders, ranging from 16 in Naunton to 54 in Mickleton; these were Great Barrington,

18			BRADLEY HUNDRED.			
Parish or Township.	No.	Christian and Surname.	Place of Abode.	Nature of Qualification.	Street, Lane, or other like place in this Parish or Township where the Property is situate, or name of the Property.	Name of the Tenant.
EASTINGTON TITHING IN NORTHLEACH.	803	Day, Edward	Eastington	Freehold House	...	Himself
	804	Eeles, Thomas	Ditto	Leasehold house and land	Cottage farm	
	805	Fricker, Edward	Grosvenor Place, Cheltenham	Trustee in possession, with beneficial interest...	Vineyard	
	806	Hewer, George	Eastington	Occupying tenant of £50 per annum	Middle-end farm	
	807	Hewer, William	Ditto	Ditto	Northleach farm	
	808	Leech, Thomas	Ditto	Freehold House	...	Himself
	809	Millard, Daniel	Ditto	Occupying tenant at £50 per annum	Upper-end farm	
	810	Parrott, George	Ditto	Freehold House	...	Richard Ferris
	811	Parrott, Thomas	Ditto	Freehold Houses	...	Joseph Tea
	812	Spindlo, Charles	Ditto	Occupying tenant at £50 per annum	Northleach Mill	
	813	Starkings, Richard	Ditto	Lifehold	...	Himself
	814	Saul, Thomas	Milton	Freehold House	Eastington	Richard Moss
	815	Tayler, Thomas	Eastington	Occupying tenant at £50 per annum	Coal Yard farm	
	816	Wilkinson, Jacob	Ditto	Ditto	Winterwell	
NOTGROVE.	817	Johnson, Thomas	Notgrove	Occupying tenant at £50 per annum	Manor house	
	818	Pyrke, Joseph	Little Dean	House and land	Folly farm	
	819	Wetherell, Richard	Pashley House, Ticehurst, Sussex	Rectorial house and lands	...	Robert Comely
	820	Williams, Thomas	Notgrove	Occupying tenant at £50 per annum	Near the village of Notgrove	
	821	Wood, Edward	Ditto	Ditto	Folly farm	
	822	Wood, John	Ditto	Ditto	Roberts's farm	
SHIPTON OLIFFE.	823	Bee, Richard	In this parish	Occupying tenant at £50 per annum		
	824	Bee, John	Ditto	Ditto		
	825	Barnfield, William	Ditto	Freehold House	...	Himself
	826	Chapan, William Posthumous	Crane street, Salisbury	Freehold Farm and Lands	...	Richard Bee and Self
	827	Cook, William	In this parish	Occupying tenant at £50 per annum		
	828	Fletcher, George	Shipton Sollars	Freehold land	...	Himself
	829	Griffin, William	In this parish	Freehold House	...	Ditto
	830	Handy, Thomas	Hampen Farm	Occupying tenant at £50 per annum	Hampen farm	
	831	Hathaway, Daniel	Shipton Oliffe	Freehold House and Garden	...	Ditto
	832	Tuffly, William	In this parish	Freehold House and Land	...	Ditto
	833	Williams, William	Ditto	Freehold house	...	Ditto
SHIPTON SOLLARS.	834	Gegg, Richard	In this parish	House and garden held for lives	In this parish	
	835	Handy, Avery	Ditto	Occupying tenant at £50 per annum		
	836	Meadows, Edward	Frog Mill, in this parish	Ditto	Frog Mill	
STOWELL.	837	Councer, Richard	Stowell	Occupying tenant at £50 per annum		
SALPERTON.	838	Browne, John	In this parish	Freehold House and Estate	...	Himself, John Cook & others
	839	Barnfield, Thomas	Ditto	Copyhold House and Land	...	Himself
	840	Barnfield, Daniel	Ditto	Freehold House and Land	...	Ditto
	841	Cook, John	Ditto	Occupying tenant at £50 per annum		

114. The different categories of voters are illustrated in a page from the first electoral register made as a consequence of the 1832 Reform Act.

THE DECLINE OF VILLAGE AND TOWN

Bledington, Bourton on the Water, Mickleton, Naunton, Oddington, Great Rissington, Little Rissington, Stanton, Taynton, Weston Subedge, Willersey and Withington. In many of these places there is evidence that copyholders had been converted to freeholders in the 16th or 17th centuries. Mickleton is most striking, with more freeholders than most of the small towns. Blockley, Broadway, Burford, Chipping Campden, Stow on the Wold and Winchcombe all had between fifty and seventy, Northleach 34 and Moreton in Marsh thirty. This shows the continuing effect of the medieval creation of burgages or small freehold plots of land when the towns were founded. Between 1712 and 1832, a marked reduction in freeholders occurred in every agricultural parish, excepting Bourton on the Water and Naunton. In Buckland, Notgrove and Upper Swell, the only registered voters were the rectors, in Sezincote only the owner, Charles Cockerell. In some there were no registered voters at all: Eyford, Hailes, Hazleton, Roel, Shipton Solers, Sudeley and Yanworth. Only in Compton Abdale and Shipton Oliffe had there been a small increase. Even in Mickleton the number of freeholders had fallen from 54 in 1614 to 32 in 1832. Rudder noted that the population had declined during the 18th century, and 'the whole parish is in dairy and grazing, in which fewer hands are employ'd than in tillage'.

The Barringtons are an example of how the ownership of an open parish was completely altered in the course of the 18th and early 19th centuries. There were 20 freeholders in Great Barrington and six in Little Barrington in 1712; when Little Barrington's open fields were enclosed in 1759, 12 small allotments of land were made and three large ones. Gradually the Ellis family, lords of the manor of Little Barrington, bought up freehold estates south of the river Windrush and when Giles Greenaway bought the estate in 1779 and rebuilt Barrington Grove, his property covered nearly all of the parish. Similarly in Great Barrington, the Talbot and Talbot Rice family of Barrington Park bought up freeholds north of the Windrush, though not until the 1930s was the whole parish in the Wingfield family's ownership, with the purchase of 37 acres of church land. The 1832 electoral register listed three freeholders in Great Barrington and five in Little Barrington, of which two were the respective vicars, and one was Charles Greenaway of Barrington Grove; George Talbot Rice, Baron Dynevor, owner of Barrington Park, was not of course an elector of members of the House of Commons since he sat in the House of Lords.

Together with the reduction in the number of owners of land, in many places the number of farmers had been halved between 1608 and 1831. Longborough had 24 husbandmen in 1608, but only 11 in 1831; Buckland had 23 in 1608 but 15 in 1831; Sherborne had 24 in 1608 but 15 in 1831. Farms were correspondingly much larger. Only one farmer in every five in 1831 relied on the family to work the holding and did not employ labourers. If 25 acres of arable could be cultivated by one man in the early 19th century, four fifths of farms were larger than this in 1831. Small farms had not survived even in those places where copyholders had become freeholders in the 16th or 17h century, and so were free from the pressure of landlords wanting to create larger farms. The only places where they were at all numerous were Blockley and Campden, each with 21, Broadway where there were 14, Mickleton, 17, and Winchcombe, 25. These places probably shared the market gardening specialisation of the Vale of Evesham, which made small holdings viable. In his survey of Gloucestershire carried out during the Second World War, Payne particularly noted the market gardening specialisation in Mickleton, where he also remarked on the 'family' spirit in the area and said it was quite usual to find two or more brothers or fathers and sons operating one holding. A large number of holdings were under an acre, and were cultivated by agricultural workers in their spare time; this encouraged diversity. The main crops were brussels sprouts, cabbages, cauliflowers, potatoes, 'a very fine asparagus', apples and plums.

Whereas in other parishes in the Vale of Evesham, like Willersey, Broadway, Buckland, Stanton and Stanway, about 2½ per cent of the land was devoted to market gardening, in Mickleton and also in Saintbury the proportion was 20 per cent. Payne linked Campden with the market gardening area, too.

Enclosure had encouraged the creation of large farms and made their operation more practicable. 'In new enclosures, it was an object of considerable consequence to place as much land as could conveniently be managed, under one tenant, to reduce the necessity of buildings'. Farms were still not entirely within a 'ring fence', as the effect of the terrain itself, and of the habits of mind created by centuries of common-field operation, made commissioners allocate each owner areas of meadow, pasture and arable which were often not contiguous. John Bravender, who was a land agent and surveyor in Cirencester, wrote a prize essay for the Royal Agricultural Society of England in 1851. He observed that larger holdings predominated in the north Cotswold region, 'varying from 200 to 1,000 acres and upwards. I know several above 1,000; one or two above 2,000 acres'. In 1939, a high proportion of Cotswold holdings were above 300 acres, 500 to 1,000 was said to be 'common' and some holdings were over 2,000 acres. Farms of 300 acres were then considered small for the Cotswolds. Few were owned by the farmer himself, and for a farm to be still in the hands of the same family for well over a hundred years, like Lower Hampen in Shipton, is thought to be very unusual.

Farmers and Labourers
Fifty years of rapid population growth all over the country preceded the 1831 census, and in many rural parishes there was a strong impression that there were more labourers than could possibly be employed. Cotswold village population reached a peak in 1831, but there were still less than 500 inhabitants in three quarters of Cotswold places and less than 300 in more than half. Enclosure may have led naturally to some increase in population, as open downland pastures were converted to arable, which required more labour. It was Marshall's impression, and that of the Dursley man who wrote a chapter on Gloucestershire for *England Delineated* in 1800, that the Cotswolds were 'at present principally devoted to the growth of corn'; a poem was quoted about the greedy plough preying on the sheep's carpet of grass—a reversal of the 16th-century belief that sheep were devouring men's sustenance. By 1851 'nearly the whole of the downs is now broken up, and produces moderate crops, with paring and burning and a liberal use of artificial manures'. This was the most prosperous period for arable farming, when rural population reached its peak.

Cotswold villages in 1608 had been inhabited in about equal proportions by husbandmen, labourers and craftsmen, but at the end of the 18th century Marshall thought that 'labourers are remarkably numerous for the nature of the country' and in 1831 there were six times more labourers than farmers. In at least a third of Cotswold parishes there were as many as 12 labourers for every farmer. A Royal Commission was set up in 1832 to investigate the operation of the Poor Laws, because there was widespread concern about the growth of rural poverty and the increasing cost of poor relief, which was the responsibility of each parish. Questionnaires were sent out to sample rural and urban parishes. The rural queries asked, amongst other things, for estimates of labour requirements and supply, and for information about the ownership of land and cottages. Replies were received from Great and Little Barrington, Broadway, Donnington and Maugersbury, the three Rissingtons, Upper Slaughter and Temple Guiting. They reveal some surplus labour in a number of these parishes. At Little Barrington 25 or 26 labourers were needed for the proper cultivation of the land but there

THE DECLINE OF VILLAGE AND TOWN

were actually 30 in the parish, and two were said to be 'out of employ'. In all three Rissingtons, there was surplus labour. The rector of Upper Slaughter, F. E. Witts the diarist, however, found demand and supply perfectly balanced; 'there is no superabundance of labour in this parish', Witts wrote, and the overseer of Maugersbury said the same.

Sir Thomas Phillipps of Middle Hill, who wrote the Broadway replies to the Rural Queries, put forward a rule of thumb for estimating labour requirements of one man to 25 acres of arable or one man and a boy to 100 acres of pasture. A few years later Bravender's researches into eight Cotswold farms, ranging in size from 100 acres to 1,000 acres, confirm the general applicability of Phillipps' ratios. In winter rather less labour was required than in summer: a 1,000-acre farm, which was largely arable, normally employed 34 men but 42 to 44 in summertime. The rector of Little Rissington told the Poor Law Commission that 35 men were needed in the least busy period but 'more of course required in hay and corn harvest', and the same comment was made by Wyck Rissington's overseer. When ripening and weather conditions were favourable, the more hands that could be mobilised, the faster the harvest could be successfully gathered. In the winter, therefore, some labourers were unemployed. Also the amount of arable varied from year to year; 'seeds', that is, various grasses, were sown to create temporary grassland.

A factor in determining the size of a village's population was thought to be cottage ownership. Sir Thomas Phillipps suggested that small tradesmen in Broadway 'have added much to our Pauper population by building new Cottages and charging high rents'. Certainly Broadway's population had grown, from 1,117 in 1801 to 1,517 in 1831. Labourers owned cottages in Great Rissington, probably some of the former copyholders' cottages, and here population had grown from 277 in 1712 to 468 in 1831, and the surplus of labourers was the largest of the three Rissingtons. In Little Rissington there were nine freehold cottages belonging to the labourers, though one labourer owned five; the term 'labourer' must have described a man who did not farm for himself. Another 11 cottages belonged to the parish and were occupied by poor people, and 20 belonged to the proprietors of land. In Wyck Rissington, however, apart from the eight which the parish had owned since enclosure, all the cottages belonged to the landowners. On the other hand, in both the Barringtons, the lords of the manor owned all the cottages, yet the population of Great Barrington had risen from 120 inhabitants in

115. The curfew was rung in Moreton in Marsh curfew tower until 1860. In Winchcombe in the 1870s the curfew was still being rung from the time of the Autumn Stow Fair until the spring fair in May. 'The tolling lasts about ten minutes and is immediately followed by the deliberate tolling of the day of the month'. It was a simple way of controlling the population of the streets at night.

116 & 117. A stronger sense of time seems to have developed in the mid-18th century. The sundial on Whittington cottages *(left)* was probably provided by the lord of the manor and the sundials in Naunton *(right)* (a second one is painted on the south wall) were commissioned by the rector, who also started a Dame school to teach poor children.

1712 to 532 in 1831. The farmers, however, kept close watch on residents and those who could not claim a legal right to poor relief from Great Barrington were made to move out, or obtain guarantees from other parishes that the costs would not fall on Great Barrington.

After 1831, Cotswold villages generally lost population. The concentration of ownership, both of land and cottages, prevented the villages from growing further. By 1861 decline was evident throughout the area, a decade at least before the 'Great Depression' in arable farming led to a general exodus from the countryside; between 1882 and 1907, the years of the Great Depression, the amount of arable declined by a third in Gloucestershire. Arthur Gibbs thought that 'the country is rapidly going back to its original uncultivated state'. 'Now that farming is no longer remunerative, the whole country seems to be given up to hunting. Depend upon it, it is this sport alone that circulates money through this deserted land'.

By 1931 many places had returned to their 18th-century levels of population. A sample of 33 farms investigated by Payne had an average size in 1938 of just under 500 acres and half employed at least five labourers; one employed more than twenty. Vale farms averaged only about 150 acres and employed 3.5 men per farm. Neither 20th-century commuting nor tourism has radically altered the small size of the Cotswold villages.

Old Cottages and Model Cottages
Very few real cottages in the villages have survived. A cottage in the 16th century, with its small garden plot, would have been tiny and possibly built of wattle and daub or rubble; it would certainly have been thatched. Stone-tiled roofs seem so much a part of the Cotswold landscape that it is difficult to realise that nearly all the houses were once thatched; of 30 buildings in Buckland at the end of the 16th century, houses, cottages, barns and cowhouses, only two were tiled, and two were partly tiled. There seems to be no particular social distinction

THE DECLINE OF VILLAGE AND TOWN

about which were tiled; one was a stable and cowhouse, one a six-bay cottage, which seems to be so large that it was perhaps a row of cottages. Two bays of one of the larger houses were slated and the rest were thatched. A survey of Stanway at the end of the 18th century shows that most of the houses were thatched. When Rudge wrote, in the early 19th century, thatch 'was rapidly falling into disuse'. In the 19th century, therefore, many houses were either re-roofed or were rebuilt. It is probably significant that from the beginning of the 19th century rectories and vicarages begin to be described as tiled.

Cottage improvement often involved inserting a floor in a one-storey building to create a bedroom upstairs. This development sometimes followed the erection of a brick chimney in a house where formerly there had been an open hall with the fire on a hearth in the centre of the floor. The low walls of single-storey thatched cottages made it necessary to insert the characteristic dormer windows to light the rooms upstairs. The internal walls of old Cotswold houses were wattle and daub, according to Guy Dawber's observations at the end of the 19th century, and so the buildings lacked transverse ties; the weight of the new stone roof frequently pushed the walls out of plumb. As a result, dormers tend to lean backwards.

Landowners in the 19th century began to feel responsible for the cottages on their estates; awareness of poor housing standards grew and led to a great deal of cottage building. When Marshall surveyed the agriculture of Gloucestershire at the end of the 18th century, he made no mention of cottages; Rudge, however, a few years later, perhaps because he was a clergyman, spoke with concern about the standard of rural housing: 'the popular complaint against the dilapidation of cottages is but too well founded ... more families are crowded together, than is either consistent with comfort, health or decency'. He thought landowners should have been encouraged to build or repair cottages because it would improve the chances of securing good tenants. Cottages were usually let with the farms. A particular point

118. A cottage at Sevenhampton displays a variety of roofing materials: thatch, local stone and Welsh slate.

was made, when Wyck Rissington was sold in 1868, that the 26 cottages, which made up a large part of the village, were 'not let with the farms'. Tenant farmers were not inclined to spend money improving or rebuilding their workers' cottages.

E. Chamberlayne Esq., of Maugersbury, built model cottages in 1800 in a crescent, facing south and near a convenient spring; each cottage had a lower room and pantry downstairs and two bedrooms upstairs with a low room in the attic 'capable of containing beds'. In the centre of the crescent there was a Sunday School room, a public oven and furnace in a basement, and a coal house opposite. Lord Sherborne also built 20 model cottages in Eastington in Northleach soon after enclosure, each with a garden. He went on to rebuild nearly all the houses in his own village. Plans dated 1818 for 10 cottages arranged in pairs show each with a living room and kitchen, a pig sty conveniently close to the kitchen door for feeding household waste to the pig, a woodshed and a garden. Allotments were provided for the villagers. The value of a garden and a pig was recognised by Rudge, though he thought labourers should not aspire to a cow, the management of which

> is attended with considerable trouble, requires more utensils than the earnings of a day labourer can well supply, and more conveniences of building than are usually attached to a cottage...The greatest of evils would be to place the labourer in a state of independence, and thus destroy the indispensable gradations of society.

Thomas Phillipps, of Middle Hill, Broadway, father of Sir Thomas Phillipps the book collector, had

119, 120 & 121. Model cottages: at Sherborne they are mainly early 19th century; at Hawling the Public Elementary School was built in 1860 for 50 children with a residence for the schoolmistress; at Buckland and Laverton James Orchard Phillipps built several sets of cottages in 1875 and 1876.

Laverton cottages surveyed soon after he had bought the estate from Lord Viscount Weymouth in 1799. It seems that they were very overcrowded. One cottage had 18 people in it, three families with 11 children between them and 'a very poor' old widow. Another cottage had 14, two families and seven children, two widows and a daughter; a third had 12, two families, seven children and another 'very poor' old widow. These were perhaps former farmhouses with two or three rooms downstairs. Altogether 16 cottages contained 95 people, and only one widow lived alone; there were 10 old people amongst this population. Against each cottage he noted the terms on which it was held. One cottage belonged to the parish, and several were copyhold. Phillipps was worried when he bought the estate that there were not enough trees growing to repair the houses. Major building was not undertaken until after the death of Sir Thomas Phillipps in 1872. The Middle Hill estate, including Buckland and Laverton, was left to his son-in-law, James Orchard Halliwell, a famous Shakespearean scholar. He adopted the surname Phillipps, and within four years had built eight pairs of cottages in Laverton, a row of four in Buckland Fields and a pair in Buckland, all built of stone but with Welsh slate roofs, and all carrying an engraved stone with his initials, J.O.P. and the date, 1875 or 1876. A few years earlier, the Earl of Eldon had built five pairs of cottages in Yanworth, some with a date stone 1863.

While there was growing interest in the late 19th century in the major buildings of the past, churches and manor houses, and their restoration, the vernacular architecture of more

122 & 123. Smaller Cotswold houses were not generally stone-slated until the 19th century, and much more thatch would have been seen a hundred years ago than there is now. A slate roof *(left)* at Upper Slaughter is being relaid. At Broad Campden *(right)*, there are several thatched houses and one is receiving a new top layer to give it a longer life.

humble cottages was hardly yet appreciated. Guy Dawber was responsible for awakening interest in the Cotswolds; he gave a paper to the Bristol and Gloucestershire Archaeological Society on 'Old English Architecture with special reference to the Cotswolds' in 1896. He later wrote a book, published in 1905, describing his exploration, titled *Old Cottages, Farmhouses and other stone buildings*, but his descriptions were not of really humble homes of the farm labourers but of small farmhouses. He noted that many cottages had been demolished in the 19th century, 'so that they should not be a burden on the landowners' and thought that there were almost none left from the period 1700 to 1850 for this reason. The date is significant. An act of parliament in 1857 had altered the basis of charging for the relief of the poor; a parish's rate-payers were no longer charged according to the number of their poor people, but there was a standard charge for the area of a Poor Law Union. A landowner did not need to restrict housing to minimise the chances of poor people finding homes in the parish, and much cottage building dates from the later 19th century as a result. A few Elizabethan cottage rows did survive, like Bagehotts Cottages in Upper Slaughter, remodelled by Lutyens early in the 20th century.

Dawber was writing when the railway was enabling building materials to be brought from a distance. He lamented the introduction of Welsh slates, and said that the craft of the thatcher and slater was almost lost. As a consequence, buildings were losing their restful harmony with the surrounding countryside.

> New buildings should be designed in as modern spirit as we wish, but using the materials at hand. The very fact that in so doing we shall be more or less governed by the same conditions and limitations as these old builders, will give our work to-day a continuity in design and feeling, in harmony with the old, and will help to carry on in a certain sense the spirit and tradition of bygone days, which surely in these times of change and hurry, will appeal to many.

He foresaw the effects which planning authorities would have. 'Building Byelaws are bound in the course of years to have a disastrous effect, even if they have not done so already'. Sir Phillip Stott might have read these words with wry recognition. Having bought the Stanton Court estate together with 29 cottages, he planned in 1921 to build cottages in the local vernacular style.

> The Ministry of Health, who afterwards took up the matter, insisted on a window-space of one square foot of glass for every ten square feet of floor. In order to attain the necessary window-space it was found impossible to adhere to the traditional type, so the long windows in each gable were introduced. On comparing these cottages with others in the village one clearly sees how departmental interference with local traditions and styles would affect the character and charm of an old English village.

Dawber's fears for the Cotswolds were not altogether well-founded, because the falling population reduced the pressure to build new houses. There were 229 vacant houses in the North Cotswold Rural District and 162 in Northleach Rural District in 1939, out of a total housing stock of 7,286. In the Northleach district there had been little building in the previous decade, in fact the lowest rate in the county. A field survey by the county planning officer, in Blockley, Moreton in Marsh, Northleach and Stow on the Wold, in the early years of the Second World War, found about 17 per cent of housing 'obsolete'. The rebuilding and refurbishment of the past century left the Cotswolds with a nearly adequate and characterful set of houses and cottages.

Chapter Twelve

In Search of Old Cotswold

Because the Cotswolds did not experience population growth in the late 19th and early 20th centuries, an impression was created of stability and peace; tourists and people wishing to escape the increasing noise and hurry of industrialised Britain began to be attracted there, but books of nostalgia for the old country way of life may over-emphasise for later readers the undisturbed character of the area. There was modernisation, to a lesser extent perhaps than in other areas, but modernisation nonetheless. The railway made relatively little impact; the greatest changes were accomplished by motor cars and the tractor.

The Railway Age
Though railways soon passed to east and west of the uplands, no line was built across the Cotswolds until the last quarter of the century. The Birmingham to Gloucester line, opened in 1840, followed the valley of the river Severn, and the Oxford to Worcester, opened in 1853, followed the valley of the Evenlode. The hills and scarp edge of the Cotswolds, however, were just high enough to deter railway development. Nevertheless there was interest in providing Cheltenham with a direct link with Oxford and London. The first stage of an east-west route was the result of pressure and capital supplied by William Bliss, owner of the tweed mills in Chipping Norton, who wanted a cheaper way of bringing coals to his mill steam engines. A junction with the Oxford, Worcester and Wolverhampton railway was made in 1855, later called Kingham, and a branch line opened to Chipping Norton. Seven years later the Kingham junction was used again to bring a line westwards to Bourton on the Water, where a timber-framed station was built, somewhat out of keeping with the Cotswold stone vernacular style. The station was rebuilt some twenty years later, in stone and to the same design as Stow on the Wold. At the same time this railway finally reached Cheltenham. It had involved building a tunnel, several cuttings and embankments, and a viaduct to take the single track over the hills and valleys; the highest point was on Aylworth Down, later called Notgrove station. Some relics of the civil engineering remain in the landscape. Andoversford became a junction in 1891 for a branch line from Cheltenham to Cirencester, and as late as 1900 Andoversford to Cheltenham was made into double track. From 1906 one train a day in each direction travelled through from South Wales to Newcastle, but this was the first service to be withdrawn, even before the Second World War. Finally, the Cheltenham to Honeybourne line was opened in 1908, bringing trains much closer on the west to the Cotswold edge. The Honeybourne line was helpful in marketing the produce of the Vale of Evesham; in 1914 a special train was run to London to 'convey asparagus to Covent Garden from the Broadway and Childs Wickham districts'.

Arthur Gibbs wrote in 1898, 'until the new railway between Andover and Cheltenham was opened, four years ago, with a small station at Fosscross, there were many inhabitants of these old world villages who had never seen a train or a railway'. The great difference which railway development made to the Cotswolds, he suggested, was to kill the coaching trade of the small towns, like Burford and Northleach. Dawber, too, wrote in 1905 about the effect of the railway on Burford.

> Fifty years ago it was a thriving and prosperous place, but the advent of the railways has long since left it high and dry and out of the world of today ... But though it has lost all its trade, and activity and bustle, yet Burford of today is a peaceful spot to visit.

On the other hand, the railway also facilitated access. Estate agents advertising big properties in 1911 were able to say:

> In order to save the time of applicants desirous of viewing the Cold Aston and Hampnett estates, the Auctioneers have instructed Mr. Stokey of the Railway Hotel opposite Bourton-on-Water station to drive applicants to and from Bourton-on-Water station to any of the estates.

Similarly, a Mr. Davis met applicants at Notgrove station to view Hawling and a Mr. Smith at Andoversford to view Compton Abdale.

About this time, a quiet summer afternoon stop at Adlestrop station inspired Edward Thomas's famous evocation of England before the First World War.

> Yes. I remember Adlestrop —
> The name, because one afternoon
> Of heat the express-train drew up there
> Unwontedly. It was late June.
>
> The steam hiss'd. Some one clear'd his throat.
> No one left and no one came
> On the bare platform. What I saw
> Was Adlestrop—only the name
>
> And willows, willow-herb, and grass,
> And meadowsweet, and haycocks dry,
> No whit less still and lonely fair
> Than the high cloudlets in the sky.
>
> And for that minute a blackbird sang
> Close by, and round him, mistier,
> Farther and farther, all the birds
> Of Oxfordshire and Gloucestershire.

In 1939, between 11 and 20 trains a day in each direction stopped at Moreton in Marsh station, and six to 10 at Blockley, Chipping Campden and Mickleton; on the Honeybourne line there were between 11 and 20 trains a day calling at Broadway, and up to 10 at Gretton, Winchcombe, Hailes, Toddington, Buckland and Weston Subedge. On the Cirencester line not more than five a day stopped at Fosse Cross, Chedworth and Withington, and five a day crossed the Cotswolds, calling at Notgrove, Stow and Bourton. The Cotswold railway encouraged a few businesses, like Thomas Comely and Sons, corn merchants and Pratt and Haynes (Shipton) Ltd., coal merchants, to open offices at Notgrove station, and Shell-Mex and B.P. Ltd., oil merchants, had depots at Stow on the Wold and the Anglo-American Oil

Co. at Moreton in Marsh; but it is uncertain whether the railway made very much difference to the Cotswold towns. In any case they were developing modern-style services as towns were in other areas.

The Bicycle Age
A simpler and humbler development in transport made more difference to the average Cotswold inhabitant and encouraged the discovery of the area: the bicycle. George Swinford of Filkins, near Burford, was a stone-mason, and so was his father. He recalled his father telling him how he walked from home to Tetbury every weekend; he stopped work at one o'clock and

> walked home, did a bit of gardening and started back to Tetbury on Sunday night as the bells were ringing for the six p.m. service at church. He was there ready to start work at six a.m. on Monday morning...The journeyman did a lot of walking...then the bicycle came and the old journeyman said it was the best friend the workers ever had.

Even using footpaths, this walk must have been over 20 miles.

For those with more leisure, the bicycle allowed them to travel further and see more of the countryside. 'I recognise the great service that had been conferred on a vast number of young men, who, by means of bicycles and tricycles, are enabled to explore the countryside ...' The Chancellor of the Exchequer forbore to impose a tax on them in 1888 for this reason. Arthur Gibbs experienced the 'poetry of motion' for the first time in 1898. 'It is probable that the bicycle will cause a large demand for the remote country houses ... the invention seems of the greatest utility. It brings places 60 miles apart within our immediate neighbourhood'. He rather exaggerated the effect of the bicycle on the un-let Cotswold mansion houses, which were un-let still even after the motor car became commonplace. Gibbs found the roads quite deserted: 'We had ridden 40 miles along the Fosseway, and save in the curious half-forsaken old towns of Moreton in Marsh and Stow on the Wold we scarcely met a soul on the journey'.

Gibbs' book, *A Cotswold Village*, published in 1898, was about his own manor house at Ablington, and was also an attempt to capture the nature of 'a quiet old-fashioned Gloucestershire hamlet and the country within walking distance of it'. Fishing and hunting were two major components of his life there. The hum of the thrashing machine reminded him of the old hand methods it replaced. In the porch of his house, there hung 'an ancient and much-worn flail'.

> Two stout sticks, the handstaff and the swingle, attached to each other by a strong band of gut, constitute its simple mechanism. The wheat having been strewn on the barn floor, the labourer held the handstaff in both hands, swung it over his head and brought the swingle down horizontally on to the heads of the ripe corn. Contrast this fearfully laborious process with the bustling, hurrying machine of today.

The thrashing machine was the first widespread mechanisation of a farming process.

Herbert A. Evans toured the Cotswolds in 1905. 'For ourselves, the bicycle is the conveyance we have chosen, and for the firm smooth main roads of our district no easier mode of travelling can be devised'. The Fosse Way was 'one of the best-kept roads in the county'. In summer, the grassy margins were used for the road, 'the repairable track in the centre being reserved for the winter, when rain and mud rendered the grass impassable'. The roads to the many villages which the cyclist visited, however, were not firm and smooth;

> ... oftener they are little more than cart tracks leading him from gate to gate across the fields in a fine, open fashion; and sometimes they are deep, well-worn holloways, full

of stones and ruts, plunging headlong down the steep sides of the valley in their haste to pass the old grey bridge and climb the opposite ascent...after a few hours' rain they become hopelessly sticky and impassable.

His tour led to the first notable descriptive history of the Cotswolds. Evans, an Oxford don, backed up his own observation of the area with research in the Bodleian Library. Although published over eighty years ago, *Highways and Byways in Oxford and the Cotswolds* can still be reckoned by a modern writer 'the best historical and topographical guide to the north Cotswolds'. The book is learned, yet the historical anecdotes are lightly sketched. Evans does not often obtrude his personal opinions, except on the subject of church restoration. While recognising the sad state of disrepair of many church buildings in the 19th century, he regretted the wholesale elimination of historical features, and described the restorers as iconoclasts equal to the 17th-century Puritans. A few churches, like Bledington, had escaped 'the no less destructive alterations of the modern church restorer, and its historic continuity with the past therefore remains unviolated'. On the other hand Icomb church had 'alas! been through the furnace of restoration' and Lower Swell had had its historical significance 'entirely destroyed'. He visited the Cotswolds just before the opening of the Honeybourne railway line. The villages under the edge were still 'secluded and unspoilt; ... but a time of probation is approaching, the new railway will soon be open—and then? But I will not forestall the date of grief'.

Algernon Gissing, like Evans, came to the Cotswolds on a bicycle, and carried nostalgia much further. By the time *The Footpath Way in Gloucestershire* was published in 1924, the motor car had started to impinge on the upland roads and tracks.

It is no good grumbling about the desecration of our quiet roads by the noise and dirt of alien traffic, which has at last taken possession of them. We must make the best of it, and slink as far as possible into impracticable byways if we want to study or enjoy the last relics of our wild or picturesque life.

124. On his way back to Oxford at the end of the long vacation, after his bicycle tour of the Cotswolds, Evans visited Shipton Court just as the pillared entrance was removed. The Court's present appearance is illustrated on page 21.

Despite his strictures, there were still in 1924 places like Hailes approached along a cart track across fields and through several gates.

Gissing's book is slighter than Evans', and he describes fewer villages, but it is a second marker for the growing tourist attraction of the Cotswolds. Broadway was already noted for its transatlantic popularity; in 1905 Evans wrote that it had been 'discovered by Americans some years ago'. By 1924 all the area was becoming much better known:

> ... during the last twenty years or more the district has been discovered by the outside world, and this has brought about many changes...It does not seem to be realised how rapidly in many parts of the country our charming old villages are simply slipping away from us through the neglect or inability of the owners to repair. If by a sacrilegious touch two crumbling cottages are transformed into one little tasteful holiday residence, this is surely better than the loss of them altogether by collapse.

Gissing was less an historian than a naturalist, though he thought local history could be the means of persuading the countryman of the beauty of his surroundings. His book was written in an attempt to distil some of the essence of the Cotswolds, and at the same time to convince his contemporaries that rural life was being destroyed by universal education and the motor car. He had known the Cotswolds for 50 years, and the reminiscences told him by the elderly parish clerk of Saintbury, where he lived, made a link with mid-Victorian Britain; the parish clerk had sung in the choir at the dedication of Broadway's new parish church in 1840.

The End of the Horse-drawn Age

Although railway development created bustle in a few Cotswold places, most public transport of both people and goods was horse-drawn until the early 20th century. Horse-buses met the trains at Bourton on the Water and Stow on the Wold stations. The carriers' carts took people from the villages once a week to the nearest market town, and the towns were also linked by carrier services. From Chipping Campden carriers went three times a week to Evesham and twice a week to Stratford; a carrier went daily from Broadway to Evesham. Northleach, positioned near more important roads, had Bourton on the Water, Cheltenham and Cirencester within reach at some time each week.

The early horse-drawn tramway on the edge of the Cotswolds, from Stratford on Avon to Moreton in Marsh, was horse-drawn until 1884, despite the success of steam engines generally. William Jones, a colliery owner and railway projector, planned to develop a London to Stratford railway, to connect with the Stratford canal in which he was also involved. No part of the tramway might have been built, but for the financial support and enthusiasm of Lord Redesdale, who saw an opening for the revival of Moreton-in-Marsh market. The act of parliament which had authorised the tramway in 1821 actually prohibited the use of steam, a provision which had to be amended when the Great Western Railway Company wished to upgrade it, as far as was practicable. Steam was then used on part of the line for a number of years, the tramway being closed for passengers in 1929. A description of a journey on the horse-drawn tramway creates an impression of the leisurely, though hazardous, nature of the ride. These recollections were published first in 1864 but refer to a somewhat earlier time; even in 1864, the writer thought the tramway worthy of the archaeologist. The traveller concerned sat outside, on top of the carriage, as many coach passengers did:

> Attached to the carriage in front was a platform, on which the sagacious horse (the only locomotive used on the Stratford and Moreton railway) mounted when it had drawn our carriage to the top of an incline, thus escaping being tripped up as we descended at a

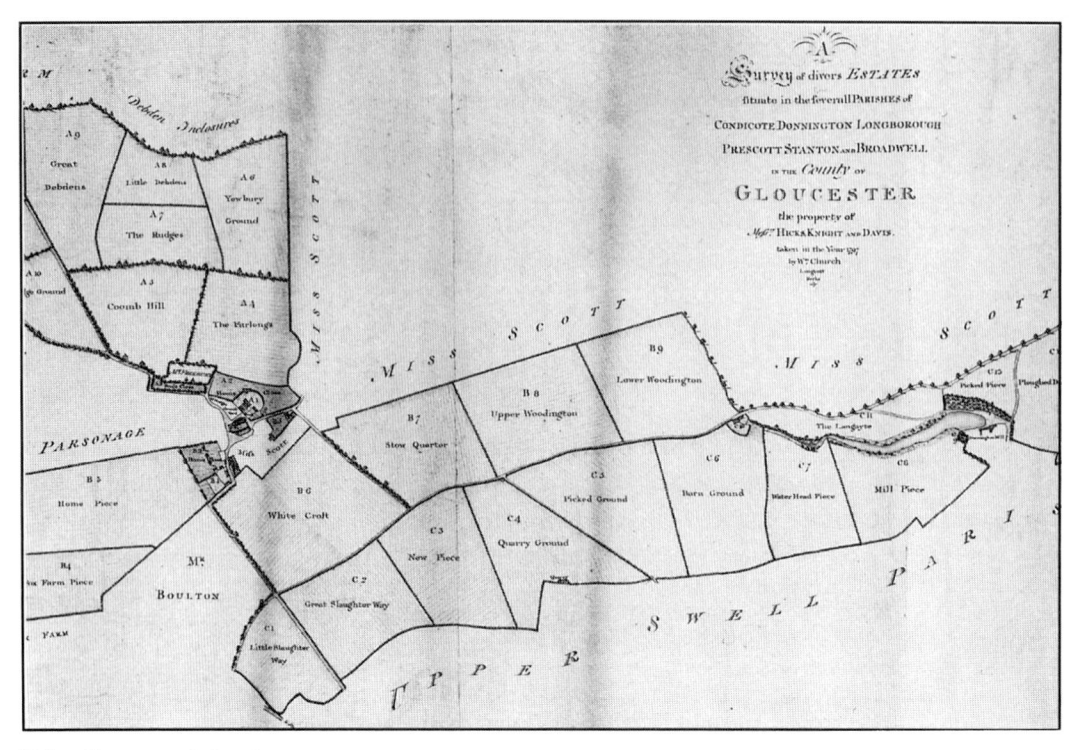

125. The map of Condicote of 1797 depicts a simple layout of fields which was only 20 years old; prior to enclosure in 1778 the land was divided into strips. The cross, illustrated in plate XXXV, is near a large pool on the Green and the village pound is marked.

126. On the Ordnance Survey map of 1922, Condicote's many antiquities are shown. The village green survives, but the pool has been filled in and replaced with a pump and the cottages in the north-west corner have been demolished.

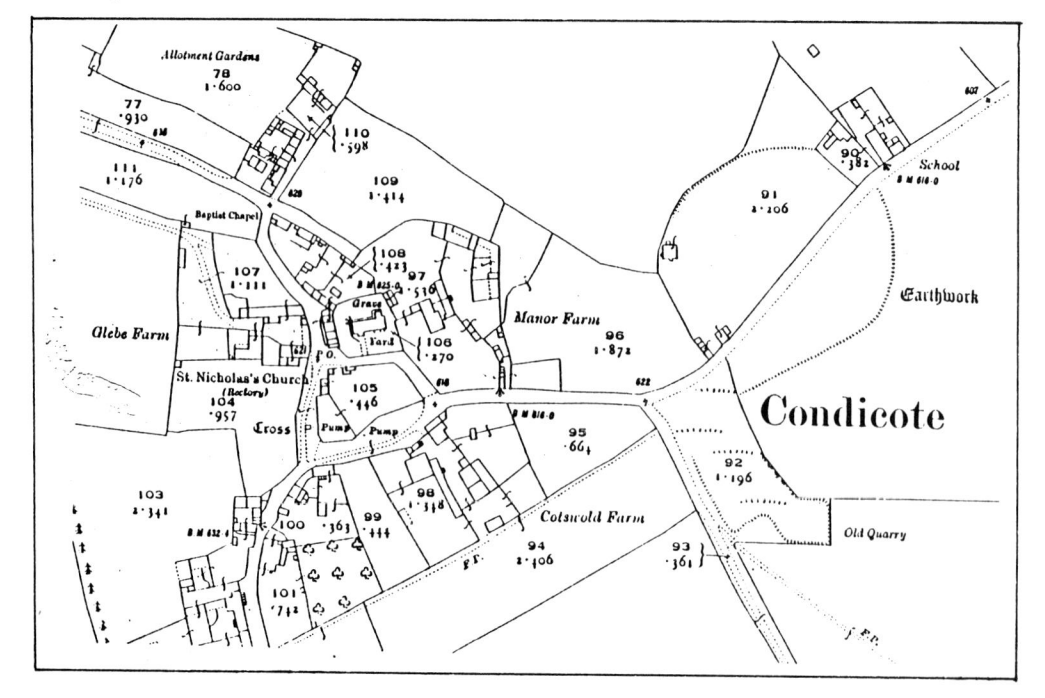

rattling good speed ... When we came to the foot of the incline the guard applied his break as tightly as he could; we all, to the best of our individual capacities, held on to our seats, and if we had taken firm hold we thus managed to avoid being pitched off head-foremost. When the carriage came to a stand, the horse dismounted, and drew us along as before. There was a tunnel, too, on approaching which the driver was kind enough to suggest that such of the outside passengers as thought it likely they would have any further use for their brains, should duck their heads as low as possible, and carry their hats in their hands. And thus, following chiefly the course of the river Stour, we wound very pleasantly through shady lanes where the high hedgerows, forming a grateful screen from the hot sun, could be reached by the hand on either side. Or we ran along the public highway, not separated from it by any fence, stopping now and then to take up or set down a wayfarer, or to refresh our thirsty selves with beer ... We are of opinion that, except on the break-neck inclines, no great dispatch was either sought after or obtained, and it would generally have been quite safe to get down and walk a little. There was always pleasant matter for speculation, too, as to what county we were in at that particular moment. For, starting in Gloucestershire, we found ourselves presently in Worcestershire, forthwith in Warwickshire, then for another breathing space in Worcestershire, anon again in Gloucestershire, back into Worcestershire, thence once more into Gloucestershire, until at last the graceful spire of Stratford rising before us, we trundled across the beautiful Avon, and ended our journey in Warwickshire,—the shires in these parts being intermixed very singularly, and we having in our short journey made no less than seven changes of this kind.

In *Kelly's Gloucestershire Directory* for 1902 there was only one entry under 'motor', a motor-car builder in Cheltenham. By 1914, motor buses had effectively displaced horse-drawn buses from the roads of London, but not in a country district like the Cotswolds. Four men in Gloucestershire advertised themselves as motor-car proprietors in 1914, including one based at the *Noel Arms Hotel* in Campden and one at the *Wheatsheaf* in Northleach. Under the heading 'Omnibus Proprietors' *Kelly's* referred readers to 'Jobmasters', who hired out horses and carriages. Even in 1939, the motor revolution was not entirely complete as far as rural transport was concerned and a few carriers were taking passengers to Cheltenham, Campden and Stow, but local motor buses had taken over from most carriers' services, with a once-a-week service on market day, or perhaps two or three return journeys a week. Burford and Northleach had the advantage of several bus services a day. Most significantly, *Kelly's* said under 'Omnibus' see 'Motor Omnibus'. There were small motor-bus businesses in Gretton, Guiting Power, Naunton, Stow and Winchcombe, but the bigger Gloucestershire bus companies neglected the Cotswold uplands. Motor-car and motor-cab proprietors were also to be found in Bourton on the Water, Moreton in Marsh, Blockley, Gretton, Stanton and Stow on the Wold. Long-distance Black and White Coaches linked Burford and Northleach with Oxford, London, Gloucester and Cardiff.

On Cotswold farms, horses only finally replaced oxen about 1900, a change which was as much regretted by writers as the subsequent replacement of horses by tractors in the thirties. About 1800, Marshall saw oxen worked on Cotswold farms five to a team and 'perfectly handy'. As to using horses, he wrote of the 'folly of sending elephants to plough', though overall he thought that twice as many horses were then in use as oxen. Rudge, too, said oxen were generally used on the Cotswolds. 'It seems to me more the effect of ancient prejudice than experiment, that they are not used with profit even on stiff soils'. Oxen were 'easily brought into the habit of working' and 'can do nearly as much work as horses'. In mid-century, according to Bravender, 'a considerable number of oxen are worked in the spring and summer months'. But when Gibbs wrote in 1898, horses were usual on Cotswold farms.

127. At the Cotswold Farm Park, oxen are being yoked. Joe Henson, the founder chairman in 1973 of the Rare Breeds Survival Trust, says oxen are more intelligent than horses: they refuse to pull unless it is easy.

128. A Cotswold wagon and other old agricultural implements are preserved in the Cotswold Countryside Collection at Northleach.

> One does not often see teams of oxen ploughing in the fields nowadays. Within a radius of 100 miles of London town this is becoming a rare spectacle. They are still used sometimes in the Cotswolds, however, though the practice of using them must soon die out. Great slow lumbering animals they are, but very handsome and delightful beasts to look upon. A team of brown oxen adds a pleasing feature to the landscape.

In her childhood, Margaret Westerling had seen the last working team of eight oxen which were regularly used until 1920 at Spring Hill near Broadway; she is particularly firm that this was the correct date and not 1931 as stated by Massingham. She based her book, *Country Contentments*, published in 1939, on conversations with older Cotswold inhabitants, as well as being able to draw on her own memories. Some of her Cotswold informants had worked with oxen: 'memory here always comes back to ox ploughing as a thing many of them have known and only lately lost'. The one remaining team at Cirencester, as she observed, was being kept 'more as a curiosity than as a true survival, with no certainty of continuance'; the two teams of eight oxen maintained at the end of the First World War had been reduced to one team of only five oxen. Cotswold Farm Park now has a team of six oxen which is being accustomed to draw a plough or waggon, building on the experience of one of the men who handled oxen at Cirencester, so that the tradition is not quite lost.

The use of tractors was encouraged during the First World War, as the government was anxious to reduce the amount of food consumed by horses, as well as enable much larger amounts of land to be ploughed in the critical situation of 1917, when foreign imports were very seriously disrupted by the German submarine campaign. Only 2,500 tractors in the whole country were delivered in 1917-18, but gradually the number increased; by 1938 there were about 38,500. The imminent elimination of horses on the farms was already clear to Margaret Westerling; around Ford, she estimated with some gratitude, 'there is probably as much land ploughed by horses as by the tractor'. As the numbers of horses fell, there was a corresponding decline in village blacksmiths and farriers. Many villages had their own blacksmith's shop in 1914, but in 1939 nearly half had gone. The Second World War provided another enormous stimulus; the government again tried to persuade farmers of the economic good sense of using a tractor. One advertisement proclaimed:

On a ten-acre farm, four had to feed the horse and the farmer had to work 1,000 hours to cultivate his land; with a Ferguson tractor he could do it in 200 hours, decrease his costs, keep more hens or extra pigs and cattle, and at the same time save his country.

In his survey of the area during the Second World War Payne noted that: 'mechanisation is being developed increasingly on the plateau, and very large fields, some 400 by 450 yards (more than 60 acres) make this economically possible. The face of Gloucestershire will alter considerably as a result of the increased use of machines'.

As soon as petrol and materials were released from war production, horses quickly became unnecessary and in 1947 and 1948 they rapidly disappeared.

129. An early 'International' tractor, purchased in 1927 by Mr. J. H. Clifford of Whalley Farm, Whittington, when tractors were by no means commonplace, and used at first mainly to drive a thrashing machine. It was rebuilt by his grandson in 1970 and is now used for ploughing competitions.

The Search for Old Cotswold

After reviewing the industry and occupations of Gloucestershire about 1939, Payne's judgement was that, except in isolated cases, the Cotswolds had no industry. The exceptions he mentioned were two large brickworks near Blockley, each of which employed nearly one hundred men, a sawmill also near Blockley, employing 40 workers, a manufacturer of metal windows and leaded glazing at Moreton in Marsh, with thirty to forty men working there, canning and preserving works at Winchcombe and Toddington—the latter employing 300, mainly women, and paper-making at Postlip near Winchcombe employing nearly one hundred. 'The busy, prosperous woollen towns of past ages are now quiet little country communities, often containing beautiful churches and buildings which remind the tourist and the seeker after peace and quietness, of their prosperity in the past.' Payne reviewed future developments which might occur in Gloucestershire. The importance of the motor-car was recognised but he also predicted an extraordinary development in air travel. Noting the growth in civil aviation before 1939 he said, 'it is probable that towns or areas without aerodromes or landing grounds will become as stagnant in the future as those did which were not served by the coming of the railways'. He foresaw particularly 'a tremendous development of family planes of the autogyro types, as much in use as present-day family cars'. Amongst five locations for small aerodromes in the county, he suggested one between Stow on the Wold and Moreton in Marsh.

Paynes's verdict on the Cotswold towns did not altogether give credit for their apparently thriving commercial life, though he added 'there are numerous small firms catering for local needs'. *Kelly's Directory* for 1939 shows the amount of modernisation which had occurred, however small the towns were. Moreton in Marsh seems to have been the most flourishing, although Broadway and Bourton on the Water were two places which had expanded between 1831 and 1931. In all there were modern facilities like banks: usually two, Midland and

Lloyds, or Barclays in Burford; doctors in all and district nurses in most; cottage or district hospitals in Bourton on the Water, Burford, Moreton in Marsh and Winchcombe; a peripatetic dentist who called at least once a week in all; an optician in Moreton in Marsh; solicitors in all except Blockley; architects in Burford and Chipping Campden. Garages and motor engineers were to be found in all the towns except Blockley, showing the motor-car well-established; everywhere, bicycles could be bought or repaired. Gas or electrical engineers were to be found generally. There were cinemas in Moreton in Marsh and Winchcombe. Very few chain stores had yet reached these market towns—only Moreton in Marsh had the International, the London Meat Company and United Dairies. Although the Guild of Handicrafts had come to Chipping Campden with forty to fifty men in 1902, the numbers employed fell rapidly to 16 in 1914, including three apprentices, and in 1939 only three craftsmen were mentioned, George Henry Hart, silversmith, Alec Miller, architectural carver and J. W. Pyment and Sons, builders and ecclesiastical woodworkers. Burford was undoubtedly the town catering most for the tourist, with eight hotels, nine inns, three boarding houses and one tea room, together with two antique dealers. The *Cotswold Gateway Hotel* advertised 28 bedrooms and garage, with an 18-hole golf course adjacent. The most famous hotel in the area, however, was the *Lygon Arms* at Broadway, which produced its own guidebook to the area in 1933. The writer extolled the hotel somewhat fulsomely; it is

130. Broad Campden Norman chapel was restored by C. R. Ashbee between 1905 and 1907. (The doorway is illustrated on page 4). Inspired by Ruskin and Morris, Ashbee founded the Guild of Craftsmen in 1888, and moved to Campden in 1902. Houses restored by Ashbee include Woolstaplers' Hall and Braithwaite House in High Street, which provided lodgings for Guildsmen; F.L.Griggs stayed there in 1904-5.

interesting to find that seven gardeners were employed in the Lygon's own gardens to supply the hotel table. The re-creation of the inn by S. B. Russell after it had fallen into considerable decay was also described; 'he was lucky to set out on his venture just as the motor-car was to people again the English road'. The motor-car, in fact, was carefully catered for at the *Lygon*.

> Lastly, if master is well-served, so too is his chauffeur and his car. Two or three expert mechanics are always at hand in the Lygon's own garage, which is heated and will take 24 cars in comfort. If you ask overnight to have the tank filled you can rely on it being done and charged correctly. There is a workshop for any running repair.

In the course of his *English Journey* in 1933, J. B. Priestley came by car to the Cotswolds, 'the most English and the least spoiled of all our countrysides ... In no other part of the country do we see so large a tract of the beautiful old England still unspoilt ... a national heritage of great value'. He was pleased that 'the Cotswolds is singularly remote from the railway, for only one line finds its way across these hills'. He also reported a conversation with an inhabitant of Chipping Campden about whether the town had changed. 'It has changed a lot', he says grimly. 'They don't bake their own bread anymore there. They used to have three flour mills in the town, but now they have gone. The home-made bread was fine stuff'. He concluded that 'the beauty of the Cotswolds belongs to England'.

131. Gloucester Street, Winchcombe, about 1905, by F. L. Griggs. When the illustrations for *Highways and Byways in Oxford and the Cotswolds* were complete, Griggs settled in Campden and contributed a great deal to awareness of the need for conservation and sensitive development in the town.

A number of books about the Cotswolds were written in the 1930s, which looked for still-remaining traces of the old hand-tool agriculture. Massingham's books were a lament for industrial development, and J. B. Priestley shared something of this attitude. Margaret Westerling's book was a more serene account of Cotswold life written between 1936 and 1938. She lived at Ford, and walked great distances round the area, but was also aided in her exploration by a motor-car; she lamented that formerly white country roads were now black with tar, but acknowledged the gains in speed of travel which they provided. She creates a strong impression that change was coming rather more slowly to the Cotswolds than to some other areas, but she was not sentimental and appreciated the benefits for the farm-worker of less physical labour. Hay making, for instance, had become less exhausting because of the mechanical elevator, and threshing, too, with the threshing machine; one of her informants remembered vividly hitting herself over the head with the jointed end of the flail.

Margaret Westerling saw Cotswold sheep being sheared by hand at Aldsworth. She thought there were then two flocks left in England, the other being in Norfolk, though this was not quite accurate, as there was at least one other flock nearby, at Stowell. For the farmer at Aldsworth, William Garne, 'it is a struggle against circumstances going on before our eyes,

132. *The Lygon Arms* in Broadway was a notable hotel from its restoration at the beginning of the 20th century; it soon catered especially for chauffeur-driven motorists.

133. Gordon Russell established his business after restoring antique furniture for the *Lygon*.

134. The youth hostel in Stow on the Wold was opened at the end of 1935, five years after the first hostel in Wales. It was requisitioned by the army and was returned to the YHA in November 1945. The *White Hart* next door was an inn in the late 17th century.

a breed of sheep that once represented a country's wealth being forced out of existence by altered conditions'. She was told that the sheep were no longer washed in the local streams before shearing, because washed wool earned so little more it was not worth the time and trouble. Examples of sheep washes, the ponds specially constructed for the purpose, particularly next to mills where the dammed-up mill pond could supply a good quantity of water, may still be seen, though crumbling and overgrown like the water wheels and channels of the mills themselves. Amongst the survivals of old methods which she was searching for, Margaret Westerling found quarry men were still working stone by hand in a number of the Cotswold quarries, at Coscombe, Temple Guiting, Kineton Thorns, and Eyford, but at Huntsman's quarries she found machinery. One quarryman who talked to her was a Hughes, and Norman Hughes of Temple Guiting Quarry remembered that her book had included his mother's wheat and mangold wine recipes. Plenty of the countrywomen apparently still made wine which they were proud to let her taste. She visited one working water mill at Lower Slaughter, but the miller had not ground wheat for bread flour 'for many years' and the baker's part of his business was much the busier. The miller said he recalled folk bringing to the mill their 'leasings' of corn gleaned from the fields after the main harvest had been carted, and he kept the bran as his payment. Local farmers no longer carted their spare wheat to Tewkesbury mill, either, though she was told tales of the turnpike road down Stanway Hill which the carts travelled at night to arrive at the mill early in the morning. She was delighted to find one place, in Naunton, where cider was being made by crushing the apples in a mill turned by a horse. The maypoles at Cutsdean and Ford, she was told, had only 'recently' gone. Thus her book

135. Farm workers *(above)* have maintained the craft of stone-walling, as at Hampen, and there is a revival of interest in this feature of the Cotswolds.

136. Norman Hughes, quarryman, slater and quarryowner of Temple Guiting *(left)*. The craft of making Cotswold stone slates is no longer taught and he may be the last to have learnt the old time-consuming process.

draws together many of the last signs of the older countryside of the Cotswolds before it was completely changed but shows clearly how the modern scene was largely in existence.

Is it right to see the changes in the Cotswolds since 1945 as more dramatic than any in previous centuries? Each older inhabitant is inclined to see his lifetime as a period of great change, one of the main themes which emerges from oral testimony about the past. Probably the generation in which the open-field system was extinguished witnessed the greatest revolution in this countryside, but since 1945 a process has been completed, which has removed the men and horses from the farming landscape. Even so, the past of the Cotswolds is still visible, and each person who explores the area can find on a small scale a rich historical record and a scene with a special claim to timelessness.

Sources

Abbreviations

BOD	Bodleian Library, Oxford
GCL	Gloucester City Library
GRO	Gloucestershire Record Office
OA	Oxfordshire Archives
WRO	Worcester Record Office
IPM	Inquisitiones Post Mortem
TBGAS	Transactions of the Bristol and Gloucestershire Archaeological Society
VCH	Victoria County History

Section One: Manuscript and Printed Sources used in Accounts of Individual Parishes

Aston Blank: Dyer, C., 'The rise and fall of a medieval village: Little Aston (Aston Blank), Gloucestershire', *TBGAS* 105 (1987) 165-181

Bledington: Cutts, J. E. C, 'Bledington church', *TBGAS* 7 (1882-3) 81-6; *VCH* Glos.VI, 27-33

Blockley: Eyre, W. T., *A Guide to Blockley* (Evesham, 1827); Hilton, R. H. and Rahtz, P. A., 'Upton, Gloucestershire, 1959-1964', *TBGAS* 85 (1966) 141-154; Icely, H. E. M., *Blockley through twelve centuries* (1974); *Red Book of Worcester* III, 295-311, 312-3, 314-7: Extents of 1299, 1282 and 1166; *VCH* Worc. III, 265-77

Blockley—Northwick Park: Barnard, E. A. B., 'The Rushouts of Northwick Park, Blockley', *Transactions of the Worcester Archaeological Society* 16 (1940) 22-39; Barnard, E. A. B., 'An old Worcestershire Mansion: Northwick House in 1705', *Transactions of the Worcestershire Archaeological Society* 21 (1944) 54-60; **WRO**, 705:66/BA228/78 Inventory 1705, BA4221/Box 13 Inventory 1859, Box 14 Servants book, Box 17 do., Box 23 do., BA4839/1 (iii) Stock book

Bourton on the Hill: *VCH* Glos.VI, 197-207

Bourton on the Water and Clapton: *VCH* Glos. VI, 49-63; **GCL**, sketch of church, BGAS Library, Dr. Moore's Notebook; **GRO**, GDR/V5/53 Glebe

Broadway: Habington I (1895) 107; II (1899) 34; Houghton, C. C., *A Walk About Broadway* (1980); *VCH* Worcs. IV, 33-43; **WRO**, 705:962/8656/2 (i) Court rolls, 705:960/8965/4 (vii) Schedule of lands, 307:3/r143/3 Enclosure

Broadwell: *VCH* Glos. VI, 49-59; **GRO**, D612/13 Tithe case

Buckland: Bazeley, W., 'Notes on Buckland Manor and Advowson', *TBGAS* 9 (1884-5) 103-124; *Historia et Cartularium Monasterii S. Petri Gloucestriae*, III, 61-4: Extent *c*.1266; 302-3: Inventory 1518; **GRO**, D2857/2/4 Rectory, GDR/V5/61 Glebe, Map No.2001; **Longleat House**: Thynne papers Book 65 Box 69 Survey 1548, WMR Gloucestershire: Buckland and Laverton—Survey 1590, NMR 2230 Survey 1673, WMR 13 A viii Survey 1746, WMR Gloucestershire: Buckland and Laverton Sale papers 1799, NMR 2210 Enclosure Act; **WRO**, 705:962/8965/10 (i) 6 Rectory and Laverton cottages

Burford: Gretton, R. H., *The Burford Records* (Oxford, 1920); Moody, R. & J., *The Book of Burford* (1983), **OA**, Misc.Dors.iv/ii/1

Campden: Pennington, D. H., 'Chipping Campden', *History Today* Jan. 1952, 45-52; Powell, G., *The book of Campden* (1982); Richardson, L., 'The Chipping Campden Area and its Industries Past and Present', *Transactions of the Worcester Naturalists Club* VI (1918) 177-183; Whitfield, C., *A History of Chipping Campden* (1958); Whitfield, C., 'Lionel Cranfield and the Rectory of Campden', *TBGAS* 81 (1962) 98-118; IPM IV 63-9, 80-83; **GCL**, Hockaday Abstracts 140; **GRO**, D2857/2/2 Court Books, 2/9 Enclosure claims, P81a/45/1 Enclosure, GDR/V5/66 Glebe

Cutsdean: *Liber Elemosinarii* 2-3; *Registrum Prioratus Beatae Mariae Wigorniensis*, 103a-b: Extent *c.*1249; **GRO**, Q/RI 51 Enclosure; *VCH* Worcs. III, 284-286

Eyford: *VCH* Glos. VI, 72-6

Farmington: **GCL**, Hockaday Abstracts 195; **GRO**, GDR/V5/132 Glebe, D1445 Enclosure

Hailes: St Clair Baddeley, W., *A Cotswold Shrine—being a contribution to the History of Hailes* (1908)

Hawling and Roel: GRO, GDR/V5/157 Glebe, D363/E1 Survey 1748, E2 Survey 1755, E3 Survey 1821, D363/P4 Map 1748; Aldred, D. and Dyer, C., 'A medieval Cotswold Village: Roel, Gloucestershire', *TBGAS* 109 (1991) 129-170

Hazleton: Bill 1766 to confirm enclosure (courtesy Mr. D. Tongue)

Icomb: Anon., *Plain Facts in a Country Dress by A. Farmer* (1861); Habington I (1895) 185-6, 517; II (1899) 323; Royce, D., 'Icomb Place', *TBGAS* 20 (1895-7) 172-90; Royce, D., *Icomb—Its History, Topography and Archaeological Antiquities* (1869); *Parliamentary Survey of the lands and possessions of the Dean and Chapter of Worcester made in or about the year 1649*, 88-91; *Registrum Prioratus*, 104a-b: extent *c.*1249; **GCL**, Hockaday Abstracts 249, RF 330.2 Manor; **GRO**, D4143/1 & 2 Icomb Place terrier 1797, D334/T13 do., P185/VE/3/1 & 2 Map 1847, /SD1/1 Enclosure, Q/RI.85 do.; **WRO**, 736/2006/52/71-127 Bishop's Transcripts, b009:1/1230/7 Survey 1771

Mickleton: GRO, P216 IN 3/5 Tithe book

Moreton in Marsh: *VCH* Glos. VI, 240-250

Naunton: *VCH* Glos. VI, 76-87; **GRO**, AP31 Enclosure Act, D1395 I/19 Westfield deeds, P224/IN3/1 Survey 1830 and Communicants Register, and /5 Rectory Farm, /SD2/1 Tithe, /a/SD1/1 Enclosure, GDR/V5/211 Glebe

Northleach: Fallowes, W .C., *Northleach Brasses* (n.d.); Monk, W. J., *Northleach and Around* (*c.*1936); *Calendar of the Charters, Rolls and other documents ... in the muniment room at Sherborne House* 8-9; *Historia et Cartularium* III, 176-183: Extent *c.*1266; **GCL**, Hockaday Abstracts 300; **GRO**, GDR/V5/217 Glebe, D391/1 Town book, Q/RI 107 Enclosure

Rissington, Great, Little and Wyck: *VCH* Glos. VI, 98-120

Sevenhampton: 'Will of John Camber', *Gloucestershire Notes and Queries* II (1882) 444-5; Hall, J. Melland, 'Sevenhampton', *TBGAS* 14 (1889-90) 328-355; 'A Transcript of "The Red Book" of the Bishop of Hereford' 27-9: Extent *c.*1290; **GRO**, D444 M2 manor, T66 common

Sherborne: Hilton, R. H., 'Winchcombe Abbey and the Manor of Sherborne' in H. P. R. Finberg, *Gloucestershire Studies* (Leicester, 1957) 89-113; *VCH* Glos. VI, 120-127

Shipton Oliffe and Solers: GRO, AP 33 Enclosure Act, GDR/V5/267 Glebe, D245 I/26 Court Rolls, D1930 Survey 1764 and map, P290/SD1/1 Enclosure

Slaughter, Upper and Lower: Cutts, J. E. K., 'St. Peter's church Upper Slaughter' *TBGAS* 7 (1882-3) 126-130; 'Enclosure Act', *Gloucestershire Notes and Queries* 8 (1889); *VCH* Glos. VI, 128-142; **GRO**, GDR/V5/272 & 273 Glebe, D4084/14/12 Deeds

Snowshill: Mason, C., *Snowshill* (Cheltenham, 1987); **GRO**, GDR/V5/275 Glebe, Q/RI 130 Enclosure

Stanton: Barnard, E. A. B., *Stanton and Snowshill* (Cambridge, 1927); **GRO**, GDR/V5/283 Glebe, Wills & Inventories, D476/E1 Enclosure and T4 & 29 Deeds etc., D4262/E3 Enclosure and F2 Deeds etc., P307/IN3/1 Tithe Book

Stanway: Earl of Wemyss and March, 'Stanway' in *The Sudeleys* (1987) (for title see **Sudeley**); Neidpath, J., *Stanway House* (1982); Mrs. Winkless, 'Five Tracy Diaries' in *The Sudeleys* (1987); *VCH* Glos. VI, 223-232
Stow on the Wold: *VCH* Glos. VI, 142-165; **GRO**, GDR/V5/290 Glebe
Sudeley: Dent, E., *Annals of Winchcombe and Sudeley* (1877); *The Sudeleys—Lords of Toddington* (Manorial Society of Great Britain, 1987); *IPM* V, 255-6
Swell, Lower and Upper: *VCH* Glos. VI, 165-172 (Lower Swell); **GRO**, P323 SD1 Enclosure (Upper Swell) and; **WRO**, 705:66/BA4221 Box 23: Accounts
Taynton: Bod. Oxon Rolls 64, 96 & 107 Court rolls,; **OA**, Tice IV/1 'Lots'
Westcote: *VCH* Glos. VI, 172-178; **GCL**, Hockaday Abstracts 392
Whittington: GRO, GDR/V5/338 Glebe, D444/T74 Corn mill
Winchcombe: Bassett, S. R., 'A probable Mercian Royal Mausoleum at Winchcombe, Gloucestershire', *Antiquaries Journal* LXV (1985); Dent, E., *Annals of Winchcombe and Sudeley* (1877); Donaldson, D. N., *A Portrait of Winchcombe* (Winchcombe, 1978); *Landboc sive Registrum Monasterii de Winchelcumba* I 'Introduction' by D. Royce; **GRO**, GDR/141A Easter book
Windrush: *VCH* Glos. VI, 178-184
Withington: Finberg, H. P. R., *Roman and Saxon Withington* (Leicester, 1955); **GRO**, GDR/V5/347 Glebe, P 374 a/SD1 Enclosure

Section Two: General Manuscript and Printed Sources
These have been arranged under chronologcal headings:
1. Anglo-Saxon and Domesday Sources
2. Medieval Sources
3. Modern Sources

1. Anglo-Saxon and Domesday Sources
Early Charters:
  of the West Midlands ed. H .P. R. Finberg (Leicester, 1972)
  of the Thames Valley ed. M.Gelling (Leicester, 1979)
Domesday Book, ed. J. Morris (Phillimore, Chichester): Gloucestershire (1982); Oxfordshire (1978); Worcestershire (1982)
'Duties of a Reeve', in Cunningham (1915)
English Historical Documents:
  I ed. D. Whitelock (1979): Laws of Edgar
  II ed. D. Douglas and G. W. Greenaway (1981): 'Rectitudines Singularum Personarum'
Grundy, G. B., 'Saxon Charters of Worcestershire', *Transactions and Proceedings of the Birmingham Archaeological Society*, 52 (1927)
Grundy, G. B., *Saxon Charters and Field Names of Gloucestershire* (BGAS 1935-6)

2. Medieval Sources
'Aid levied in Gloucestershire in 20th Edward III (1349)', ed. J. Maclean, *TBGAS* 10 (1885-6)
'A Transcript of "The Red Book" of the Bishop of Hereford', ed. A. T. Bannister, *Camden Miscellany* 15 (1929)
Historia et Cartularium Monasterii S. Petri Gloucestriae, ed. W. H. Hart, 3 vols. (Rolls Series, 1863-67)
Inquisitiones Nonarum (Record Commission, 1807)
Inquisitions and Assessments relating to Feudal Aids II (1900)
Inquisitiones Post Mortem for Gloucestershire, ed. S. J. Madge and E. A. Fry, IV, V, VI (British Record Society, 1903, 1910, 1914)
Landboc sive Registrum Monasterii de Winchelcumba, ed. D. Royce, 2 vols. (Exeter, 1892 and 1903)
Lay Subsidy, 1327, I Edward III: for the county of Gloucester (Middlehill Press, n.d.); for the

county of Worcester, ed. Rev. F. J. Eld (Worcester Historical Society, 1895); for Burford, see Gretton (1920)
The Lay Subsidy of 1334 ed. R. E. Glasscock (1975)
Liber Elemosinarii - The Almoner's Book of the Priory of Worcester, ed. Rev. J. H. Bloom (1911)
'Pegolotti's List of wools' in W. Cunningham, *The growth of English Industry and Commerce* (Cambridge, 1915)
Red Book of Worcester, ed. M. Hollings, 4 parts (Worcester Historical Society, 1934-50)
Registrum Prioratus Beatae Mariae Wigorniensis, ed. W. H. Hale (Camden Society, 1865)
Taxatio Ecclesiastica Angliae et Walliae auctoritate P.Nicholai IV circa 1291 (Record Commission, 1802)
Valor Ecclesiasticus temp. Henr. VIII Auctoritate Regia Institutus, 6 vols. (Record Commission, 1810-34)

3. Modern sources
(i) Manuscript material:
Auctioneers notebooks **GRO**, D2080
Freeholders list **WRO**, 3762/8 Foley scrapbook III
Hearth Tax **GRO**, D383
       WRO, 900:4001/7449
Land tax **GRO**, Q/Rel 100 (1775)
       WRO, BA 823 (1787)
Dr. Parsons' Notebook c.1700 (for Gloucestershire) in **BOD**: Rawlinson 323
Rating appeal **GRO**, D2299/5917 (1934-6)
Register of electors **GRO**, Q/REr (1832/3)
Sales particulars **GRO**, D476 E3; D1388/SL3-8; D2299; D2582; D4858; D5658; SL 158, 159, 174, 573

(ii) Printed material:
Bateman, J., *The Great Landowners of Great Britain & Ireland* (Leicester, 1971)
British Universal Directory (1793-8)
Calendar of the Charters, Rolls and other documents (dating from AD 1182) as contained in the muniment room at Sherborne House (privately printed, 1900)
Census and Census enumerators' books
Cotswold Sheep Society Flock Books (Cirencester, 1892 onwards)
'Dring's list of Compounders', *Gloucestershire Notes and Queries* I (1881) 375-6
Kelly's Directories: Gloucestershire 1871, 1902, 1914, 1939; Oxfordshire 1939; Worcestershire 1912, 1936
Knighthood Fines, Maclean, *TBGAS* 9 (1884/5) 345-353
Men and Armour for Gloucestershire in 1608 (Gloucester, 1980)
Oxford Record Society:
    1 (1919): Chantry Certificates
    2 (1920): Parochial collections
   21 (1940): Hearth Tax returns for 1665
   38 (1957): 'Articles of enquiry addressed to the clergy of the diocese of Oxford at the Primary Visitation of Dr. Thomas Secker 1738'
Parliamentary Survey of the lands and possessions of the Dean and Chapter of Worcester made in or about the year 1649 (Worcester Historical Society, 1924)
'Replies to Rural and Urban Queries', *Parliamentary Papers* (1834) XXX - XXXVI
'Returns of Owners of land, 1872-3', *Parliamentary Papers* (1874) LXXII, i, ii & iii

Bibliography

1. Books covering numbers of individual parishes:

Atkyns, R., *The ancient and present state of Glostershire* (1712)

Buildings of England, ed. N. Pevsner: 'Gloucestershire: The Cotswolds' by D. Verey (2nd. edition, 1979); 'Oxfordshire' by J. Sherwood and N. Pevsner (1974); 'Worcestershire' by N. Pevsner (1968)

English Place Names Society volumes: Gelling, M., *Place-Names of Oxfordshire*, 2 vols. (Cambridge, 1953-4); Mawer, A. and Stenton, F. M., *Place-Names of Worcestershire* (Cambridge, 1969); Smith, A. H., *Place-Names of Gloucestershire* 4 vols. (Cambridge, 1964-5)

Habington, T., *A Survey of Worcestershire*, ed. J. Amphlett, 2 vols. (Worcester Historical Society, 1895 and 1899)

Nash, T. R., *Collections for a History of Worcestershire*, 2 vols. (1781)

Noake's Guide to Worcestershire (1868)

Perceval, A., 'Gloucestershire village populations', *Local Population Studies* 8 (1972)

Rudder, S., *A New History of Gloucestershire* (1779, reprinted 1977)

Victoria History of the County of Gloucester: vol. II ed. W. Page (1907); vol. VI ed. C. R. Elrington (1965); vol. VIII ed. C. R.Elrington (1968)

Victoria History of the County of Worcester: vol. III ed. J. Willis-Bund (1913); vol. IV ed. J.Willis-Bund (1924)

2. General works:

Addleshaw, G. W. O., *The beginnings of the parochial system* (n.d.)

Addy, S .O., *Church and Manor* (1913, reprinted New York 1970)

Alldridge, N., *The Hearth Tax: Problems and Possibilities* (n.d.)

Armitage, P. L. and Goodall, J. A., 'Medieval horned and polled sheep: the archaeological and iconographic evidence', *Antiquaries Journal* 57 i (1977) 73-89

Astill, G. and Grant, A., *The Countryside of Medieval England* (Oxford, 1988)

Baker, J. H., *Introduction to English Legal History* (1979)

Barlow, F., *The Early Church 1000-1066* (2nd edition, 1979)

Beckinsale, R. and M., *The English Heartland* (1980)

Bettey, J. H., *Church and Community* (Bradford-on-Avon, 1979)

Blair, J., ed., *Minsters and Parish Churches: The local church in transition 950-1200* (Oxford, 1988)

Bond, C. J., 'The estates of Evesham Abbey: a preliminary survey of their medieval topography', *Vale of Evesham Historical Society* 4 (1973) 10-43

Bond, C. J., 'Church and Parish in Norman Worcestershire', in Blair (1988) 119-158
Braun, H., *Parish Churches* (1970)
Bravender, J., 'Farming of Gloucestershire', *Journal of the Royal Agricultural Society of England,* 11 (1850) 132-145
Campbell, J., ed., *The Anglo-Saxons* (Oxford, 1982)
Cheltenham Guide (1781)
Christiansen, R., *A regional history of the Railways of Great Britain:* 13 *Thames and Severn,* (1981)
Clay, C. G. A., *Economic expansion and social change: England 1500-1700,* I (Cambridge, 1984)
Cobbett, W., *Rural Rides* (1973)
Cook, G. H., *The English Medieval Parish Church* (1954)
Copus, A. K., 'Changing markets and the development of sheep breeds in Southern England 1750-1900', *Agricultural History Review,* 37 i (1989) 36-51
Cunningham, W., *The growth of English Industry and Commerce* (Cambridge, 1915)
Dawber, G., *Old Cottages, Farmhouses and other stone buildings in the Cotswold district* (1905)
Defoe, Daniel, *A Tour thro' the whole island of Great Britain,* (1724-6)
Dictionary of National Biography
Ditchfield, P. H., ed., *Memorials of Old Gloucestershire* (1911)
Dyer, C., *Lords and Peasants in a Changing Society* (C.U.P. 1980)
Dyer, C., 'Deserted Medieval Villages in the West Midlands', *Economic History Review,* 35 i (1982) 19-34
Ellis, W., *A Compleat System of Experienced Improvements made on Sheep, Grass-Lambs and House-Lambs,* 3 vols. (1749)
England Delineated (1800)
Evans, H. A., *Highways and Byways in Oxford and the Cotswolds* (1st. ed.1905, reprint 1919)
Everitt, A., *Continuity and Colonisation* (Leicester, 1986)
Finberg, H. P. R., ed., *Gloucestershire Studies* (Leicester, 1957)
Finberg, H. P. R., *The Gloucestershire Landscape* (1975)
Finn, R. W., *Domesday Book: A Guide* (Chichester, 1973)
Florence of Worcester, A History of the Kings of England (Llanerch Enterprises, n.d.)
Freeman, E. A., *The History of the Norman Conquest of England,* 4 vols. (Oxford, 1869-70)
Garne, R., *Cotswold Yeomen and Sheep* (1984)
Gelling, M., *Place Names in the Landscape* (1984)
Gelling, M., *Signposts to the Past* (Chichester, 1988)
Gibbs, J. A., *A Cotswold Village or Country Life and Pursuits in Gloucestershire* (1st.ed. 1898, reprint 1942)
Gissing, A., *The footpath way in Gloucestershire* (1924)
Glass, D. V. and Eversley, D. E. C., *Population in History* (1969)
Glass, D. V., 'Two papers on Gregory King' in Glass & Eversley (1969) 159-220
Gomme, G. L., *The Village Community,* (1890)
Grant, A., 'Animal Resources', in Astill & Grant (1988) 149-187
Hanham, A., *The Celys and their World* (Cambridge, 1985)
Harrison's Description of England, ed. F.J. Furnivall (1877)

Harvey, P. J., 'Taxation and the Ploughland in Domesday Book', in Sawyer (1987)
Harvey, S., 'The Knight and the Knight's Fee in England', *Past and Present*, 49, Nov. 1970
Henson, E., *British Sheep Breeds* (Shire Album 157, 1986)
Hicks Beech, Mrs. William, *A Cotswold Family* (1909)
Hilton, R. H., *The English Peasantry in the Later Middle Ages* (Oxford, 1979)
Hilton, R. H., *A Medieval Society* (Cambridge, 1983)
Hilton, R. H., *Class Conflict and the Crisis of Feudalism* (1990)
Holt, J. C., *Domesday Studies* (1987)
Hooke, D., 'Open-Field Agriculture—The evidence from the Pre-Conquest Charters of the West Midlands', in Rowley (1981) 39-63
Hooke, D., 'Two documented Pre-Conquest Christian sites located upon parish boundaries: Cada's Minster, Willersey, Gloucs. and "the holy place", Fawler in Kingston Lisle, Oxon.', *Medieval Archaeology* 31 (1987), 96-99
Hooke, D., *The Anglo-Saxon Landscape* (Manchester, 1985)
Jessup, M., *A History of Oxfordshire* (Chichester, 1975)
John, A., *Land Tenure in Early England* (Leicester, 1964)
Keyser, C. E., 'An essay on the Norman Doorways in the County of Gloucester', in Ditchfield (1911)
Kingsley, N., *The Country Houses of Gloucestershire, I* (Cheltenham, 1989)
Kingsley, N., *The Country Houses of Gloucestershire, II* (Chichester, 1991)
Leech, R., ed., *Historic Towns in Gloucestershire* (Bristol, 1981)
'Leland in Gloucestershire', ed. J. Latimer, *TBGAS* 14 (1889-90)
Low, D., *On the Domesticated Animals of the British Isles* (1845)
Luccock, J., *An Essay on Wool* (1809)
Maitland, F. W., *Domesday Book and Beyond* (1897, reprinted Cambridge, 1987)
Maclean, J., 'On feudal and compulsory knighthood', *TBGAS* 9 (1884/5) 345-353
Marshall, W., *The Rural Economy of Gloucestershire*, 2 vols. (1796)
McGrath, P. and Cannon, J., eds. *Essays in Bristol and Gloucestershire History* (BGAS, 1976)
Miller, C., ed., *Rain and Ruin: The diary of an Oxfordshire Farmer* (Gloucester, 1983)
Moore, J.S., 'The Gloucestershire section of Domesday Book: geographical problems of the text', 4 parts, *TBGAS* 105 (1987) to 108 (1990)
Norris, J., *The Stratford and Moreton Tramway* (1987)
Payne, G. E., *Gloucestershire: A physical, social and economic survey and plan* (n.d., c.1947)
Power, E., *The Wool trade* (Oxford, 1941)
Priestley, J. B., *English Journey* (1934)
Rackham, O., *The History of the Countryside* (1986)
Rowley, T., ed., *The origins of Open-Field Agriculture* (1981)
Rudder, S., *A New History of Gloucestershire* (1779, reprinted 1977)
Rudge, T., *General View of the agriculture of the County of Gloucester* (1807)
Ryder, M., 'Medieval Sheep and Wool Types', *Agricultural History Review* 32, i (1984) 14-28
Saul, N., *Knights and Esquires: The Gloucestershire Gentry in the Fourteenth Century* (Oxford, 1981)
Savine, A., *English Monasteries on the Eve of the Dissolution* (Oxford, 1909)

Sawyer, P., ed., *Domesday Book: A Reassessment* (1987)
Schumer, B., *The evolution of Wychwood to 1400* (Leicester, 1984)
Sims-Williams, P., *Religion and Literature in Western England 600-800* (Cambridge, 1990)
Smith, B., *The Cotswolds* (1976)
Strong, R., Binney, M. and Harris, J., *The destruction of the Country House* (1974)
Swinford, G., *The Jubilee Boy*, ed. J. Fay and R. Martin (Filkins, 1987)
Tawney, R.H., *The Agrarian Problem in the Sixteenth Century* (1913, reprinted New York)
Taylor, C. S., 'The Origin of the Mercian Shires', in Finberg (1957) 17-51
Thirsk, J., 'Projects for Gentlemen, Jobs for the Poor : Mutual Aid in the Vale of Tewkesbury 1600-1630', in McGrath & Cannon (1976) 147-169
Thomas, Edward, *The Collected Poems* (Oxford, 1981)
Thompson, F. M. L., 'Nineteenth Century Horse Sense', *Economic History Review*, 2nd.series, 29 i (1976) 60-79
Turner, G., *General view of the agriculture of the county of Gloucester* (1794)
Verey, D., *Cotswold Churches* (1976)
Verey, D., ed., *The diary of a Cotswold parson* (Gloucester, 1986)
Westerling, M., *Country Contentments* (1939)
Wood, M., *The English Medieval House* (1990)
Woolrich, A.P., 'An American in Gloucestershire and Bristol', *TBGAS* 92 (1973) 169-179
Wright, S., ed., *Parish, Church and People* (1988)
Whybra, J., *A lost English County: Winchcombeshire in the 10th and 11th centuries* (Woodbridge, 1990)

Index

Spellings of place-names are drawn from the English Place-Name Society's volumes. Great and Little, Upper and Lower, are not used as main index titles.

Abbotswood (Lower Swell), 173, 174, 177
Ablington, 201
Adlestrop, 16, 200
advowson, 36, 133, 136
Aelfric, abbot, 76-77
air travel, 207
Alderton, 15, 106
Aldsworth, 75, 93, 103-4, 188, 209
Alfred, King, (871-899) 16
Andoversford (Dowdeswell), 5, 16, 32, 103, 199, 200
Angles, 17
Anglo-Saxon estates & boundaries, 4-5, 22-33, 59, 68, 71-73, 76, 77, 86, 125-26, 129; invasions, 18; landowners, 9-12
appropriations, 40
arable cultivation, 2, 12-14, 74-77, 79-89, 179, 181, 192, 194
Ascot under Wychwood, 18, 19
Ashbee, C. R., 208
Ashfielde, Michael, 67
Asthall, 118
Aston Magna (Blockley), 49, 151, 154
Aston Somerville, 106
Aston Subedge, 12, 161, 173
Aston Blank (Cold Aston): 12, 16, 26, 27, 29, 40, 44, 46, 106, 157, 180, 200; Little Aston, 30, 49, 50
Atkyns, Sir Robert, 114, 116, 136, 188
Augustine, St, 38
Avon, river, 2
Aylworth (Naunton), 8, 10, 26-27, 29, 36, 79, 86, 199

Badsey, 73
Badgeworth, 76
Bakewell, Robert, 101
Bank's Fee (Longborough), 49, 50, 86, 172
Barrington 5, 8, 10, 14, 15, 18, 22, 23, 30-31, 40, 79, 91-93; hundred, 23; tithings, 31
Barrington, Great, 23, 30-31, 66, 74, 131, 160, 171, 190-91, 192-94; church, 30, 43, 45, 47; Park, 118, 164, 181
Barrington, Little, 23, 30-31, 40, 74, 118, 120, 136, 172, 173, 191, 192-94; church, 42-43, 45, 47
Barton (Temple Guiting), 15
Baskerville family, 26, 107
Bateman, John, 178-79

Bath, 18
Bath, Marquess of *see* Thynne family
Bathurst, Lord, 67
Batsford 40, 41, 68, 154, 160, 170, 172, 173, 176, 181, **plate XXVIII**
Bazley, Sir Thomas, 174-75, 179
Beach, Susan Hicks, 114
beakhead carving, 31, 43, 50
Beckford, 16
Bede, the Venerable, 8, 18, 36
Bedwell, Thomas, 138
'beorg', 22
Berrington *see* Campden
Betson, Thomas, 94
Bibury, 10, 20, 66, 79
bicycle, 5, 201-2, 208
bishops *see* deanery & diocese
Bishop's Cleeve, 16, 91, 95
Blaket family, 107-9
Bledington, 12, 14, 24, 39, 45, 46, 98-99, 131, 157, 190, 202
Bliss, William, 199
Blockley, 14, 15, 17, 18, 20, 21, 40, 41, 53, 68, 74, 79, 84, 93, 154, 186, 198, 200, 205, 207-8; church, 157; freeholders, 191; labour services, 92; population, 184; Upton, 53, 90, 95; vicarage, 149, 151; Worcester church estate, 1, 5, 12, 38
'bordars', 16
Bordesley Abbey, 41
'borough', 22
Boteler family, 56, 111
Bourton on the Hill, 7, 16, 21, 68-69, 76, 91, 159, 161, 164, 170, 171, 176; church, 45; House, 114-15; rectory, 149; Westminster Abbey manor, 12
Bourton on the Water, 7, 14, 15, 17, 22, 28, 29, 74, 76, 80, 93, 102, 106, 154, 156, 164, 171, 173, 184, 205, 207-8, **plate XXXII**; church, 29, 36, 150, 155; Evesham Abbey manor, 12, 16, 38, 62; freeholders, 131, 190-1; Manor, 176-7; population, 183-84, 207; railway, 5, 199-200, 203; rectory, 40, 144, 149-50, 159; Salmonsbury, 2, 22, 30
Bradley hundred, 7, 23
brasses, monumental *see* Northleach
Brassey family, 175
Bravender, John, 192-93

221

Bray family, 118, 160-61
Bredon, 38, 75, 149
Bristol & Gloucestershire Archaeological Society, 109, 118, 119, 156
Broad Campden, 64-65, 80, 82, 86, 141-43, 154, 160, 197; Norman chapel, 48, 208
Broadway, 5, 7, 18, 20, 40, 41, 51, 52-53, 70-73, 74, 86, 94, 120-22, 124, 129, 154, 164, 170, 172, 181, 191-94, 199, 203, 207-10, **plate XXXIII**; church, 44, 45, 70, 72-73, 154-55, 203; Court 72-73, 120-21; enclosure, 71, 72-73, 121; freeholders, 121, 131, 191; Pershore Abbey manor, 1, 12, 38, 41; population, 207; railway, 200; Upend & Westend, 70, 72-73
Broadwell, 4, 7, 12, 14, 15, 16, 20, 38, 40, 62, 63, 86, 87, 106, 114, 144, 147-48, 159, 160, 164, 171
Brockhampton (Sevenhampton), 126-27; Park, 4, 172, 173, 181-82
Browne, T. B., 179
Bruern Abbey, 56, 79, 89, 90-91, 164, 172
Buckland, 14, 20, 22, 72, 93, 123, 126, 127-30, 135, 171, 194-97; church, 44, **plate I**; copyholders, 127-30; customs of the manor, 127; enclosure, 129-30, 152; Fields, 48, 152-53, 197, **plate VIII**; freeholders, 190-91; Gloucester Abbey manor, 12, 38; Manor, 106, 127-30, 164, 171, 173, **plate I**; railway, 200; rectory, 145-47, 151-53
Buckle Street *see* Ryknild Street
Burford, 5, 7, 14, 16, 40, 52-53, 58-61, 80, 93, 102, 118, 154, 164, 185, 186, 187, 188, 200, 205, 208, **plate XII**; church, 3, 43, 45, 49, 61, 95, 98, 155-56; enclosure, 60, 120, 151; freeholders, 191; Guild, 61, 98; Hospital or Priory, 4, 56-57, 60-61, 89, 118-120, 164, 172; lot meadow, 81-83; population, 184, 207; rectory & vicarage, 41, 151; Upton & Signet, 58-60, 75, 95, 118, 120
burgage & burgess, 15, 16, 52-53, 55, 57-58, 63, 66-67, 68, 70, 191
'burh', 22, 60
Bury St. Edmund's Abbey, 16
Busshe family, 67, 93-95, 99
'byrig', 63

Calcot (Coln St Denis), 36
Caldicote *see* Westfield
calendar, Old Style & New Style, 141-42
Calvert, J., S., 175
Camber, John, 99
Campden, including Chipping Campden, 5, 7, 11, 14, 15, 17, 20, 41-42, 52-53, 63-66, 74, 84, 91, 92, 93-94, 97, 114, 135, 154,160, 161, 162, 164, 171, 173, 185, 186, 191-92, 203, 205, 209, **plate X**; Berrington, Westington & Combe, 21, 41, 64-65, 106, 141-43, 160, 173; church, 3, 45, 46, 49, 95, 97-98, 155; Court House, 65, 163; deanery, 41; enclosure, 80, 82, 142-43, 151; freeholders, 191; Guild of Handicrafts, 208-9; labour services, 89; manor courts, 141-43; population, 55, 184, 207; railway, 200; rectory & vicarage, 41-42, 151; *see also* Broad Campden
'campi', 84, 86

carriers, 203, 205
Cassey Compton (Withington), 12, 31
Castlett (Guiting Power), 10, 36
Cely family, wool merchants, 90, 93-95
ceorl, 39
Cerne Abbey, 76
Chamberlayne family, 62-63, 160-61, 171, 179, 196
'champagne countryside', 84
Chandos, Lord, 111-12, 161
chantries, 42, 49, 61, 154
chapels of the Church of England, 40, 48, 66, 73, 153-55, 156; *see also* Nonconformity
Charlton Abbots, 12, 39, 79, 164, 172, 190
charters, Anglo-Saxon, 35; borough 52, 61, 66, 68, 70
Chedworth, 14, 31, 52, 85, 95, 103, 156, 181, 200
Cheltenham, 2, 16, 170, 171, 187, 199, 203, 205
Chester, Earl Hugh of, 11, 14, 17
Chester, St Werburgh's (cathedral), 41-42
Childe, Thomas, 165
Childswickham, 15, 72, 199
Chipping Campden *see* Campden
Chipping Norton, 5, 93-94, 103, 167, 199
Christianity, conversion to, 36-38
church buildings, 42-46, 95-99, 144; nave & chancel, 45, 51, 96-98, 145, 155, 158; font, 45; pews, 44; pulpit, 44-45, 46; tower, 3, 35, 36, 46-47, 96-99; Victorian restoration, 3, 144, 145, 155-58; *see also* Norman churches and wool churches
Church Icomb *see* Icomb
church services, 44
Churchdown, 163
Cirencester, 18, 22, 38, 94, 102, 192, 199, 200, 203, 206; Abbey, 56, 67; deanery, 41; Seven Hundreds, 67
Civil War, 112, 130, 148, 160-63
Clapley (Sezincote), 21
Clapton, 28, 29, 75, 77, 144; Bridge, 28
Clifford, J. H., 207
Clopton, 15, 132
Coates *see* Winchcombe
Cobbett, William, 81
Cockbury (Winchcombe), 57
Cockerell family, 167, 170, 174, 191
Cod *see* Cotswold—origin of name
Colburn, Oscar, 104
Cold Aston *see* Aston Blank
Colesborne, Little (Withington), 7, 12, 106
Coln, 20, 22, 23, 40, 74
Coln, river, 15, 20, 22, 23, 31-32
Coln Rogers, 7, 23, 42, 46, 93, 95, 102, 184
Coln St Denis, 7, 12, 17, 20, 23, 42, 45, 46, 95, 158, **plate XXVI**
Combe in Campden q.v.
Combe *alias* Icomb q.v.
common fields *see* open fields
common grazing rights, 66, 68, 78, 80-84, 123, 138, 139, 142, 143
common pastures, 2, 15, 66, 78, 81-83, 89, 110, 126, 132, 133, 143, 146; *see also* downs
Compton Abdale, 12, 46, 74, 95, 103, 155, 180, 181, 190-91, 200

INDEX

Condicote, 11, 12, 36, 40, 204, **plates VI & XXXV**
Cope family, 109
Copse Hill (Upper Slaughter), 173, 175-76, 181
copyhold & copyholders, 3, 84, 87-89, 123-33, 138, 139, 141, 143, 183, 191, 193
Corndean (Winchcombe), 57, 111-12
Coscombe (Didbrook), 49, 50, 211
Cotswold, 18, 90; Collection at Northleach, 206; Farm Park, Guiting Power, 100, 104, 206; origin of name, 20-21, 74; sheep, 99-104, 167, 209, 211, **plates XVI, XVII & XVIII**; Sheep Society, 102-4; Woollen Weavers, Filkins, 104; *see also* wold
cottages & cottagers, 16, 87, 92, 128-31, 132, 138-39, 141, 193, 194-98, 203
Cotterell family, 141, 143, 151-52
Council for British Archaeology—list of towns, 5
Council for the Preservation of Rural England, 178
County boundaries, 1
court rolls *see* manor
Coventry, Lord, 121-22
Cranfield, Lionel, 42
Craven, Lord, 178
Culpepper, Sir Anthony, 160
curfew, 193
customary tenants *see* copyhold
customs of the manor *see* manor
Cutsdean, 1, 17, 18, 20, 38, 40, 76, 86, 149, 190, 211; church, 47, 155; enclosure, 138, 149; labour services, 87-88
Cutts, J. E. K., (architect), 156-58

Daglingworth, 102
Daston family, 120-21
Dawber, Sir Guy (architect), 140, 175, 176-78, 195, 198, 200
Daylesford, 18, 20, 38
deanery & diocese, 3, 35, 38, 41, 62
Deerhurst, 15, 16
Deerhurst, Lord, 170
Deerhurst Priory, 12, 14, 19, 68, 76
Defoe, Daniel, 1
demesne, 3, 39, 40, 66, 72, 86-87, 88-89, 125, 145, 147, 148
'den', 86
Dent family, 47, 110, 112-14, 156, 171, 179
deserted villages, 5, 27, 32
Didbrook, 46, 71, 124, 160, 184
Dikler, river, 2, 23
diocese *see* deanery
dissenters *see* Nonconformity
dissolution of the monasteries *see* monasteries
Dolman, Mathias & Thomas, 133-34
Dolphin, V., 158
Domesday Book, 3, 4, 7-17, 20, 38, 40, 52, 62, 89, 127-28
Donnington, 20, 23, 38, 49, 50, 62, 86, 131, 147, 192-94
Dorn (Blockley), 18, 49, 68, 77
Dowdeswell, 2, 7, 12, 16, 32, 75, 76, 77, 95, 106, 114, 161, 171, 172, 173
downs, 15, 68, 71, 74-75, 78, 91, 101, 138-39, 141, 192, **plate XII**

Drayton, Michael, 99-100
Droitwich, 19, 20
Dulverton, Lord, 176
'dun', 22, 32, 75
Dutton family, 67, 114, 116, 117, 146, 161, 175, 178, 190, 196
Dynevor *see* Talbot family

'ea', 22
Eabba, 36
Eadburgha, St, 42, 44, 73
Eastington (Northleach), 20, 49, 50, 66, 79, 93, 95, 102, 145-46, 173, 196
Eastleach, 66
Ebrington, 7, 10, 46, 173
Edgar, King (959-975), 38, 39
Edward the Confessor, 8, 10, 12, 16, 109
Edward the Martyr, King (975-979), 62
Elcho, Lady *see* Tracy family
Eldon, Lord, 103, 178, 181, 197
Ellis family, 191
Ellis, William, 100-1
enclosure, 2, 3, 81, 86, 89, 121, 123, 132-33, 139, 183, 188, 191-92; by act of parliament, 79, 129-31, 136-41, 142-43, 144, 148-152
English Heritage, 182
Enstone, 19
estates *see* landowning
esquire *see* knights
Ethelred, King (Unraed) (979-1013; 1014-1016), 62
Ethelred of Mercia, King (674-704), 38
Evans, Herbert, 4, 5, 122, 156, 158, 201-3
Evenlode, 18, 75
Evenlode, river, 1, 18, 20, 199
Evesham, 21, 192, 199, 203; Abbot & Abbey, 12, 15, 16, 36, 40, 52, 56, 62-63, 90-91, 106, 147
Eye, river, 2, 22, 175
Eyford, 29, 50, 158, 172, 173, 174-75, 177, 180, 190-91, 211; House, 180
Eynsham Abbey, 12, 76, 132

fairs *see* markets
fallow, 13, 79
Faringdon, 31
'farm' (rent), 16, 66, 124
Farmcote (Guiting Power), 10, 36, 48, 57, 114, 160-61, 164, 172, **plate V**
farmers & farm sizes, 16, 77, 91, 123-24, 126, 130, 131, 136, 139, 141, 142, 152-53, 183, 188, 190-94, 205
Farmington, 74, 77, 93, 95, 101, 126, 156, 160, 171, 172, 173, 180; church, 45, 46, 48; enclosure, 136, 138-39, 148; freeholders, 190; rectory, 148, 151
'feld', 86
fells (sheep), 93
Fifield, 8, 9, 14, 40, 118, 155; labour services, 89
Filkins, 95, 201
Finberg, H. P. R., 76
'fine' (legal), 88, 127, 129, 131
Fisher, Sir Edward, 114, 132-33
FitzHamon, Robert, 52
Florence of Worcester *see* Worcester

Ford (Temple Guiting), 49, 206, 209, 211
Fortey, John, 95-96, 99-100, 145
Fosse Cross station, 200
Fosse Way, 2, 29, 38, 41, 62, 66, 68, 69, 187, 201
Foxcote (Withington), 12, 32, 36, 106
Frampton *see* Winchcombe
'freebench', 127
freehold & freeholders, 39, 52, 58, 70, 73, 84, 87-89, 105-6, 121, 123, 125-27, 130, 131-36, 138-39, 141, 143, 188, 190-94
'freeman', 16
Freeman family, 69-70, 149, 151, 154, 160, 170, 176, 178, 186, 203
Fulbrook, 8, 14, 15, 41, 59, 60, 184
furlong, 12, 79-81

Gainsborough, Earl of *see* Noel family
Ganborough (Upper Swell), 22
Garne family, 102-4, 209, 211
'gate', 24
Gawcombe (Westcote), 24, 26
geld, 8
Gelling, Margaret, 75
gentlemen & 'gentry', 3, 105-137, 148, 160-182
George III, 112
George, Sir Ernest (architect), 176
Gibbs, Arthur, 194, 199-201, 205-6
Gilpin, Joshua, 112
Giraldus Cambrensis, 21
Gissing, A., 202-3
glebe, 3, 36, 40, 138, 139, 144-47, 159; terriers, 144-47
Gloucester, 16, 18, 22, 199, 205; Abbot & Abbey, 12, 19, 38, 53, 56, 66, 67, 76, 79, 91, 92-93, 96, 102, 106, 127-28, 145, 146; bishop, 151; diocese, 3, 144
Goda, Countess, 10, 109
Godwin family (including Harold, Earl & King), 11, 41
Goizenboded, William, 8, 10
Gomme, G. L., 84
Greenaway family, 120, 179, 191
Greet, 48-49, 54, 57, 156
Gretton, 48-49, 54, 154, 156, 200, 205
Grevil, William, 64, 92, 97-98
Griggs, F. L., 4, 208-209
Grundy, G. B., 72
Guild of Handicrafts *see* Campden
Guiting, 10, 14, 15, 17, 20, 22, 23, 26, 40
Guiting Power, 8, 28, 37, 43, 46, 49, 53, 79, 80, 86, 95, 154, 158,160, 184, 205, **plate XXXI**; Grange 49, 172; Oldchurch, 49

Habington, Thomas, 18, 70-71, 74, 107, 120-21
Hailes, 15, 17, 20, 40, 41, 44, 45, 54, 109, 114, 155, 160, 172, 190 91, 200, 203; Abbey, 40, 56-57, 79, 90-91, 182, **plate XXXVI**
Hakluyt, Thomas, 26
Halliwell, J. O., 197
Hampen, Lower (Shipton Oliffe), 32, 36, 76, 77, 192, 212; Manor (Shipton Oliffe), 77-78, 85; Upper (Sevenhampton), 32, 180

Hampnett, 15, 20, 22, 40, 44-45, 46, 74, 95, 102, 147, 156, 158, 180, 190, 200
Harford (Naunton), 26-27, 29, 36, 86
Harman, Edmond, 118
Harnhill, 138
Harold, Earl & King *see* Godwin family
Harrison, William, 84, 183, 184
Harroby, Earl, 178
Hawling 10-11, 15, 40, 74, 75, 76, 79, 95, 102, 106, 145, 154, 160, 180, 196, 200; church, 11; copyholders, 141; enclosure, 86-87, 136, 139-41, 148; Manor, 114, 121, 164, 172; open fields, 139, 141; rectory, 86-87, 148
Hazleton, 10-11, 20, 40, 75-76, 81, 86, 95, 106, 145, 149, 159, 160, 180, 190-91; church, 11, 46
Hearth Tax. 112, 128, 140, 160, 163-64, 174
Hemming of Worcester *see* Worcester
Henmarsh, 65, 68
Henry VIII (1509-1547), 12
Hereford, bishop & diocese, 12, 106, 126
'heriot', 88, 126, 127, 131
Heythrop, 175
Hicks, Baptist (Viscount Campden), 42, 65, 161-63
Hidcote, Bartrim & Boyce, 7, 12, 16, 36, 132, 141, 173, 182
'hide', 8-9, 13, 18, 38, 39, 40, 71-72, 105, 127
Hilcot (Withington), 12, 36, 106
Hinchwick, 23, 79, 89, 172, 174
Hinton on the Green, 20
'hitching', 32, 142
Holford hundred, 23, 49
Horniman, E. J., 120
horse-buses, 203, 205
Hughes family, 211-12
'hundred', 3, 7, 21, 38
Hundred Rolls, 87, 89
'husbandman', 124, 128, 134, 191
Hwicce, 18, 20-21, 36-38, 42

Icomb, 1, 7, 18, 20, 22, 23-26, 63, 126, 153, 156, 190; church, 45, 107, 202; Church Icomb, 23-26, 38, 88-89; copyholders, 130-1; enclosure 131; labour services, 88; Place, 3, 22, 23-26, 51, 86, 105, 107-9, 131, 172, 173
Idbury, 8, 14, 22, 23, 40, 45, 164; labour services, 89
impropriator *see* appropriations
inclosure *see* enclosure
Ingles, R., 134-5
inhabitants, numbers of, 183-84, 192-94, 198, 199
Inquisitions Post Mortem, 87
Ireland, T., 149
Isbourne, river, 15, 55, **plate IX**
Izod family, 133-36, 160

Jackson *alias* Booth family, 133-34
Johnston, L., 173
Jones, W., 203

Kelly's Directories, 172-73, 205, 207-8
Kelmscott, 95
Keynsham Abbey, 41, 118
Kidderminster, Richard, abbot of Winchcombe, 57

INDEX

Kiftsgate Court, 173
Kiftsgate hundred, 7
King, Gregory, 183, 184
Kingham railway junction, 199
Kip, J. (engraver), 116
Kirkham, N., 133
knighthood fines, 135, 160
knights, 105-6, 107, 109-10, 135, 137, 138, 190
Knights Templars *see* Templars

labour services, 16, 52, 74, 87-89, 92-93, 123
labourers, 123, 130, 131, 136, 138-39, 141, 183, 191-93
Lambeth, St Mary's church, 12
Landboc (Winchcombe cartulary) *see* Winchcombe Abbey
landowning, 9-12, 22-23, 35-36, 77, 86, 105, 144, 178-82, 183, 188, 190-94, 195, 198
Laverton (Buckland), 47, 50, 94, 127-30, 153, 196, 197, **plate VIII**
Lawrence family, 179
Lawton, W. F., 179
Lay subsidy, 53, 55, 64, 66, 68, 70, 77
Leach, river, 15, 22, 66, 93
'league', 14
'leah', 20
leases & leaseholders, 123, 128-30, 131, 138, 141
Lechlade, 15, 66, 102
Leland, John, 51, 55, 111, 116
Lenthal family, 60, 119-20
Leominster, 100
Leonard Stanley, 67
'lifehold', 125-26, 138, 143
Llanthony Priory, 30-31, 79, 91-93
'long & short' masonry, 42
Longborough, 10, 20, 22, 46, 75, 79, 86, 184, 191
lord of the manor *see* manor
'lot' meadows, 81-83
Ludlow family (wool merchants), 65
Lutyens, Sir Edwin (architect), 174, 175, 198
Lygon, General, 122
Lysons, Samuel, 95, 110, 135

Maitland, F. W., 13, 131
manor & lordship, 3-4, 5, 8, 15, 22-34, 49, 52-73, 74, 78, 83-84, 86, 138, 139, 142, 153, 160, 186, 188, 191, 194; & parish 5, 18, 31-32, 39, 41, 43, 49, 73; court, 58, 67-68, 70, 73, 77, 78, 88, 123, 124-25, 141-42, 160; customs of the manor, 77, 126-27, 132; houses, 3-4, 64, 66, 78, 105-6, 109, 110, 121, 128, 133, 135, 140, 150, 156, 173, 175-77, 179-80, 201, **plates I, XIX, XX, XXI, XXII**; *see also* copyhold and labour services
market-gardening, 133, 191-92
markets & fairs, 5, 53, 58, 63, 66, 70
Marshall, William, 78, 81, 84, 101-2, 126, 138, 148-49, 192, 205
Maugersbury, 8, 9, 10, 12, 16, 22, 23, 38, 62-63, 86, 131, 147, 160, 161, 163, 164, 170, 171, 192-94, 196
meadow, 14, 81-84, 88-89, 128
meerstones, 24

Men & Armour (1608) *see* militia lists
Meon Hill, 1
'merchet', 87
Mercia, 18, 19, 53
Mickleton, 1, 12, 20, 41, 57, 97, 114, 161, 164, 171, 172, 173, 183-84, 190-92, 200; freeholders, 131-33, 184
Midwinter, William, 93-96, 99-100, 101
Milcote, 97
militia lists (musters), 124, 128, 133, 134
mills, 15, 33
Milton under Wychwood, 18, 177
'minster' churches, 35, 36-40, 41, 53-54
monasteries, 35, 40, 43, 76, 90-93, 100, 132; dissolution, 3, 12, 105, 111, 132; as landowners, 11-12, 38, 147, 164
Moore & Sons, auctioneers, 113
Moore, John, 25
More *see* Northmoor
Moreton in Marsh, 5, 65, 68-70, 91, 186, 191, 193, 198, 200-1, 203, 205, 207-8; church, 154; Old Town, 68, 70; population, 184, 207; rectory, 149; Westminster Abbey manor, 12, 52-53, 68
Morris, William, 156, 158
motor transport, 199, 202, 205, 207-10

National Trust, 116, 160, 182
Naunton, 4, 18, 21, 23, 26-27, 28, 74, 95, 205, 211, **plate II**; church, 46, 98-99, 194; freeholders, 131, 191; rectory, 40, 145, 147, 149, 159; Little Worth, 26
Naunton in Winchcombe q.v.
Nether Swell Manor (Lower Swell), 173, 176-77
Noel family, 114, 142-43, 151, 161, 163, 178
Nomina Villarum (1316), 22
Nonconformity, 144, 153-55
Norman churches, 3, 30, 31, 37, 43-45, 47, 158; south doorways, 31, 37, 43-44, 153
Northleach, 5, 7, 14, 17, 22, 52-53, 66-68, 74, 86, 92-96, 101-2, 104, 114, 155, 156, 164, 185, 186, 188, 198, 200, 203, 205, **plates XVI & XVII**; brasses, 90, 93, 95-96, 99-100; church, 3, 45, 46, 95-96, 99-100; freeholders, 191; Gloucester Abbey manor, 12, 38, 53, 66, 145; population, 184, 207; vicarage, 145-46, 150-51
Northmoor, 14
Northwick (Blockley), 18, 53, 143
Northwick, Lord, 142-43, 165, 167-70, 178
Northwick Park, 4, 160, 164, 165-70, 171, 173, 181-82
Norton, Lower (Weston Subedge), 49
Notgrove, 12, 16, 26, 29, 38, 44, 95, 106, 114, 156, 157-58, 172, 173, 180, 190-91, 200
Notgrove station, 199

occupational structure, 5, 55, 66-67, 183-84, 185-88, 207-9
Oddington, 12, 14, 17, 24, 44, 45, 46, 114, 131, 154-55, 156, 159, 160, 171, 173, 191
Offa, king of Mercia (757-796), 23, 25
Ogilby's Road Maps (1675), 71
Oliffe family, 32, 145

open fields, 2-3, 23, 26, 31, 32, 34, 60, 65, 66, 68, 72-73, 74, 79-89, 101, 123, 126-28, 139, 141-42, 144, 147, 183, 192; *see also* enclosure
oratories, 35, 39, 51
Osney Abbey, 90
Oswald, bishop of Worcester (961-992), 38
Oswaldslow hundred, 7, 38
Owdeswell (Withington), 32, 49, 77
ownership of land *see* landowing
oxen, 12-14, 66, 77, 80, 84, 126, 142, 205-6
Oxenton, 16, 75
Oxford: diocese, 3; University, 139, 140

parish, boundaries, 23, 72-73, 87; creation, 35-36, 39-41, 46-47; significance 3, 36, 46-47, 51; *see also* manor
Parker, Thomas, 67-68
parks, 110, 114, 116, 118, 167, 170
parson & parsonage *see* 'rectory'
Parsons, Dr. Richard, 50, 116, 133, 136, 147
pasture, 14, 84; *see also* common pastures
Paxford (Blockley), 15, 151, 154
Payne, G. E., 191-92, 194, 198, 207
Peachey family, 32, 85
'peasant', 123-24; *see also* copyholder
Pegglesworth (Withington), 12, 32, 36
Peggolotti's list of wool suppliers, 90-91, 101
'pen', 32, 76
Pershore Abbey, 1, 12, 38, 41, 42, 53, 70, 71, 73, 86, 90-91, 120-22; hundred 7
Phillipps family, 53, 121, 122, 130, 137, 141, 151, 170, 174, 178, 179, 193, 196-97
Pinnock, 15, 16, 20, 50, 76, 190
Pinswell (Colesborne), 14, 76
place-names, 4, 7, 12, 18, 20-23, 24, 26, 32, 52, 60, 63, 75-76, 84, 86, 126
'plough' in Domesday Book, 12-14, 17, 127
plough-teams, 12-14, 66, 84, 86
Poll Tax (1381-2), 55, 164
Poor Laws, Royal Commission into, 192-94
Pope Gregory, 17
Pope Nicholas taxation (1291), 40-41
population *see* inhabitants, numbers of
'port', 52
Postlip (Winchcombe), 15, 44, 48, 57, 156, 173, 188, 207
Power, Eileen, 101
Prescott, 57
Prestbury, 12, 16
Priestley, J. B., 209
priests, 16, 20, 35, 38, 39, 40
Puckham (Sevenhampton), 126
Puesdown (Hazleton), 74-76
Pynnok, John, 98

railways, 5, 198, 199-201, 202, 209
Rating Appeal (1934-5), 181-82
Rectitudines Singularum Personarum, 77
'rectory', rector & vicar 3, 35-36, 39-41, 78, 81-83, 86-87, 96, 118, 132, 134, 135, 138, 139, 144-53, 175, 188, 191, 194
Redesdale, Lord *see* Freeman family
Rendcomb Park, 103

Returns of owners of land (1872-73), 178-79
'reversion' (legal), 125, 126, 130
ridge & furrow, 2, 80-81, 116, **plate XI**
'riding-men', 16
Rissington, 8, 10, 22, 75
Rissington, Great, 41, 95, 118, 131, 136, 149, 160, 164, 172, 173,181, 191, 192-94
Rissington, Little, 45, 77, 131, 136, 140, 159, 191, 192-94
Rissington Wyck, 20, 36, 131, 140-41, 148, 157, 160, 179-80, 192-94, 196; church, 46; enclosure, 136, 139, 148
Roel, 12, 40, 50, 76, 81, 86-87, 112, 141, 181, 190-91
Rogers family, 179
Royce, Rev. David, 25, 36, 107, 109, 156
Rudder, Samuel, 101, 109, 133-34, 135, 154, 174, 176, 184, 188, 191
Rudge, Rev. Thomas, 101-2, 171-72, 195-96, 205
Rushout family, 139, 151, 165-70, 174, 179
Russell, G. & S., 209-10
Ryknild Street (or Buckle Street), 2, **plate VI**

Saintbury, 20, 41, 43, 46, 114, 172, 192, 203
Salmonsbury, 2, 22, 30
Salmonsbury hundred, 30
Salperton, 20, 40, 74, 77, 105, 172, 173, 179, 190
saltways, 19, 20, 24, 38
Sandywell (Dowdeswell), 171
Sartoris, Alfred, 174, 179
Savage family, 120-21
Scarborough, Earl of, 138, 148
Scotman, Thomas, 151-53
Scott, Sir G. G. (architect), 114
'serf', 16
Sevenhampton, 12, 17, 20, 32, 106, 126-27, 160, 195; church, 46, 99; labour services, 89
'severalty' (legal), 80
Severn, river, 199
Sezincote, 11, 40, 50, 114, 164, 167, 171, 173, 174, 179-81, 190-91, **plate XXIX**
sheep & shepherds, 13-14, 20, 67, 71, 74-79, 89, 128, 133, 135,139, 142, 143, 146, 149, 167, 192, 209, 211, **plates XIII to XVIII**
Sheldon family, 120-21
Sherborne, 12, 14, 17, 22, 39, 40, 66, 91, 93, 95, 102-3, 106, 117, 118, 183, 184, 190-91, 196, **plate XXIV**; church, 43, 48-49, 155, **plate XXVII**; House, 3, 114, 116, 117, 118, 164, 171, 173, 181-82, **plate XXVII**; labour services, 92
Sherborne, Lord *see* Dutton family
Shipton (Oliffe & Solers), 5, 14, 18, 20, 23, 31-33, 74, 76, 95, 105, 160, 164, 172, 180, 190-91; church, 45, 46, 85, 156; open fields, 32, 85; rectories, 40, 145, 147, 149, 159
Shipton under Wychwood, 18, 21, **plate XXV**; Court, 21, 202
shires, 1; Four Shire Stone, 1, 4
Signet *see* Burford
Slaughter, 5, 8, 18, 22, 23, 27-30; enclosure, 29, 136, 139, 149
Slaughter hundred, 7, 23, 30
Slaughter, Lower, 23, 30, 114, 144, 147, 149, 155,

INDEX

164, 172, 176, 184, 211; church, 29, 30, 155
Slaughter, Upper, 22, 23, 29, 74, 77, 103, 156, 170, 172, 192-94, 197, 198; church, 29, 46, 157-58; Manor, 139, 175-76, **plate XXII**; rectory, 145, 147, 175
slaves in Domesday Book, 16, 17, 86, 128
smallholders, 2, 52, 58, 63, 132-33, 136, 139
Smyth, John, 160 *see also* militia lists
Snowshill, 12, 39, 40, 70, 71, 78, 79, 106, 114, 133, 172, **plate XXXIV**; church, 154; enclosure, 136; Manor, 171, 182
Society for the Preservation of Ancient Buildings, 144, 156, 158
Solers family, 32
Somery, Roger de, 63, 91, 97
Southrop, 20
Spoonley (Sudeley), 20, 40
Stanley Pontlarge, 54
Stanton, 20, 45, 125, 133-36, 160, 176, 178, 192, 198, 205, **plate XXIII**; church, 46, 134, 178; copyholders, 125, 133-34; Court, 133, 135-37, 172, 173, 178; enclosure, 133, 136; freeholders, 131, 136, 191; rectory, 78, 80, 136, 147; Winchcombe Abbey estate, 12, 39
Stanway, 12, 15, 20, 38, 71, 79, 114, 160, 171, 184, 190, 192, 195, 211, **plate III**; church, 20, 46, **plate VII**; House, 3-4, 116, 118, 164, 171-72, 173, 181, **plates XIX & XX**
'staple' of wool, 99
Staple, Company of, 94-95
'stints' (for grazing), 77
Stoke, 16
Stott, Sir Philip, 133, 178, 198
'stow', 10, 62
Stow on the Wold, 1, 5, 9, 20, 21, 52-53, 56, 62-63, 102, 142, 154, 156, 161, 185, 186-87, 188, 198, 201, 205, 207-8, 211, **plate XXX**; church, 10, 46, 63, 155; deanery, 41, 62; freeholders, 191; population, 184, 207; railway, 199, 200, 203; rectory, 41, 147; *see also* Maugersbury
Stowell, 44, 77, 105, 164, 171, 172, 173, 190, 209; Park, 103-4, 181-82
Stratford family, 57, 114, 160
Stratford on Avon, 203, 205
'strips' in open fields, q.v.
Sudeley, 15, 20, 40, 45, 53, 54, 57, 81, 83-84, 109, 156, 190-91; Castle, 3, 55, 105-6, 109-14, 156, 171, 173, 181
Swell, 7, 11, 23
Swell, Lower, 23, 25, 36, 62, 79, 131, 155, 156, 177, 190, 202; Wold, 20
Swell, Upper, 12, 16, 20, 22, 23, 38, 40, 62, 86, 147, 148, 179, 190-91; enclosure, 136, 139, 148
Swinford, George, 201
Sylvester, Edmond, 118
Syreford, 15, 32, 33

Taddington (Stanway), 12, 36, 49
Talbot & Talbot Rice family, 160, 171, 178, 179, 181-82, 191
Tanfield, Sir Lawrence, 61, 118
Taynton, 8, 12, 14, 15, 16, 18, 19, 22, 41, 59, 95, 118, 164, 181, 191; court rolls, 125; labour services, 89; 'lot' meadows, 83; stone quarries, 4, 43, 89, 181
Taylor, Jenkin & John, 93, 95, 99, 101
'teign', 22
Templars, 15, 26
Temple Guiting, 8, 36, 76, 82, 95, 157, 172, 192-94, 211-12
Tetbury, 94, 201
Tewkesbury, 52, 211; Abbey, 12, 20, 38, 43, 56-57, 65, 78, 79, 90-91, 116, 118, 125, 184
Thames, river, 14
thegn, 9, 10, 39
Thomas, Edward, 200
threshing machine, 201, 209
Thynne family, 127-30, 197
tithes, 3, 35-36, 39-41, 96, 135-36, 138, 139, 143, 144-53, 154; abolition, 136, 139, 144, 148-52, 158; 'great' & 'small', 40, 144, 145-46
Toddington, 54, 57, 106, 116, 135, 156, 200, 207
'ton', 18, 21-22, 68, 75
Tracy family, 57, 109, 114, 116, 118, 160-61, 170, 171-72, 178
tractor, 199, 206-7
tramway, 203, 205
Turkdean, 7, 26, 29, 46, 95, 126, 161, 173, 180
turnpikes, 71, 188

Universal British Directory, 186-88
Upton *see* Blockley or Burford
Upton Wold (Blockley), 20, 21

Valor Ecclesiasticus, 12, 56-57, 79
Verey, David, 174
vernacular building, 156
Vestey family, 104
vicar & vicarage *see* 'rectory'
vicus, 19
vill, 22, 123
villagers, 16, 39, 78, 80-81, 84, 87-89, 91, 124-6, 132-33, 144
villas (Roman), 20, 31-32, 36, 53-54, 174
'villein', 16, 123
virgates *see* yardlands
voters, 126, 130, 188, 190-94

Wagborough (Upper Slaughter), 22
'wald', 20
Waller family, 179, 180
Warne or Warren, Thomas, 133-34
Wars of the Roses, 111
Warwick, 97
'well', 4
Wemyss, Earl of *see* Tracy family
Werburgh, St *see* Chester
Westcote, 23, 25, 26, 159
Westerling, Margaret, 206, 209, 211-12
Westfield (Hawling), 8, 10
Westington *see* Campden
Westminster Abbey, 12, 16, 38, 53, 68-69, 91, 186
Weston on Avon, 16
Weston Subedge, 2, 10, 20, 41, 46, 106, 172, 191, 200
Westwell Manor, 102
Weymouth, Lord *see* Thynne family
Whitmore family, 58, 179

Whittington, 12, 15, 17, 31-32, 40, 95, 106, 126, 145, 172, 190, 194; church, 106; Court, 102, 171, 173, 181, **plate XXI**
'wic', 19
Widford, 14, 36, 118
Willersey, 12, 16, 40, 41, 46, 86, 144, 160, 173, 191-92
Winchcombe, 2, 5, 7, 11, 18, 42, 52-58, 71, 77, 109, 112, 154, 160-61, 185, 187-88, 189, 193, 205, 207-8, **plate IX**; burgesses, 15-16; church, 45, 51, 56, 114, 155-56; Coates & Throp, 53-54, 57, 81; deanery, 41; Frampton & Naunton, 12, 54, 106; freeholders, 191; population, 57, 184, 207; railway, 200; shire (Quarter), 1, 16, 39; St Nicholas's, 50, 51; vicarage, 40-41, 147, 149
Winchcombe Abbey, 17, 19, 53, 54, 55-57, 111; estates, 8, 24, 39, 78-79, 81, 86, 89, 90-93, 106, 110, 114, 117, 121, 133-36; *Landboc*, 51, 106; minster parish, 40, 54; Three hundreds, 38
Windrush, 2, 8, 11, 12, 14, 20, 22, 30, 31, 43, 46, 47, 79, 81, 93, 175
Windrush, river, 14, 15, 18, 22, 23, 26, 28, 29, 36, 60, 75
Wingfield *see* Talbot family
Winson, 10, 95
Withington, 7, 12, 14, 15, 16, 20, 21, 22, 31-32, 40, 75, 79, 86, 95, 106, 164, 172, 183, 191, 200; church, 10, 46; minster, 32, 38; rectory, 41, 149, 151
Witts, Rev. Francis, 158, 170-71, 175, 193
'wold', 20; *see also* Cotswold and downs

Wontley (Bishops Cleeve), 75, **plate IV**
wood, 2, 14, 15, 20, 79, 81, 84, 111-12, 139, 141, 170, 174, **plate III**
Woodchester, 8
Wood Stanway *see* Stanway
Woodstock, 18
wool trade, 77-78, 90-99; churches, 3, 90, 95-99; merchants, 67, 93-94, 95, 97-99; *see also* Cely family
Worcester Abbey & Priory, 23, 25, 38, 40, 53, 56, 87-89, 91-93, 130; bishop & diocese, 1, 3, 7, 12, 13, 17, 38, 42, 77, 79, 84, 90-91, 95, 106, 126, 130-31, 151; cartularies, 7, 16, 35; Hemming the monk of Worcester (*c*.1091), 16, 35; Florence the chronicler (died 1118), 109
Wormington Grange, 170
Wright, Richard & Humphrey, 133
Wychwood forest, 14, 15, 18-19, 21, 89
Wyck Rissington *see* Rissington
Wynniatt family, 133, 135-37, 178, 179
Wyndham, William, 139

Yanworth, 10-11, 15, 76, 86, 160, 181, 190-1, 197
yardlanders *see* villagers
yardlands, 2, 8, 39, 77, 80-81, 87-89, 118, 123, 128, 130-31, 132, 133, 139, 144, 148, 149
'yeoman', 124, 134, 136, 137, 185
York, Archbishop of, 12, 14, 17, 24
Young, Arthur, 12
Youth Hostels Association, 211

II.

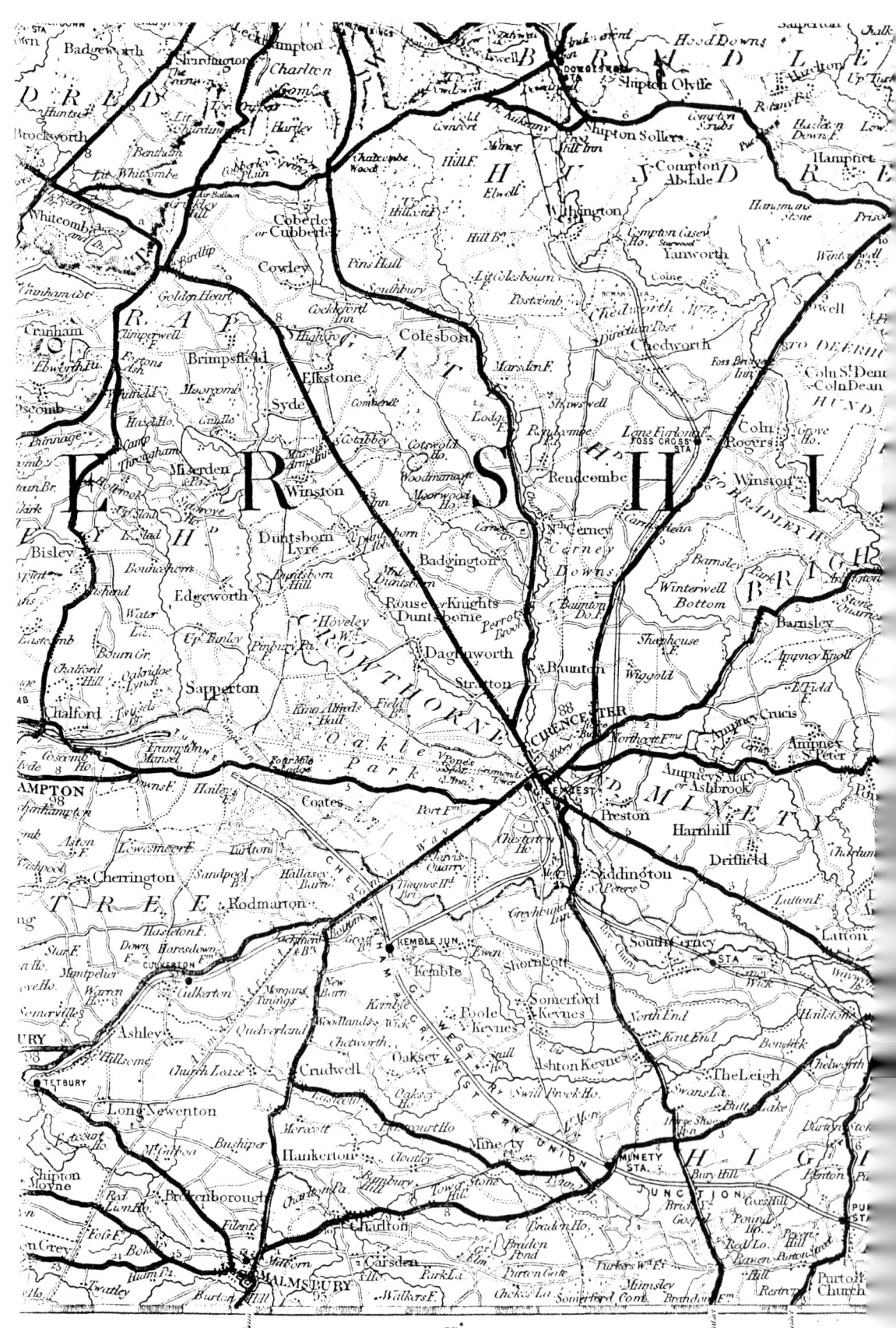